D0871874

02-08-19

Tim,

WISH YOU ALL THE
BEST! KEEP YOUR HEAD UP.
I WILL MISS YOU!!

JOEL

"Marty's book is not an autobiography. It's a personalized, guided tour through the mind and consciousness of genius. I thought I knew my friend from our many years of association. But not until I read *The Hope Circuit* did I really understand how Marty's life is a reflection of the unimaginable purity of one man's creative and unparalleled intellect."
—Major General Robert Scales (retired)

"Here is a major thinker who sees deeply into human nature and tells a good story. In *The Hope Circuit*, Marty Seligman displays both these gifts. This book is his best writing and thinking yet." **—Angela Duckworth,**
CEO of the Character Lab and
bestselling author of *Grit*

"Martin Seligman is an intellectual giant, and readers will look to his memoir *The Hope Circuit* for secrets to his phenomenal impact as a scholar. What they will find is a deeply human story of his own struggles, hopes and ideas, told in an inspiring way. *The Hope Circuit* is more than an autobiography; it is handbook for each of us to build a life dedicated to human flourishing." **—Arthur C. Brooks, PhD,**
President of the American Enterprise Institute

"*The Hope Circuit* is a masterful blend of memoir and recent intellectual history—specifically, the history of trying to understand how we can live richer and more meaningful lives. This book could only have been written by someone who has played a vital role in that inquiry, cares passionately about it, and has the literary skill to carry that passion onto the page. The result is a vivid, bracing and sometimes poignant story of unfolding synergy between a psychologist's life and his work." **—Robert Wright,**
author of *Why Buddhism is True*

"For half a century Martin Seligman has enlightened and inspired students of the human mind with his arresting findings and his visionary insights. He has been unafraid to plumb the dark recesses of the psyche, and just as bold in illuminating our better angels. This book combines a history of psychology by a man who shaped it, an explanation of powerful ideas about mental life, and a delightfully candid and reflective memoir."
—Steven Pinker, Johnstone Professor of Psychology,
Harvard University, and the author of
How the Mind Works and Enlightenment Now

"In this revealing memoir, the founder of the Positive Psychology movement recounts the experiences that shaped his work—from early childhood through his academic studies and research to the present. Martin Seligman has transformed the field of psychology to the benefit of all of us. It is fascinating to read the story of how he did that."　**—Andrew Weil, MD,**
author of *Spontaneous Happiness* **and**
Eight Weeks to Optimum Health

"One of our most important psychologists alive takes us on a surprising personal journey—through his own highs and lows, twist and turns, overcoming tremendous obstacles to discover some of the most groundbreaking and iconic concepts in psychology. For a time his concept of 'learned helplessness' dominated the field as we looked to undo the past and now has us looking forward with positive psychology to grow our resilience, gratitude and hope. If you have an interest in the human condition, you will love this book."　**—John Ratey, author of** *Spark* **and** *Driven to Distraction*

"This warm, lively, beautifully written book tells the stories behind some of the grand ideas and developments that have reshaped psychology—as well as the struggles, missteps, conflicts, and misunderstandings that nearly derailed them. Through it all emerges the author's infectious excitement about exploring the human mind and his roaming quest for how to make life better for the mass of humanity."　**—Roy F. Baumeister, author of**
Willpower: Rediscovering the Greatest Human Strength

"With a mix of humility and insight, Marty Seligman walks us through the full arc of his life, offering his theories on tectonic shifts in both himself and the field of psychology. In *The Hope Circuit*, Marty uncovers a view of human nature that is as surprising as it is inspiring. Dive in for a fascinating disciplinary history seen through the eyes of one of the most influential psychologists of our time."　**—Barbara Fredrickson, author of**
Positivity **and** *Love 2.0*

"This inspiring and rewarding well-documented record of a lifetime is a beautifully written page-turner. In addition, *The Hope Circuit* is the saga of how American psychology came of age."　**—George E. Vaillant, MD,**
author of *Triumphs of Experience*

"Martin Seligman provides a riveting autobiography about his discovery of 'learned helplessness' and 'positive psychology' with *The Hope Circuit*. Interwoven within the carefully scripted storytelling, Seligman takes the reader in a journey of self and intellectual discovery that explains why he is one of intellectual icons of our times. Woven throughout is a story of discovery, resilience, passion, and drive to not only understand self but

to understand and remedy the maladies of life. The 2017 recipient of the prestigious American Psychological Association's Lifetime Achievement Award employs a unique, simultaneous combination of both fast reading and soul-scratching to deliver a timely and critical message of hope."

—Antonio Puente, President of the
American Psychological Association

"*The Hope Circuit* is riveting. It turns out that one of the greatest psychologists of all time is also one of our greatest storytellers. Offering an unparalleled glimpse into a particular time and place and history of science, Marty Seligman's book will entertain you, fascinate you, disabuse you, and move you. Along with Marty, you will laugh, grieve, and rage and, alighting on the last page, insist on a sequel."

—Sonja Lyubomirsky, Ph. D., professor of
psychology at the University of California, Riverside,
and author of *The How of Happiness:*
A Scientific Approach to Getting the Life You Want

"Martin Seligman has written a fascinating and intimate portrait of both his own life and the discipline of psychology. A deeply gifted scholar, practitioner and communicator, he reminds us that positive psychology has profound implications for the way we live and work—and for public policy. Through his unique insights, relentless work ethic and infectious enthusiasm, Marty has helped many children and adults around the world—and especially in Australia—live more engaged, happy and meaningful lives. For that we should be most grateful." **—The Honorable Kevin Rudd,**
26th Prime Minister of Australia

"Martin Seligman is simply the most important and influential psychologist of the last 30 years. This stunning memoir will tell you why, and reading it will change your life for the better."**—Sir Anthony Seldon, vice-chancellor**
of the University of Buckingham

"This valuable memoir reveals how an influential new approach in psychology is intertwined with the life story of its leader."

—Howard Gardner, Hobbs Professor of Cognition and Education at
Harvard University and author of *Multiple Intelligences*

"The positive psychology movement is a beacon of hope in our contemporary culture. Its founder, Martin Seligman, is one of today's most influential psychologists. In this book, he tells his remarkable journey—from studying failure to promoting human flourishing. It is a fascinating story."

—Richard Layard, Director of the
Well-Being Program at the London School of Economics

"In my life, Martin Seligman rapidly evolved from just brilliant scientist, to become my good friend and mentor after we started the Comprehensive Soldier Fitness program in 2008. This book, *The Hope Circuit*, which is both entertaining and refreshingly honest, helps me understand how he become the scientist, visionary and patriot I met and admire today."

—Rhonda Cornum, Brigadier General (retired),
PhD, MD, and Director of Health Strategy for TechWerks

"There are only a handful of living psychologists who would be worthy of an autobiography. Martin Seligman is one of that handful—one of the very most eminent psychologists alive today. Seligman's life and career are both models for how one can find meaning in life. Seligman not only reminds us of the tremendous positive impact he has had—through his studies of learned helplessness, depression, and positive psychology—but also of how even the greatest of professionals must overcome the many obstacles strewn in their path. Seligman shows that greatness does not derive from a life without obstacles, but rather from viewing those obstacles as challenges and learning experiences. He demonstrates how he and anyone else can meet challenges in life to reach ever-growing heights not despite the challenges, but often, because of them. This is a wonderful story masterfully told."

—Robert J. Sternberg,
Professor of Human Development, Cornell University

"*The Hope Circuit* is a remarkable blend of personal growth and scientific discovery. Seligman is one of the giants of science and in this treatise he bares his sole as to how he came to the revelations that have so changed the field. Preparedness, safety signal, learned helplessness, and positive psychology are among the most original and important contributions to psychology in the last half century. The treatise reads as a character study and as a road map for how to do science and it is always fascinating and illuminating."

—Steven Hollon,
Gertrude Conaway Vanderbilt Professor of Psychology,
Vanderbilt University

"Martin Seligman is renowned for his contribution to the field of positive psychology—and in this thought-provoking and surprisingly candid memoir, he explains how hard-won his wisdom has been."

—Gretchen Rubin, author of
The Happiness Project* and *The Four Tendencies

The Hope Circuit

The Hope Circuit

A Psychologist's Journey from Helplessness to Optimism

Martin E. P. Seligman

PublicAffairs

New York

Copyright © 2018 by Martin E. P. Seligman

Hachette Book Group supports the right to free expression and the value of copyright. The purpose of copyright is to encourage writers and artists to produce the creative works that enrich our culture.

The scanning, uploading, and distribution of this book without permission is a theft of the author's intellectual property. If you would like permission to use material from the book (other than for review purposes), please contact permissions@hbgusa.com. Thank you for your support of the author's rights.

PublicAffairs
Hachette Book Group
1290 Avenue of the Americas, New York, NY 10104
www.publicaffairsbooks.com
@Public_Affairs

Printed in the United States of America

First edition: April 2018

Published by PublicAffairs, an imprint of Perseus Books, LLC, a subsidiary of Hachette Book Group, Inc. The PublicAffairs name and logo is a trademark of the Hachette Book Group.

The publisher is not responsible for websites (or their content) that are not owned by the publisher.

Print book interior design by Timm Bryson, em em design, LLC

Library of Congress Cataloging-in-Publication Data
Names: Seligman, Martin E. P., author.
Title: The hope circuit : a psychologist's journey from helplessness to optimism / Martin Seligman.
Description: New York : PublicAffairs, [2018] | Includes bibliographical references.
Identifiers: LCCN 2017052870 (print) | LCCN 2017054667 (ebook) | ISBN 9781610398756 (ebook) | ISBN 9781610398732 (hardcover)
Subjects: LCSH: Seligman, Martin E. P. | Psychologists—United States—Biography. | Positive psychology. | Optimism.
Classification: LCC BF109.S426 (ebook) | LCC BF109.S426 A3 2018 (print) | DDC 150.92 [B] —dc23
LC record available at https://lccn.loc.gov/2017052870

ISBNs: 978-1-61039-873-2 (hardcover); 978-1-61039-875-6 (e-book)
LSC-C

10 9 8 7 6 5 4 3 2 1

For my father,

ADRIAN SELIGMAN,

and for my mother,

IRENE BROWN SELIGMAN

CONTENTS

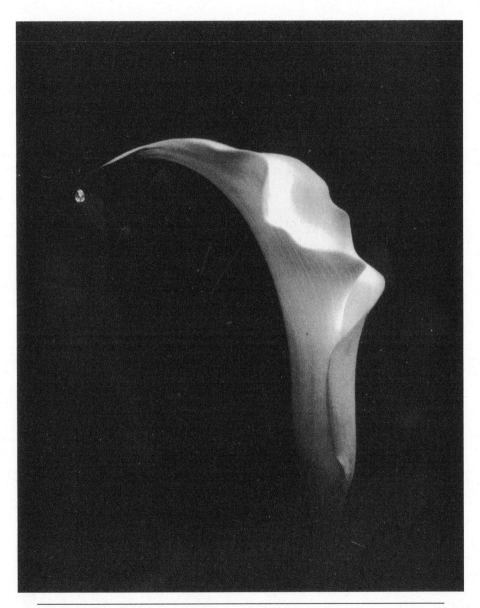

Photo courtesy of Mandy Seligman.

Follow, poet, follow right
To the bottom of the night,
With your unconstraining voice
Still persuade us to rejoice;

With the farming of a verse
Make a vineyard of the curse,
Sing of human unsuccess
In a rapture of distress;

In the deserts of the heart
Let the healing fountain start,
In the prison of his days
Teach the free man how to praise.

—W. H. AUDEN (1939)
In Memory of W. B. Yeats

Part 1

Beginning

Chapter One

Lightning Bolt

MY FAMILY AND I were driving through Yellowstone Park in the late spring of 1996 when I got the news that changed the course of my life. I went to a pay phone and found out that I had been elected president of the American Psychological Association (APA). It was then, and remains now, one of the greatest honors of my life.

A few months later, I attended the APA convention in Toronto as president-elect-elect (I'd become president-elect the following year and president the year after that). I was told that there was no place for me to sit on the floor of council, and while the rank and file greeted me warmly, even effusively, I got one cold shoulder after another from the establishment, whose chosen candidate I had soundly defeated in the election. I returned from Toronto dismayed, wondering if I could be effective on this national stage.

The answer came by way of epiphany.

"GET TO WORK, Nikki," I shouted irritably. It was three weeks after the Toronto convention, and I was low. We were supposed to be weeding. Nikki, however, was having a great time, throwing weeds in the air, dancing, and singing. She startled when I shouted at her, walked away, and slowly walked back.

"Daddy, can I talk to you?"

I nodded.

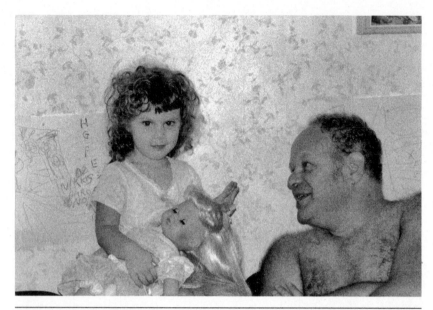

"Well, on my birthday, I decided that I was going to stop whining, and that was the hardest thing I've ever done," Nikki Seligman said. "And if I can stop whining, you can stop being such a grouch." Nikki Seligman and the author, 1996. Photo courtesy of Mandy Seligman.

"Daddy, do you remember before my fifth birthday I was a whiner, I whined every day?"

I nodded.

"Have you noticed that since my fifth birthday, I haven't whined once?"

I nodded.

"Well, on my birthday, I decided that I was going to stop whining, and that was the hardest thing I've ever done. And if I can stop whining, you can stop being such a grouch."

I was stunned. Nikki was exactly right.

First, I was a grouch and proud of it. But it occurred to me for the very first time that maybe any success I'd had was not because I could see every flaw—because of my "critical intelligence"—*but in spite of it*. If Nikki could change, so could I. I decided to change.

Second, my "remedial" view of raising my children was wrong. If I could correct all my kid's errors—shouting at Nikki's indolence—I would somehow end up with an exemplary child. What nonsense.

Instead I had to identify what Nikki was really good at—and I'd just seen it: gleaning insight into other people—reward it, and help her to lead her life around her strengths, not waste her time thanklessly correcting her weaknesses.

Most significantly, I got the idea that powered the rest of my life: psychology could be explicitly about building the good life. The current practice and science of psychology was half-baked. Psychology started with the premise that not getting it wrong equaled getting it right. If psychology could somehow eliminate all the ills of the world—mental illness, prejudice, ignorance, poverty, pessimism, loneliness, and the like—human life would be at its best. But the absence of ill-being does not equal the presence of well-being. Psychology could be about the presence of happiness not merely about the absence of unhappiness.

Not getting it wrong does not equal getting it right.

IN JANUARY 1997, I threw myself into my work as president-elect of APA. The possibility of a psychology of well-being had been percolating. But it seemed like a long shot, and I wanted my presidency to leave a mark. So on the day my term began, I hit the ground running and started work on other, less adventurous initiatives. I visited with Steve Hyman, the young director of the National Institute of Mental Health (NIMH). Steve was no colorless Washington bureaucrat, but a world-class intellect and former professor of neuropsychiatry at Harvard. He and I shared a passion: empirical *evidence* in treatment.

"Steve," I said, "I won by the largest vote in APA history, and I have a mandate. We have an opening here to change the course of APA. Let's launch a program on evidence-based psychotherapy."

"If you can bring recalcitrant-old-APA into the fold, Marty," Steve said, "I will find $40 million to support the research."

VISIONS OF COOPERATION between science and practice and the salvation of APA danced in my head. I asked to attend a meeting of the influential Council for the Advancement of Private Practice and Science (CAPPS)—which had backed the losing candidate in the APA election but remained vitally important to the discipline—to explain

my vision. The council deigned to allot me fifteen minutes, and I had my first encounter with the machine I had just humiliated.

It did not go well.

About twenty stony-faced committee members sat around an enormous table in one of the many well-appointed seminar rooms in the luxurious new APA office building. APA's treasurer, Jack MacKay, had wisely invested in Washington, DC, real estate, and APA was now worth $100 million. It was perhaps the only national professional organization well in the black.

I launched into my pitch. The council members stared at me as if I were an exotic bird that had flown in off course from another planet, and my voice got louder than I wanted it to be. They stared. I couldn't seem to make my voice softer and less shrill. These people hated me. I thought, "I have defeated them in the election, and they will have their revenge." As I described the possibilities for putting psychotherapy on a lasting evidence-based platform, their faces got even stonier and their stares more hostile. I concluded by telling them that NIMH was willing to spend an unheard-of amount—$40 million—to underwrite the search for evidence.

This was my applause line. There was dead silence. One question cut through the quiet, asked by Stan Moldawsky, the group's next president-designate.

"What if the evidence does not come out in our favor?"

RON LEVANT, STAN'S right hand, took me out for a drink. Brimming with good cheer and friendliness, he said, "Marty, you are in deep shit."

I HAVE HAD a lot of good advice in my life, but since my student days, I'd had only one true mentor: Ray Fowler. Ray was the CEO of APA, and unlike the presidents who come and go, he was its institutional memory. He defined his role as bringing out the best in its presidents. Years after that meeting he confided in me that his best quality was his willingness to suffer fools gladly, and at that moment I knew whom he had in mind.

Ray hailed from Alabama, where he was a well-known personality psychologist, dissecting the characters of such celebrities as Howard

Hughes, and chairing the department of psychology at the university. He was the soft-spoken, moderate, and civilized face of the "dirty dozen," the practitioners who had seized power from the science wing fifteen years before, and he was immediately elected president of APA.

APA happened to collapse at that moment. Having invested heavily in *Psychology Today*—a more foolish investment than Washington real estate—it was penniless. The administration was fired, and Ray was called on to become CEO. He did so, rescuing the organization, and became its near-permanent chief executive.

Ray was the very soul of patience and moderation. He was the only APA officer who advised me that my running for president was not impossibly quixotic, and he encouraged me to go for it.

In deep shit, I turned to him now.

"There are two kinds of leadership," Ray told me after listening patiently as I described the CAPPS fiasco, "transactional and transformational. You cannot possibly out-transact these people. They sit on all the committees, and they have great sitting power. They will out-sit you. If you are not to fail, you will need to be a transformational president.

"Your job, Marty, is to transform American psychology."

WHEN I FIRST encountered psychology, more than thirty years before my stint as APA president, two warring factions in the field—the behaviorists and the Freudians—were at a standoff. For all their differences, they shared many of the same dogmas. Both focused on misery. Neither took evolution seriously. Both believed that the past, especially childhood trauma, frog-marches us into the future. Both considered thinking and consciousness mere froth. They also shared many of the same blind spots: happiness, virtue, free will, meaning, creativity, and success. In short, they both missed everything that makes life worth living.

I have witnessed the transformation of psychology, and at more than one pivotal moment, I led the transformation. Psychology in my lifetime rejected these premises in order to remove four huge blind spots. First, the discipline abandoned behaviorism to embrace cognition and consciousness. Second, it realized that evolution and the brain constrain what we can learn. Third, it ended its fixation on only

curing what is wrong to include building what is right and positive in the world. Finally, it discovered that we are drawn into the future rather than driven by the past.

Together these make up the new psychology of hope.

This book tells the story of these sweeping changes in psychology over the last five decades. I too came to reject these four dogmas, and I tell the story of how the field was transformed through the medium of how one psychologist was himself transformed.

Chapter Two

Childhood

*I*T BEGAN, AS for many psychologists of my generation, when I first read Sigmund Freud. I was thirteen years old, and my sister came home from the University of Rochester for her summer vacation. Beth was my exuberant and affectionate mentor from the time I was six. When I was seven she taught me what a factorial was. Showing off to my second-grade class may have been my first display of academic hubris. When I was nine, she read *Flatland* aloud to me,[1] unveiling the marvels of geometry. At twelve, I confessed to her that I had never read a whole book and merely bluffed my way through seventh-grade book reports. So she locked me in my bedroom with *The Count of Monte Cristo* and did not let me out until I had read all of it. Eighteen hours later, I emerged, peed copiously, and passed her quiz. I have never been without a novel since.

In the summer of 1955 she brought home Freud's *Introductory Lectures on Psychoanalysis*.[2] So I lay in the navy surplus hammock that stretched between two emaciated pine trees outside our little camp in Lake Luzerne, New York, and I could not put Freud down.

Counting forward from the date of the Japanese attack on Pearl Harbor, I was born almost exactly nine months later. My conception, I surmise, was a declaration of optimism about the future by my parents, Irene and Adrian. Both of them had lived troubled lives, and optimism did not come at all naturally.

My mother, Irene Brown, was born in 1905 in Nagyvarad (meaning "big town"), Hungary—now Romania. She changed her birthdate to 1906 when she married my father in 1931 since it was unseemly for the bride to be older than the groom. Nagyvarad was a center of fashion and culture and Jewish life until the Nazis "cleansed" it of Jews in 1944. My grandmother (Elsa Bet Weinstock) died giving birth to Irene. It was December 1905 in the Carpathians, and Irene, premature, was incubated in the family oven and nursed to health by my grandfather. With the death of his wife, Marten Brown lavished all his affection on tiny little Irene. Bathed in such love, the first three years of my mother's life must have been idyllic. But scarring events would soon cast her out of paradise.

Marten was a tailor who designed women's clothes, and he was ambitious. This was the height of the Belle Époque, and Vienna at the turn of the twentieth century was the center of the intellectual and artistic universe. This was the Vienna of Freud, Ludwig Wittgenstein, Gustav Mahler, Gustav Klimt, Karl Kraus, and the Strausses—it was the place to be, but it was also a place of rising anti-Semitism. Marten, in his mid-twenties, must have yearned for Viennese life and applied to the Academy of Fine Arts to study haute couture. Just a Jew from the countryside, he was summarily rejected (as was Adolph Hitler, twice). So he packed up Irene and decided to try his luck in Berlin.

But not before acquiring a second wife. I knew her only as "Granny Brown." Petite, solid, outspoken, determined-jawed, fiery . . . and jealous, she was a stepmother right out of Cinderella. The love that Marten lavished on his firstborn daughter his wife should have instead, and she let him know it. Marten withdrew from Irene, and even in her late eighties, Irene teared up when she spoke about this rejection, a rejection that no three-year-old could possibly understand, a rejection that any three-year-old would only attribute to herself.

Berlin proved no more promising than Vienna, and Marten's haute couture hopes were again dashed. So in 1911 he took his five-year-old daughter and his pregnant wife to New York. They settled in the town of Tuckahoe, a few miles north of the Big Apple, and Marten opened a tailor's shop. Irene's first day of school was bittersweet. This was the age of the welcomed huddled masses coming to America, and her

class was full of newly landed kids. The kindergarten teacher called on the children to share songs from their homelands, and a Scottish girl sang. Irene knew exactly what was going on and bursting with excitement waved her hand to be called on. She so wanted to sing a Hungarian song. But since she spoke no English, the teacher passed over her for the Irish girl on her right.

As she grew into a teenager, she was not passed over any more. She was gorgeous—there is no other word: five-foot-one, full-figured, blonde, and blue-eyed. She was well-spoken but reserved and very sympathetic of manner—a girl you could pour your heart out to. But poverty took its toll. Marten's tailor shop burned to the ground. Irene dropped out of high school to help support the family as a legal secretary. In the early hours of the morning, she often heard Marten sobbing in his bedroom in despair over their dwindling finances.

But all her suitors during the Roaring Twenties may have been ample compensation. One of them, a most persistent young law student, she brushed off repeatedly. Not to be deterred, he sat mooning on her porch steps all evening, waiting for Irene to return from her dates. By now she was engaged to a wealthy dentist (there are family rumors of six engagements), and the Great Depression had begun. One evening Adrian must have finally caught her in the weak moment he was waiting for. He pounced, and their romance began.

Persistence was only one of Adrian's strengths. He was handsome, but not head-turningly so like Irene: five-foot-nine, blonde, barrel-chested, and blue-eyed, with the deepest dimple in his chin. He was also dazzlingly clever, ingratiating of conversation, and extremely quick of mind. His parents, Sigmund and Matilda (née Beringer), had emigrated from the Dutch border of Germany and from Alsace, respectively, in the 1890s and married in New York City on the very last day of the old century. Their firstborn, Bert, Adrian's big brother and my uncle-to-be, was a strapping, ruddy, and domineering lad. He became a millionaire in his twenties on the eve of the Great Depression and founded a Wall Street trading firm. In a family scandal, he changed his name to Sinclair upon marrying a Catholic—a cause for ostracism by the Seligmans. Adrian, in contrast to Bert, was a sickly child, prone to hiding at home from school when things

got too rough. He had a childhood lump in the throat that impeded swallowing, likely an anxiety condition known as *globus hystericus*. It was quite prevalent in the days of Freud but is rarely seen today. (If I think too hard about my own Adam's apple, I can almost feel the lump arising. I will refrain and put off a discussion of heritability until later in this book.)

But Adrian skipped four grades in school, zoomed his way through City College, got his bachelor of laws degree from New York University School of Law and then a Juris Doctor from Columbia, when the *D* in "JD" meant that you wrote a real doctoral dissertation. His was about Benito Mussolini's rise to power. He courted Irene successfully, and they married in 1931, honeymooning in Atlantic City, then a classy destination.

And then came the crucial decision of his life.

He was a brilliant young lawyer, armed with a doctorate from Columbia Law School. But it was the second year of the Great Depression. Lawyers were not out of work, but much of the rest of America was, and clients were having trouble paying up. Lawyers were still drawing salaries, but many of them were poor. He was newly wed, and he and my mother both saw potential disaster looming more readily than they saw opportunity.

So he chose a secure path: civil service. Low pay, steady work, no chance of ever losing your job, but also no chance of scaling the heights of money or power. No chance of standing eye to eye with Bert.

Adrian took a job reporting judges' decisions at the Court of Appeals (New York State's highest court) and moved with Irene from the center of power—Manhattan—to the provinces: Albany.

Albany in 1931 was not a boomtown and, in fact, hadn't been since the building of the Erie Canal more than a century before. Its population had held steady at 130,000 for those one hundred years. While it was the capital of New York State and domicile of politicians on the rise—Theodore Roosevelt and Franklin Roosevelt, soon to be president, to name just two—the brightest lights escaped every weekend on the express train back to Grand Central Station in Manhattan.

Albany was settled by the Dutch in the 1620s, and the prominent wealthy families were still named Ten Eyck, Schuyler, VanDerZee,

Pruyn, and Van Renselaer, with a couple of Townsends and Living-stons thrown in for diversity. The decaying estate of the patroon still stood high o'er the Hudson River. But the old families eventually lost their political power to the Irish, who had come en masse as labor-ers after the 1845–1852 potato famine. By 1920 Dan O'Connell's po-litical machine—a machine so all-powerful as to make Jersey City and Chicago look like democracies—ran the city. O'Connell passed out twenty-dollar bills from the living room of his unpretentious row house in Colonie to voters in need, and the machine's front man—Mayor Erastus Corning IV—lent it all a veneer of gentility.

Albany was as grubby as it was corrupt, and the Great Depression made it worse. Large numbers of "bums," looking for any work at all, roamed the streets during the day and slept in cardboard boxes on the banks of the Hudson River by night. The bums were white, and beneath them on the social scale were the blacks, who were even more miserable and drew even less public sympathy and attention. This was in good weather. In the winters, when snow could pile up to four feet and the temperature could sink below zero for a week, life was brutal, fragile, and cheap.

Civil servants and merchants made up the middle class, some of whom hailed from Albany's sizable enclave of Jews. There were the old Jewish families: the Sterns, Nathans, Mendelsons, and Barnets, the Jewish upper crust. They had come to Albany in the mid-1800s, founded Reform Judaism in America, owned the factories, and be-come prominent pillars of the community—although they still could not join the Fort Orange Club. Then there were the nouveau riche Jewish families, newer arrivals, who ran very prosperous businesses. They were the upper middle class, and they could join the Colonie Country Club—but not Wolfert's Roost. And then there were the rest of us, the civil servants and just-hanging-in-there merchants, who could not join Colonie but could join the synagogues.

Adrian and Irene joined T'Firith Israel, the conservative syna-gogue. I came to know, under tragic circumstances, that my father was an atheist, but my mother was very strongly attached to Juda-ism. Marten had been pious (as well as a loyalist admirer of Emperor Franz Joseph of Austria, who had given a medal to his second wife for

The Seligman family in 1945 at the Fulton Chain of Lakes in upstate New York: Martin (three), Adrian, Beth (ten), and Irene. Courtesy of the author.

her apple strudel). My father's attachment to Judaism was political. A mover and shaker, he became president of the synagogue and was instrumental in transforming it into Temple Israel, which became the largest and most powerful of the Jewish institutions in Albany.

SO YOU NOW know the world as I found it when I arrived one gestation period after Pearl Harbor.

"Just in time for lunch," were the first words my mother heard on August 12, 1942, after the delivery at 11:58 a.m.—an exclamation we will soon hear William James make under more momentous circumstances. I came late, and Irene was forced to walk and walk and walk

to induce labor. It must have been traumatic, because after that I was never late again: a compulsion to get stuff done and show up early is an emblem of my life that I am proud of.

There was no doubt that I would be named for my saintly grandfather, Marten, who had died of a sudden heart attack in 1940. Elias was chosen as my middle name to honor Irene's Weinstock grandfather. But all this upset my naming-deprived six-year-old sister, who was then given naming rights. So I acquired a second middle name, Peter.

Martin Elias Peter Seligman.

Somehow the unmyelinated oblivion of childhood blanketed World War II right up to its close, and my first memory, no less disturbing, dates from the very end of the conflict. It was April 1945, and a blue-eyed boy with ringlets of platinum blonde hair was playing on the linoleum floor of the kitchen. All the photos from that era—and my father took hundreds of them—show me to be unfailingly merry and beaming.

I heard heartbroken sobs and gasps from the next room and soon found my mother on the second step of the stairs under the newel post, her head in her hands. I tried to comfort her but could not. She would not stop. She sobbed and sobbed.

What had happened? The thirty-two-month-old boy was mystified, and he knew only that the person at the center of his universe was in the throes of grief and that he was helpless to do anything about it. Many years later, my mother explained that she must have just heard that President Franklin Roosevelt had died or, even worse, that she had just found out about all the Jews—much of her family abandoned in Hungary—murdered.

Or both.

I can't say for sure if the sunshine went out of my life just then, but the photos of me as a young child—merry and beaming—do look different from those taken in later childhood, and they look very different still from those of my teenage years. The smiles are a shade or two less bright after age three, and by late childhood I am usually tight-lipped and unsmiling. When that beaming two-year-old looks up at me from the old photos, I do not recognize him. But I do recognize myself in the teenage photos. By then I look serious. Considering

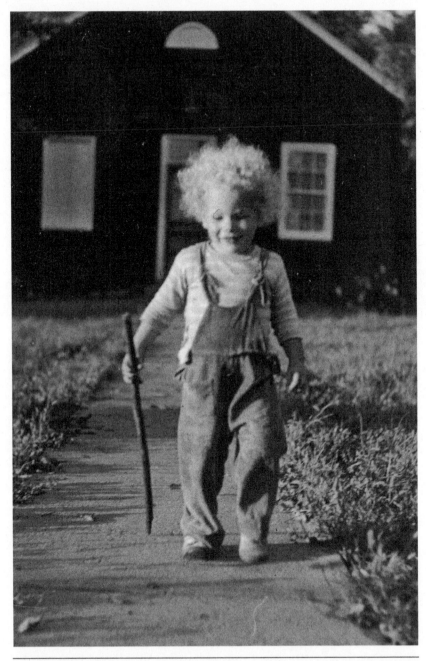

Martin in 1946, the blue-eyed boy with ringlets of platinum blonde hair. Photo by
Adrian Seligman.

my lifelong skirmishes with my own depression and the fact that my early work in psychology centered on helplessness and depression, this must have been a turning point in my life.

I was indeed a serious student once school started. My parents first tried nursery school when I was four, but the moment my mother left, I wailed and did not stop until my parents retrieved me. So school was postponed until I was five.

School 16 was only two blocks from our house on South Main Avenue. The ten-minute walk took me first for a long hug from Milton, the crippled and basset-eyed newsboy peddling the *Times Union* outside Mack's corner drug store; then past Stittigs, where the cherry parfaits at thirty-five cents were Beth's highest reward for me; then past the Madison Theater, where every Saturday morning Hopalong Cassidy outgunned Peg Leg and his gang of seedy Mexicans; across Madison Avenue under the watchful eye of the huge, merry policeman in black leather; and onto the packed-dirt playground of the school yard, where two hundred scruffy kids stood awaiting the rattle of the morning bell.

What awaited us on the inside of School 16 was . . . well, not much. Teaching kids in the public schools of Albany was the female extension of the O'Connell machine's hiring dozens of men to plant tulips in slow motion in Washington Park. In addition to legions of unemployed males in need of featherbedding, there were legions of unemployed spinsters to pay off as well. These were my teachers.

We spent countless hours singing about Ireland.

> *And if there is going to be a life hereafter*
> *And somehow I am sure there's going to be*
> *I will ask my God to let me make my heaven*
> *In that dear land across the Irish Sea.*

(It makes me sick even now that my seventy-five-year-old mind is still cluttered with this junk rather than with Shakespeare or the Gettysburg Address or even the Bible.) Irish songs were broken by an occasional song about America. We had dancing lessons next to the monstrous coal-blackened furnace in the basement.

Papa loves Mambo
Mama loves Mambo
Swings like a gate with it
He loses weight with it
Uhh

We memorized times tables and practiced penmanship. "Duck and Cover," diving under our desks and covering our heads with our hands to survive a Russian nuclear attack, was a fun break in the otherwise mindless school day. Try as I might, I cannot recall a single intellectual moment until the fourth grade.

I soaked up a storehouse of knowledge through this period—but not from going to school. I had a stamp collection from which came unbidden the geography and political makeup of the world. I could feel the German inflation of 1920 as I glued in the stamps overprinted with 1 million marks and then 1 billion marks. The dignified visage of a youthful King George VI on British colonial stamps told me of a vast empire that stretched across the globe, an empire that kids who went to better schools learned about from Rudyard Kipling. Without any effort I absorbed a lot of American history from the president series (Woodrow Wilson on the one-dollar stamp, Warren Harding on the two-dollar stamp, and Calvin Coolidge on the five-dollar stamp). I had a drawer full of comic books, including Classic Comics, from which came, again unbidden, rudimentary space science, the plots of the great novels, and countless portraits of what it is to suffer and what it is to be a victim and what it is to have courage.

"AND NOW FOR the finals. The fourth grader who gets all of these right will be Albany's Quiz Kid," said the announcer to the expectant audience of about two hundred parents, teachers, and students assembled in the Madison Theater.

"There are only two of you left. Martin Seligman, you have ten seconds. What state ends in 'ut'?"

"Connecticut," I snapped back.

The heroes of the Seligman household in 1952 were not Douglas MacArthur, Dwight Eisenhower, or even Mohandas Gandhi. Not

Albert Einstein and Robert Oppenheimer, though they were runners-up. Rather, the big names were Joel Kupperman, Joan Alizier, and Dickie Freeman. They were Quiz Kids. Once a week Beth and I sat in the kitchen on the edge of our chairs, glued to this popular radio show from Chicago. Five kids, chosen for IQ, poise, and quick wit, competed to answer listener-sent-in questions. "President Truman must fly over eight states to go to Washington from his home in Independence, Missouri. Name five."

I raced the Quiz Kids, often winning to Beth's cheers. The Chicago celebrities, it was announced, were chosen from local playoffs. *Imagine, Martin, that you can win a playoff in Albany and get to Chicago.*

The moment actually arrived. "Connecticut is right, Martin. Now, Rocco, your question. How many Little Peppers are there?"

Rocco Giaccomino, from somewhere in lower Albany, a place my family wouldn't even drive through, pondered.

"Five," he ventured. I was sure he was guessing. I didn't know why, but I too would have guessed five.

"Correct!"

And so it went through six more rounds.

"Martin. Who wrote 'Flow Gently Sweet Afton,' and where it is?" I'd never remotely heard of this. The Afton must be a river. In Ireland? But not in any song we sang in School 16.

"England," I blurted out right before the bell.

"Incorrect! Rocco?"

"Scotland. 'Flow Gently Sweet Afton' is a poem by Burns . . . Robert Burns," said Rocco with finality.

On the way out of the theater, Beth said disconsolately, "How can they expect an eight-year-old to know Robert Burns?"

I took home a Mickey Mouse watch with a fire-engine-red wristband. Rocco, unfairly all of nine and taught by Scottish spinsters, went to Chicago.

HEBREW SCHOOL WAS held in the basement of the Federal Street Synagogue. Mrs. Mordkoff, four-foot-six, hair dyed orange-red, with disfiguring scars on her cheeks, taught Jewish history. Neatly crayoned drawings of ancient Jewish conquests—the sword-wielding Amalekites,

Albany *Quiz Kids* final, 1950. Rocco Giaccomino wins. Photo courtesy of Adrian Seligman.

the Phoenicians tending miniature sailing ships, and the giant be-skirted Philistines fallen under Jewish spears—adorned the walls.

The heat of the ovens of Bergen-Belsen was palpable in this basement. Our teachers were refugees from Hitler, and they were militant Zionists. The phrase "never again," though unspoken, was omnipresent. As in School 16, there was never an intellectual moment. We memorized the twelve tribes of Israel—they were up there in crayon if we forgot. Manasseh was huge and purple. We recited Hebrew we didn't understand and sang songs in Hebrew and English.

> *Israel, Israel lives again*
> *For the greatness and courage*
> *Of her men . . .*

Beth interjected loudly

> *And Women*

IF WE MEMORIZED enough Hebrew, we got promoted to memorizing Rashi, a rabbinic commentator of the fifteenth century whose
Hebrew was in a different script, and obediently we read Rashi aloud
still minus understanding. I was reading Rashi aloud and recovering
from a bug that had kept me home the week before. The teacher, a
grizzled ancient in a threadbare black suit with a pocket watch on a
silver chain, towered over me, glaring. I read on. I came to a word I
had not seen before and sounded it out: "Yee . . . yaw."

Lifted by the scruff of my neck into the air and tossed out the door,
I landed on the polished wooden floor outside. Much later, I was told
that I had sinned by saying the name of the Lord out loud. My class
had learned the previous week that this was forbidden.

The best moment of Hebrew school was right after it ended. Like
released prisoners, Howie Berkun, David Grand, and I shot out the
double doors and raced up to the greasy spoon at the corner of Federal and Delaware. A deep fryer redolent of boiling pork fat dominated the tiny room. For a quarter it produced the most delicious fries
I had ever tasted. The secret was smearing them with catsup and salt
and eating the potatoes immediately out of the fryer.

Adrian, elected president of the synagogue, had sold the old building to the Jehovah's Witnesses (as a child I hadn't the foggiest idea
what they were) and merged the congregation with one of the other
conservative congregations; he was now running for president of the
newly minted Temple Israel. The internecine rivalries were fierce, and
dinner conversation was all about what a "dope" Kibby Koblenz, his
opponent, was and how Adrian's young handler, Leo Pfaff, was bringing the Lorvans around. My bar mitzvah was scheduled for October
1955 in the spanking new building.

But my little world was about to be turned upside down.

Chapter Three

Youth (1955–1960)

Taller, I walk through the shrunken corridors
On the cross of whose walls I was nailed
My gelatinous mind impaled
My gelatinous heart jelled[1]

BY AGE TWELVE, I was brainy. Teachers liked me. Miss Eldred in the fourth grade was the first to dote on me and to tell me that I was unusually bright. Beth and my parents said so, but Miss Eldred was more credible, since she penciled my report card and therefore was harder to discount. I was fast and confident in class—if not on the street or the Little League diamond—and liked to show off my smarts. I had my hand in the air before almost all my classmates—except Gary Hoke, who mercifully decamped to Cleveland midyear. Facts stuck to me, and learning was effortless. When it did demand effort— like plowing through a whole book—I didn't do it. I bluffed my way through the long stuff.

I strongly identified as Jewish. You (and I) should find this noteworthy, even provocative, given the dark stories I've just narrated and the absence of any positive memories that come to mind. But tribalism is surely not about the good times, and it penetrated to my soul. When I scanned the front page of the *Knickerbocker News*, as I did every evening after reading *Alley Oop*, the *J*-word just popped off the page. I was part of a minority and a persecuted one at that. It was dangerous to be Jewish. They might descend on us in the middle of the night and

cart us off to the gas chambers. I was chicken-shit Jewish, not proud Jewish like my Hebrew school teachers. Most of our neighbors were Catholic, and they were also tribal. But they were not hostile, and we were tolerated, at least to our faces. I was never called a dirty Jew, but this did not weaken my lurking paranoia. At Christmas, Easter, and especially on Sunday, the difference between the Seligmans and the Campbells and Buccis was stark. My parents almost never socialized with the goyim, and unlike our Reform Jewish friends, we didn't have a Hanukkah bush.

Lastly, I was déclassé. I was soon to find out what this meant.

MY FATHER DROPPED me off at the bottom of the circular, elm-lined driveway of a stately Georgian edifice surrounded by a green-sward of tennis courts and football fields. I was not allowed to walk up the white marble steps and go in by the front door. Rather I was ushered around the side and into the "buttery," a cavernous, low-ceilinged, wood-paneled affair. I sat on one of the long benches set at a gleaming hardwood table. There were about fifty boys of my age so seated, and on the hour we were each presented with a booklet, a pencil, and blank answer sheet. This was the entrance competition for admission to the Albany Academy for Boys. It was (I now know) just an IQ test. No need to bluff here. I breezed through it and finished minutes before any other boy.

Weeks later my parents told me that I would be attending the academy in the fall of 1955 for second form (the British public school term for eighth grade). My father was very proud. He and Irene had decided to make a big sacrifice for my future. Adrian, as deputy state reporter of the Court of Appeals, earned less than $7,500 before taxes, and the tuition they shouldered was $600 plus uniforms, lunches, bussing, and fees.

Why this sacrifice? Not only did the teachers at School 16 not teach anything, but college admissions officers had sniffed this out. Even the valedictorian from Albany High School must have struggled to get into Cornell—the zenith of aspiration for students of the Albany public schools. Harvard, Yale, and Princeton were out of reach. Beth had been admitted to Radcliffe, but my parents would not pay for

a girl to be so expensively educated. So she went to the University of Rochester for just one year and then to the free New York State Teacher's College in Albany. The best graduates of the Albany Academy for Boys, however, sometimes got into the great universities, and my assigned role was to burst the chains that had shackled the family since Marten's rejection by the Viennese Academy of Fine Arts, Big Brother Bert's Millions, the Great Depression, and the gray civil service.

I was told none of this of course, not even about Radcliffe.

IT IS 1998. Darryl, my son, is four years old. I am fifty-four years old. My wife Mandy and I tell Darryl that he has to have exploratory surgery, a colonic biopsy. He is scared and bewildered. He goes out the kitchen door and sits on a low wall. Over and over he drops polished stones one at a time into his hand, empties his hand, and does it again. And again. After an hour he comes back in.

"I'm ready," he says, and lightning arcs across the generations.

IT WAS THE last day of August 1955. I was scared and bewildered. I would be bussed to a new school, a military school, all boys, uniforms, a battalion, rich kids, and only male teachers. I didn't know a single person. I would be kept there every day until 5 p.m. My bar mitzvah was in two months. My very body was erupting: a four-inch black hair had sprouted in my groin. In the gray drizzle, I took foul shots over and over for two hours. With every clunk of the basketball against the backboard, the haze of childhood dropped away.

"I am ready," I said out loud.

I TOOK THE same walk as before, but now I stopped at the corner of Madison and Allen and waited for the school bus. I was in uniform, my black knit sweater tucked neatly into the heavy gray woolen trousers. An older boy in uniform waited on the corner.

"Hi, I'm Jerry Spector," he said, "and your sweater is on wrong. It isn't supposed to be tucked in." Blushing self-consciously, I pulled my sweater out of my trousers. Before the bus could arrive, a huge, be-finned Cadillac pulled over, and we were offered a ride. Jerry got in.

"Hail dear Academy, school that we love."

The Albany Academy for Boys. In the spring of 1955 my father dropped me off at the bottom of the circular, elm-lined driveway of a stately Georgian edifice. Here are the stairs I was not allowed to walk up until my senior year. Photo from *Cue*, 1960 yearbook.

Sheepishly I slinked in behind him. The driver was Mr. Titus, and his son, David, in the front seat, was, like Jerry, a fourth former.

As we alighted in the circular driveway, Jerry whispered to me, "Wow. Their older son was the major of battalion, the pinnacle position in the student body, last year. The major—John Abel Titus, and Mr. Titus is 'Mr. Major-maker.'" Jerry said this reverently.

"WHAT IS THE story of the Hayes-Tilden election of 1876?" Mr. Steck asked in a sharp midwestern twang. It was second-form American history, a continuation of first-form American history, which must have left off with Ulysses Grant. My hand shot up. Puzzled,

Mr. Steck called on me. I narrated the electoral vote tie and then the sellout to the southern forces in the House of Representatives. As I talked, Mr. Steck's face got redder and redder. He cut me off at the word "Reconstruction." I had answered a rhetorical question. I was told to stay after class and wrote "soybeans are better" one hundred times, covering three blackboards before he dismissed me.

The day ended on the football field. To my surprise I recognized the coach, Bob Olcott. Burly Bob had been the amiable swimming instructor at the Stratton Mountain Boy Scout camp the previous summer. He had failed me on my swimming merit badge for doing a scissors kick, rather than a frog kick, with my breast stroke. Duly corrected, I finally got the badge.

"Hello, Bob," I said. His jaw dropped. There was a stunned silence from the football kids within hearing range.

"It is 'Mr. Olcott,' and it is 'Sir,'" he said. Not a perfect start to my five years at the Albany Academy for Boys.

I made some friends in the first two weeks: red-headed Charlie Witherell, who sat noisily behind me in first-year Latin, whose older brother, Warren, was a renowned water-skier; and Charles Lansing Pruyn Townsend, star athlete who bounded like a mountain goat down the marble steps three at a time. The very same name was also up on the mahogany Class of 1927 plaque listing the majors for the last 140 years. In that case it was Charlie's father's name, and Charles senior was now the PMS&T, or professor of military science and tactics. I never discovered what that meant that he did.

One boy had been unaccountably absent for the first two weeks and was whispered about in tones of awe. He was a star student, a poet, and the fullback. His father, Sidney, owned swaths of downtown Albany and Troy. (A decade later William Kennedy would defame Sidney on the front page of the *Times Union* as a "slumlord.")

Sight unseen, I was starstruck.

The young man finally appeared. He had been on a family vacation. Strikingly handsome, a shock of red-brown hair combed insouciantly over his left eye, more mature than his prepubescent classmates, and quietly aloof, he exuded mystery. If the second form could be said to have a god, it was Jeffrey Albert.

With more than a touch of hero worship, I focused on befriending Jeff. He and I had in common "pre-intellectualism," a better trait than pseudo-intellectualism, but not much better. We asked profound questions (two years too soon to be sophomoric) about God, truth, meaning, and death, and we looked down on those boys who were not as profound. Jeff and I did not, however, have in common spending money, popularity, athleticism, tailored uniforms, good looks, and a gaggle of lovelorn second formers from the Albany Academy for Girls. Jeff had all of these.

Jeff lived in a mansion at the bottom of Marion Avenue, *the* place to live. My parents had walked me to that part of Albany on Sunday strolls, imagining the lives of the other half.

I was invited for dinner. The Alberts had a live-in Negro maid—Eppsie—and she served us each a whole guinea hen with raisins. We sipped a French wine. Beatrice Albert presided. She was gaunt and deeply bronzed, her lustrous black hair was regally coiffed, and she spoke with a southern accent. She used words like "trepidation." The conversation was about golf at the Colonie Country Club and the doings of the Barnets and the Sterns, the old Jewish families of Albany. I did not yet know the term "nouveau riche" or even have an inkling of the concept.

There were bowls of fresh fruit in the basement, a pool table, a ping-pong table, and a pinball machine. Beatrice, who unbeknownst to me had clawed her way up from southern poverty to marry the richest lawyer in Albany, immediately sensed my true social standing and almost by telepathy communicated it to me. I blushed violently and found myself saying "social climber" over and over to myself about myself.

IT IS A perfect spring day in late May 2013. Acres of tulips are out in Washington Park. It is the day of the two hundredth anniversary of the founding of the Albany Academy. I receive the distinguished alumni award and am invited to give a speech. The academy's headmaster introduces me as its "most important graduate since Herman Melville." Puffed up, I decide to take a memory jaunt around Albany. I walk three miles all the way to Jeffrey's house. There is a new wing jutting

*from its west end. I stare up at the vast pile. I want to ring the doorbell
and tell Mrs. Albert about Herman Melville and me.*

*I stand transfixed for a full minute. I tremble violently and then
slink away. Beatrice Albert haunts me all the days of my life.*

MY BAR MITZVAH was an unusual double event, with Gerry Shay
and me having to share the spotlight. The Kibby Koblenz wing had
wrested control of the synagogue from my father and vengefully
slighted the son of the outgoing president of Temple Israel to deliver
their message. Decades later my sister told me that Adrian's name was
not even on the plaque memorializing the past presidents of Temple
Israel.

I was told none of this, but I could sense my father's frustration and
helplessness . . . and something even worse, something that felt like a
boil about to burst.

The reception was a meeting of oil and water. Enthusiastic but
clueless, I had invited my old friends from School 16 and from the Boy
Scouts and my new friends from the Albany Academy: Jews and non-
Jews, rich and poor, the old gentry and the newly arrived, the tailored
and the shabby. The girls also came from all these strata. Except for
the mysterious magnetism by which the pretty girls attracted an ad-
venturous boy or two across the invisible boundary, the worlds didn't
mingle. They rarely jitterbugged together and never slow-danced to-
gether. It was an awkward afternoon and exposed for all the Acad-
emy boys and girls to see what Beatrice Albert instantly recognized:
Martin did not belong.

My mother asked me that evening if I would be continuing my
Jewish education. I emphatically told her that this was my last day in
a synagogue and that I did not believe in God. Late that night I heard
her sobbing softly in the next bedroom.

MY FATHER HAD arrived at a turning point in 1955. Young newly-
weds of the Great Depression, he and Irene had chosen the safe life:
civil service and a guarantee of lifetime employment. They watched
in surprise as the economy boomed after World War II and into the
1950s. No depression returned. Their peers—whom they often called

"dopes"—turned out not to be so dopey. Many of them were becoming really prosperous, leaving my family in the dust. At least the civil service promised advancement for talented lawyers, and my father was talented. Irene told me that he was fast, so fast that he could do in one hour what other lawyers took a full day to do, and so he had seven extra hours to make his work perfect. He was forty-nine years-old, and the next big job opened up: state reporter of the Court of Appeals. The job after that might even be justice of the Court of Appeals. Blue skies. Adrian was a shoo-in. No one else was nearly as talented.

Shortly after my bar mitzvah, he came home in the middle of the day, close to tears. He had not reckoned on Irish politics. James Flavin, a favorite of the O'Connell machine, was promoted over him. Just as he had as a child, Adrian went into hiding. He stayed home for weeks with a cold.

But he emerged from this dark night of helplessness with a big plan. He would run for office, and not just any office—for the second-highest office in New York State: comptroller. He was a natural politician. I had watched him work the beach in Lake Luzerne. He often approached strangers, asked them questions that he knew the answers to, and so got them talking about themselves. After fifteen minutes he had a new friend. He approached all these friends for campaign money and began to build a war chest. He angered easily now and was feverish with activity.

I HAD BEEN doing very well academically. An A was a rare grade at my school, and I was getting lots of them—even in Mr. Steck's American history class. Mr. Santee, the second-form English teacher, was underwhelmed, however. He kept me after class for talking out loud without raising my hand and had me write a spontaneous one-page essay on John Buchan's racist novel *Prester John*. I handed it in confidently after ten minutes—like my father, I was a fast worker. Mr. Santee was delighted: I had fallen into his trap. He warned expectantly, "Unless every *i* is dotted and every *t* is crossed, Seligman, you fail for the period." Each *i* was dotted, and each *t* was crossed. Mr. Santee was visibly annoyed.

But I was not doing well socially. I manned up and asked Mary Ellen Fisher on a date to the movies. It seemed to go well, and her

mother told my mother that I was a "perfect gentleman." Mary Ellen threw a big party a month later for the whole "crowd," the big social event of the fall. I was pointedly not invited. Except for what was soon to befall me, this was the worst thing I experienced in second form.

I was also not doing well with the boys. I loved food. Lunch in the buttery—white bread with browned chicken gravy—was a blissful break in the eight-to-five Academy day. When I am happy eating, I hum. It was a fiercely cold winter lunchtime. I was happily eating and noticed that the entire room had fallen silent. I looked around. Everyone was staring at me and listening to my humming. The older boys were beside themselves with laughter. I turned beet red. I wanted to die.

There was one other new boy in second form who shared my status: half Jewish, no money, brainy, not an athlete, nomadic, with a civil servant father. His name was Robert Kaiser. His father was an aide to the governor. Bob and I let down our guard with each other, and we spent weekends comfortably together. Governor Harriman, broomstick stiff and overly meticulous of speech, came to dinner at their house, and he was the first dignitary I ever met. Mr. Kaiser actually called him "Averill."

The Kaisers had a drafty weather-beaten farmhouse in Guilderland with a large empty pasture. Bob and I scraped together fifty dollars and bought a green 1948 Ford. We were both just thirteen, but you did not need a license to drive on private property. We mowed an oval track into the pasture, and Bob's mother showed us how to work the balky stick shift. She made us wear our football helmets. We spent heavenly afternoons racing at top speed around our little track. We went to the drag races on Saturday nights.

One perfect May Saturday, Adrian drove Bob and me in our family's 1950 black Chevrolet to the golf course. As he departed, Adrian remarked casually that he couldn't feel his left arm. I caught his nervous chuckle and worried all through the afternoon. But when he picked us up, after an afternoon of campaigning, he seemed fine.

He went to see Dr. Drapkin, the doctor around the corner. Adrian's blood pressure was sky-high: 300/180! Dr. Drapkin dismissed him with the advice "Take it easy." An effective antihypertensive drug, warfarin, had recently come on the market, but this life-saving

knowledge had not yet made its way up the Hudson River to the general practitioners of Albany.

The next Friday I overnighted after school at Jeffrey's house. I walked home in the morning, and as I rounded the corner of South Main and Madison Avenue, I saw flashing red lights in front of our house. I raced down the block to see my father being wheeled on a gurney into an ambulance. I could hear him speaking, but I couldn't make out the words. It was apparently an attempt at humor since the paramedic feigned a laugh. They drove off at top speed, siren blaring.

Adrian had a stroke, a cerebral thrombosis. It was serious but not life threatening. I was afraid, actually petrified, to visit the hospital. I couldn't bear to see him so struck down. His big brother, Bert, rushed up from Manhattan and visited for two hours. Irene heard a loud argument from inside the hospital room. Bert exploded out the door and left. Irene rushed in. Adrian was unconscious. He had suffered another stroke, this one massive and irreversible. We never found out what Adrian and Bert had argued about.

When Adrian woke, he was paralyzed on his left side and not expected to live. Against the odds, he survived and spent the next two weeks in Albany Hospital. Then he was transferred to a nursing home in Guilderland, where he spent the next two months without improvement. I finally steeled myself for a visit. I could see in a glance that he had lost twenty pounds, and his left arm and left leg were withered and motionless. He was overcome with tears when he saw me. His speech was unimpeded, and except for being more emotional than before, he seemed quite lucid.

At the end of the visit, he told us in a choking sob, "I don't believe in God. The only thing I believe in is *you*—Irene, Martin, and Beth—and I don't want to die."

Adrian never recovered. By the end of the summer he was sent home, still paralyzed, still emotionally labile, and wholly drained of his hallmark vitality.

"HI THERE. SORRY to bother you, but I've been talking to all the folks here in Greenwich [pronounced 'green witch,' not to be confused with the posh suburb in Connecticut], making a sort of survey. I'm not here to sell you anything," I lied.

Bob Kaiser had seen an ad in the *Knickerbocker News* from the Keystone Readers Service offering to hire boys as young as thirteen. We needed the money. Irene had called a family council. She told us that the nursing home costs had wiped out almost all our savings and all their insurance, and now Adrian would need round-the-clock nursing care when he came home. Beth all too eagerly suggested that I return to public school, saving almost $1,000, and Irene very reluctantly agreed. A year ago I would have burst into tears, but now I was a man, and *the* man of the house, so I quietly decided to go looking for a job with Bob.

Bob and I appeared for the interview on the fifth floor of a run-down office building in lower Albany. There was no interview. All the boys who showed up were hired on the spot. There was no salary, only a commission, four dollars on the thirty-six-dollar deal. Those few boys who didn't quit the first week would be the summer sales force. We were door-to-door magazine salesmen. The customer got four three-year subscriptions to Curtis Publishing House magazines. Five boys were packed into each car and driven to hamlets all over upstate New York. We avoided rich places (residents were too smart not to realize that thirty-six dollars is no bargain, since they would pay exactly that if they wrote in for subscriptions), and we avoided poor places (where people didn't have the two-dollar down payment). We met hundreds—and in my case thousands—of young housewives from poor working families.

"Would you mind telling me which three of these [I tried to hand her a laminated card with a list of magazines—*Ladies Home Journal, Better Homes and Gardens, Field and Stream, Jack and Jill*] are your favorites?" If she opened the screen door and took the card, I was halfway home. If she did not—saying, "Books! We don't want any!"—I reassured her that I was not there to sell anything; I was just taking a sort of survey. Forty years later, New York's state legislature would outlaw this as a deceptive sales practice, but in June 1956 it was legal.

Bob Kaiser quit in disgust after the first week. I, however, had made forty sales and was handed eight twenty-dollar bills, $160—more than my father, with a doctorate in jurisprudence, took home from the Court of Appeals. I did this for five summers, and by the time I was ready to graduate and had a driver's license, I had my own crew of young boys.

I made more money selling magazines than I would make again until I was an associate professor. When I was seventeen, Mr. Hunter, the owner, told each boy on the way out the door, "Touch the lucky stones." Some of them obeyed reluctantly, but I recoiled at this mysterious sexual overture. He did not ask me again—but he did offer me the whole company in the summer of 1960 if I gave up my college dream.

When the Academy reopened in late September 1956, Headmaster Harry E. P. Meislahn called me into his office and told me that he was giving me a full scholarship. Beth and my friend Jerry Spector had been to see him to tell him I would have to withdraw because we were too poor. I had to wash dishes at lunchtime, but between that and my magazine sales, I was saved.

Henceforward, adopting my headmaster's double middle initials, I would be Martin *E. P.* Seligman.

I was now a third former. I stood first in my class of fifty academically. But I was not brimming with confidence; quite the opposite: my father's helplessness had affected me in ways I could not begin to fathom. I was ambitious to achieve the heights at the Academy, to become a major or at least a captain, and I was elected class president—the last presidency I would hold until I won that of the American Psychological Association. About eight of the third formers were promoted to private first-class—the very rich boys, Mr. Meislahn's son, Findlay, and Charles Lansing Pruyn Townsend, the winner of competitive drill. I remained a private.

Bob Kaiser decamped for the Loomis School in Connecticut. His parents were in better touch with the real old-boy system than were the more provincial Albany parents. After Yale, Bob would be a journalist and historian, then famously the managing editor of the *Washington Post* under Ben Bradlee. He never had to sell another magazine. Dan Chirot took Bob's place.

Dan was the most exotic kid in school. He was French, his blonde hair was wildly uncombed, and he spoke with just a trace of an accent. Despite being very middle-class—his father was an anesthesiologist in Troy—Dan was supercilious. Somehow, I felt honored when he deigned to chat with me. Even Beatrice Albert was taken in. When Dan and I arrived for dinner together at the Marion Avenue mansion, Mrs. Albert brightened visibly and hugged him. Mr. Albert asked Dan

(who was just fourteen) to sip and then approve the red Bordeaux. "Quite potable," he said.

I was chopped liver.

And Dan was superbright. The highest grade at the Academy was an A. Dan took French, and suddenly an A+ was publicly awarded. By the middle of fourth form, Dan did something no one else had ever done in the Academy's 140 years: a headline in the *Fish and Pumpkin* announced that Daniel Chirot had gotten all A+s. I was being bettered, but not to be wholly outdone, I soon became the second boy to achieve this.

He joined Jeff and me as the class "intellectuals." He was sophisticated. He read *Le Monde* and told us it had footnotes. He read *Doctor Zhivago* when it first came out. He talked about Napoleon's exiles and about French socialism. Dan and I played chess every day, since we were excused from study hall because of our grades and, as nerds, didn't play football. Dan read chess columns. I played a bold and unlettered game. He usually beat me.

IT WAS THE first day of fourth form, and the battalion promotions were posted. I raced down the white marble steps to the basement bulletin board. Half the class would be promoted to corporal, the must-have next step on the way to leadership at the Academy. My promotion was a near certainty: president of the class and a close second in the class academically. I scanned the corporal list: Sangster . . . Siebert . . . Townsend . . . VanDerZee. No Seligman. Surely this was a mistake. It was not. I was promoted to private first-class on the list below. Dan Chirot remained a private . . . in his case proudly so. As for me, this was perhaps the most disappointing day of my life. I was heartbroken.

THIRTY-FIVE YEARS LATER, I attend an alumni event at the Union League in downtown Philadelphia. The speakers are Mr. Steck and Mr. Olcott, both legendary Academy coaches, both now almost eighty. I invite them to overnight at our spacious home on the Mainline, and both accept enthusiastically. The next morning, while Bob Olcott sleeps in, Ernie Steck and I have breakfast.

"You may have wondered, Marty," begins Ernie, "why you were not promoted to corporal in the fourth form."

Jeff Albert, Dan Chirot, and Martin Seligman. From *Cue*, 1960 yearbook. Photo courtesy of Ruth Andrus.

I am taken aback. How could he know about the trauma I have kept so secret? "Actually it really hurt and has baffled me all these years," I confide to Ernie.

"You probably have no idea how anti-Semitic the Academy was in the 1950s. I arrived, as a newly minted teacher from Iowa, three years before you did. The Santees had us over to dinner, and Harold [who later became headmaster] asked me where I went to church. I told him I sometimes attended the Reform Synagogue. Harold left the table and did not reappear that evening. That is also, by the way, Marty, why you were rejected by Harvard."

It had never—not even once—occurred to me that Mr. Steck was Jewish.

JEANNIE ALBRIGHT, Barbara Willis, and Sally Eckert were the *it* girls and the unattainable romantic interests of this chubby fourth former. What could I possibly do to interest spit-curled, ski-sloped-nosed Jeannie, or full-breasted Barbara, the voluptuous fount of pubescent gossip, or, most impossibly, winter-tanned Sally? Jeff, who had already cornered Jeannie, was almost every girl's dream come true. Tony VanDerZee, though slow-witted, was from a family that had reigned in Albany for three centuries. Barbara already had her cap set at Charlie Townsend, or if that failed, at Tony as runner-up. Sally was the princess of the Catholic girls. She would marry the major of the battalion of the Class of 1959.

Jonathon Gordon—handsome, confident, and the likely major from our Class of 1960—it was rumored, had already gotten laid. How could I even get to first base? *I could talk to them about their troubles.* What a brilliant stroke! I was willing to bet no other guy ever listened to them ruminate about their insecurities, nightmares, and bleakest fantasies. I tried on the role, spending three hours a night on the phone listening to Sally or Jeannie or Barbara. I did not score or even come close, but I snuggled comfortably into my new niche—these were the baby steps to becoming the psychologist I would be.

In sixth form Mr. Charles Colton helped me take my first real steps. He had taught me Caesar in third form. One day I came in

unprepared. When he called on me, I glided my way through a passage on Germania.

"You're bluffing, Seligman," he interrupted. "Zero."

This was the only failing grade I ever got. I was never unprepared again, and except in poker, I never bluffed again. Not ever.

Three years later, Mr. Colton did me a momentous favor. He invented a new course called "The Humanities." I had no idea what that was, but Jeff, Dan, and I and all the other cum laude boys took it. Paul Monaco was not one of the cum laude boys. He was the quiet, unassuming one. We shared a deep bond. His father, a daring star columnist for the *Times Union*, dropped dead at about the same time as Adrian had his strokes. Paul turned out to be the most loyal of my friends, and he, like me, had his life changed by his first encounter with the humanities.

We read Will Durant on religion and philosophy. We listened to Beethoven's Fifth Symphony. We read Dylan Thomas, lots of dark Dylan, as you can see from the poem at the beginning of this chapter. An unbounded new world opened. There *was* a life of the mind, and it was different from getting A+s and being a snobby intellectual. It was where I wanted to spend the rest of my life.

Graduation was a glum affair for me. Dan was valedictorian of our class—although fifty years later, my friend Doug North, valedictorian of 1958 and the new headmaster, sent me an official transcript stating that I had actually graduated first in the class. I did not receive the various academic prizes that I felt I had earned. Instead they were distributed to the boys whose families were most likely to support the Academy financially in future years. I felt more a failure than a triumphant graduate sallying forth to conquer new worlds. I was going to Princeton, and that should have been cause for celebration, but so were four of my classmates, and I was, after all, a Harvard reject. Beth and Irene hosted a lifeless party for me in the backyard with tables set up around our sour cherry tree. My cousins, aunts, and uncles were all there, but I was a zombie going through the motions. I did not belong to their underclass world any longer. My father was conspicuous, hobbled and unable to control his emotions, both positive and negative. He was proud. He had achieved what he sacrificed for, and I was no longer the poor Jewish boy I had been before the Academy.

Chapter Four

Miseducation (1960–1964)

AT EIGHTEEN, I was still brainy, but now I was in the big leagues, at Princeton University, and I had no idea how brainy I was relative to the amazing other freshmen I met: National Merit Scholars, winners of national science competitions, math and physics geniuses already publishing, even speed readers. I asked Bob Darling, later my roommate, how long it took him to read Thomas Mann's dense *Tonio Kruger*. He said, "About three minutes." It took me five hours.

I was no longer *Jewish*, but I was still very much *lower caste*, although I didn't know exactly which variety of low. As I walked down Prospect Street past the Ivy Club, which had a larger endowment than the University of Pennsylvania, I knew that I would never walk up the path to its doors. Princeton's social strata made Albany's seem scalable. I desperately needed to avoid this nasty, inaccessible part of Princeton, but I couldn't imagine how.

I was *depressive*, and I was a *pessimist*. I toyed with writing about death and dying, and I wore black much of the time. I was morbidly introspective and through freshman year kept a handwritten journal full of dark thoughts.

I was *ambitious and hungry*. I wanted Mrs. Albert to know my name.

I was an *intellectual*, and I was at home in the *life of the mind*. My caste problem and my craving for the life of the mind were addressed in one fell swoop. Darwin Labarthe was president of the Class of 1961,

that year's senior class. I never personally met him as an undergraduate, but he was my hero. On our first day as freshmen, we assembled in the ornate Victorian Alexander Hall. Darwin told us in his crisp staccato about the honor code—either giving or receiving aid on an examination automatically led to expulsion and the extirpation of one's name from all records—and about what was expected of us: Princeton in the nation's service. It was a stirring speech, but Darwin was much more than a speech maker.

The year of "dirty bicker," 1958, was a bad one for Princeton's reputation. Bicker was Princeton's equivalent of fraternity "rush." A week of interviewing sophomores culminated in their admission to one of the fifteen Prospect Street eating clubs, which were the centers of social life for upperclassmen. The clubs were selective, and every year some unfortunate sophomores were "hosed," rejected by all the clubs. There was a gentlemen's agreement that these losers would be absorbed into the fold, one per club. In 1958 twenty-three sophomores were hosed, mostly Jewish and mostly National Merit Scholars. No club was willing to absorb them, and Princeton's anti-intellectualism and racism made headlines the world over.

Attempts to work around the clubs had a long and bitter history for Princeton's presidents. Woodrow Wilson tried to abolish them, and the trustees asked him to resign for this heresy. He exited to the lesser posts of the New Jersey governorship and the American presidency, harboring deep animosity toward his Princeton foes until his death.

Darwin approached Robert Goheen, the very young new president of Princeton. In 1957, in a single electrifying hour, Goheen had been promoted from lowly assistant professor of Greek and Latin to associate professor with tenure to full professor and then to president. It would be his job to drag the southern gentleman's resort that was Princeton belatedly into the twentieth century of civil rights for black people. His encounter with Darwin was defining. Darwin asked him to underwrite a rival system to the clubs—a nonselective eating facility that would become an epicenter of undergraduate intellectual life. President Goheen, knowing well Woodrow Wilson's fate, at first demurred. But the persistent Darwin brought the valedictorian and

the celebrated Princeton Tiger mascot into President Goheen's office to lobby and threatened a public walkout from the club system. President Goheen saw the wisdom of the idea and grasped it with both hands. The new "alternate facility" was duly named after Woodrow Wilson.

Wilson Lodge was flooded with takers, not just the most intellectually serious of the undergraduates but many distinguished faculty as well. And it solved both my problems. I joined in my sophomore year and found myself surrounded by people just like me. We engaged every evening in some of the most stimulating discussions of my life. About fifty faculty, including President Goheen himself, Walter Kaufman, Hans Aarsleff, James Ward Smith, Sam Glucksberg, Julian Jaynes, Malcolm Diamond, John Wheeler, Bruce Goldberg, Richard Rorty, and Robert Nozick, could be found there every evening, dining with rapt undergraduates. I have spent much of my academic life trying to replicate those evenings—since they are the very essence of what a university is about.

IN 2010 I go with my sixteen-year-old son Darryl on the campus tour of Princeton. Wilson Lodge and its descendants—the "college system"—have grown and flourished to such an extent that the tour guide, as we walk down Prospect Street, calls the eating clubs the "alternate facility." I write President Goheen an admiring letter saying that he succeeded where Woodrow Wilson failed. In one of his last letters before his death, Robert Goheen agrees. I treasure his handwritten letter.

THE GRANDEUR AND grandiosity of Freud's vision stayed with me all through high school and into my first year at Princeton University. I took no psychology courses early in my undergraduate days but rather immersed myself in the life of the philosophy department. I avoided psychology courses because the sophisticated upperclassmen called them "guts"—populated by the jocks and gentleman's C students—and at Princeton in the early 1960s, the psychology department was undistinguished, utterly without gods. On the other hand, the philosophy department was chock-full of great men.

Of the greats, the one who became my friend was Robert Nozick. He was a mere graduate student at the time, only four years older than I, but his unique brilliance was obvious even then. He paced up and down in his baggy brown suit—graduate students wore academic robes at dinner but suits in class—and told us freshmen that Descartes was wrong and that Aristotle could be greatly improved upon. This was nothing short of astonishing. Philosophy was alive, something one can do rather than just study. Bob went on to become one of the preeminent philosophers of the twentieth century, with a range of philosophical contributions from the foundations of logic to happiness to liberty and ethics and everything in between. At the Harvard memorial service for Bob (he died of intestinal cancer in 2002 at age sixty-three), his son said, "Some boys brag about their fathers, saying he was the strongest man in the world, or the handsomest man in the world. Well, my father was the smartest man in the world." Many of us could only nod agreement.

In the mother's milk of meeting the first world-class intellects that I had ever known, I also imbibed their unspoken premises. There were two. The first premise in the Princeton philosophy department was rigor. It was not enough to know what was true; you had to be *entitled* to know what was true by the rigorous and compelling argument that got you there.

Poor Freud. His work was rich with insight, and the landscape of his vision was almost boundless. His intuition leapt from mountaintop to mountaintop, but the valleys were too shrouded in mist to make out clearly. Rigor? This Freud did not have, as emblematized by his nomination for the Nobel Prize in literature, not medicine. Was there some way, I wondered, to answer the great questions that Freud investigated with the rigor so prized by my mentors?

In psychology, as in many disciplines, the degree of rigor and the importance of a problem are all too often reciprocal. This dilemma goes under the name "internal versus external validity," or, without the jargon, "rigor versus reality." The more the method captures the real-world issue (external validity), the less rigor (internal validity) it has. Conversely the more rigor the method has, the more poorly it captures the real world. How unfortunate. This is the "white rats and

college sophomore" issue: researchers can control and measure what rats and sophomores do in the laboratory, but any finding's application to real human problems is always a strain. Are stomach ulcers in the rat exposed to unpredictable electric shocks really the same thing as duodenal ulcers in a woman who has lost her job?

Freud was aware of this dilemma, and the story attributed to him—a man looks under a streetlight, where the light is better, for a watch he has dropped elsewhere—is about just this. It tells us where Freud stood on the importance of external validity over rigor. Freud believed that the possibility of a revolutionary insight could justify going way beyond the evidence.

In direct contrast, the behaviorists—militantly—looked where the light was good, even at the cost of not finding their lost watches. The behaviorists are the direct descendants of what I call "atomism."

ATOMISM—THE SECOND AND more insidious premise slipped into the mother's milk of my Princeton education—is the thesis that real understanding comes only by working from the ground up. We can gain clarity about real-world issues only if we first discover and analyze the simple building blocks of the complex real world and then reassemble them to reconstruct reality. The model is the periodic table of the elements. Chemistry was a muddle until the relationship among elements was first understood and codified in the periodic table. Only then could molecules be understood and could chemistry take off.

Philosophical atomism began at the turn of the last century with the work of Bertrand Russell and Ludwig Wittgenstein and had its full flowering in logical positivism and behaviorism. Russell and Alfred North Whitehead[1] showed that arithmetic, which seemed sloppy to them, could be derived from just a few premises of logic and thus placed on much firmer ground. Only on such firm ground could indubitable truth rest. In his *Tractatus logico-philosophicus*,[2] Wittgenstein took this much further. To understand reality, he argued, one must discover its "logical atoms" and how they combine. Absent such bedrock, alleged understanding is just confusion. This idea is famously distilled in the Wagnerian close of the *Tractatus*:

Wovon man nicht sprechen kann, so muss man schweigen.
Whereof one cannot speak, so must one consign to silence.

Matters of good and evil, of beauty, of politics, of science, of re-ligion, in Wittgenstein's view, lacked the bedrock and could not be rigorously and thoroughly understood. It is commonly thought that Wittgenstein was drawing the boundaries of the island of what could be known. A more romantic interpretation offered by one of the many followers who fell in love with him is that Wittgenstein was "drawing the boundaries of the ocean."

A cruder interpretation is that of logical positivism, which trans-muted the closing epigram of the *Tractatus* into the "verification principle": only statements that can be verified empirically (or are tautologies) are meaningful. Logical positivism enjoyed its moment in the sun in the 1950s but fell out of fashion because, among other problems, it could not be applied to itself: the verification principle is itself neither a tautology nor verifiable.

When applied to what philosophy should work on, atomism urges that before real-world problems—ethics, science, politics, morality, beauty, happiness, and the like—can be tackled, the basic philosoph-ical confusions about language, knowledge, and the mind must be sorted out.

This issue formed the nub of the dramatic story of Wittgenstein's poker.[3] In 1946, in the shadow of the Holocaust, Karl Popper rebuked the members of the Moral Philosophy Club in Cambridge, the very den that Ludwig Wittgenstein and his besotted lion cubs inhabited. Wittgenstein was by then the leading "analytic" philosopher in the world, and his cubs were fierce in their devotion to him. Popper con-tended that there were real problems in the world, and it was the job of philosophy to tackle them. Wittgenstein, he contended, had suborned an entire generation of philosophers by seducing them into working on the preliminaries to the preliminaries—puzzles rather than problems. Wittgenstein reacted by brandishing a fireplace poker at Popper and then walked out, slamming the door.

Most of my teachers at Princeton worked in the deep shadow of Wittgenstein, and the careful, logical analysis of puzzles was the work

Robert Nozick, pictured here as a second-year graduate student at Princeton, was in 1961 my first teacher in philosophy. He went on to become one of the world's preeminent philosophers and played a major role in the founding of positive psychology thirty-five years later. Courtesy of Getty Images.

given to good students there. The iconoclasts, like Professor Walter Kaufman, who worked on atheism and morality, and Professor Arthur Szathmary, who worked on beauty, were ostracized. Bob Nozick survived because he played the analytic game as well as anyone. But as we shall see, it was not the only game he played superbly.

Logical atomism and logical positivism eventually fell out of favor in philosophy; they did not, however, fall out of favor in scientific psychology. They found their voice in "operationalism," psychology's attempt to imitate physics. A notion such as "intelligence" was too fuzzy for science, but if translated—"operationalized"—into an IQ test score, intelligence suddenly became an object whose presence or absence—and even amount—science could measure objectively.

My senior thesis in philosophy solved a small puzzle. It was a careful analysis of the difference between "same" and "identical," a step

on the road to undermining the thesis that mind and body are identical, because "identical" entails having the same spatiotemporal coordinates. Mind and body have the same temporal coordinates (they occur at the same time) but not the same spatial ones (they do not occur in the same place). So mind and body are not identical. QED. My thesis even won the philosophy prize at graduation.

In the summer between my junior and senior years, I did my first laboratory work in psychology, another small school-boy puzzle. In Byron Campbell's lab, I looked at the effects of electric shock as punishment. I disconfirmed a current theory about masochism in rats by showing that they would stay away from shock, and the stronger the shock, the more they stayed away. Both my senior thesis and this first bit of psychology were atomistic and rigorous approaches to well-defined issues. Both were of journal quality. The rat study led to my very first publication[4] (in the top journal), and the argument of my senior thesis found its way, not under my name but rather under that of my advisor, George Pitcher, into the philosophical literature. Both were just baby steps in a professional academic career, and I was quite proud of them.

But neither was deeply satisfying. Although I did not know it yet, the battle line was drawn. How much rigor? How much reality? This was a central theme of the transformation of psychology over the next fifty years and my role in it.

Although I could not articulate why then, both these professional steps were indeed preliminaries to the preliminaries, and neither shed light on the place where I had dropped my watch.

MY LIFE WAS, of course, not all philosophy and psychology. Dating played a large, preoccupying role, but I was ill prepared. From the onset of puberty through the end of college, I was stuck in all-male settings. Women were mysterious and exotic, and I was not at ease with them. Vassar and Bryn Mawr were the women's colleges that Princeton men most looked to for being "fixed up." The Vassar freshman yearbook had photos, and a busload of Princeton freshmen traveled to Poughkeepsie to meet the photo of their choice. But first there was a lottery, and I actually won it. So I had the very first pick. A gorgeous Swedish blonde, Monica Skenske, stood out head and

shoulders, and she was mine. We arrived at Vassar and exited the bus in order of the lottery. Monica was there in the front of the line waiting for me. She was indeed spectacularly beautiful, but she was also a foot taller than I am. We were a nonstarter.

More than a year later, I spent the summer before my junior year at Berkeley. I was mostly playing bridge at the Bear's Lair and shyly ogling women. But there I took my very first psychology course. Martin Orne, a bear of man at six and a half feet tall and nearly three hundred pounds, was a social psychologist and the very model of an enlightened psychoanalyst, with more than a trace of a Viennese accent. He offered a small seminar with an opaque title: "Demand Characteristics in the Social Psychological Experiment." I signed up. "Demand characteristics" turned out to be the artifacts that bias subjects in experiments to do just what the experimenter wants them to do. So if a subject walks into a room labeled "Sensory Deprivation Laboratory," is greeted by a researcher wearing a white coat and stethoscope, and signs onerous waivers about hallucinations and danger of death, sure enough, when deprived of sights and sounds for a few hours, she will have hallucinations. If the sign said, "Meaning Deprivation Laboratory," the researcher wore jeans, and there were no waiver forms, there would be no hallucinations. This kind of debunking appealed to my critical intelligence, my negativity, and my search for "relevant" science. I was hooked in the very first half hour. Martin was the perfect blend of the clinic and the laboratory, and in later years he would wind up at the University of Pennsylvania as a professor in the psychiatry department. We would be colleagues and friends through his wrongful persecution by the American Psychiatric Association for allegedly mishandling Anne Sexton's privacy[5] until his untimely death in 2000.

I was also one of three hundred students in an art history lecture course. On the first day, I spotted a statuesque blonde and grabbed the seat next to her. She looked familiar, and thrillingly she did not move her foot when mine brushed it. At the end of the lecture she stood up. She was a foot taller than I. It was Monica Skenske.

I had better luck with the Bryn Mawr college women. My roommate and bridge partner, Brian X. Schmidt, introduced me to his high school friend and weekend date, Kerry. A Bryn Mawr sophomore

majoring in Greek and Latin, she regaled me with descriptions of her research into Greek mythology and her wondrous professor, Mabel Lang. I was fascinated—she was actually the first female I had met who was both comely and, like me, serious about academic work.

Serendipity interceded. Two weeks later I was on a train to Philadelphia, and a frumpily dressed middle-aged woman struck up a conversation. She told me she was a professor at Bryn Mawr.

"Do you know a Mabel Lang? I just heard such glowing things about her from one of her students," I asked.

"I am Mabel Lang," she said, "and who said such nice things about me?"

"Kerry Mueller."

"Oh, yes, Kerry. I am so pleased to have such an enthusiastic student of Greek. My work is so arcane, the mysteries of Linear B and all that, most of my students—even the brightest of the Bryn Mawr girls—don't much care, but to find an undergraduate so devoted . . ." Mabel said, and she went on and on.

I was now smitten, not with Mabel (with whom Kerry was smitten) but with Kerry. We began to spend weekends together, and as captain of the Ivy League championship bridge team, I had car privileges; my little red VW plied US Route 1 between Princeton and Bryn Mawr most weekends.

We lived through two national traumas together.

"I think we are all going to die this weekend," pronounced my roommate, Wilfrid Schmid, to Kerry and me from the top of our two-story suite in Dodge-Osborn. Wilfrid was as sober an undergraduate as I knew. His father was a noted Greek scholar, resident at the Institute for Advanced Studies, and his mother, he reminded us, was murdered by the Americans in the fire-bombing of Dresden. Wilfrid was a math major. The highest grade at Princeton in the 1960s, the equivalent of an A+, was a 1. A 1+ equaled 100 percent. Wilfrid would graduate valedictorian with all 1+s, except for a single 1 in a politics course. We had hoped that Princeton would trot out *insigne cum laude* (used only once, a century previously) for him, but Wilfrid and two of his other roommates (eight of us roomed together in the suite) were relegated to a mere summa cum laude.

"Politics is hard," he muttered, excusing his poor grade and also commenting on the Cuban Missile Crisis now upon us. We were glued to the radio in our suite for days, awaiting the end, but it did not come, and we staggered on to November 1963.

"YOUR PRESIDENT HAS been shot," a German graduate student, Helmut Lamm, shouted to me as I crossed Washington Road to the psychology laboratory.

"President Goheen?" I asked.

When I look back and ask myself which was the saddest event of my life (and which the happiest), I am surprised. Not the death of my mother, or the miscarriage of one of my children, not even close. It was the slaying of John F. Kennedy and equally the slaying of Robert F. Kennedy. Kerry and I hunkered down in front of the oversized black-and-white television at Wilson Lodge with about one hundred Princetonians and their dates (it was supposed to have been a party weekend) and a dozen of the faculty. Few of us were not red-eyed with weeping. Back then, before the revelations about his private life, he was our hero. We personally identified with him in ways we could not with his predecessor or his successor. He set forth our vision, and we became the bearers of his torch: "Let the word go forth from this time and place, to friend and foe alike, that the torch has been passed to a new generation of Americans—born in this century, tempered by war, disciplined by a hard and bitter peace, proud of our ancient heritage— and unwilling to witness or permit the slow undoing of those human rights to which this nation has always been committed."

Soon we got further tragic news. The body of one of our roommates, Alan Toll Dunham, an unstained golden boy from Toll Valley, Colorado, was fished out of the Hudson River. On November 22, he apparently jumped off the George Washington Bridge and shot himself in the head. I never discovered why, but even fifty years later I still glimpse him from behind on busy streets and rush up to embrace him once again, as I did on his very last day at Princeton.

Kerry and I were not overthrown by the rush of events. The very next weekend, we drove to Albany and announced to my parents that we were engaged. We were married the day before graduation.

PETER MADISON TRIED to help me find where I had dropped my watch.

Princeton hired Peter, a fish-out-of-water faculty member, during my sophomore year. Almost every other one of his colleagues in the department was an experimental psychologist who tilted toward rigor rather than reality, and this profile characterized almost all the faculty of the prestigious psychology departments in America. I used to wonder how this came about, so I asked Jerome Bruner, one of the deans of American experimental psychology.

Jerry, recently dead at age one hundred, said, "It happened in 1946, and I was there." The decisive moment came in a smoke-filled room at the annual conclave of the Society of Experimental Psychologists, an honorary fraternity (now a sorority as well) of the most senior and most rigid professors in the field. (I am a member, though increasingly marginalized for reasons that will become clear.) By 1946 this group was professing operationalism in the hope that by imitating physics—the top dog in the scientific hierarchy—psychology would gain the status of a real science and win the prestige and funding it so craved. But pressure was building in the other direction: America's soldiers were returning from war, suffering countless injuries of body and mind, and the Veterans Administration Act of 1946 promised employment and grants for psychologists, potentially transforming psychology from an academic backwater into a health-care (read "illness-care") profession. Three powerful chairmen of psychology departments, Gary Boring from Harvard, Samuel Fernberger from Penn, and Herbert Langfeldt from Princeton, huddled and then announced to the society that in the future their great departments would "hire no applied psychologists." Psychology would be the physics of the mind.

Peter Madison was a personality psychologist, not an experimental psychologist, and he certainly did not do physics of the mind. Princeton would not have hired him had the University Counseling Service not needed a new head and had benighted undergraduates not been demanding, even then, courses on "relevant" issues such as mental illness and sex—problems rather than puzzles. Peter was recruited from Swarthmore College, where he studied the lives of individual

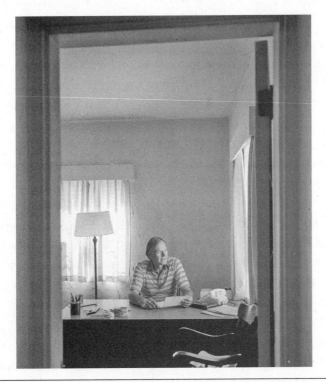

Peter Madison (born Patras Matuliatis), 1928–2009. Peter taught me personality psychology at Princeton and, at a crucial moment of professional choice, set me on the path of psychology rather than philosophy. © 1978 David Madison.

college students intensively, a project he continued at Princeton. I volunteered to be a subject. This entailed writing my autobiography—now lost[6]—of which the present book is my second attempt.

In writing my autobiography I had to choose a pseudonym. I chose "Jeffrey." Peter asked me why. I told him about Jeffrey Albert. Midway through my explanation, Peter stopped me, puzzled. He knew of Jeffrey. Jeff entered Princeton with me, but by sophomore year he had crashed and burned. He had been expelled for using hard drugs and was now hospitalized at an expensive private sanitarium. En route Jeff had casually stolen a girlfriend from me, sleeping with her and then discarding her, but not until she had discarded me. Peter asked me why I would name myself after such a shipwreck—exactly the right question. Why would I, now just beginning to blossom, nevertheless still envy Jeffrey?

I took the entire gamut of personality and intelligence tests and was interviewed at length by Peter's "Advanced Personality" class. I did all this not out of mere narcissism and curiosity about myself; it seemed like a better way of learning about "soft" psychology from the inside rather than taking one of those notorious "gut" courses. One of his personality inventories asked me what my "ideal" future self was. I wrote, "To be like Wittgenstein, surrounded by devoted students and followers." Another measured my IQ with a test that was sensitive to the upper end. Peter told me my IQ was 185.

I GOT TO know Peter well. He was tall, soft-spoken, self-effacing, and, like I am now, very hard of hearing. I leaned on him for personal advice, which I badly needed by the tail end of my senior year. In April 1964, I opened one fat envelope and was thrilled to find that I had been granted a National Science Foundation graduate fellowship to study experimental psychology wherever I chose. But another fat envelope arrived shortly thereafter, and I found that I had also been offered a Fulbright fellowship to study analytic philosophy with Geoffrey Warnock at Magdalen College, Oxford. A psychologist or a philosopher?

Actually it was a trilemma. I had been an avid tournament bridge player since my teens, and I was captain of Princeton's championship team. (In fact I am writing this paragraph while waiting for the next hand to be dealt in a large internet bridge tournament.) At about the same time as the two fat envelopes arrived, Mark Blumenthal, the captain of the University of Pennsylvania's second-place bridge team, asked me to turn pro with him. I gave this serious thought since I loved the game of bridge.

Unlike academia, bridge has a clear bottom line: either you win or you lose. Even better, bridge knowledge is cumulative: it is perhaps more of a science than psychology or philosophy. In those days progress in bidding systems was really being made, and bridge had almost as many serious journals as psychology.

But three facts eliminated bridge as a profession for me. First, I really was not all that good at it. There are "naturals" in bridge. The cards just fly off their hands, and they often can't even tell you how

they know what to do. They just do it. I, in contrast, was a "student." I usually had to think, sometimes for minutes, getting a headache in the process and, more often than not, arriving at the wrong answer. Second, making a living was chancy. The pros, other than the very top ones, slept in their cars and were grateful to land a novice partner who would pay them twenty-five dollars a day. Within a year Mark, astonishingly, went on to become one of the highest-paid professionals in bridge, joining the Dallas Aces. But I never believed that I played at his level. Academia, at least, paid a (barely) living wage, even for the less-than-stellar professor. Third, and this was decisive for me, bridge is just a game, even if the best of all games. I wanted to help human beings, not just play.

So the choice came down to academic psychology or philosophy. I asked Bob Nozick what I should do, and imparting the cruelest and kindest advice I have ever gotten, he said, "Marty, philosophy is a good preparation for doing something else." Bob was telling me that I would never scale the high peaks of philosophy—the peaks that he was ascending even then.

THE ROAD NOT TAKEN. Just as I was finishing this book, fifty-three years after mulling Bob's words, I made my first visit to Magdalen College as the guest of David Clark, now the most eminent clinical psychologist in Great Britain. Is there an opposite of déjà vu—reexperiencing an alternate life? If so, I had it.

When I entered the gates, with the huge deer park on the left and the greenswarded sixteenth-century quadrangle on my right, my jaw dropped, and I felt that I had finally—after an enormously long and exhausting journey—arrived home. When I plopped down in an overstuffed easy chair under a Turner waterscape, I thought I might never get up again. At High Table, I engaged the professor of philosophy in a recounting of Wittgenstein's wielding the poker to threaten Popper for daring to trivialize him, and then over an old Madeira, the professor of English and I discussed whether one could use my big-data methods for measuring happiness (or its lack) in Henry James. The Princeton philosophy department and all the evening dinners at the Wilson Society had groomed me for this. I knew how to be charming at High

Table and how to fit right in with Oxford philosophy. In 1964 I had not the slightest idea of how to be housebroken as a student of experimental psychology, and that made all the difference. Given Bob's advice, I decided not to go to the trouble and expense of crossing the Atlantic that April to scope out Magdalen. Had I visited, I know I would have stayed forever, and the world would have had one more mediocre analytic philosopher, accepting the premises of analytic philosophy, instead of a psychologist eager to overthrow the dogmas of experimental psychology.

I ASKED PETER MADISON what I should do. He said that in me he recognized a natural psychologist. I recognized it in myself when he told me this: the cards often just flew off my hands in psychology. Listening to a lecture or hearing what a colleague was puzzling about, it seemed that I knew—often deeply and right away—the answer long before I could explain how I knew it. This kind of intuition did not sweep over me in philosophy. As in bridge, I had to think headache-hard in philosophy, and I often came up with the wrong answer. I take intuition seriously as a mode of knowing, and being a natural is one theme of this book. For now, suffice it to say that, at the most pivotal moments in my life, I did psychology by epiphany and by intuition.

By the time I graduated from Princeton, the very texture of my mental life had changed. I recognized scientific intuition, and I took my first-blush intuitions seriously. But my daydreaming—the reverie that went through my mind hours a day—had also transmogrified. I paid attention to my daydreams—the routine material that floods the mind of a college student—and their idleness: sexual fantasies, revenge, social and material success, even death. How useless! I *decided* to tame my reverie. My reverie henceforward would be about problems in psychology and in philosophy. It actually worked, and to this day my daydreams, and even my night dreams, are not idle. In them I constantly turn over issues in science, in the same way someone visual might rotate and examine a complex three-dimensional figure. I work 168 hours per week. I entertain and welcome outlandish and even bizarre perspectives, especially waiting for a feeling of

"rightness" to strike me. What goes on in my reverie is "scaffolding," the construction of shortcuts and of modules about issues I have already visited and revisited. And unlike thinking about bridge or philosophy, this is effortless and headache-free.

Peter Madison, in parting, told me something else on that late April morning in 1964. "There are two reasons people go into psychology. One is not to be wrong. The second is not to be boring. I hope you choose the second."

With Peter's and Bob's advice, I had, by the end of April of my senior year, decided to go to graduate school in experimental psychology. It was between Yale and the University of Pennsylvania, and so I visited both places. My first stop was New Haven and the laboratory of the renowned Neal Miller. Neal, a ruddy-faced bull of a man both in stature and in personal style, was my host. He radiated confidence as befitted the world's reigning monarch of experimental psychology. His work bridged both the animal laboratory and the analyst's couch. He was especially famous for his attempt to operationalize Freudian concepts at the more basic level in rats. This was a perfect fit for me—taking clinical insights out of the consulting room and into a setting where they could be tested.

But something bothered me about Neal. He was not at all bewildered. He knew exactly what he wanted to do next and how he and his students were going to do it. There are two basic learning processes, he asserted to me in his nasal twang. There is "instrumental learning," in which an apparently "voluntary" response like pressing a bar for food is rewarded and so increases in strength. And there is "Pavlovian conditioning," in which an apparently "involuntary" response, like fear as shown by a high heart rate, is preceded by a conditioned stimulus like a tone, and the tone alone comes to increase the heart rate. But these two processes, he believed, were really one and the same. To find out if this was true, you needed to see if you could increase an involuntary response like heart rate by rewarding it or decrease it by punishing it. Neal had a team of polished postdocs and ambitious graduate students grinding away at this problem. If they succeeded, Neal Miller would go down in history as having discovered the unifying building block of all learning.

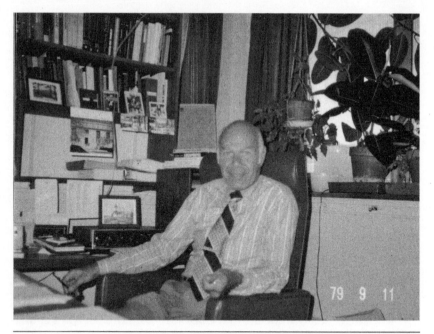

Richard L. Solomon (1918–1995) was my *Doktorvater* and one of the most influential learning theorists of his time. His crowning achievement was his election to the National Academy of Sciences.

He invited me to join the team and offered me a $500 supplement to the National Science Foundation graduate fellowship. I was tempted, since the amount of my fellowship was a mere $200 per month. But I would be a mere yeoman cog in a wheel of a big machine working on an idea that was not my own and about which I had doubts anyway, since neither instrumental learning nor Pavlovian conditioning struck me as "basic."

My next stop was the University of Pennsylvania, where Richard L. Solomon greeted me in his College Hall office. Well-tanned, bald, dapper, and wearing a brown Harris Tweed jacket, he exuded openness. Dick was one of the young Turks that Penn had rustled away from Harvard. Reputed to be the first Jewish scientist to get tenure at Harvard, Dick was famous for his work on the irreversibility of fear conditioning. In the early 1950s he trained dogs to avoid shock by jumping over a barrier when a tone went on that heralded shock. First the animals escaped the shock by jumping over the barrier, but they

soon learned that if they jumped over the barrier earlier—as soon as they heard the tone and before the shock—they would avoid the shock altogether. The memorable result was that even if the shock was never presented again, the dogs just kept jumping. Avoidance never extinguished. Dick argued that the learning of fear might be irreversible. If true, this would have profound clinical implications for curing problems like phobias, and this intersection between rigorous laboratory studies and mental illness made Dick Solomon an attractive mentor.

Unlike Neal Miller, Dick did not talk about himself or his own research program, but he did try to elicit my vision, if any. He did this in a nondirective, bubbly way, chatting about the issues that puzzled him in his laboratory, hoping I would "free associate" creatively from his puzzlement.

I did not say anything particularly creative, and in fact I made the mistake of asking Dick if he would supplement my fellowship by $500. He agreed, but his daughter told me many years later, after Dick's death, that he never forgave me for such an "unacademic" request. At any rate I was favorably impressed, and one of Dick's rambles stuck with me permanently.

"I think the dogs in my lab are helpless, and I don't know why."

Chapter Five

Twitmyer's
Breakthrough

I N THE ROOM that housed my desk in graduate school, one of the great fiascos of science had taken place sixty years before: Edwin Burket Twitmyer's announcement of his momentous discovery to the psychological world. It was not auspicious that my desk sat exactly there.

On the morning of December 29, 1904, the leading lights of American psychology assembled to listen to each other's papers. The occasion was the thirteenth annual meeting of the American Psychological Association (APA), held appropriately enough on the West Philadelphia campus of the University of Pennsylvania. Penn was home to the very first department of psychology in America, established in 1887. Its founders had taken inspiration from Leipzig's Wilhelm Wundt and his brave band of breakaway German-speaking scientists—brave because they sought nothing less than a science of mental states, a science of psychology. College Hall, a Victorian pile of green and brown stone, sat in the center of the few buildings that constituted the University of Pennsylvania. To attend the paper reading, these professors, the men wearing heavy dark suits and white shirts with rounded collars, trudged up the twelve concrete steps and through the heavy double doors. It is noteworthy that the assemblage was not solely male since the next APA president, Mary Whiton Calkins, was

among them. They turned right, strode the length of the wide corridor with its fifteen-foot ceiling, and entered the large classroom.

On the dais sat William James himself, the newly inaugurated president of the American Psychological Association, holding that post for the second time. James was a founder of American psychology, having established the first American "psychological laboratory" at Harvard in 1875, even while teaching physiology. His was an awe-inspiring presence. Erect and wiry, with striking blue eyes, his light beard now mostly gray, James was an affable and witty conversationalist. Like his dour brother, novelist Henry James, William was quite fragile, having suffered at least two "nervous breakdowns," and he was a prolific but much less fusty a writer than Henry. His acclaimed 1,200-page *Principles of Psychology* was already the classic textbook, and his influential essay "Does Consciousness Exist?" had just come out.[1]

James called the morning session to order, and the reading of papers began. You, my reader, and even I would have found the session dull—our knowledge of what was about to happen notwithstanding—and we would have spent our time gazing out the twelve-foot windows onto the green fields. R. S. Woodworth reported a high correlation between the strength of the right hand and the left. Margaret Washburn discoursed on the difference between a "feeling" and a "sensation." Hugo Muensterberg somehow united the truth of arithmetic with the values of morality and religion. Lightner Witmer, director of the psychological clinic of the Penn department, reported on the accuracy of guesses about the heaviness of very similar weights. A polite, low-key discussion lasting about ten minutes followed each paper.

At least one person in the audience was terrifically excited, barely able to contain himself. Thirty-one-year-old Edwin B. Twitmyer was about to report on his 1902 doctoral dissertation. He suspected that he had captured the most fundamental particle of learning.

This was a grand venture with a venerable provenance. David Hume (1711–1776), the founder of "associationism," claimed that we could never observe *cause* directly; rather we could only observe the *contiguity* in time between two events. The red billiard ball strikes the white ball, and the white ball shoots off into the pocket. We infer

that the motion of the red ball caused the white ball's motion, but all we ever see is an *association* in time. Such associations are the fundamental building blocks of all learning, since for the British empiricists, of whom Hume was the leading light, the mind is but a blank slate that experience writes on. And what does experience write on the blank slate? Only these associations, and so all that we learn, all that we know, is merely the combination of countless pairings.

This became a program for scientific psychology. If science could isolate and measure such associations in the laboratory, science would be able to measure learning objectively and get on its way to unraveling the mysteries of all knowledge. The scientist who discovered how to do this would achieve immortality.

Twitmyer believed he had done it. When the human kneecap is struck—just right—with a rubber hammer, a large kick ensues. This is called the patellar reflex. Reflexes are not learned; they are the nervous system's inevitable and unconscious reaction to a stimulus. Twitmyer, ingeniously, rang a bell half a second before each hammer blow. Sure enough after 150 or more pairings, the bell itself was followed by the kick—even before the hammer blow. This worked for every one of Twitmyer's six subjects.

This should all sound familiar, because in Saint Petersburg at just the same time and for similar reasons, Ivan Petrovich Pavlov was doing essentially the same thing—independently. Pavlov paired the clicking of a metronome with food powder injected into the mouths of dogs and found that the clicks alone came to elicit salivation. Pavlov added an important wrinkle: digestive surgeon that he was—not a psychologist—he extruded the salivary gland of the dog, and so he could count precisely the number of drops of saliva elicited by the clicks, rather than just weighing some mushy food. Pavlov, already renowned for his work on digestion for which he got the Nobel Prize in 1904, trumpeted these results in Madrid in 1903 in his Nobel acceptance speech. Pavlov achieved immortality for discovering this, the "conditional reflex."[2]

Twitmyer did not achieve immortality. For at the close of his paper, James said, "Just in time for lunch. I guess there won't be any discussion of this paper. Let's go eat."

Edwin Twitmyer (1873–1943), Penn professor. He codiscovered what came to be called "Pavlovian conditioning" with Ivan Pavlov, but he was completely overlooked. Photo courtesy of University Archives, University of Pennsylvania.

Why didn't Twitmyer get any credit at all for this important discovery? For one thing Twitmyer's 1902 dissertation was privately printed and so inaccessible, while Pavlov—already an international icon—was able to spread the word of his latest discovery in his Nobel acceptance speech. Twitmyer, in contrast, was a newbie and seems to have shyly avoided anything that smacked of self-promotion. For another, American psychologists at this time focused on consciousness, whereas a reflex was merely physical and mechanical, hardly the key that would unlock the mind. But it is also a sad fact that William James was bored and hungry.[3]

Kneecapped, Twitmyer dropped his conditioning work and turned his attention to his wife's specialty, speech defects in children.

Sixty years later this wound to the collective psyche of Penn's proud department still festered, and I could sense it as Professor Francis

W. Irwin related the Twitmyer story to us. Frank had been at the center of the only psychology coup d'état of the last century. Since Twitmyer's time Penn's department had gotten sleepier and sleepier, and by 1955 it was snoring audibly. As the longtime editor in chief of the prestigious *Journal of Experimental Psychology*, Frank was one of the only faculty members who still had his finger on the pulse of any living science. He persuaded Penn's high administration that a rustling was in order, and the victim of the raid was to be Harvard's psychology department. Two rival tyrants then reigned over Harvard: B. F. (Fred) Skinner, the star of 1950s behaviorism, and S. S (Smitty) Stevens, the world's leading mathematical psychophysiologist. But chafing under their whip hands were a half dozen brilliant young psychologists. Penn contacted Robert Bush, the political leader of these young Turks, and in one fell swoop Penn offered all of them full professorships. All of them accepted, and you will meet this cast of characters shortly. Nothing like this had ever happened before in psychology; nor has it since. So in 1958 a rejuvenated department under the chairmanship of Bob Bush suddenly appeared at 121 College Hall. Penn became—overnight—the place to be.

Frank told us the Twitmyer story on the very first day of the proseminar, the grueling yearlong, five-day-a-week course in which every single faculty member taught, seriatim, his (pronoun accurate) personal research in detail. Frank (PhD, Penn 1931) was the senior member of the faculty, and he actually knew Twitmyer. Austerely dressed in a threadbare gray suit and gray-blue tie, he looked considerably older than his sixty years—although everyone over fifty looked ancient to me at the time. He chain-smoked and at one point had three cigarettes smoldering—he was every bit as nervous as the twenty graduate students newly arrived at the place to be.

He had every right to be nervous since he was presenting the culmination of his forty years' work on learning to a hypercritical audience. Young as we were, we were up to date about the very latest in learning theory—trends Frank was deeply skeptical about. He did not believe in stimulus-response-reinforcement theory, which held a monopoly in the field of learning.

Frank came to maturity as this monopoly grew. To appreciate why behaviorism came to exert over the world of psychology a hold so strong that Frank spent his entire career fighting it, let's return to William James's shooing everyone out to lunch.

William James was likely bored by the reflexes of the knee and for good reason. The associationists were thoroughgoing mentalists: an association was the pairing of two mental states: the idea of wooden false teeth evokes an image of the unsmiling George Washington. James believed that mental states—ideas, images, knowledge, attention, and awareness—were the true subjects of psychology. You can bet that James began to gaze out the window soon after the talk started, thinking that this Twit-fellow was irrelevant: no science of mind would ever come from low-level reflexes.

But James did not reckon on behaviorism, the up-and-coming movement that dispensed with mental life altogether on the grounds that only behavior can be reliably measured.

The psychological world listened to Pavlov, if not to Twitmyer, with growing—and then exploding—interest. Through the first decade of the twentieth century, discontent was rife in the field. The mentalism that pervaded the 1904 meeting increasingly clashed with the materialism of the harder sciences, spurred on by the remarkable success of Einsteinian physics in the first twenty years of the twentieth century. Not only were ideas, sensations, images, and awareness "soul" stuff and science "body" stuff, but, even worse, these mental states were notoriously hard to measure. If two introspecting subjects might disagree about what they saw when light of a given wavelength was flashed—blue, dark blue, reddish purple, or deep purple—what of their even bigger disagreements when introspecting about images and ideas?

Behaviorism was elegant. It sought to rid psychology of the quicksand of mental stuff and to place measurable behavior as the concrete footing that real science requires. A rat turning left or right in a maze was more measurable and more replicable than the sensation of slimy as composed of the sensation of warm plus that of wet. John Broadus Watson ignited the revolution in 1913 at Columbia

W. Irwin related the Twitmyer story to us. Frank had been at the center of the only psychology coup d'état of the last century. Since Twitmyer's time Penn's department had gotten sleepier and sleepier, and by 1955 it was snoring audibly. As the longtime editor in chief of the prestigious *Journal of Experimental Psychology*, Frank was one of the only faculty members who still had his finger on the pulse of any living science. He persuaded Penn's high administration that a rustling was in order, and the victim of the raid was to be Harvard's psychology department. Two rival tyrants then reigned over Harvard: B. F. (Fred) Skinner, the star of 1950s behaviorism, and S. S (Smitty) Stevens, the world's leading mathematical psychophysiologist. But chafing under their whip hands were a half dozen brilliant young psychologists. Penn contacted Robert Bush, the political leader of these young Turks, and in one fell swoop Penn offered all of them full professorships. All of them accepted, and you will meet this cast of characters shortly. Nothing like this had ever happened before in psychology; nor has it since. So in 1958 a rejuvenated department under the chairmanship of Bob Bush suddenly appeared at 121 College Hall. Penn became—overnight—the place to be.

Frank told us the Twitmyer story on the very first day of the proseminar, the grueling yearlong, five-day-a-week course in which every single faculty member taught, seriatim, his (pronoun accurate) personal research in detail. Frank (PhD, Penn 1931) was the senior member of the faculty, and he actually knew Twitmyer. Austerely dressed in a threadbare gray suit and gray-blue tie, he looked considerably older than his sixty years—although everyone over fifty looked ancient to me at the time. He chain-smoked and at one point had three cigarettes smoldering—he was every bit as nervous as the twenty graduate students newly arrived at the place to be.

He had every right to be nervous since he was presenting the culmination of his forty years' work on learning to a hypercritical audience. Young as we were, we were up to date about the very latest in learning theory—trends Frank was deeply skeptical about. He did not believe in stimulus-response-reinforcement theory, which held a monopoly in the field of learning.

Frank came to maturity as this monopoly grew. To appreciate why behaviorism came to exert over the world of psychology a hold so strong that Frank spent his entire career fighting it, let's return to William James's shooing everyone out to lunch.

William James was likely bored by the reflexes of the knee and for good reason. The associationists were thoroughgoing mentalists: an association was the pairing of two mental states: the idea of wooden false teeth evokes an image of the unsmiling George Washington. James believed that mental states—ideas, images, knowledge, attention, and awareness—were the true subjects of psychology. You can bet that James began to gaze out the window soon after the talk started, thinking that this Twit-fellow was irrelevant: no science of mind would ever come from low-level reflexes.

But James did not reckon on behaviorism, the up-and-coming movement that dispensed with mental life altogether on the grounds that only behavior can be reliably measured.

The psychological world listened to Pavlov, if not to Twitmyer, with growing—and then exploding—interest. Through the first decade of the twentieth century, discontent was rife in the field. The mentalism that pervaded the 1904 meeting increasingly clashed with the materialism of the harder sciences, spurred on by the remarkable success of Einsteinian physics in the first twenty years of the twentieth century. Not only were ideas, sensations, images, and awareness "soul" stuff and science "body" stuff, but, even worse, these mental states were notoriously hard to measure. If two introspecting subjects might disagree about what they saw when light of a given wavelength was flashed—blue, dark blue, reddish purple, or deep purple—what of their even bigger disagreements when introspecting about images and ideas?

Behaviorism was elegant. It sought to rid psychology of the quicksand of mental stuff and to place measurable behavior as the concrete footing that real science requires. A rat turning left or right in a maze was more measurable and more replicable than the sensation of slimy as composed of the sensation of warm plus that of wet. John Broadus Watson ignited the revolution in 1913 at Columbia

University.[4] Psychology, he thought, should be "a purely objective experimental branch of natural science," aiming not to understand the fluff of the mind but to predict and control behavior. Introspection was a muddle, and behavior was the right unit for scientific analysis.

Within two decades, behaviorism had swept away introspection entirely, and its experimental psychologists ascended to the top professorships of American psychology. The science of mind had transformed into the science of behavior, and "learning theory" now sat on the throne.

Learning theory had three basic elements: stimulus, response, and reinforcer. "Stimulus" and "response" were the American derivation of Ivan Pavlov's work, the leading exemplar of good behavioral science. Food was the "unconditioned stimulus" and salivation the "unconditioned response" elicited by the food. The clicking of the metronome became the "conditioned stimulus" when paired with food, and the little bit of salivation that occurred in response was the "conditioned response."

"Reinforcer," the third element of the behaviorist triad, descended from Edward L. Thorndike's work at Columbia Teacher's College. He put cats in "puzzle boxes," in which pulling a string would open a door leading to food and freedom. The cats learned only gradually, not by sudden insight, and Thorndike proposed the "law of effect": associations followed by a "satisfier" are strengthened; those followed by an "annoyer" are weakened.[5] This was solid behavioral work, but Thorndike's language needed purging by the language police.

So, stripped of Thorndike's mentalism, a "reinforcer" was an event that, when made contingent on a response, increased the probability of that response—no need to postulate mental satisfaction or reward. Out of these simple elements, so the program went, the entire edifice of all learning would be constructed. When my parents asked me on one of my visits back to Albany what I was, I proudly *responded*, "I am a learning theorist."

Frank Irwin would also have said, "I am a learning theorist," although he would have termed this his "action" and not his "response." Frank told us on that first day that stimulus, response, and reinforcer

were bosh. Instrumental behavior is not governed by blind reinforcement but rather is *intentional*—even in rats. Rats (and certainly people) are cognitive and choose their most highly preferred available outcome. Frank's skepticism resonated with me; that animals might be cognitive was on my mind when I later undertook my work on learned helplessness.

So, a central premise of psychology as I first knew it was that the discipline could safely ignore thinking and consciousness, could ignore all of "mind." For the behaviorists, impeccable measurement topped everything. Behavior could be known with certainty, but mind could not, so mind was outside science. And it was not just the behaviorists who eschewed mind. For the Freudians, it was no accident that Freud used *die Seele*, the soul, to describe the scope of his endeavor. *Seele* was then crudely mistranslated as the "mind," which is not at all what Freud meant. For Freudians, mind is merely the froth on the cappuccino, and Freud was not much interested in the froth of the conscious mind. Freud was after the espresso, the roiling deep of negative emotion that drives the meanderings of consciousness.

These militant denials of cognition led to blind spots: that consciousness is not causal, that imagination has no role, and that free will is an illusion. I could not begin to articulate these blind spots when I entered graduate school, but contrary to the prevailing wisdom of 1964, today, fifty years later, we know the following:

- Conscious thoughts powerfully influence emotions. Thoughts of helplessness produce passivity. Thoughts of loss produce sadness. Thoughts of trespass produce anger. Thoughts of a better future produce hope. A science of behavior without the mind is hopelessly insufficient.
- We continually imagine different futures, we evaluate them, and we choose among them. Try as we might, we cannot shake off free will. A science that is only about the past (memory) and the present (perception) without an account of future-mindedness is hopelessly insufficient.
- A science that is only about negative emotions is hopelessly insufficient.

Much of my own story over the next fifty years would be about the struggle to carve out a scientific psychology congenial to these truths.

EVEN THOUGH MY fellow graduate students were the cream of the next generation of behaviorists, one among them shared my deep doubts. Steve Maier was his name.

We met on our very first day at Penn, standing at the departmental reception desk waiting for the ever-harassed department administrator, Ada Katz, to give us our course schedule. Steve told me that he hailed from the City College of New York and before that from Bronx Science, the legendary high school for the brightest kids from New York. Within the first three minutes, he startled me with the information that he had made his living in high school running numbers in Harlem. He wanted me to know that he was a tough New York City street kid. When he made a point, he did not waste words, and he tended to repeat his same words for emphasis. But it was more than just "no nonsense, please": I sensed immediately that he had an active bullshit detector always on high gain. We talked about learning theory, and he chuckled a lot, giving voice to the inchoate contempt for conventional thinking we shared. At the end of our thirty-minute wait, I said, "Let's work together."

"Sure," he replied without a hesitation. Steve and I would be friends and collaborators for the rest of our lives. Steve would, four decades later, make what I consider to be the most important discovery ever in the neuroscience of emotion: the hope circuit.

Chapter Six

Learned Helplessness
(1964–1967)

*T*HE STORY OF learned helplessness began well before that day in 1964 when Steve Maier and I arrived at the University of Pennsylvania. As Steve and I were looking for a project to do together, Dick's bewildered mention of "helplessness" came back to me, and I talked with Bruce Overmier, Dick's most senior graduate student, the person who, as best I could ascertain, first discovered it.

For Bruce, two years earlier in 1962, it had been an annoyance to root out, not a phenomenon to investigate. In his first year as a graduate student, he, like many of the brightest kids in the field of learning, wanted to know how the two "basic" learning processes interacted and if they could be unified. This endeavor was a first cousin of Neal Miller's obsession with finding a single basic process. Bruce's question was this: If a dog first had Pavlovian fear conditioning in which a tone preceded a shock, then the dog learned to jump a barrier to escape a shock not preceded by a tone, would the tone increase fear and propel the dog to jump even faster?

This was a simple enough question, so Bruce and Russ Leaf, then the senior graduate student, built the equipment and carried out the study. It involved two distinct settings. The first was a comfortable rubber hammock in which the dogs lay, with shock electrodes attached to their back paws. A loud tone sounded, and five seconds

later a mild shock—strong enough to make the dog bark but much too weak to do any tissue damage—started, lasting for five seconds. They repeated this sixty-four times over the course of one hour, ample Pavlovian conditioning trials to make the dog fear the tone. This first part went according to expectations.

The second part introduced the big, unexpected problem. Russ and Bruce built a shuttle box, a six-foot-long, two-chambered room with steel grids on the floor and a low barrier between the two sides. In the shuttle box, dogs learned easily to avoid shock: the lights dimmed and five seconds later the grid floor was electrified—again with a mild-moderate shock, just strong enough to provoke a jump over the barrier to escape. The idea was to turn on the tone from the earlier session in the hammock and see if it made the dogs jump faster.

But the experiment fizzled. The dogs conditioned in the hammock did not jump the barrier. They just lay down and did not try to escape the shock. This was unprecedented and enormously frustrating for the investigators.

This I had to see. So Bruce took Steve and me up to the lab on the third floor of the decrepit Hare building, just around the corner from College Hall, to show me the dogs. Indeed the dogs looked helpless— whatever that might mean in scientific terms. Bruce also showed me the two-inch-deep gouge in the sickly green wall where a furious Russ Leaf threw his clipboard in frustration.

What Bruce and Russ saw as an annoyance,[1] Steve and I saw as *the phenomenon*, one of much farther-reaching importance than unifying Pavlovian conditioning and instrumental learning. Helplessness in humans is ubiquitous and the source of endless suffering. Could we capture it in the laboratory? Could we discover what causes it? Could we discover how to reverse it? Could we discover its brain physiology? Could we discover how to prevent it?

This was why I became a psychologist.

FROM THE BEGINNING I thought the phenomenon looked like helplessness. But what, we puzzled, were the elements of helplessness? How did it come about? How could we test for it? What were its consequences? How did it relate to mental illness? How could we

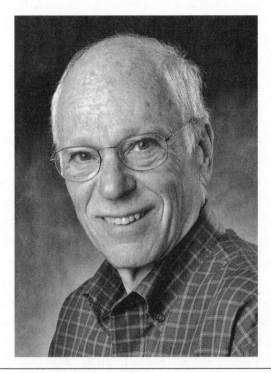

I met Steve Maier on my first day in graduate school at Penn, and we agreed to collaborate on the spot. He became a serious neuroscientist and upended our theory of learned helplessness. Steve is pictured here at the time he made his major discoveries that overturned our original theory. Photo courtesy of Steve Maier.

begin to do serious science on the mere intuition that the dogs had become helpless?

We began by defining it. Central to our intuitive notion of helplessness was the belief that nothing one does matters. This was subjective helplessness, but what, first, were the conditions of objective helplessness that might lead to such a belief? This was a thorny question, and its solution ran afoul of the most sacred premises of the learning theory that ruled academia. Formally, an animal or a person is *objectively helpless* about an important outcome, such as shock offset, if the probability of that outcome, given a response, does not differ from the probability of that outcome in the absence of that response. When this is true of all responses, objective helplessness exists.

Notice—as every learning theorist had previously failed to—that all Pavlovian conditioning is helplessness: no response of the animal

made any difference to the outcome. The food came whether or not the dog salivated. The shock followed the tone whether or not the rat's heart rate rose. Pavlovian conditioning entails objective helplessness by definition, and it seemed never to have dawned on anyone that animals might learn this and that they might find this more urgently important than the Pavlovian part of the experiment. A strong theory, such as Pavlov's, tells scientists what to look at and what to ignore, and around Pavlovian conditioning there descended a hegemony of silence about what to ignore.

Once you digest this unpacking of "nothing one does matters," helplessness seems straightforward—there is no relation between what happens to the dog and what the dog does. So we proposed that animals (and people) could learn that they were helpless, and for that to happen, the animal had to "detect" this lack of relation and so must be able to learn that outcomes like shock offset were independent of its responses. This was a radical suggestion for the 1960s. The learning theorists of that era, the grandchildren of early behaviorism, were stubbornly "associationistic" and militantly anti-mentalistic. Cognition was to be shunned, and the underlying program was to show that the "illusion" of cognition entailed nothing more than simple stimulus-response associations. Animals can learn only pairings—for example, a response paired with shock, strengthening the association (acquisition), or a response paired with no shock, weakening the association (extinction). These pairings are the only two kinds of "magic moments" that can produce learning. It seemed to us that the integration of two conditional probabilities—the probability of shock given a response and the probability of shock in the absence of that response—was an act that required brain power rather than mere behavioral conditioning. For this reason we called our theory "learned" helplessness rather than "conditioned" helplessness, in the process rejecting the simple premises that both Pavlovian conditioning and instrumental learning held so dear.

Emblematic of the tension between learning theory and cognitive theory was a standoff between Dave Williams, a young radical behaviorist professor, and me in the first-year learning proseminar.

"So you think, Marty, that animals have a rich mental life?" Dave asked, as if mockery should end the argument. I did indeed think that

higher mammals were richly cognitive and that the ability to form expectations about the future had given us an edge in the never-ending competition to survive. But these beliefs were so out of keeping with behaviorism that one either shut up or one endured mockery. I didn't shut up, and neither did Steve.

All of this made us outcasts on our home turf by putting us squarely in the camp of what would soon be called "cognitive" psychology. Two winds were already blowing in the gathering storm of the cognitive revolution. The first was Jean Piaget's sound scientific observations on the mental processes of children. The second was Noam Chomsky's devastating review (1959)[2] of B. F. Skinner's long-awaited volume (1957)[3] allegedly demonstrating that language could be understood in strictly behaviorist terms. Chomsky, a rebellious linguist and talented polemicist, argued that the essence of language was not reinforcement—the repetition of old verbal habits—but generativity: speakers could produce and understand entirely novel utterances, such as "There is a purple Gila monster flying through the kitchen," never before encountered by anyone. Learned helplessness, arguing that animals were cognitive, was the third wind, and the fourth wind, the one that transformed this into a hurricane, got started in 1965 at Penn.

Ulric Neisser, on sabbatical from the Brandeis University psychology department, was spending 1965–1966 at Penn writing his great book *Cognitive Psychology*.[4] He offered us a graduate course, which consisted of discussing his working manuscript. Dick, as we all called him, argued that behaviorism got its sea legs by somehow convincing psychologists that replicable, objective science on mental life was impossible. New experiments showed that they were wrong, and this kind of work justified a new science of the mind. Just one example suffices.

Briefly flash up on a screen a brightly lit ten-by-ten matrix of random letters. Turn it off two seconds later. It disappears from the screen, but the subject still has an "afterimage" of the matrix before his eyes. Now flash an arrow where the third row of the matrix used to be, and ask the subject to read off the letters still in his afterimage. The subject gets seven of the ten right, and this quantifies how much information is still there in the mind's eye two seconds after the objective stimulus is gone. How long does the afterimage last? Instead of

waiting two seconds, vary the interval, and discover the rate at which the afterimage melts to nothing. This is a rigorous measure of the rate of decay of a mental image.

The scientist can even tell precisely how bright the afterimage in the mind's eye is. During the interval, flash up masking lights of differing intensities and discover the brightness at which the afterimage is exactly masked. The duration, the amount of information, and the brightness of a mental image can be exactly measured. So very fine, quantitative science can be done on mental life.

Dick published his blockbuster book the following year, and the cognitive revolution—which is still with us in 2018—began to sweep behaviorism away, just as behaviorism had swept mental life away at the end of William James's life.

Steve and I, deeply impressed, were also in midst of testing whether animals were cognitive. How could we find out if it was the lack of contingency between response and shock and not the shock itself that produced the profound failure to escape in the shuttle box? How could we find out if animals actually learned that nothing they did mattered?

To assess this question, we had to isolate the noncontingency from the shock. So three groups were needed. One group got escapable shock (ESC), where shock offset was contingent on the animal's response. So in our first helplessness experiment,[5] these dogs learned in the hammock to press a panel with their noses to turn off the shock. The second group was yoked to the ESC group, getting exactly the same duration, intensity, and pattern of shocks, but their responses had no effect on the shock. In this inescapable shock group (INESC), shock offset and all the animal's responses were noncontingently related. A third group (Zero) got no shock.

The next day the dogs were tested in shuttle box escape. We ran twenty-four dogs through our new "triadic" design and found that all the dogs in the ESC group and all the dogs in the Zero group readily learned to escape in the shuttle box, but five of the eight dogs in the INESC failed altogether to learn to escape. Importantly the ESC and the Zero group learned to escape equally well. We concluded that the animals in the INESC group learned in the hammock that shock offset was independent of their responses, and when shock occurred

the next day in the shuttle box, they expected that its offset would once again be independent of their response. This expectation undermined their trying ("response initiation") to escape. They had *learned* helplessness.

Our first publication on helplessness, outlining our cognitive theory, was, to our surprise, published as the lead article in the prestigious but archconservative *Journal of Experimental Psychology*.[6] The reviews contained only one criticism: "paralyse is usually spelled with a 'z.'" We briefly harbored the illusion that learned helplessness would be well accepted, and it would be smooth sailing from there, but we were wrong. The learning theorists, sensing that the rising storm would soon pose a mortal threat, closed ranks against cognitive theorizing in all forms, particularly in animals. There was a hostile encounter at the Princeton University conference where Steve and I first unveiled the theory to the major learning theorists:[7] Dick Herrnstein, B. F. Skinner's right-hand man and articulate gunslinger, retorted, "You are proposing that animals learn that responding is ineffective. Animals learn only responses—they don't learn *that* anything." Animals for the behaviorist are stimulus-response machines, not creatures that can ever learn propositions.

We defined a dimension that we called "control over outcomes," with control being present whenever the probability of an outcome, given a response, differs from the probability of that outcome in the absence of that response. Clearly, the escapable subjects controlled an aspect of the aversive event (when the shock went off), and the inescapable subjects did not. This was exactly why we developed the triadic design and included the escapable subjects as a control group as well as the zero group, because it isolated the element of uncontrollability: if failure to escape in the shuttle box was caused by learning uncontrollability, then this failure should not occur if uncontrollability was removed but the shocks stayed identical. That is, we assumed that uncontrollability was the active ingredient in producing passivity and that escapable subjects were later escaping normally in the shuttlebox because they lacked this critical learning ingredient.

We found out, almost fifty years later, when Steve finally unraveled the brain processes, that our theory was 180 degrees off. Steve

discovered that helplessness is not learned; rather it is mammals' default response to prolonged bad events. What is vouchsafed to mammals is learning that bad events can be controlled. One of the privileges of doing science for fifty years is that it is long enough to find out that you were wrong, and I will tell you the story of Steve's discovery of the Hope Circuit in Chapter 28.

Much of the work Steve and I did in graduate school centered on testing the theory of learned helplessness. But I became a psychologist not to test theories but to relieve suffering, and animal experiments really only mattered to me if they could lessen the amount of misery on the planet. I was sure that what we had seen in our dogs was about something larger. So I began to study abnormal psychology under Jim Geer, a behavior therapist newly arrived at Penn as an assistant professor. I told Jim about our dogs, and he came up to the lab to see them.

"Those dogs are depressed," Jim told me.

"What is depression?" I asked Jim. I spent much of the next ten years trying to answer my own question.

So in addition to theory testing we did two kinds of experiments anticipating the clinical applications of learned helplessness. First, we asked about prevention—we called it "immunization," influenced by the Salk and Sabin vaccines that had recently put an end to polio. If our dogs first learned that they could control shock and then experienced inescapable shock, would they *not* become helpless? Immunization worked: dogs that first learned to turn off shock in the hammock by pushing a panel with their noses, then had enough inescapable shock to make naive dogs helpless, later easily learned to escape in the shuttle box by jumping the barrier. These dogs, we believed, expected that they could control shock and so did not give up. They were immunized against helplessness.

We also worked on "therapy." Once a dog was helpless in the shuttle box, what could we do to cure him? We took inspiration from "exposure" work in behavior therapy. Spider-phobic people, for example, who are forced to endure being in the presence of spiders until they discover that nothing bad happens, are cured. So we decided to show the helpless dogs that they had control over shock. We dragged them

across the shuttle box and out of the shock that they were passively enduring. We showed them that getting to the other side worked. After a few draggings, the dogs perked up and began to jump on their own. This was true of every dog, a 100 percent cure.[8]

Ethics

There was a snowy-white, long-haired dog in the laboratory. I spent a lot of time with him. I loved him, and he loved me. I wanted to adopt him, but Steve and I weren't allowed pets in our apartments. So after the experiment we took him in Steve's aging Plymouth Valiant to Fairmont Park, the Manhattan-sized park in the middle of Philadelphia, and we set him free. Two weeks later he reappeared in our laboratory, captured once again by the people who rounded up stray dogs and sold them to laboratories. I do not know his fate, but I have dreamed about him at least once a month for the rest of my life.

Running dog experiments was a harrowing experience for us. We were both dog lovers, and had we not found ourselves in a laboratory in which dog experiments were already underway and unquestioned, we would not have chosen this path. As soon as I could I stopped experimenting with dogs; I ran rats and then people in helplessness experiments, with exactly the same pattern of results as with dogs. I have not run an animal experiment in more than forty years, and I have thought long and hard about the practice.

There are three kinds of issues that bear on the "ethics" of animal experiments such as ours. The first is "sentimental." It feels bad to do these experiments. Unlike some scientists, I never habituated to feeling bad. I cringed then and I still cringe remembering them. I still dream of the white dog, with love and with guilt.

The second issue is "moral." Peter Singer, a critic of learned-helplessness experiments, has put it well.[9] To wit: all life is sacred, and a civilized morality extends the human moral circle to animals. Animals are equally entitled to our sympathy and protection as other human beings are. Singer considers it "speciesism" to believe that humans deserve special rights. In this view, even if the shock was mild to moderate in our experiments (and I tested it on myself, producing

a sudden startle but no pain), it is always and absolutely wrong to shock animals.

I strongly disagree with this kind of moral absolutism. Inflicting pain on animals (or people) is wrong, but not *absolutely* wrong. This is but one value in a complex world of clashing values. Curbing the epidemic of depression, suicide, and posttraumatic stress is another value. Markedly decreasing the tonnage of human suffering in the world matters more to me and to most other people as well. These are difficult choices, particularly when the cringe factor is strong and one cannot see clearly into the future. The progress that was made over the next decades in curing and preventing mental illness as a result of our studies—which I discuss in later chapters—tells me that we saw into the future with considerable accuracy.

The final ethical issue is "scientific." All animal experiments that try to make inferences to humans must tangle with the problem of *external validity*. This is a crucial, neglected, and really hairy issue. Experimental psychology's rigor, its *internal validity*, had attracted me to the field. A controlled experiment is the gold standard of internal validity because it discovers what causes what. Does the fire cause the water to boil? Turn on the fire, and the water boils. Without the fire (the control), the water does not boil. Do uncontrollable bad events spur tumor growth? Implant tumors in rats and then give one group of rats inescapable shock, give another group identical escapable shock, and compare them to a group that receives no shock. Rats that get inescapable shock grow a cancerous tumor at a greater rate; hence, inescapable shock causes tumor growth in rats.[10]

But what does this tell us about the causes of cancer in human beings, and what does that tell us about how helplessness influences cancer in human beings? This is the problem of external validity. When laypeople complain about psychology experiments with the gibe "white rats and college sophomores," it is external validity that is in dispute. It may seem simplistic, but it is a profound complaint. Human beings differ in many ways from the white laboratory version of *Rattus norvegicus*. Inescapable shock differs in many ways from finding out that your child drowned in a boating accident. The tumor implanted in *Rattus norvegicus* differs in many ways from the

naturally occurring tumors that afflict human beings. So even if the internal validity is perfect—rigorous experimental design, the exactly right control group, large enough numbers to insure randomization, and impeccable statistics—we still cannot infer with confidence that this illuminates the effect that uncontrollable bad events will exert on cancer in people.

I have come to think that establishing external validity is an even more important, but much more nettlesome, scientific task than establishing internal validity. Academic psychology requires all serious psychology students to take entire courses on internal validity. These "methodology" courses are entirely about internal validity and almost never touch on external validity, which is often passed off as mere philistinism about science on the part of ignorant laymen.

Hundreds of professors of psychology make their livings teaching "scientific" method and statistics, the trappings of internal validity, but no one makes a living teaching about external validity. Unfortunately, public doubts about the applicability of basic, rigorous science are often warranted, and this is because the rules of external validity are not clear.

As you will see in later chapters, I went on to work for years asking if the helplessness experiments in dogs and then rats and then people had external validity and if they illuminated real helplessness in real human beings.

They did.

So learned helplessness in dogs was the choice I made, and if it were offered to me again, I would steel myself and make the same choice.

Chapter Seven

A Clinical
Psychologist (1967)

I SPRINTED THROUGH THE Penn PhD program in two years and eight months, eclipsing the all-time Penn psychology record. The disenfranchised life of a graduate student grated on me, and I soon accepted my first job: assistant professor of psychology at Cornell University. I asked my students to call me Marty, the nickname I've had since Dickie Fink bestowed it upon me at age eleven, rather than "Doctor Seligman." I hoped this would break down the psychological distance between undergraduate and professor, and I've kept this moniker all my life. No one but my sister Beth and my parents—and I myself—calls me Martin.

In work and in life, I strove to be an intellectual, the old-fashioned kind. My loyalty was—and still is—to the big questions, not just to those that were fashionable within psychology or philosophy. I read widely, from literary classics to thrillers to history to the obscure academic journals. I listened to classical music—Monteverdi to Mahler—in my "spare" time. I kept trying to "improve" myself. I took no time off.

I also had a skeptical nature. I scoured for the most "basic" accepted premises in psychology and asked what followed if the premises were wrong. My reflexive loyalty was to the ideas that needed defenders.

As with my PhD studies, I tried to do all of this in a hurry. I wanted to finish things, and I was brash. I took shortcuts. Wrapped up in my own thoughts, I didn't listen well, drifting inward almost immediately to play mentally with how what I was hearing fitted the issues I had been pondering. People thought that I was riding roughshod over them, but I think this was a side effect of such self-absorption. I was puzzled about why they didn't much like me.

I was ambitious, and I knew what I was ambitious for. Peter Madison's personality inventories stayed with me, and my ambition was to be like Wittgenstein, surrounded by devoted students and followers.

Finally, I was negative. The academic questions I asked were about helplessness, hopelessness, trauma, fear, and depression. My critical antennae were always up, and I easily found flaws. My mood was congruent: I was anxious and grumpy a lot.

"THEY'VE GOT YOU by the balls, Joe," shouted Jim Geer merrily.

This was my introduction to the haute monde of psychiatry. Philadelphia in 1967 was right at the cutting edge of a revolution. The epicenter of the revolution was Joe Wolpe's monthly salon, held in the cavernous living room of his hypermodern house in Merion, a western suburb of Philadelphia. His salon had become a magnet for behavior therapists from all over the northeastern United States.

Psychoanalysis had dominated American psychiatry—both in academia and in the therapy trenches—for forty years. This was not a benign tyranny. Following Freud's example and that of the traditional, authoritarian European professor, dissenters were drummed out of the profession. But the dike had sprung two leaks, and the torrent was starting.

One was drugs.[1] In the 1950s Thorazine was tried out on paranoid schizophrenics, and their delusions seem to melt away. Depressives given imipramine, an antitubercular, sang and danced in the corridors. Worried housewives took Valium and, Stepford-like, seemed content.

The other was behavior therapy. Its founder was Joe Wolpe, the guy Jim thought we had by the balls. Joe was a recent emigrant from a hostile—both to his politics and to his science—South Africa. He was in his mid-forties, bald, pugnacious, outspoken, and iconoclastic.

In his horn-rimmed glasses, he reminded me of an owl, wise, yes, but also ready to pounce on a prey. He had accomplished something that no one else in psychiatry had done before.

Joe treated anxiety disorders, his specialty being phobias. Phobics are deathly afraid of specific objects, such as cats or spiders or going shopping. They were routinely treated by psychoanalysts who probed for the underlying, unresolved childhood conflict of which the object of the adult fear was but a symbol. In the classic case, Little Hans,[2] at the age of four, saw a horse fall down in a Vienna street. He became terrified of horses. Freud interpreted this as a fear that his father would castrate him, a fear that Hans had displaced onto horses. Hans, duly enlightened, was said by his father to recover.

Crucial to the Freudian theory of phobia, and to Freud's theory of all mental disorders, was the premise that an underlying problem causes the symptoms, just as an underlying spirochete causes the symptoms of syphilis. Joe thought this was hogwash. The symptom of the phobia itself caused the phobia. A cat phobic had no underlying conflict; she was just terrified of cats. Period.

And Joe set out to prove it. The cat phobic, he theorized, must have previously had a traumatic experience in a place where cats happened to be. Her father might, for example, have spanked her when a cat was in the same room. By Pavlovian conditioning, the previously neutral cat became a stimulus that now evoked fear. If Joe was right, the therapeutic course was clear. Extinguish the conditioned fear, and the phobia would vanish!

Extinction should occur if the therapist got the patient up off the couch and presented cats to her now, but paired with no fear. Easier said than done, since presenting a cat in the consulting room would precipitate panic, not extinction. But Joe invented a way to do it and dubbed it "systematic desensitization."

First Joe had the patient learn "whole body relaxation," in which she relaxed every muscle in her body. Profound relaxation is a motor response incompatible with fear—you can't be afraid when you are relaxed. (Joe liked incompatible motor responses as explanations of extinction, and we will soon hear him invoke them in an argument with Steve and me.) Next Joe had the relaxed patient imagine someone

named "Katz." No fear occurred. Then he had her imagine the word "cat." No fear occurred. Joe kept going up her fear hierarchy while she relaxed, being careful to be sure she exhibited no fear, only relaxation. Joe had her imagine a cat. Finally he brought a cat into the consulting room and sprung it on the patient. Lo and behold, the phobia was gone.[3]

This actually worked. Joe cured several patients and showed thereby that a mere symptom of a mental illness, not some underlying conflict, was its cause. He did it by actually curing the mental illness and thus became the most famous heretic in the world of psychiatry. Systematic desensitization and its first cousins are still the treatment of choice for phobia sixty-five years later.

Joe, also a foe of apartheid, became persona non grata in his racist homeland. He fled South Africa for Thomas Jefferson's University of Virginia and finally settled in Philadelphia at Temple University in 1965. He and his quiet wife, Stella, held a monthly salon, and Steve and I attended. Aside from Jim Geer, there was Arnold Lazarus (soon to be expelled, and never forgiven, for the heresy of eclecticism—using cognition in therapy excluded him from the ranks of pure Wolpean therapists), Albert Stunkard (obesity researcher and the chair of psychiatry at Penn), Aaron (Tim) Beck (soon to become the leading light in depression), Paul Brady (who had cured stuttering behaviorally), and more than a dozen others.

We were invited to present our work on learned helplessness. About ten minutes into our presentation, Joe—who had been scowling since our first mention of cognition—burst in. "Cognitive? Nonsense—your 'helpless' dogs have learned a competing motor response. In the hammock shock goes off every so often when the dog happens to be still. That reinforces the motor response of lying still. In the shuttle box, when shock goes on, they lie still because they have been rewarded for not moving before in the hammock, and they get further reinforcement for lying still when the shock finally terminates. So learned helplessness is completely explained by tried-and-true behavioral principles."

Steve and I had anticipated this clever objection. In fact, it was by then the very subject of Steve's doctoral dissertation. Like Joe, the

Skinnerians proposed a "superstitious" reinforcement explanation of helplessness. They claimed that in the hammock, shock offset occasionally got paired accidentally with not moving, and this "superstitiously" reinforced the association of not moving with relief. Hence, in the shuttle box the "helpless" dogs engaged in not moving and eventually shock ceased—further strengthening the association between no-movement and relief. So learned helplessness was fueled not by a cognition that actions didn't matter but merely by good old Skinnerian response-reinforcement learning.

"Joe, make a prediction," I ventured. "Imagine that instead of accidentally allowing just a few accidental pairings of shock offset and motionlessness in the hammock, we go one better. We turn the shock off *only* when the dog is motionless. Every time the dog is completely still for five seconds, the shock stops. What would be learned?"

"The dog will learn to stand still, of course," Joe answered.

"Now imagine we yoke another dog to the first one, with shock going off at exactly the same time, but independent of its responses. It might get an occasional superstitious pairing, but which dog will have learned the stronger competing motor response?"

"The first dog," Joe said.

There are not many entirely decisive experiments in the history of science, but this was one. Steve had run a special escapable-shock group in the hammock: for this group shock terminated only when the dog held still, explicitly reinforcing not moving—one-step stronger than mere superstition. The cognitive theory predicted that these animals would *not* lie still in the shuttle box since they had learned that they could control shock—albeit by not moving, whereas behavior theory predicted that they would show the competing response of lying still, which according to behaviorists was all that "helplessness" amounted to.

Steve told Joe the results: all the dogs in this motionless escapable-shock group easily learned to escape in the shuttle box by jumping the barrier. Learned helplessness was cognitive, not the competing motor response of not moving reinforced by a few accidental shock offsets.[4] QED.

"They've got you by the balls, Joe!" shouted Jim merrily.

Joe conceded gracefully. He cornered me at the end of the meeting and invited me to spend time with him at his anxiety ward to show me how very powerful behavioral principles were in the clinic. He took me under his wing, and I had my first actual look at mental illness.

"SEE THAT FELLOW who just walked into the men's room? Follow him in," Joe instructed me. We were in the anxiety ward of Haverford State Hospital, and the gentleman whom Joe told me to follow into the bathroom was middle-aged and beautifully attired in a tailor-made dark blue suit.

"When he goes to pee, take the next urinal, unzip, and stare at him," Joe instructed.

I did as Joe asked. Next urinal, unzip, stare. The man peed, he zipped up, he stepped back, and so did I. Joe walked in beaming. The gentleman threw his arms around me and exclaimed with tears in his eyes, "You've cured me!"

Joe explained. This patient had a urinary phobia. He couldn't pee in a public restroom. He stood in front of the urinal waiting until the room emptied out, which in his office building could take fifteen minutes or more. He then let go, but if anyone walked in, he froze again. His absences had been noted, and people were gossiping about all the time he spent in the men's room.

He had been through systematic desensitization for the last month, starting with relaxing while hearing Joe say the word "urinate" and progressing upward through more fearful, imagined scenarios. The acme of his fear hierarchy was actually peeing with a stranger standing next to him and staring. He did it. He peed. Joe asserted that the urinary phobia stemmed not from an underlying conflict, like anxiety that he might be homosexual, that required resolving but merely from a fear of peeing in public. The gentleman was cured.

JOE AND I became friends, and although he disagreed with me about cognition in mental illness until the very end of his life, we found common ground, and he held my hand on my first baby step to becoming a clinical psychologist.

Part 2

Becoming

Chapter Eight

Cornell (1967–1969)

"Snow!" EXCLAIMED KERRY, looking out the second-floor bedroom window. We were scoping out Ithaca, guests in Jim Maas's house in Brooktondale. It was late May 1967—hence the exclamation point. Indeed, a glaze of new-fallen snow covered Jim's sloping lawn and his emerging crocuses. There was snow at the beginning and more snow at the end of our time at Cornell.

I had been offered two good jobs. One was at the University of Michigan, and at the end of my visit, I had a memorable and ominous conversation with Norman R. F. Maier. He was in the final year of a distinguished career and one of my heroes. His work bridged the animal laboratory and the clinic, and he had rediscovered "experimental neurosis" (Pavlov first named it[1]). Rats were taught to jump to the left window or the right window for food, but eventually the problem became unsolvable, and no window was consistently correct.[2] The rats froze at the starting post and became vulnerable to auditory seizures produced by loud, high-pitched sounds. To my eye it looked like learned helplessness in the nontraumatic, positive case. I gushed at Professor Maier, and he blushed, seemingly quite unaccustomed to praise.

"Watch your back," he warned me in hushed tones. "No one ever cites my work. My students can't get jobs. You have embarked on a dangerous path. What you don't know is that the academic establishment, those pure experimental psychologists, secretly despise our

kind of work. I don't know why, but my trying to apply experimental psychology to the clinic—as well as the existence of the entire profession of clinical psychology—embarrasses them, or worse."

As Professor Maier was warning me, I flashed back to two recent puzzling incidents at Penn. In Dick Solomon's Thursday lunch seminar, I mentioned Joe Wolpe's work as a good example of straightforwardly applying basic behavioral principles to real-world troubles. Dick, who insouciantly applied laboratory findings to the real world in his teaching—but almost never in print—reacted with contempt for Joe. He did not explain the ground for his contempt, but its vehemence was patent and wholly out of keeping with Dick's sunny, tolerant character.

And just the week before my visit to Michigan, I had my first and only long conversation with Bob Bush. Bob, you may recall, had led the Harvard young Turks when they exited en masse to Penn. He was a mathematician by training and famous for the rigorous statistical modeling of stimulus-response-reinforcement learning. His work inspired the new generation of aspiring mathematical psychologists. He became the first chairman of the remade Penn department in 1958 and left the chair to Henry Gleitman just as I arrived. I told Bob about our work on learned helplessness and how our tests demonstrated that animals must integrate two conditional probabilities. I emphasized that this pointed directly to cognition and not to stimulus-response learning.

He listened patiently and clearly got it. At the end of the hour, he said, "If you are right, Marty, I've wasted my life." Not long thereafter, Bob Bush killed himself. He had a complicated personal life, and I have no direct information about why, but when I heard the news, I could not help wondering.

"Watch your back, Mr. Seligman," Norman Maier concluded. "You don't want to end up like me."

Except for the awful weather, Cornell contrasted sharply with Michigan. Its homey department had only about twenty-five faculty members, completely dominated by one faction, the perception psychologists led by husband and wife team Jimmy and Jackie (Eleanor J.) Gibson. Jimmy was the brains and Jackie the enforcer. The Gibsons

were the opposite of behaviorists in ideology, but they were just as cultish, tyrannical, and narrow-minded. They worked on the "affordances" that the environment lends to perception. The department had been hemorrhaging psychologists recently and was rebuilding. It made many job offers: the recipient most distinguished was Dick Neisser, who eagerly accepted. They tendered five assistant professorship offers, one to me.

Kerry cast the deciding vote between Michigan and Cornell. She had put her PhD ambitions on hold during our three years at Penn and wanted to get on with her career. Cornell has a good classics department, so we accepted Cornell's offer.

WE RENTED A cozy sabbatical house on forty acres of woods on Ellis Hollow Road, east of campus, and finally I got a dog. Apollo, my blonde golden retriever puppy, and I spent hours exploring the woods and just sitting together outside in the cold, cuddling. My office was the fourth-floor attic of Morrill Hall, and my laboratory, Liddell Laboratory, a converted sheep barn, was about five miles away. My salary was $9,500, soon raised to an even $10,000 through the generosity of Harry Levin, the chairman. Harry assigned me to teach "Introduction to Experimental Psychology."

On the first day, I took a seat in the middle of the lecture room and narcissistically relished the collective gasp when I came to the podium and the undergraduates found that their professor was not much older than they were. This was the first time I'd designed and taught my very own course, and I did not do it the usual way. I used no textbook, only original journal articles, and created my own tour of what I considered "hot" across the discipline. My love of psychology came across, and the students were enthralled. I chose the topics according to my enthusiasm for them, and my enthusiasm was contagious.

Unexpectedly, this kind of teaching turned out to be a lightning rod for my own creativity. As I lectured, I found myself knitting together an entire area of psychology whose texture had previously been invisible to me. Today it is known as "evolutionary psychology." Fifty years ago it did not exist.

John Garcia, a maverick who worked on animal learning in a radiation lab, had published a two-page article that went almost unnoticed for two years.[3] When I first read it—and it was so badly written that I had to read it three times—I felt the earth move, but until I taught about the article, I did not fully understand why.

As I recounted the history of behaviorism to my students, I began to see that it was a rock-bottom premise of learning theory that John Garcia had obliterated. When John B. Watson, the founder of behaviorism, famously wrote, "Give me a dozen healthy infants, well-formed, and my own specified world to bring them up in and I'll guarantee to take any one at random and train him to become any type of specialist I might select—doctor, lawyer, artist, merchant-chief, and, yes, even beggarman and thief, regardless of his talents, penchants, tendencies, abilities, vocations, and race of his ancestors,"[4] the political and scientific appeal was electric. This justified the egalitarian social program that underpinned American democracy as well as the Bolshevik and French revolutions.

"Pavlov and Skinner," I recounted to my undergraduates, "believed fervently in 'equipotentiality,' the idea that any stimulus that is paired in time with any other stimulus will produce learning."

"Hold on, Marty," objected Susan Mineka, a sophomore who twenty-five years later became editor of the *Journal of Abnormal Psychology*. "It can't be any old stimulus. The animal has to perceive it and respond to it."[5]

"Of course, Sue. But the crucial point is that these are exactly the associations that David Hume and John Locke argued make up the experience that writes on the blank slate," I continued, making a mental note to invite this very bright sophomore into my laboratory. "It is just this flexibility of the brain that with the right experience will make of any man or woman a genius, the president of the United States, or a bigoted ignoramus."

I decided to ease into the complicated Garcia experiment with an anecdote that captured its essence, and this juxtaposition of anecdote and hard data later became the hallmark of my teaching and writing.

"Sauce béarnaise," I told my class, "is an egg-thickened tarragon-flavored concoction that used to be my favorite sauce. A few months

ago, my wife and I had a delicious meal of filet mignon with sauce béarnaise. About three hours later, I got sick to my stomach, so sick that Kerry had to take me to the emergency ward to get an injection to stop my vomiting. I now hate the taste of this sauce. Just thinking about it—right now—sets my teeth on edge.

"Strangely," I continued, "filet mignon did not become aversive, nor did my wife, nor did *Tristan and Isolde*, the opera I was listening to right before throwing up. Only the sauce did. What's going on?"

"It's just Pavlovian conditioning, Marty," said one of the students. "The taste was paired with throwing up. Now the taste makes you sick to your stomach."

"Anything wrong with that?"

"Plenty," piped up Jim Johnston, a member of Cornell's elite, experimental six-year BA-PhD program. "First, Marty learned with just one trial, and conditioning takes more pairings than that. And there was a three-hour gap between the taste and throwing up. I'll bet if Marty wired up your chair, played a tone, and three hours later shocked your butt, you would not become afraid of the tone. Second, *Tristan* and the beef didn't become nauseating even though they were just as well-paired with vomiting. The toilet seat was even closer in time to vomiting, and do toilet seats now make Marty sick?"

Wow, I thought to myself, *Jim is amazing.* He spoke in full paragraphs with no "uhs" or "likes." Jim would go on within a decade to become one of America's leading young cognitive scientists.

"Let me tell you all about the Garcia 'double-dissociation' experiment," I continued. "Garcia works in a radiation lab and he gives X-rays to rats, which makes them sick to their stomachs. A few seconds before receiving the X-ray, the rats drink saccharin-tasting water, and with each lick they hear a loud tone. Good old Pavlovian condition, right? Both the sweet taste and the tone are paired with sickness. Later Garcia finds that the rats now hate sweet tastes but are completely unperturbed by the tone.

"Maybe the rats just didn't notice the tone. So Garcia now does the same experiment, but with shock to the feet as the bad event rather than radiation sickness: loud tone plus sweet taste are both paired with foot shock. Now the rats come to fear the tone, but they still love

sweet tastes! So they could perceive the tone after all. What is learned selects the 'right' conditional stimulus, depending on what kind of noxious event follows. Stomach illness selects for tastes and ignores the tone. Foot shock selects the tone and ignores the taste.

"Why?" I asked. The class looked puzzled. "What would Darwin have said about Garcia?"

As I thought over my education, nothing stood out as more egregious than third-form biology at the Albany Academy a decade earlier. F. Norton (Skippy) Curtis marched us through species, genus, phylum, and kingdom but omitted one thing: natural selection. I suppose he can be forgiven since it had been only a century since the publication of *On the Origin of Species* and the news may have traveled slowly up the Hudson River to Albany. We had pop quizzes, the most memorable question being "Name the authors of your textbook." None of the forty-seven of us third formers got that one right (Moon, Mann, and Otto), but the name Mr. Curtis never mentioned was Charles Darwin.

When I first heard the principles of evolution from Colin Pittendrigh in my introductory biology course at Princeton (Pittendrigh's own textbook), I lived through a thunderbolt of just the sort that must have shaken the fellows of the Royal Society in 1859. Natural selection reframes almost everything, and it has pervaded my thinking about psychology since. But like Skippy Curtis's students, learning theory also missed out on evolution. How else could equipotentiality have remained a first principle?

Could learning itself be just as subject to evolution as the makeup of the eye and the ear? In the reality of mammalian evolution, distinctive tastes herald poisonous stomach illness, but sounds do not. Animals that could ignore external stimuli but selectively learn that tastes go together with illness—even with just one experience—would avoid those tastes in the future, survive, and pass on the genes that allowed such selection. Animals that could selectively associate sounds with pain and ignore co-occurring tastes would have a similar survival edge.

"Consider the evolutionary basis of learning itself," I told my class. "Learning that mirrors the actual causal skein of the world will be

favored and selected. Evolution may have prepared us to associate tastes with illness even over a several-hour gap. Evolution may have contra-prepared us to associate external events, like sounds, with stomach illness."

My two teaching assistants, Meredith West and Drew King, chimed in. They had been studying birds over in the biology department. "It's not just mammals that learn so selectively. Birds learn to sing in just the same way. They selectively imitate the songs of their parents and not the songs of bypassing strangers. And human language is like this too. This is at the heart of Chomsky's theory that language is a species-specific human adaptation. Babies show 'babbling drift,' the accent of their babbling drifting in the direction of their parent's language."

Drew and Meredith were already an item and they went on to become world-class avian ethologists together.

Out of this course a *Psychological Review* article and my very first book, *The Biological Boundaries of Learning*,[6] written with my graduate student Joanne Hager, emerged, as did a snide comment from the behaviorists calling my sauce béarnaise story the "most publicized meal since the Last Supper." Most importantly, I joined the battle against the "blank slate" brand of psychology that ignores natural selection and insists that while having a brain is nice, that brain is just a means of faithfully transcribing what experience writes.

CORNELL NOT ONLY stimulated my creative juices but became a political hotbed as well. I got my first taste when I volunteered to serve on the undergraduate admissions committee. This was huge fun, particularly for me, since I liked spotting brilliant prodigies, such as stars like Jim Johnston and Sue Mineka, for admission into the six-year BA-PhD experiment. Toward this end, each faculty admission committee member got wild cards—applicants we could admit based on just our lone vote—*if* we agreed to mentor them through Cornell.

But President James Perkins played a wilder card than any faculty member had.

The issue was black admissions. The Black Student Association was agitating loudly for more black students, and we were very

sympathetic—this in the first blush of enthusiasm for Lyndon John-son's vision of affirmative action. We had been bending over backward to take more and more black applicants. We reached deep into a small pool—students that all the Ivies were competing fiercely for—and we were hopeful that lots of academic talent might lie hidden beneath low Scholastic Aptitude Test (SAT) scores and low grades, particu-larly when the kid came from a poor neighborhood and a fatherless family. So we took lots of chances, admitting kids who showed glim-mers of promise, particularly high determination in overcoming ob-stacles, even if they had mediocre high school grades and low SATs.

But we still were not keeping pace with the administration's quota for black students, and an order came down from President Perkins. We didn't hear from on high often, and the only other communi-cation we'd had from him had been a cause for hilarity: I was going through a folder of a potential freshman from the Bronx and stuck upside down in it was a letter on the president's stationery to the head of Knight Newspapers as well as the original letter to which it was a response. The Knight person endorsed a woman applying for the PhD program (this had nothing to do with undergraduate admissions), and President Perkins's letter reassured him that his letter would "not get lost in the shuffle."

The present order was not a cause for hilarity, and it would not get lost in the shuffle. We were instructed to take 100 percent of black applicants whose SATs averaged 600 or better. The SAT is a barely concealed and more publicly acceptable surrogate for the IQ test, correlating almost perfectly with IQ scores. An average of 600 was near the seventieth percentile for all college-bound applicants across America, and we were pretty much already admitting all black appli-cants in this range. No problem. We were further instructed to take 60 percent of all black applicants whose SATs averaged 500 or better, somewhat below the fiftieth percentile for all applicants. This was a push, but we guessed we could comply. And then came the wildest card in the pack.

We were instructed to take 40 percent of all black applicants with an SAT average of 400 or better. This was the bottom 25 percent of the entire American pool. (Do you see the problem before you read on?)

"Hold on," said my fellow faculty committee member Thomas Sowell. Tom was a sober black economist who later became famous for his courageous take on the miseducation of young black kids.[7] He pointed out a gaping statistical anomaly to us.

"Think about the bottom 40 percent of the pool of kids who average 500, the half we are instructed to reject. Such a kid might score 530 on average. What we are now told to do is to discriminate against this kid in favor of kids who score in the upper 40 percent over 400, say 460 on average. We are told to favor less talented (460) black kids over a large number of more talented (530) black kids. President Perkins's theory seems to be that the lower the IQ, the more deprived and deserving the applicant is."

"I quit," Tom said, and he did. He left both the admissions committee and Cornell, but the admissions committee and Cornell continued to knuckle under. This foreshadowed the racial politics soon to come.

"HOW CAN YOU possibly claim that there are more than 10,000 advanced technical civilizations in the galaxy?" I challenged the brash, confident, and outspoken new arrival at the astronomy department. We were at a welcome dinner given by Bob and Jennifer Schneider. Bob taught calculus, and Jenny was jaw-droppingly beautiful—so beautiful that in Bertolt Brecht's *The Good Woman of Szechuán*, she played the daughter, and at the serious line "Am I pretty, Mother?" the audience actually broke into gales of laughter. The new arrival had left the astronomy department at Harvard bitterly, denied tenure, and was holding forth unstoppably about intelligent life. He was strikingly handsome, gifted with a deep, mellifluous voice, and spoke in cogent full paragraphs. His name was Carl Sagan.

"I just wrote a long book about how widespread intelligent life must be with the Russian astronomer Shklovskii, Marty," he replied handing me a copy. "Read it."

And I did. I stayed up for the next twenty-four hours digesting his argument. The book culminated in a "qualitative equation" (I had not heard this term before), the Drake Equation, named after Frank Drake, a senior member of our astronomy department. On the

Carl Sagan arrived at Cornell in 1968, rejected for tenure in astronomy at Harvard. We became fast friends. Carl embodied the responsibility of science to communicate effectively with the public, even at the cost of professional jealousy. Photo courtesy of Getty Images.

left-hand side was "the number of advanced technical civilizations in this galaxy," meaning civilizations that used radio waves for communication. On the right-hand side were the estimates for more than ten parameters to be multiplied together, such as the number of Sol-like stars in the galaxy, the percentage of those with planets, the percentage of those with planets far enough away from the star to be temperate, the percentage of those with atmospheres, and the longevity of an intelligent civilization (which was bimodal, either short and destroying itself right away or wise and long). The solution blew my mind: there are, right now, between 10,000 and 2 million advanced technical civilizations just in our galaxy.

Understanding the human mind and the search for intelligent life in the universe were for me the two grandest of scientific pursuits. I

chose the former for my life's work because my mathematical skills for astronomy were not good enough. In Sagan, I met someone respectable who had chosen the latter.

We became fast friends and began to spend huge swaths of time together. We read each other's manuscripts. He gave me an early draft of his *Dragons of Eden*, a book about the brain. The psychology in it was too sloppy, and I advised him not to publish it. It won the Pulitzer Prize. We swapped books that we read overnight and then discussed over breakfast.

"Read this one, Carl," I insisted. "It might change your mind about truth." I handed him the latest rage in the philosophy of science, Thomas Kuhn's *The Structure of Scientific Revolutions*.[8] Kuhn argued that science was more about fashion than about absolute truth. He contended that in any current science, a "paradigm" dictated the right questions and created a hegemony of silence about those that should not be asked. The old guys died off, and the new guys then came along and swept away the old paradigm, replacing it with their own new paradigm. This sure looked right to me for psychology. Behaviorism swept away introspection, and now cognition was sweeping away behaviorism. Kuhn had created a sensation, and it fit the relativism that was just starting to overtake the humanities, as English and history departments started to switch from Shakespeare and Columbus to a focus on race, class, and gender.

The next morning over very strong coffee at Carl and his wife Linda's apartment, Carl told me, "This is about bad science, Marty. Good science makes absolute predictions that can be proved or disproved. Good science is about the truth, not about fads. There are two theories about the origin of our solar system. One predicts that the moon is covered with a deep layer of dust. The other predicts that the moon's surface is solid. Next year we will find out for sure."

We watched the moon landing together at the faculty club. Neil Armstrong did not sink into a layer of dust.

"That's good science," Carl said with finality.

Carl had saved a book to read aloud to me for a very special occasion. Kerry and I were expecting our first child. Kerry went into

labor, and I started our Buick and pointed it toward the Tompkins County Hospital eight miles away. Mindlessly, I then just let it idle in the driveway for six hours, and the car ran out of gas. Carl came to the rescue with a can of gas. After another twelve hours, the four of us raced off to the hospital, where Linda held my hand, and Carl read from J. B. S. Haldane's essays on science. Amanda Seligman was safely delivered in the wee hours of a spring morning in 1969.

CARL AND I experienced together the assassination of Martin Luther King Jr. and Robert Kennedy, the exit of Lyndon Johnson from the presidency, and the black revolution at Cornell. We both started out left of center and reacted to the same events in diametrically opposite ways. In the middle of all this, however, we had a personal rupture that was not about politics but about Carl's physical health.

Carl had a ferocious temper and was easily offended. Kerry and I gave a dinner party in which Carl and L. Pearce Williams, a noted historian, faced off about the Boxer Rebellion. Williams sided with the imperialists and Carl with the Chinese. At first the mention of "yellow peril," Carl stomped out, shaking his fist at Pearce. I had managed to stay on Carl's good side up until then. Carl was going off to Boston for the first of the surgeries on his esophagus stemming from a rare cancer that would eventually kill him at the tragically young age of sixty-two. Kerry and I supplied Carl with our dozen favorite science fiction classics to read. Carl had never read any science fiction, saying that real science was much more interesting. But he agreed to read them during his recuperation and emerged from the hospital with the idea that became his novel, *Contact*.[9]

Linda called me from the hospital right after surgery and told me that Carl was in critical condition.

"You might give blood," Linda suggested.

About six of our students and I drove to the donation center. I fainted while giving blood, and the doctor warned me never to do it again, but we did manage to donate a few pints. Within hours, Carl called me from his hospital bed. He was shouting, beside himself with fury.

"My illness was a secret. You betrayed me and told my students." I'd had no clue. Carl recovered rapidly, but we would never be close again.

MY ACADEMIC WORK was going superwell. Steve Maier and I had found that learned helplessness was temporary: twenty-four hours after inescapable shock, the animals remained helpless, but if we waited a full week, the animals had recovered and escaped shock in the shuttle box easily. Then I found a condition under which learned helplessness was permanent. If animals had not just one but multiple sessions of inescapable shock, helplessness did not go away in time.[10]

Word of our work was spreading. I had been offered an assistant professorship at Harvard. My chairman, Harry Levin, mocked the offer: "Every Jewish boy wants to be at Harvard." He hit the target and shamed me, and so I turned Harvard down. Steve Maier had taken a plum assistant professorship at Illinois. Princeton offered me an endowed bicentennial preceptorship, which came with an assistant mastership at my beloved Woodrow Wilson Society under Julian Jaynes, a former teacher. This dream offer from my alma mater was very tempting, but Dick Solomon told me to wait, saying many more offers would come my way. I turned Princeton down. (Many more offers did not come my way and never again from my beloved Princeton.)

I was initiated into the Psychological Round Table, a secret fraternity of haughty under-forty male experimental psychologists. It met once a year in a New York City mansion, and each member delivered a scholarly paper interlaced with humor. I was the youngest and least humorous initiate and worried that when they discovered my loyalty to applied psychology, I would be expelled. Dave Williams reported on Wilhelm Wundt: "Wundt was so disciplined that he wrote two thousand words every day for his entire career. Eighty-eight volumes in total. And in German. The last four volumes were all verbs."

Tenure was all but certain at Cornell. My courses were oversubscribed. I had a large coterie of enthusiastic undergraduates working in my laboratory and a passel of sleepier graduate students. Senior

professors from across the university invited me onto the right committees. They seemed to be grooming me for higher Cornell office. I had just received my first grant from the National Institute of Mental Health for research on learned helplessness.

"YOU REALLY DON'T know anything about clinical psychology, do you?" said Suzanne Bennett Johnson. Suzanne was a perky, freckle-faced senior and not at all intimidated. She got a rare A+ in my experimental psychology course, and I invited her into my laboratory, where she continued to shine. Cornell, being without a medical school, did not teach about mental illness, and I was now offering an advanced course on psychopathology—even though I was a novice. Suzanne was taking this course and saw my ignorance right away. She would become a clinical psychologist working on juvenile diabetes and was elected president of the American Psychological Association in 2012.

"You have us reading about learned helplessness and experimental neurosis in animals. Rats? Dogs? But what about people? What about schizophrenia, drug addiction, manic depression, and suicide?" chimed in Chris Risley, another senior not intimidated by me. (This "Marty" stuff had perhaps gone too far.)

On the first day of my experimental psychology course two years before, Chris, a wet-behind-the-ears sophomore, came bouncing into my office, beaming. "Hi, Marty. My name is Chris Risley. You should get to know me. I am really worth getting to know!" No undergraduate, before or since, has approached me in this bold way, and Chris turned out to be right. We became good friends, and he and Suzanne spent much of their time with Kerry and me at our house eight miles west of campus. Our house was now the watering hole for a dozen of my students.

When two of my best students, Suzanne and Chris, who were also now my close friends, told me that I didn't know what I was talking about, I listened. They told me to get into the trenches and learn something about real mental illness.

I intended to take time off to learn clinical psychology, but such a profession barely existed. Psychiatry was the only profession that

Suzanne B. Johnson was a sparkling Cornell undergraduate. She went on to become president of the American Psychological Association in 2012. Photo courtesy of Suzanne B. Johnson.

officially treated mental illness, and it was a guild that did not readily open its doors to people who were not medical doctors. Qualified psychologists were not welcomed and were allowed to enter only as handmaidens and supervisees of psychiatrists. Furthermore, I was not qualified to treat patients, and there was no well-charted trail for an experimental psychologist like me to follow to retool as a clinical psychologist. I was, however, about to have one blazed for me.

"CLINTON ROSSITER IS a racist and will die in the gutter like a dog. Allan Sindler is a racist and will die in the gutter like a dog. Walter Berns . . ." The litany went on, naming the faculty members who were to die. (I was not among them, being far too junior, obscure, and apolitical to be noticed by the leaders of the increasingly frenzied Black Liberation Front.) This was our local campus radio

station, and the speaker was Tom Jones, Class of 1969, president of the group. Tom was a shape-shifter and somehow later shed his radical skin with a huge "gift" to Cornell in 1995. He went on to become the head of TIAA-CREF, the custodians, ironically, of my retirement money. But his threats were not hollow. Clinton Rossiter committed suicide. Allan Sindler and Walter Berns left Cornell. Physical assaults on faculty went unreported in the newspaper, but we heard about them at the Faculty Club. Black students, protesting his teachings about poverty, wrestled the microphone away from an economics lecturer, then walked in and took over the economics department. They went unpunished. Fire swept through the six-year BA-PhD program dormitory, and eight of the students died of asphyxiation. It seemed to have been arson, and this marvelous program was aborted, but the case was never solved. Charles Thomas, one of my advisees, told me that female black students chased him down and stuck him with pins for the crime of dating white girls.

IT WAS PARENTS' WEEKEND, April 1969. I reverted to my *Quiz Kid* role and was named captain of the Faculty College Bowl team. We planned to face off against four undergraduates to see who could answer trivia questions fastest. The contest was aborted as news of heavily armed black students swept the campus. The epicenter was Willard Straight Hall. A parent had either jumped from a window or been defenestrated, with at least a broken leg as a result. Bristling with rifles and ammunition, a large group of black students entered Willard Straight, threatened all those inside, and forcibly ejected them. They were now occupying the building, and the photo of the armed black students entering the Straight flashed around the world. The 1960s revolution had come to the Ivy League.

Rumors flew. A group of armed vigilantes was gathering near campus to retake the Straight from the "niggers and commie Jews." President Perkins's dog had been kidnapped. They had threatened to kill President Perkins's children. They had threatened to kill President Perkins. What did the black students want? Their demands were nebulous—more black faculty members, more black students, more black scholarships—but one "nonnegotiable" demand stood out: amnesty.

The black takeover of Willard Straight Hall (April 18, 1969). Capping mounting intimidation against whites and nonmilitant blacks, members of the Afro-American Society violently took possession of the student union. This led me to quit my job at Cornell Library. Photo courtesy of Cornell Library.

The administration trembled. The faculty trembled. Emergency faculty meetings were held, and the meetings broke all attendance records. Max Black, the universally respected silverback of the philosophy department, urged, "When in doubt, stand on principle." The faculty declined and voted to give the black students whatever they wanted, and most certainly, amnesty.

A minority of the faculty, including me, was scandalized. Relinquishing the freedom to teach what one believes, giving in to violence, allocating scarce resources to the loudest group for academically dubious projects like the Ujamaa Residential College—this was not what a university was about. A "Committee of 41" was formed and included the most distinguished of the centrist members of the faculty: Nobelist Hans Bethe, Paul Olum (later president of the University of Texas), Fred Kahn (later dean of the faculty), Max Black, and Dale Corson (who soon succeeded President Perkins). I was the forty-first, the token junior faculty member. The senior notables told me that they saw me as a future dean, someone who believed in traditional academic values. I did not see myself as a future dean or university president (my mother, however, would have loved me to have those roles), but I was honored to join their cause. Carl Sagan did not join. From identical experiences, he had moved far left, and I had become markedly more conservative. What I most valued in a university— arguably the best human institution ever created—needed defenders.

The last straw for me happened in my experimental psychology course. I'd prepared a lecture on intelligence. Arthur Jensen, a distinguished Berkeley professor of education, had recently published a well-reasoned but explosively controversial article in the *Harvard Educational Review*.[11] He argued that IQ was heritable and that the IQ difference between American blacks and whites was genetic. He cited a bushel of evidence, such as the IQ gap remaining constant at every level of income. Jensen was vilified in the press. The ordinarily disinterested *New York Times*'s railing against Jensen notwithstanding, this was a very complex issue with serious arguments and counterarguments on both sides. It was also certainly a topic that would engage the students to come to grips with behavioral genetics. As I

began my lecture, I noticed that several of my black students appeared to be scowling at me from the back row.

I was afraid. I even trembled. I stumbled on, omitting all mention of race and heritability. I was intimidated. I knew that the time for me to leave Cornell had come.

I voted with my feet.

Chapter Nine

Penn Psychiatry
(1970–1972)

"**N**oooo," BURBLED AMANDA from the car seat.

"SNOOOOW," corrected Kerry. "Look at all that snow."

On either side of the road as we sped away down Van Ostrand Road, snowdrifts stood taller than the car. It was the last day of a turbulent decade: December 31, 1969. I was leaving Cornell.

As we drove out of Ithaca, I congratulated myself for showing at least a shred of courage. I thought about Adrian at just my age. Forty years before, faced with the Great Depression, he had been afraid. He decided to forgo possible fortune and fame for a lifetime of financial security. I guessed I had more backbone, but I was staring at joblessness. So I was driving our pale yellow bottom-of-the-line Buick, fleeing from a badly broken university. But I was also heading for something positive.

ALBERT STUNKARD AND Tim Beck had blazed a trail for me to learn some real psychopathology back at Penn in the psychiatry department. Albert was called "Mickey," I guess because of his Mickey Mouse outsize ears. In the mid-1960s, with Tim Beck at his right hand, Mickey had wrested control of the psychiatry department from the psychoanalysts and had since been busy reshaping this huge, amorphous department. He was determined to build a field of

research-based psychiatry with Penn at the center. Mickey saw me as a possible recruit and rescued me from joblessness and poverty. He found private donors to support my stay at Penn, and Louise Harper, a generous Washington socialite, pledged $10,000. So Mickey offered me a two-year psychiatric residency to train in psychiatry. I went on to learn about mental illness firsthand and was given the strange, long title of "visiting associate professor of psychology in psychiatry." Tim Beck was my mentor. I was twenty-seven, and Tim suggested that I grow a beard to try to look as old as my fellow residents.

I was given an office in the psychiatry department and spent the next two years on the inpatient and outpatient floors of the ramshackle University of Pennsylvania Hospital. Henry Bachrach, a PhD psychologist, was director of residency training and my first therapy supervisor. His high training position was an encouraging sign of how well Mickey and Tim's regime tolerated psychologists. I did not know about Henry's biases, but I soon found out.

"Marty, you'll never believe what I just heard about Arnold Lazarus." Arnold, you may recall, was the behavior therapist expelled from Joe Wolpe's inner circle for introducing *cognition* into Joe's orthodox behavior therapy.

"A patient came to see him, worrying that his penis was too small," Henry continued.

"Well, let's measure it," Arnold said.

After a few seconds of silence, I realized that this was a punch line, and I was supposed to laugh. I chuckled, but the gulf between the old Freudians and the new cognitive behaviorists had never seemed more unbridgeable.

I was decidedly nervous about seeing my first real patient, but Henry reassured me. "You're smart, Marty. Don't forget you have that edge, but never take a patient who is smarter than you."

My first patient may not have been smarter than I was, but he was slyer. Jerry, in his early twenties, was a mustachioed, ghostly pale college dropout. He was markedly depressed according to the standard symptom checklist, which I made a habit of using early in therapy. His eyes were downcast, he told me tearful stories of one failure after another, and his speech and gait were painfully slow. He told me he

Aaron Temkin (Tim) Beck and I first met in 1967. Tim was my principal teacher of psychopathology, particularly depression. A model of how to age, Tim turned ninety-six in July 2017. I still have the privilege of a once-a-month research lunch with him. Photo courtesy of Aaron Beck.

had just shaved his head. When I asked Henry about head shaving, he told me that it was a textbook red flag for suicide, although quite unproven. I saw Jerry once a week, using the new moves that Tim Beck was in the process of inventing with his residents for what would soon be called the "cognitive therapy" of depression.

After three months, Jerry appeared at my office without an appointment. Bright-eyed, brisk of gait, tan, and normal of speech for the first time, he was grinning broadly. His hair was growing back. *My very first case is a success. This new cognitive therapy sure works wonders*, I thought to myself.

"I am here to terminate," Jerry gushed, "but I want to thank you for all you did. Particularly for the letter you wrote to my draft board about my depression. They have reclassified me 4-F. No Vietnam for me!"

Tim Beck and I met once a week with Igor Grant, the chief resident, and Dean Schuyler to discuss our cases from the point of view of the new cognitive theory of depression—that depression stems from thoughts of loss—which Tim advanced in 1967.[1] These meetings were the seedbed from which cognitive therapy emerged five years later.[2] Dean was the most acute teacher of therapy I'd ever had. Tim formulated the abstractions—for example, "That's an automatic thought about her husband's never reciprocating"—but Dean hit the nail on the head with the concreta: "When she gives him a Hershey bar, he never gives her back a Baby Ruth." Igor kept us focused on the case, and I sat in deep respect for their different skills, skills uncommon in the airy world of psychology departments.

I contributed by extrapolating the current scientific literature to the cases: for example, that childhood experience with helplessness should lead to automatic thoughts of being a victim and a loser. Tim called himself "Mr. Outside" and me "Mr. Inside," using a West Point football metaphor to say that he viewed his theories as far out, while mine were nestled cozily inside academia. That was not my view, however, since I also saw myself as an iconoclast.

MY TWO YEARS of clinical training left me with an open, even a credulous mind about therapy and what causes mental illness. By the end of my residency in 1972, I believed that large swaths of mental illness were straightforward. Unfortunate Pavlovian conditioning, maladaptive instrumental habits, debilitating automatic thoughts, learned helplessness, stunted social skills, malign genetics, and neural imbalance were at play. The new cognitive and behavior therapies seemed useful here. And never to be derided or ignored was a big "placebo" benefit: to the extent a disorder involved the loss of hope, entering therapy in and of itself provided some. Often patients just needed a supportive, nonjudgmental listener. Therefore eclectic techniques in the hands of a skilled therapist would do considerable good.

But I also believed that deep, mysterious forces were at play that we had barely glimpsed, and in the hands of a witchy therapist, dramatic relief could come. By the end of my residency I came to regard the human psyche and its deformations as objects of awe.

WHILE MY PROFESSIONAL life was expanding, my parents' lives were crumbling. Adrian had not been expected to survive his strokes, but he had an unbreakable will to live, still on display fifteen years later. He had been kept on at the Court of Appeals and, with enormous determination, had returned to work as deputy state reporter within the year. He would always be paralyzed on his left side and was but a shadow of his former self intellectually. He was also emotionally labile, and I often saw him burst into tears. All this made him an object of pity at the office, and I was sure he knew it. By the time I finished college, he'd cashed in his generous disability pension and decamped to an apartment in Miami Beach. Irene and Adrian had been squabbling more and more, and she stayed in Albany. They talked of separation, but it never became official.

Irene was relieved when Adrian moved to Florida and he was out of her hair. She continued her job as the head stenographer for an office full of New York State lawyers. Her many "girls" there prized her as fair-minded and turned to her for wise advice. But her arthritis became severe, and by the time I left college, I'd seen her at her worst, on all fours crawling up two flights of stairs to the bedroom, unable to walk. We drove up to Lake Luzerne one rainy autumn afternoon, and she told me that she had expected the last third of her life to be "golden years." She tearfully confessed that they were far from it.

Watching my parents' marriage fall apart and their health deteriorate made me feel helpless and sad. I thought about my own work on helplessness, and search as I might, I found no answers. I was good at compartmentalizing, however, and had my own consuming work and a growing family to distract me.

But things got worse.

Adrian flew up from Florida to visit Kerry and me and to meet his grandchild. While this gave him some pleasure, he was morose and talked of suicide. As I drove to the supermarket, he threw open the door of the speeding car and made the gesture of throwing himself out. I yanked the door closed but knew that this was beyond anything I could handle. I checked him into the inpatient psychiatry ward of Philadelphia General Hospital, where on heavy tranquilizers he regained some stability. I was mortified to have to turn my own father

over to the care of my colleagues. A few days later, I drove him to the airport, and he flew back to Florida. This was the last time I saw my father.

MY RESEARCH TOOK a decided turn toward mental illness in humans. I began looking for point-to-point mapping between learned helplessness in the lab and depression in the clinic. The question I had asked Jim Geer five years before, "What is depression?" was now getting answered with some welcome precision, and this was a sea change in psychiatry. Tim Beck's Beck Depression Inventory, published in 1961, was now in widening use. It asked patients to report on a zero-to-three scale the severity of each of twenty-one symptoms of depression. Now these symptoms were being codified into a diagnosis of depression in what would soon become *DSM-3*, the third edition of the *Diagnostic and Statistical Manual* of the American Psychiatric Association. The categories began as mere research tools that made their way in draft around the scientific end of the therapy community. This community was trying to get some purchase on a very slippery thing: diagnostic agreement from hospital to hospital. What was called schizophrenia in New York City was often called manic depression in London. Without consistent diagnostic agreement, serious research on therapy could not even start.

Depression was a fine test case. As codified in the new diagnostic manual, depression was sensibly split in two. Bipolar depression (manic depression) involved moods that alternated over long periods from irrationally high to extremely low. Unipolar depression had only lows, broken down into nine symptoms:

- Sad mood
- Loss of interest
- Weight loss
- Sleep problems
- Psychomotor problems
- Fatigue
- Feelings of worthlessness

- Indecisiveness or poor concentration
- Thoughts of suicide

"Those dogs are depressed," Jim had said, and I now thought about the formal requirements if learned helplessness was truly a model of unipolar depression in patients. A laboratory model had great advantages for science. It could allow systematic exploration of what drugs and what therapies would work in depression. So I began a research program to pin down the parallels. Ultimately I found that learned helplessness induced experimentally mapped to eight of the nine symptoms, the only exception being suicide and suicidal thoughts—an unlikely symptom for mild bad events to produce in the laboratory. Not only did inescapable shock and inescapable noise produce the symptoms of depression, but the converse occurred as well: depressed people who did not experience inescapable events behaved in the laboratory as if they had, showing passivity in the shuttle box and giving up on cognitive problems.[3]

My other niche in academic psychology was biological constraints on learning, and the heavyweight *Psychological Review* published the fruits of my undergraduate lectures.[4] The blank slate view of learning had exerted a dead hand on the theory of mental illness, and I began to wonder if biological constraints applied to mental illness just as they did to learning. Phobias fit. Recall John Garcia's finding that rats learned in one trial, and retained over long delays, a sense that a distinctive taste goes with stomach illness but distinctive sounds do not. This made very good evolutionary sense, and other features of prepared learning also stared me in the face. Unlike ordinary Pavlovian conditioning, taste aversions do not go away. I still hated the taste of sauce béarnaise a good five years after the incident. Furthermore, Pavlovian conditioning appeared cognitive. Bob Rescorla was gathering mounting evidence that conditioning was just an expectation (e.g., that a shock would follow the tone), thus a rational cognition that mirrored accurately the real contingencies of the world.[5] But taste aversions crept under the cognitive radar. Once I had recovered from my seeming food poisoning, I found out that a flu had swept

through the lab. So I knew that the sauce had not caused my illness, but that did not weaken my distaste.

Phobias look a lot like prepared learning. First, they are highly selective for objects that long ago in our primate history were common and dangerous: snakes, spiders, lightning storms, strangers, the dark, and going outside alone, for example. And despite their modern, but not ancient, dangerousness, there do not exist knife phobias or electric outlet phobias. A young girl sees a snake in a park in England (quite unusual for that country) and a bit later goes back to the family car and has her hand smashed in the car door. She develops a lifelong fear of . . . snakes but not car doors.

Also phobias don't extinguish readily and are decidedly irrational—merely knowing that you will not jump or be pushed off the cliff does not remotely stifle your fear of heights. And so I extended my work on preparedness to phobias and obsessive-compulsive disorders, arguing that as a species we are evolutionarily prepared for them and the objects they focus on and that some individuals might be more genetically vulnerable to specific disorders than others.[6]

I was not yet thirty, and these two contributions attracted considerable academic notice. Mickey and Tim asked if I might be willing to stay on in the psychiatry department. I was aware, however, that medical departments in America had very shaky funding. There was almost no "hard" money (Mickey had the only assured salary out of his two hundred faculty members), and so, for the research professors who populated the great departments, salaries depended almost entirely on either getting large federal grants or seeing patients, the latter generally dreaded. This meant that psychiatry departments, just to survive, were in a never-ending scramble to keep up with the latest trends that were popular in Congress. In fact, the National Institute of Mental Health (NIMH) had by this time, despite its "health" charter, become the National Institute of Mental Illness, and it was the sole institution that kept the great psychiatry departments from bankruptcy. So having a tenured appointment in a psychiatry department amounted to having a concession stand to try to absorb federal funds, and if that failed . . . you were "tenured" but with no salary.

Mickey had a scheme for me. The NIMH had just started granting "Career Scientist Awards," a way of supporting research scientists by paying their salaries within psychiatry departments for at least five years. Mickey and Tim urged me to apply, and I did, proposing a program of research to test whether learned helplessness was indeed a model of unipolar depression and whether it captured some or even all forms of these depressions. The institute received my proposal warmly, and a "site visit" was arranged. Four of America's leading psychiatrists assembled at Penn to spend a day grilling me. We were on the same wavelength, and it went swimmingly.

But there was a joker in the pack, and he was scowling at me. He was a psychologist from Harvard named Bill Morse, an acolyte of B. F. Skinner. He had discovered that when shocked, monkeys "chain-rattled" neurotically, and he and Skinner argued that this was "all in the schedule"—code for the dogma that the environment shaped behavior entirely, and cognition and evolution played no role at all. Morse challenged me, and I was fearless enough to give an evolutionary explanation of his very findings and then to reject the Skinnerian notion of "superstition" as an explanation of learned helplessness. I cited Steve Maier's crucial "holding still" experiment. A visibly exasperated Morse silently continued to scowl.

When the group reassembled in Washington, I later learned, the four psychiatrists all gave my application a "1.0," the highest NIMH score, equivalent to an A+. Morse asked the group, "What mark do I have to give Seligman to prevent him from getting any money?" They told him a "5.0," the almost never-used equivalent of an F. He did, and I now take this opportunity to thank Bill Morse for unintentionally doing me one of the great favors of my life.

In parallel with this, the University of Pennsylvania's psychology department was considering appointing me with tenure. Psychology departments, unlike psychiatry departments, were "hard" money, with the (generally much lower) salary secure for life, even without soliciting grant support or seeing patients. Indeed, this was the financial basis of "academic freedom," the freedom to write what one will, no matter how unpopular. The Penn psychology department's

considering me was almost unprecedented, since the last Penn PhD granted tenure was Frank Irwin, four decades before. Tenured appointments, it was sensibly argued, should come from the outside to avoid *nachschleppers* and so bring in new blood.

On the favorable side, there was a push for clinical and abnormal psychology in the psychology department. The undergraduates, then as now, continually complained about "rats" and demanded more "relevant" courses. The basic researchers were annoyed when pressured to offer applied courses. The department, with an aversion to anything applied, particularly anything clinical, continued to appoint only "basic" scientists, and it had successfully resisted the hue and cry from the unenlightened mob. I, of course, agreed with the mob, and the student pressure continued to build. The department thought I might "look" like a clinical psychologist and that it could fob the applied courses off on me, all the while hoping that my rock-bottom loyalty lay with basic laboratory research. This, I suspect, was much debated, and if asked, even I could not have answered definitively. But I was not asked.

The vote was taken, and I was offered an associate professorship of psychology with tenure.

By accident, I walked by the room during the debate and heard only two words. A basso profundo voice that I recognized as that of the chair of the clinical wing boomed out, "On balance . . ."

Chapter Ten

Tenured (1972)

I GOT MY IDEAL job, and it was for life. I was becoming well-known in experimental psychology, but its lack of application to real human affairs gnawed at me. I'd been hired by the most "basic" (some would say "constipated") psychology department in America partly as a sop to student demands for "relevance," and some of my colleagues already saw me as a wolf in sheep's clothing. They were looking over my shoulder, and they were right to be leery. Experimental psychology and clinical psychology were just tools—mere methods—for approaching bigger questions. There were other tools to be tried, and I wanted to spread my wings to explore the bigger questions.

As I had been five years before, when I started at Cornell, I was fast and in a hurry. When I read an article, no matter how important, I sprinted to the finish and got onto the next item of work. I missed fine points. I cut off conversations once I got the gist, which usually happened sooner rather than later, and just as they had at Cornell, people saw me as brusque or even rude and self-obsessed. I did not step back and savor what I'd accomplished.

I was out of touch with the people who loved me and with the friends who liked me. I worked eighty hours a week, and when not overtly working, I was always thinking about psychology and philosophy. I paid too little attention to my wife and daughter, to my mother and father. My only friendships were with my students and colleagues.

I was pretty negative. Considerable and unexpected success bolstered my outward confidence and optimism, but underneath I was still anxious a lot. I brooded. When thwarted, I got depressed, but unlike my dogs, I never gave up. I readily saw what was wrong in psychology, but sometimes I also saw what was correct, once in a while down to its very core.

"NEAL IS REALLY pissed at you, Marty," said Jay Weiss. It was a gorgeous late-April day in Rittenhouse Square in Philadelphia, the white apple blossoms exploding. The occasion was the annual meeting of the Eastern Psychological Association, and Jay had presented his doctoral research, conducted with Neal Miller at Yale using the triadic design in rats and looking at stomach ulcers. Jay found that the rats with inescapable shock got the most stomach ulcers.[1] This debunked a famous study in monkeys by Joseph V. Brady purportedly showing that the "executives," the monkeys who could turn off the shock, got the ulcers.[2] But Brady made the mistake of not assigning his monkeys randomly to escapable or inescapable shock; rather he made the monkeys who started to respond earliest the executives. So the monkeys most upset by the shock became the executives and got the ulcers. Brady inferred that helplessness was good for you, and control was bad. Jay got it right and randomly assigned his rats in the triadic design, and his results were clear and opposite to Brady's. It's good to be the executive and bad to be the slave. Jay's was a lovely piece of science.

"What's eating Neal?" I asked, puzzled. The last thing I wanted to do was alienate the most powerful experimental psychologist in the world.

"Your articles about controllable and uncontrollable shock and predictable and unpredictable shock don't cite him as having priority. Neal worked on this as Arlo Myers's supervisor in 1956, even though they never published," said Jay.

I had gotten pretty full of myself on the importance of learned helplessness, and this conversation was deflating. But it was also thought provoking. Naturally I thought that Steve and I "owned" learned helplessness (or at least Dick Solomon or Russ Leaf or Bruce Overmier did) and the triadic design as well. I had never heard of Arlo

Myers, and when I later looked up his dissertation, it did not seem particularly on point.

But who "owns" what? Who should get the "credit"? Who has "priority"? That someone as illustrious and established as Neal Miller worried about such stuff told me this issue was serious and deep. Priority had engendered much bitterness and lasting enmity in science, and almost everyone tended to overclaim for themselves and undercite everyone else. I knew how annoyed and resentful I felt when someone failed to cite me.

Dick Solomon provided the answer. He was intellectually generous. He was a fountain of ideas—some good, more half-baked—and he spewed them forth every Thursday in his luncheon seminar. He encouraged us to do the same. I resolved to be like Dick and not like Neal. I had lots of ideas and was not afraid to give voice to them, even if they turned out to be wrong or even foolish. I erred on the side of not being boring rather than that of being right. Ownership in my view belonged to the person who ran with the idea, not to the person who thought it up. For the rest of my life, I spewed forth ideas, not vetting them as thoroughly as others did, and I encouraged my students and colleagues to run with them. When they later asked me to be first author of a resulting article or fifth author because I had thought the original idea up, I usually declined. I made the mistake of under-citing—but usually from lack of scholarship, not from lack of generosity in giving credit. I also made the mistake of over-claiming— but usually for the sake of pushing the limits of an idea, not for the sake of pushing myself or for publicity.

I didn't have answers for the general problem of ownership of ideas, but with the hindsight of fifty years, I want to put ownership in perspective for the case of learned helplessness.

Learned helplessness illuminated a dimension consigned to silence by behaviorism and therefore unresearchable: the dimension of personal control. Control is both a cognition and a cognition about the future, both forbidden by behaviorism. To have a contingency between a voluntary response and an outcome is to control that outcome. The dog in the escape group controls the shock, and the dog expects to have control in the future.

Is the dog motivated to want control for its own sake? Do we want more than just lots of good stuff and little bad stuff? Do we also want control over the good stuff and the bad stuff? Is control a basic motivation?

"Control" meant something different in the 1960s than it means fifty years later. Then it was used not in the sense of *personal* control but almost entirely in sense of *governmental* or *organizational* control.

When our work was translated into German (and French, Portuguese, and Spanish), we were told something was "off" about our use of the term. In German, individual people don't *controllieren*; only the government does. But something was blowing in the wind, and learned helplessness was one of the squalls. It was the idea that individual people, you and I, can and should control what is important to us.

Control certainly mattered in and of itself for the white-footed deer mouse in a 1967 experiment. This creature, when captured, was in a continuous wrestling match with the humans who thought they ran the lab. The humans set the lights to bright, and the mouse could press a bar to alter the level of lighting. The mouse stepped down the illumination to live in dim lighting. Maybe the mouse just liked dimness. So the next day the humans stepped the lights down to the chosen dimness, but the mouse again fought them and set its ambient lighting up to bright. The mouse seemed to care not about any particular level of light but about having control over its light.[3]

Not just mice. Old people as well.

When I was a graduate student, an ever-smiling undergraduate worked alongside us in Dick Solomon's lab and was great fun to be around. Aside from bustling around the lab and enchanting all of us, she was also president of student government in the College for Women. Her name was Judith Seitz, soon to be Judy Rodin. Judy went on to a PhD at Columbia under one of the most illustrious social psychologists of the twentieth century, Stanley Schachter.

Just at the time I settled back in at Penn, Judy, by then an assistant professor at Yale, teamed up with Ellen Langer. Ellen was a pistol, and experimenting in the real world with real people came as second

Judith Rodin was an undergrad at Penn when I was a graduate student. She went on to become a pioneering researcher in personal control, then the provost at Yale, then president at Penn, and ultimately the president of the Rockefeller Foundation. Photo courtesy of the Rockefeller Foundation.

nature to her, as it did for Stan Schachter. She and Judy decided to look at the effect of control in a setting that often deprived human beings of it: a nursing home.[4]

On the fourth floor of the nursing home, Ellen and Judy gave forty-seven patients a lecture. The lecture stressed responsibility: *you* decide how to arrange your room, and *you* decide how to spend your time. Each patient also picked out a houseplant that was theirs to keep and tend.

On the second floor, forty-seven other patients got a lecture stressing all the good things that were done for them. The staff arranged their rooms for them and scheduled how they spent their time. Each patient was given a houseplant and told that the nurse would take care of it.

Ellen and Judy decided to measure activity. The 1970s were low-tech rubber band and paper clip days, so they cleverly put white adhesive tape on the wheels of the wheelchairs and just measured how dirty the tape got. The patients on the "control" floor were more active and healthier, and eighteen months later only seven (15 percent) had died. Thirteen (30 percent) of the patients from the second floor had died.

Ellen and Judy argued that having control was a basic source of vitality and that being deprived of it might be lethal for an otherwise weakened person. For now, keep in mind that there were only two groups in the Langer and Rodin experiment, so it was unclear if having control enhanced vitality and/or not having control diminished it. (An ideal experiment would have included a third group that received no lecture at all.) It took another thirty years before Steve Maier figured out which was likely true.

It was an indication of the growing respectability of control as a legitimate object of study that Ellen went on to become the first tenured woman in the psychology department at Harvard and Judy became provost at Yale, then president of Penn, and finally head of the powerful Rockefeller Foundation.

Other influential theorists started to talk about control beginning in the late 1950s. I omit the great historical forerunners: Pico della Mirandola, Erasmus, Francis Bacon, Arminius, Friedrich Nietzsche, and Alfred Adler, to name just six. (I hope someday to do them justice.) The first modern was Robert White, who published on "competence" in 1959: people and animals, he asserted, play and explore for their own sake.[5] This paper was widely read; indeed, it was assigned to me as an undergraduate and stuck in my memory when I went to work on learned helplessness. Julian Rotter, a social psychologist, developed the concept of "locus of control," with some people being "externals," believing that the environment or other people shape their lives, and others being "internals," believing that they themselves shape their own lives.[6] This attracted a large following in social psychology, but I did not read about it until after we published the first learned helplessness experiments. Stanford professor Albert Bandura, today the most-cited living psychologist, touted the concept

of "self-efficacy." An "efficacy expectation" is the belief that you, your-self, can bring about the outcomes you desire, whereas an "outcome expectation" is the belief that the outcome you desire will simply hap-pen. He castigated us for not making this distinction. Self-efficacy equals control.[7]

Richard Lazarus at Berkeley proposed a cognitive "appraisal" the-ory. When an event occurs, the organism first assesses the conse-quences of the event (primary appraisal), then asks if it has the ability to cope with the event and its consequences. This is "secondary ap-praisal."[8] Coping was Lazarus-speak for control.

So learned helplessness, finding the downside of *not having control*, was really just one step in a vigorous march emphasizing the benefits of the *presence of control*. While we self-centeredly thought of our own work as huge, Steve and I were in fact just part of two inter-twined developments making their way into mainstream psychology: the new acceptance of cognition and the new dimension of control. Our particular niche was the absence of control, helplessness. By the turn of the millennium, both control and cognition were firmly en-trenched in mainstream psychology.

BY 1972, the learned helplessness was catching on. Other scientists had replicated it in rats and mice, and it would soon be found in gold-fish and cats and even cockroaches.[9] This was a relief to me, since I hoped that we had found a general process, but at first I worried that we had tapped into some quirky human-dog submission pattern, and that learned helplessness was just a species-specific artifact. (Behold the external validity problem once again.) A similar worry was that the expectation *Nothing I do matters* was not general but somehow set off by trauma. Did learned helplessness occur across good and neutral events as well as bad ones? To find out, researchers gave food to rats independently of their actions, and these rats later had trou-ble learning to press a bar for food. They became passive. The same seemed to hold when lights and sounds were first presented inde-pendently of action.[10]

Yes, there was an "entitlement" effect, and "spoiled" rats learned to be lazy about good events and didn't even try to control them.

But for all that progress, I had real doubts about the external validity of the learned helplessness endeavor. Was it just a laboratory curiosity that like so many others would gather dust on library shelves? Was it a model of real depression in the clinic? Did it capture the essence of what a human being experiences when her spouse dies, or bankruptcy occurs, or she is rejected by her boyfriend? The next logical step on the path to external validity was for some brave soul to do laboratory learned helplessness experiments in people.

The answer to my prayers came in the form of Donald Hiroto. As a graduate student at Oregon State University, Hiroto built a human shuttle box, a two-chambered device about four feet long. The human subject, wearing earphones, heard a very loud tone while he rested one hand in the shuttle box. If he moved his hand to the other side of the shuttle box, the tone stopped, and people easily learned to escape the tone. Against this background, on the previous day in another room, Hiroto recreated the triadic design: all wearing earphones, one group got the tone but could escape it by pushing a button. The second group was yoked and got an inescapable tone, and the third group got no tone. The next day in the shuttle box the results exactly paralleled those in rats and dogs. Two-thirds of the individuals who got the inescapable tone just left their hands in the shuttle box passively and did not even try to escape.

An exceedingly formal Japanese American, Don arrived at Penn as my very first postdoctoral student. He was obsessively thorough, exactly the right kind of researcher needed to build the systematic case for external validity. He insisted on calling me "Professor Seligman," even though he was older and much better dressed than I.

"Professor Seligman," Don said, "let's do exactly what other people are doing in rats and find out if helplessness in people is general. If you are helpless about escaping noise, do you become helpless about solving cognitive problems and back again." He then did exactly that, looking at the interchangeability of helplessness across two instrumental and two cognitive tasks. Three groups of people got anagrams: solvable (e.g., OTAIP), unsolvable (e.g., OTEIP), or nothing, and the next day they went to the shuttle box. The solvable group and the zero group escaped the loud noise well. Two-thirds of the people in

the unsolvable group, however, just sat there passively and didn't even try to escape the noise. Similarly, helplessness regarding the loud tone debilitated people in solving later cognitive problems.[11]

I was proud of this work and gushed about it to Tim Beck during one of our monthly lunches at Kelly and Cohen's. (There was no Kelly, but it was still the most popular deli in West Philadelphia.) Tim was usually the gentlest and most nondirective of critics, so I choked on my grilled Reuben when he said, "Marty, if you continue down this path, you will waste your life."

I was stirred but not yet shaken. Tim was telling me to take up new methods and to do a better job with external validity by turning my work to deal directly with real people and real problems. But it took a numinous dream a few nights later to shake my foundations: I somehow found myself in the New York Guggenheim Museum. I was slowly plodding up its famous curving ramp. There were rooms off to the right every few paces, and in the rooms people were playing with cards. They seemed to be tarot cards.

I asked, "Why is everyone playing with cards?"

Whereupon the roof of the museum opened, and God appeared—only his head and not his body. In case you are wondering, God is very old, he is male, he has a white, well-tended, curly beard, and he has a booming bass voice. He said, unforgettably, "Seligman, at least you are starting to ask the right questions."

Chapter Eleven

Tessitura (1973–1974)

"TESSITURA"[1] IS A term for a singer's most comfortable vocal range—the range in which she will make her most beautiful music. A mezzo-soprano can hit a high C, but she has to strain to stay there, and you can hear it. Tessitura is the place where you find your true voice, where you can have a long and healthy career. The quest for my tessitura in psychology was a search in three dimensions: style, tempo, and content.

"EVERY TIME I construct a sentence," said Dick Solomon to Steve and me, "I first talk to the person perched on my right shoulder." The occasion was dinner at my favorite restaurant, Le Bec Fin. Georges Perrier had created this temple of classic French cuisine in the late 1960s, and I became one of his poorest but steadiest customers. I became comfortable there. I saved up, and whenever there was anything to celebrate, I visited. On this evening the dish was the lightest *quenelle de brochet* imaginable in a coral-hued lobster sauce, and the wine was a pale yellow Puligny Montrachet. Dick, Steve, and I were celebrating the acceptance of a paper by a good journal.

"On my right shoulder sits Harold Schlosberg, my mentor at Brown," continued Dick. "I read the sentence to Harold very slowly, and if he nods his head, I turn to my left shoulder. On my left shoulder sits my other mentor, Walter S. Hunter. I now read him the sentence very slowly, and if he also nods, the sentence goes in. If not, I start again."

Dick transported his graduate mentors at Brown in his imagination when he went off to teach at Harvard, and he then brought them to Penn. I didn't have to imagine my mentors, because they were here with me in Philadelphia. Two of them, Dick and Frank Irwin, would serve my journal style well by perching on my shoulders since each edited a major journal. I didn't need to imagine their comments, since I routinely sent each of them an early draft of any paper I was writing.

Dick and Frank were very careful in print, and so they were the ideal editors of the *Psychological Review* and the *Journal of Experimental Psychology*, respectively. In their writing they crafted long sentences, and any one lifted out of context was self-contained and likely true.

Here's a typical one from Dick:

> Because we shall show that discriminative instrumental acts can be established without those acts having been reinforced differentially (because they could not occur under curare), then a revision of theories emphasizing the importance of peripheral, skeletal responding and proprioceptive cues seems definitely to be required.[2]

And a typical one from Frank:

> The present experiment was designed to determine whether, as predicted on these grounds, the number of cards required for decisions in the expanded judgment situation would increase with the value of money prizes for correct decisions and would decrease with increased money cost per card.[3]

How many times did you have to read each sentence to understand it? Twice for me, and I know these topics well. Their style was "reviewer friendly," and indeed Dick and Frank rarely encountered a journal rejection, but their style was not "reader friendly."

I tried not to write like they did.

Most readers are busy. I sure am. Many readers just scan. I know I do. Help the scanners by using short sentences and plain words.

The big word and the long sentence must increase accuracy a lot to make up for impeded reading. And don't overwrite. Omit extra words and information that the reader already knows. Overwriting slows the reader way down and does not increase accuracy much at all.

In style, even if it defied the American Psychological Association's best-selling publication manual,[4] I had found my tessitura.

MY TEMPO WAS wrong. My father, Adrian, was fast, and Irene said that he could do in one hour what other lawyers took eight to do. But Irene also said that he then could use the extra seven hours to check and perfect. I had Adrian's speed, but I just raced on to the next task rather than checking and perfecting. My speeding was not limited to work, and I suspect that my poor tempo in part led to others' finding me brusque and inferring that I was self-absorbed.

Are there any slow psychologists? There was at least one, William K. Estes, the premier mathematical learning theorist. Conversing with Bill was agony.

"Bill," I asked at a party where he was the guest of honor, "what do you think the evolutionary function of sleeping is?" He stared at me unblinking. I waited. I waited. It was so long I started to count to myself. At forty-five, he blinked and his lips finally moved.

"What, Marty, do you think is the evolutionary function of being awake?"

Could I learn to be slow, not as slow as Bill Estes, but slow enough not to offend?

THE DEPARTMENT WAS hiring someone who worked in vision, the most scientifically sophisticated branch of psychology. Ed Pugh, the candidate, gave his job talk on how many photons of light it took to fire a single retinal cell. Between one and seven seemed to be the answer. This was all way over my head, but at the reception afterward, I managed to ask Ed a question that was not completely idiotic. Ed waited a full ten seconds and then gave me a full answer delivered at the slow pace I needed to understand him. He also made me feel that I'd asked him a first-rate question that took him to the cutting edge of visual science.

"You're really slow, Ed," I commented and immediately explained that I meant it as a compliment. "Have you always been so slow?"

"I was an all-state quarterback in my Louisiana high school. There are no slow quarterbacks," Ed replied. "I had to learn slow. After college I tried to become a Jesuit. Jesuit students have two mentors. One grades you, and the other is your 'socius.' Day after day my socius would write just one sentence and then instruct me to go sit under the tree in the cloister for the rest of the afternoon and think about that sentence."

"Can you teach me to be slow, Ed?" I asked. After we hired Ed, he took me under his wing and taught me how to be slow. For a year we met once a week in my office to read Kierkegaard's *Fear and Trembling*. We did only one page each week. I became slower.

Maybe too slow.

Alan Kors was a new assistant professor of history, fresh from his Harvard doctorate on Baron d'Holbach and the French Encyclopedists. Alan and I had been good friends for a decade. He was a classmate at Princeton, editor of our literary magazine, and the most entertaining of the undergraduate literati at Wilson Lodge. That he was an incomparable storyteller and improvised endless rhyming doggerel on his guitar at parties did not mask that he was also a serious poet. He was an outspoken atheist and, as best man at my wedding with Kerry, stood shoulder to shoulder with me against my mother-in-law-to-be, who cursed and wailed when I refused to allow the *G* word at the ceremony. It was a tremendous personal boon to me that he joined Penn's history department.

"Let's teach together, Marty," suggested Alan. We shared many mutual interests: brainwashing, religious conversion, poetry, and the history of science. I agreed instantly. Alan was also as mesmerizing a teacher as he was a conversationalist, the only Penn professor I knew of to ever get perfect teaching ratings in a huge lecture course—a 5.0 from every single student.

I tried out my new slow, noninterrupting style with Alan. I sat in the back row of the class we were to teach together. Alan began his lecture. About one hundred undergraduates were present, and the topic was science during the Enlightenment. At several points, he

brought up issues that I knew a bit about, and I was tempted to interrupt. But, no, I waited for Alan to introduce me. The lecture went on . . . and on. It was fascinating and entertaining, pure Alan Kors. But he did not introduce me. After ninety minutes, the lecture was over, and I had been silent. Alan and I walked back to the student center for coffee.

"What happened?" I asked, miffed. "You were supposed to introduce me."

"What happened?" Alan replied, also miffed. "You were supposed to interrupt—like you usually do."

My tempo was far from perfect, but it was slowing down.

CONTENT WAS THE final element of my tessitura. Behaviorism at its heart was trying to banish two things from science: mental life, of course, and the future—teleology, forward-looking explanations of action. These issues played out in my own department, often in tense conversations. One occurred in 1972 in the "chance encounter" room, the windowless, grotty basement of one of the three buildings among which the bursting-at-the-seams psychology department was scattered miserably. In the hope that some psychologists would bump into each other occasionally, a handful of us made a practice of lounging there, drinking instant coffee. Dave Williams popped in often, and we continued our endless argument over whether people and animals have a rich mental life, with Dave saying they don't and me saying they do, but I could sense that Dave was giving in and abandoning the barren world of Skinnerian psychology. He was on a new but flailing search to be someplace lusher and greener.

Even though smoking was forbidden, Frank Irwin spent a lot of time in the chance encounter room. This was his last year of teaching, and he remained the most upright pillar in the most rigid of psychology departments. All the hours he spent there were emblematic of what an upright departmental citizen he was.

I told Frank that Jim Johnston and I were slaving away on a comprehensive cognitive—"Irwinian"—theory of avoidance learning. Our theory was a stark contrast—some might say a "slap in the face"—to the pursuit to which Neal Miller and Dick Solomon had both devoted

their past two decades. If correct, our theory would not make me any more popular with my fellow learning theorists, who already saw me as suspect because of the cognitive slant of learned helplessness.

Learning how to avoid something unpleasant had become the testing ground of the entire behaviorist program. Neal and Dick wanted to show that avoidance could be completely explained without any reference to either the future or cognition. The future cannot act on the present, they reasoned, so any teleological explanation has causality working backward in time, which is a philosophical error of the first water.

In avoidance learning, animals were first given escape training in which a tone preceded a shock by five seconds. The animals could escape the shock by jumping over a barrier to the safe side. Jumping over the barrier also turned off the signaling tone. Animals quickly learned to jump as soon as the tone went on, but before the shock. This was called avoidance learning because the animals avoided more shock by jumping as soon as they heard the tone—which both prevented the shock and terminated the tone. Avoidance, to the uninitiated, looked like a prime case of a future-directed cognition, the lay explanation being *If I jump, I will avoid future shock.* So it became a crucial task of the behaviorists to show that they could completely explain the jumping without reference to the future. This was quite a trick, and an explanation of avoidance referencing only the present and the past was considered a tour de force for learning theory.[5]

Here's how the explanation—two-process theory—worked. It denied that the animals expected anything at all, claiming that a nonoccurring event—the avoided shock—could have no role in conditioning. Instead, a present event, the tone coming on, became fear-evoking by the usual process of Pavlovian conditioning, having previously been paired with shock. So jumping, by getting the fearful tone to stop, was actually instrumentally reinforced and not at all motivated by avoidance of a shock that never came on.

By contrast, Jim and I claimed that the animals learned first that the tone predicted shock and then that jumping during the tone, but before the shock went on, was followed by no shock. Thus they learned the expectation *If I jump during the tone, I will get no shock.*[6]

That expectation—an if-then conditional about a future outcome that does not happen—explained avoidance.

This was a rare instance of a head-on collision between two theories where a crucial prediction could settle the argument, in this case, about what happens during extinction. Once the animals became steady jumpers, they never got shocked again, and so the tone was no longer paired with shock. This "Pavlovian extinction" should have caused the tone to lose its fearful properties. If the animals were jumping merely to turn off the fearful tone, as two-process theory contended, they should stop after enough trials to extinguish fear of the tone. If, on the other hand, they were jumping to prevent the anticipated shock, as Jim and I contended, the jumping should continue, as every jump would bear out their if-then expectation that jumping would prevent shock—extinction breaks the *association* of tone and shock, but it does not *disconfirm* the conditional *If I jump, I will not be shocked.* In fact, every "extinction" trial continued to confirm the conditional expectation. So if this expectation underpinned the jumping, jumping would persist.

Which is exactly what happened. Hundreds of trials later, the animals were still jumping. They also looked nonchalant, not like animals escaping fear.[7]

Jim was obsessive, and it took us more than a year of arguing, sentence by sentence, with each other to work out every detail. We went through all the evidence exhaustively; it was entirely consistent with a cognitive theory of avoidance and inconsistent at the crucial points with the dominant two-process theory. Once we were sure, I sent Frank Irwin a draft to follow up our chance encounter room chats and presented a colloquium to the department. Frank had had a very long dry spell, and this was the first and only major use ever made of his theory. He sent me a handwritten letter saying how happy he was to have lived to see his way of looking at learning come to fruition. I was pleased this time to receive such a fulsome thank-you, rather than his usual lake of red ink.

This paper was a major "teaching moment" for me. I was sure we'd nailed it and that two-factor theorists would acknowledge that we were right.

But I was under a misapprehension about confrontation in science. I thought that science should proceed by looking for crucial differences between theories and then testing the opposing predictions. This is what Carl Sagan called "good" science: the moon either is or is not covered with a thick layer of dust, and when humans landed on the moon, the dust theory of the origin of the solar system was proved wrong and abandoned. By 1973, I had been in the ring for three heavyweight boxing matches with the dominant stimulus-response-reinforcement theorists.

The first was over learned helplessness. In response to our contention that learned helplessness entailed the cognition *Nothing I do matters*, learning theorists had posited that a few random shock-offsets had just superstitiously reinforced a motor response of standing still. Steve Maier killed that one by explicitly reinforcing standing still in a group of dogs and showing that they were *not* helpless. I suppose I expected the Skinnerians to stand up and concede that they were wrong and we were right, but they did not. Rather, learning theorists made almost no response and thereafter just went silent about learned helplessness. They simply excluded it from the learning theory corpus thereafter.

Then there was John Garcia and sauce béarnaise. I suppose I expected the Pavlovians, who held the premise that any conditional stimulus paired with any unconditional stimulus would result in conditioning, to hang it up and admit they were wrong. But again they were almost silent—uncomfortably so about Garcia, although they grudgingly elected him to the National Academy of Science.

Finally, there was the cognitive theory of avoidance. I was surprised by the reaction from our learning theory colleagues—there was none. Dick Solomon, perfect gentleman that he was, never said a word to me about this paper. Neal Miller, Bob Rescorla, and the rest of the learning theory gang stayed silent and stayed silent and stayed silent.

Instead of an abject surrender, there was no surrender at all, just a gradual drift. I should have known. Behaviorist learning theory eventually relinquished its ambition to explain "all behavior."[8] It abandoned wholesale anti-mentalism and subtly allowed in "expectations" to explain conditioned behavior. The picture of conditioning itself

underwent gradual revision, resulting in the view that "the organism is better seen as an information seeker using logical and perceptual relations among stimuli, along with its own preconceptions, to form a sophisticated representation of the world." Thus the great program of learning theory, the attempt to explain behavior without positing the "forbidden" mental representation of possible futures, slowly folded. Even more importantly, the possibility of a science that takes seriously thinking about the future opened.

But why were thoughts about the future "forbidden" in the first place? A huge conceptual error animated behaviorism, in which something genuinely suspect—causation backward in time, the future determining the present—was conflated with something not at all mysterious, namely, guidance by here-and-now cognitions that bear information about possible futures. There is nothing mysterious, or causally backward, about present action being guided by present thoughts of what will happen in the future.

I also suppose it should have come as no surprise that my Skinnerian and Pavlovian colleagues were not grateful to me for my part in showing them the error of their ways. Rather, to be candid, I left a bad taste in their mouths.

And my takeaway? I too had a bad taste in my mouth, but I'd come to know my tessitura, my thinking's comfort zone: I looked for the most basic premise of the prevailing theory and asked what would follow if it were entirely wrong? I was learning not to expect popularity, but in my heart I knew that truth would out.

"WHAT IS A 'trade' book?" I asked. I'd never heard of such a beast.

"It is smack in between a scholarly monograph, like you usually write, and a mass market book that you find in airports," answered Buck (Hayward) Rogers. Buck, representing W. H. Freeman publishers, took me to dinner at Le Bec Fin. "You've been writing about helplessness. This is not a dry topic only for professionals. It's of great interest to the educated public. Helplessness, you yourself have written, bears on depression, on death, and on raising kids. There has been only one such a 'trade' book in psychology, the *Social Animal*. Yours would be the second."

I took the offer seriously. Such a project would require me to organize my thoughts on external validity—whether helplessness really matters—as well as give me an opportunity to justify and explain experimental psychology to the public. It seemed like the first step on a path to the unknown. Jim Johnston, with his usual skepticism, asked me if the world needed a whole book about helplessness.

BY 1974 I had found my tessitura.

In style, I was comfortable writing plainly: few big words, short sentences, brief paragraphs, and straightforward arguments.

In tempo, I was becoming slower. I was more deliberate in speech as well as thought. My pace had improved. Though imperfect it was closer to right than it had ever been.

Content is what really matters. Physics and chemistry had engineering before they became "basic" sciences. Physics predicted eclipses and tides and the trajectories of cannonballs. Alchemy invented medicines and paints, even if it could not make gold out of lead. Basic physicists and chemists therefore knew what merited further drilling down. Psychology, in contrast, had never had engineering—it had no discoveries and inventions that worked in the real world—so what was "basic" to psychology was arbitrary. This was what bothered me so about learning theory, because it was far from evident that Pavlovian conditioning and instrumental training were basic to anything.

My tessitura followed. I would choose psychological topics anchored in the real world, document them at the real-world level, and then drill down to find their elements.

The world did indeed need a book about helplessness.

Chapter Twelve

England (1975)

KERRY, I, AND our two children, Amanda, five, and David, twenty months, boarded the British Airways flight to London on a freezing January night in 1975. We rented a three-bedroom detached house on Westover Road in a slightly gentrified district of Wandsworth, just one bridge south of the Thames from Chelsea. We bought a used Volvo station wagon for me to make the thirty-minute drive through the grotty areas of Battersea, Clapham, and then Brixton to work in Denmark Hill. I had a Guggenheim Fellowship and was to be a visiting professor at the Institute of Psychiatry of the Maudsley and Bethlem Hospitals. My principal reason for going to England was to learn more clinical psychology at the premier settings in the world. Both these institutions have glorious histories: aside from the fact that the word "bedlam" derives from the behavior of the insane inmates at the Bethlem Royal Hospital, the Maudsley was home to a distinguished line of psychiatrists, and the Institute of Psychiatry was its crown jewel, the central research and training hub for young clinical psychologists in England.

Hans Eysenck presided over this sprawling center. Hans was one of the great psychologists of the second half of the twentieth century, and his life was a portrait of moral and intellectual courage. He was born in Germany in 1916. As a schoolboy, being taught in class that the Jews had sold out Germany in the Great War, Hans (who was not Jewish) wrote an essay on the courage of those Kaiser Wilhelm Medal

winners who were Jewish. Shortly thereafter, he pointedly turned his back on a Nazi speaker in class, and his teacher secretly told him to get out of Germany as quickly as possible. Leaving his parents, he slipped away on a train, making his way eventually to England, but as a suspect German émigré, he then could not get a job there. He earned his PhD at the University of London with Sir Cyril Burt, a leading researcher on the heritability of IQ. Before long Hans was embroiled in a related controversy. He developed a theory of personality involving neuroticism and introversion and wanted to know the origin of these personality types. But this was the heyday of radical environmentalism—the belief that we are no more than what experience happens to write upon our blank slate. Personality had somehow to arise from our surroundings. This was one of the only dogmas that American ideals (all men are created equal) and Soviet ideals (the creation of the "Soviet Man") agreed about. In the wake of the eugenic program of the Nazis and their defeat, work on genetic influences in human development was anathema. Hardly a Nazi sympathizer, Hans sponsored twin studies of a host of personality traits, including IQ. The data kept showing that personality is highly heritable and IQ even more so: identical twins are much more similar for almost every personality trait than are fraternal twins. Further, adopted kids are much less similar to their parents than are biological offspring. As a reward for this research, the left-wing press called Hans a fascist. He was regularly heckled at his public speeches and even assaulted at one. Undeterred, he told me that his primary loyalty lay with the "arguments that needed hearers" and that "truth will out."

I would prefer, on moral grounds, for radical environmentalism to be true, but it is false. The Garcia effect and my own work on prepared learning demonstrate this dogma to be completely untenable. And too much human experience conflicts with it.

Could it be that we inherit from our parents not just their eye color and height or even their IQ but their personalities, their hopes, their very fantasies, and the form of their dreams? I suspect that the endeavors—nurturing, fighting, politicking, persuading, commanding, seducing, or stealing—that our parents and their parents were good at, we too will be good at—and for genetic reasons. Consider divorce:

it is highly heritable. A divorcé's identical twin is far more likely to be divorced than his fraternal twin. The inheritance of global personality characteristics—meanness, agreeableness, lust, loyalty, promiscuity—must account for this. There is no divorce gene. Evolution selects only secondarily for genes; it selects primarily for the actual large-scale characteristics that enhance reproductive success and survival: modules such as beauty, aggressiveness, smarts, speed, and strength. The modules simply drag along the genes of which they happen to be constructed. Carl Jung, on this view, was not far wrong with his "archetypes," and Hans headed a research program that led us more toward the true nature of the human beast than the dogma of radical environmentalism.

"There might be more to where personality comes from than just genes and the environment," he said when we met for the first time. Hans was tall, stiffly erect of posture, with wavy brown hair and arresting blue eyes. He looked closer to forty-five than sixty. He chose his words very carefully, but they exuded a quiet honesty, and he brimmed with enthusiasm. His soft charisma carried me away.

"How about the stars? There's an unpopular view."

"Astrology?" I asked incredulously. Talk about wading into another controversy.

"Neo-astrology. Take this home and pore through it," Hans said, passing me a two-inch-thick data printout. "Michel and Françoise Gauquelin condemn traditional astrology as unscientific, and they have done what looks to me like rigorous research. This printout purports to show that we can predict the occupations of famous Frenchmen from the positions of specific planets at the exact moment of their births. Sportsmen and military men (warlike) tend to have Mars at mid-heaven when they are born. Actors (the Jovian personality) tend to have Jupiter at mid-heaven, and scientists and doctors (saturnine introverts) have Saturn at mid-heaven.[1] And it's not just Frenchmen; this has been replicated for Belgians."

I took the pile home to Wandsworth and ran statistics on it. They confirmed what Hans said. I couldn't find anything amiss and told Hans as much at dinner in a chichi Clapham restaurant a few weeks later.

"But there is no conceivable mechanism," I said. "The hands of the midwife exert far more influence on the baby than the infinitesimal force of a distant planet. Influence falls off with the square of the distance."

"Mechanism? We don't even have a mechanism for gravity," retorted Hans.

As I leaned in to object, my head came too close to a candle, and my hair caught fire. Sybil and Kerry doused the flames with their glasses of water. I was embarrassed and singed but uninjured.

I never published on neo-astrology, and neither, I believe, did Hans. We were both singed, however, by our common belief that the universe holds many more secrets than our poor little science can detect.

HANS FLOATED ABOVE the Maudsley. He played a role I had not seen before, but it gave a shape to my future. My parents wanted an Einstein, a genius who could penetrate to the depths of scientific problems. I was no Einstein. I was no Wittgenstein. It was not just that I was not smart enough or deep enough. It was also a matter of tessitura. My comfort zone did not include taking a single problem and riding it all the way to the bottom. Rather, I was coming to realize, I had a "start-up" mentality and a broad "entrepreneurial" bent. This is pretty far from the standard mentality of an academic. I could see and then pounce on a basic issue that needed reframing, usually one at the heart of a popular enterprise that I found wrongheaded. Learned helplessness took on the dominant enterprise of stimulus-response-reinforcement learning theory, and we did the start-up work to move animal psychology in a cognitive direction. Prepared learning took on the dominant enterprise of environmentalism, and we tried to move it in a direction that takes evolution more seriously. I enjoyed laying the bricks for the new ground floor myself, but then I wanted to get my students and colleagues to complete the edifice.

This is the role of not an Einstein but an Oppenheimer. J. Robert Oppenheimer (1904–1967) was a highly competent physicist with sufficient grasp of all the relevant kinds of physics needed to build an atomic bomb, the vision to see the big picture, and the ability to coordinate all the moving parts of the physics in the Manhattan Project.

it is highly heritable. A divorcé's identical twin is far more likely to be divorced than his fraternal twin. The inheritance of global personality characteristics—meanness, agreeableness, lust, loyalty, promiscuity—must account for this. There is no divorce gene. Evolution selects only secondarily for genes; it selects primarily for the actual large-scale characteristics that enhance reproductive success and survival: modules such as beauty, aggressiveness, smarts, speed, and strength. The modules simply drag along the genes of which they happen to be constructed. Carl Jung, on this view, was not far wrong with his "archetypes," and Hans headed a research program that led us more toward the true nature of the human beast than the dogma of radical environmentalism.

"There might be more to where personality comes from than just genes and the environment," he said when we met for the first time. Hans was tall, stiffly erect of posture, with wavy brown hair and arresting blue eyes. He looked closer to forty-five than sixty. He chose his words very carefully, but they exuded a quiet honesty, and he brimmed with enthusiasm. His soft charisma carried me away.

"How about the stars? There's an unpopular view."

"Astrology?" I asked incredulously. Talk about wading into another controversy.

"Neo-astrology. Take this home and pore through it," Hans said, passing me a two-inch-thick data printout. "Michel and Françoise Gauquelin condemn traditional astrology as unscientific, and they have done what looks to me like rigorous research. This printout purports to show that we can predict the occupations of famous Frenchmen from the positions of specific planets at the exact moment of their births. Sportsmen and military men (warlike) tend to have Mars at mid-heaven when they are born. Actors (the Jovian personality) tend to have Jupiter at mid-heaven, and scientists and doctors (saturnine introverts) have Saturn at mid-heaven.[1] And it's not just Frenchmen; this has been replicated for Belgians."

I took the pile home to Wandsworth and ran statistics on it. They confirmed what Hans said. I couldn't find anything amiss and told Hans as much at dinner in a chichi Clapham restaurant a few weeks later.

"But there is no conceivable mechanism," I said. "The hands of the midwife exert far more influence on the baby than the infinitesimal force of a distant planet. Influence falls off with the square of the distance."

"Mechanism? We don't even have a mechanism for gravity," retorted Hans.

As I leaned in to object, my head came too close to a candle, and my hair caught fire. Sybil and Kerry doused the flames with their glasses of water. I was embarrassed and singed but uninjured.

I never published on neo-astrology, and neither, I believe, did Hans. We were both singed, however, by our common belief that the universe holds many more secrets than our poor little science can detect.

HANS FLOATED ABOVE the Maudsley. He played a role I had not seen before, but it gave a shape to my future. My parents wanted an Einstein, a genius who could penetrate to the depths of scientific problems. I was no Einstein. I was no Wittgenstein. It was not just that I was not smart enough or deep enough. It was also a matter of tessitura. My comfort zone did not include taking a single problem and riding it all the way to the bottom. Rather, I was coming to realize, I had a "start-up" mentality and a broad "entrepreneurial" bent. This is pretty far from the standard mentality of an academic. I could see and then pounce on a basic issue that needed reframing, usually one at the heart of a popular enterprise that I found wrongheaded. Learned helplessness took on the dominant enterprise of stimulus-response-reinforcement learning theory, and we did the start-up work to move animal psychology in a cognitive direction. Prepared learning took on the dominant enterprise of environmentalism, and we tried to move it in a direction that takes evolution more seriously. I enjoyed laying the bricks for the new ground floor myself, but then I wanted to get my students and colleagues to complete the edifice.

This is the role of not an Einstein but an Oppenheimer. J. Robert Oppenheimer (1904–1967) was a highly competent physicist with sufficient grasp of all the relevant kinds of physics needed to build an atomic bomb, the vision to see the big picture, and the ability to coordinate all the moving parts of the physics in the Manhattan Project.

He never got the Nobel Prize. My parents did not get an Einstein. At best, maybe they got an Oppenheimer.

But I did not yet know what my Manhattan Project was to be.

Hans was an Oppenheimer and the only one operating in psychology. He was the overseer of an institute that did research ranging over psychotherapy, personality, genetics, anxiety, depression, sexuality, intelligence, and more, and everyone at the institute approached these topics with a distinctive Eysenckian bent.

A LONG, DEAFENING scream froze us in our tracks. S. J. (Jack) Rachman and I were walking down the corridor to Isaac Marks's office. The scream was issuing from behind his closed door.

Isaac was my official host. Dean Schuyler, my therapy mentor at Penn, told me about the wonderful month he had spent with Isaac the year before, and Isaac then invited me to spend my sabbatical under his auspices at the institute. Isaac, an émigré from South Africa, had received his MD in Cape Town, trained as a psychiatrist in London, and, with the 1969 publication of *Fears and Phobias*,[2] catapulted to the top rank of research psychiatrists in the field of anxiety. He was slight of build, warm and welcoming of manner, and an aesthete. A walk through a flower garden with Isaac brought a running commentary on subtle variations in the scents of the roses and even the scent of the irises we passed. He and Shula, a historian of South African politics, hosted soirees in their fashionable Dulwich Common cottage, the most recent evening spent on T. S. Eliot's "Four Quartets." Isaac liked the preparedness slant on phobias, and I was flattered by his interest. He had taken me under his wing and was introducing me to some of his most exotic phobic patients.

The scream reissued from behind his door. Jack and I stood stock-still, but after a minute of dead silence, Jack knocked softly. Isaac opened the door, and we saw a man of about fifty, very well-dressed in a blue suit and red tie, sitting across from him, a beatific smile on his face. Isaac introduced us to his patient and asked him to tell us about the new therapy we couldn't help but overhear.

"I am an agoraphobic," he explained. "My biggest fear is crowds, being hemmed in by a crowd and not being able to escape. Dr. Marks

here is using what he calls 'catharsis' to cure my phobia. I find that when I let it all out and scream out my terror, I feel much, much better. So I am imagining myself crowded in the stands at a football match, everyone standing and yelling, and . . ." He stood, screamed again for about ten seconds, and collapsed back into his chair, exhausted but beaming.

"Last Sunday I actually went to a football match, and whenever the crowd stood and yelled, I stood with them and screamed out my panic. I had a great time, and I think I can handle the problem better now."

Isaac was a creative therapist. He practiced "exposure" therapy in which, instead of avoiding the phobic object, the patients were flooded with it. The logic was that the phobic object was a conditioned stimulus, and if it occurred without any unconditioned stimulus, such as actual trauma, the fear would extinguish. The trick was to keep the phobic in the presence of the phobic object long enough to discover that it was harmless. Isaac's techniques were extreme, such as locking a claustrophobic in a closet for two hours, but they worked. After the screamer left, saying thank you repeatedly, Isaac told Jack and me about a woman he was treating with flooding. She was a sperm phobic, something I had not heard of before. Her phobia had exploded, and she now avoided all contact with males, including her husband and sons.

"Her homework assignment was to wear her husband's dirty underpants all last week, and this week she is doing well," Isaac told us.

Jack Rachman, Hans's right-hand man, turned out to be my closest friend at the Maudsley. Like Isaac Marks, Jack was a South African Jewish émigré. Like Isaac, he was a behavior therapist of renown, and like Isaac his main field was anxiety. Unlike Isaac or Hans, Jack was not larger than life. He was shy, humble, easygoing, and uproariously funny. Beneath his quiet gaiety, I sensed a troubled past, someone who had been to Hades and come back scarred but stronger. His clinical skill and the understanding he radiated with his troubled patients seemed to stem from his time in the underworld.

Jack took evolutionary considerations seriously for all the neuroses. He and Padmal DaSilva introduced me to cases of obsessive-compulsive disorder (OCD) that fit the preparedness theory of phobias

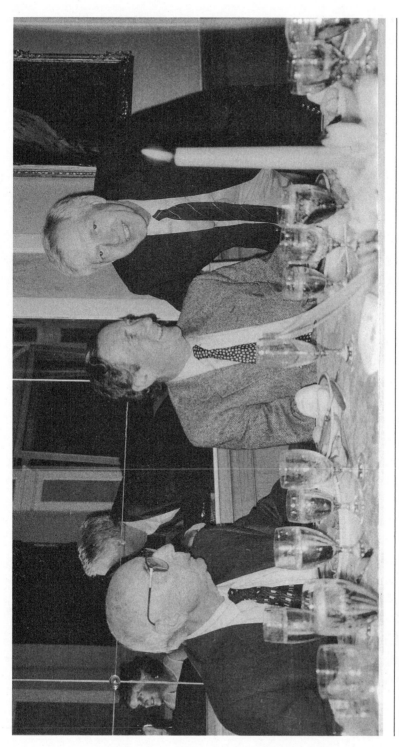

On the left is Joe Wolpe (1915–1997), a South African psychiatrist who pioneered behavior therapy. He emigrated to America in 1960 and taught at Temple University. He befriended me in 1966 and introduced me to systematic desensitization (Chapter 7). In the center, is S. J. (Jack) Rachman, my closest colleague during my year at the Maudsley Hospital. On the right is Terry Wilson, a leading behavior therapist. Photo courtesy of Terry Wilson.

well. OCD patients have very disturbing thoughts about filth, checking, injury, and doubt that do not let up unless they engage in a ritual that stops them, but only temporarily. The thoughts and the rituals made sense in the evolutionary history of humans, and so did the objects of phobias: washing to get rid of dirt, checking repeatedly to make sure the door was locked or the gas off, thinking and rethinking and rethinking again in the face of doubt. So preparedness seemed to apply to OCD as well as to phobia.

Preparedness was currently gathering steam at Arne Ohman's human-conditioning laboratory in Uppsala, Sweden. Pictures of snakes or scorpions (dangerous in evolution and so "prepared"), which in themselves do not evoke fear, were paired with electric shocks. Conditioned fear occurred with only one pairing. This fear was difficult to extinguish, and even when the electrodes were taken off and shock could not possibly occur, the photos of snakes and scorpions still evoked fear.[3] Importantly pictures of flowers (evolutionarily not dangerous) paired with shock had none of these properties. Fear took many trials to condition and extinguished rapidly—and rationally—when shock was no longer presented or the electrodes taken off. This was gratifying to me. It conformed to John Garcia's taste aversions in rats and exactly paralleled the sauce béarnaise phenomenon: evolutionarily dangerous, one-trial learning, difficult to extinguish, and irrational.

But Jack introduced me to cases of rare, unprepared phobias that violated the theory: a blind woman with a plant phobia and another woman who avoided all brown objects. Both were housebound by the severity of their phobias, lest they encounter plants or things brown, neither of which are evolutionarily dangerous—plants and chocolate seem pretty innocuous in evolution. But they were lifelong phobias, very resistant to therapy, and highly irrational. We could not explain them but were eager to find the boundary conditions of preparedness and phobia and even to overturn the theory if it was wrong, so we published "Unprepared Phobias: Be Prepared."[4]

Just as in his scientific work, Jack bent over backward to be fair-minded. He was a wine expert and twice a month took me to the tastings and then to the follow-up auctions at Christie's. Jack was a

patient teacher and highly articulate about the properties of fine wine. I started to develop a decent palette and acquire wine-discussing phrases, such as "raspberry bouquet," "undertone of motor oil," and "decent ullage for its age." Jack wrote a superb book, *A Matter of Taste*,[5] under the pseudonym Jacques Durac. (It was rumored that he had also written a gardening book by Jacques DuFleur and a betting book by Jacques DuTrac). Under his real name, he reviewed the book in *Behaviour Research and Therapy*, the journal he edited, and unceremoniously panned the wine book as naive and unscientific.[6]

I began to have wine dreams. One was prophetic. I was in fact to speak at Sussex University, and my host would be Stuart Sutherland, a renowned cognitive psychologist and an oenophile. In my dream, Professor Sutherland tried to stump me at a blind tasting with—of all things—a German *red* wine. I had never even seen one, and I was not even sure they existed. I did go to Sussex and in reality, at dinner, Stuart, in front of the entire faculty, presented me with a red wine to identify. I went through the motions of swirling, sniffing, and tasting and without a clue confidently asserted, "It is a red Rhine wine." Which it was! I could not help but recall my Guggenheim-Godhead dream with increased credulity.

Jack arranged a series of four talks for me to give at the institute, and I was gratified by the standing-room-only turnout. The institute was not only England's premier research establishment in psychiatry but also the premier training institution in clinical psychology. Part of Hans's claim to fame was his successful battle to allow clinical psychologists to practice psychotherapy legally, not just as handmaidens to psychiatrists and other physicians. The result was the institute's famed MPhil and PhD programs, with the Commonwealth's most qualified young people competing fiercely to get their clinical training under Jack, Hans, Isaac, and two dozen other research clinicians. They turned out in force for my lectures, and I found myself with a gaggle of them at tea every day in the common room.

There I met the femme fatale who would dominate my life for the next three years. Her name was Suzanne Miller, and she was a PhD student from Montreal. Jewish, short, perfect of face and body with sparkling brown eyes, and explosive, she made no bones about her

availability. I was poleaxed. Even with two young children to raise, the marital bond between Kerry and me had worn thin after ten years, and we were going our separate ways in London. My single-minded devotion to my work, which always came way before Kerry and my children, was one cause. The promiscuity of the swinging sixties in the United States was another, and the sexual atmosphere at the Maudsley in 1975 made the American sixties look puritanical. Suzanne and I began to travel together around Europe, and within a year I had left Kerry and my children for her.

This was a difficult time for me. While swept away by Suzanne, I was also wracked with guilt. Amanda's and David's futures preyed on me most. I told David, then five, that divorce meant that I would never be married to Kerry again, never, not ever, never.

"But you might," he said, looking up at me pleadingly.

Unlike me, Kerry soon landed on her feet. She married Dave Hunter, one of my roommates from Princeton. Also a philosophy major, Dave was the saintly roommate, the one who went down to Mississippi and got beaten up in 1964. The rest of us just talked the talk. After Harvard Law, Dave spent the next thirty years working in the voting rights section of the U.S. Department of Justice. At their wedding, I was pleased to hear, they pledged that they would raise the children "as Marty would have wanted." Dave was an excellent, fair-minded stepfather to my kids, but Kerry and I would never be friendly. Eventually both Kerry and Dave became Unitarian ministers and shared a congregation. I will always feel guilty about my decision to leave my kids, but without that brash move, Mandy, my next five wonderful kids, and positive psychology would not have happened.

MY FIRST TRADE BOOK, *Helplessness*,[7] had just come out. I'd spent most of the previous year writing it and found myself very much at home writing in plain English and extrapolating from laboratory findings to big real-world issues. The first half of the book went through the concept of learned helplessness and the scientific evidence for its existence. The second half speculated on how helplessness might illuminate real problems: child development as the rise out of helplessness and how to accelerate mastery in kids; learned helplessness as

a model for depression and what this tells us about therapy; learned helplessness as a cause of sudden, premature death. Isaac and Shula Marks hosted a party to celebrate the publication. During a trip back to Penn, Alan Kors took me to lunch at the campus bistro, La Terrasse, to celebrate my newly published book. "I hope your next book is about the opposite," Alan urged as we parted.

DESPITE THE POSITIVE reception that these ideas were garnering, I had growing doubts about the looseness of my inferences to human problems such as depression. It was comforting that the parallel laboratory procedures for learned helplessness in animals produced parallel passivity when applied to people, but the Guggenheim Museum dream and Tim Beck's admonition about wasting my life haunted me. All this came to a head on a sunny April day in Oxford.

I'd been invited to lecture to the department of psychology on learned helplessness as a model of depression. The large lecture room was packed to the rafters, and there was a buzz of excitement as I entered. In the audience I saw some of the stars of British academia: Jerome Bruner, American expatriate and Regius Professor; Donald Broadbent, the leading light of information-processing psychology; Jeffrey Gray, Hans's eventual successor as head of the Maudsley; Michael Gelder, dean of British psychiatry; and Niko Tinbergen, Nobelist in ethology. Those in the know (and I was not one of them) seemed to be expecting some dynamite. The format was unconventional: rather than simply my sixty-minute talk followed by an open-question session, a discussant, a young Oxford lecturer named John Teasdale, had been scheduled. I knew by reputation that he was a most highly prized student of Hans Eysenck and Jack Rachman, and he was said to be scholarly and deep, as well as a practicing clinician. He was also said to be a trenchant critic of learned helplessness.

I went through the mapping of eight symptoms of learned helplessness in the lab to nine of the symptoms of depression. I went through the fact that depressed people in the laboratory failed to escape noise and gave up easily on cognitive problems—without any helplessness induction. Given such a mapping, I suggested that the belief that nothing you do matters caused both depression and helplessness. Finally, I suggested that the therapy and prevention strategies that worked on

learned helplessness in the laboratory should guide the therapy and prevention of depression. My routine lecture.

The audience was clapping enthusiastically as John Teasdale approached the lectern.

"I wish I could share your enthusiasm for Professor Seligman's argument," John began in a clipped Oxbridge accent. He was bald and bespectacled, bent over as if from too much reading, and conveyed the impression of a monk just loosed from his cell. "But I cannot."

He then flayed the model.

"First," he said, "consider a human subject in a helplessness experiment getting unsolvable cognitive problems. What might he conclude? 'I am too stupid to solve the problems' or 'the nasty experimenter has rigged this and made the problems unsolvable?' Depression usually involves the belief in one's own inadequacy and accompanying low self-esteem, not the belief in a malign world.

"Second, when is helplessness temporary and when is it general? A laboratory subject failing to escape noise might conclude that this is just a laboratory trick and that outside the laboratory or on another day, problems will be solvable. Or he might conclude, as depressives seem to, that he will *always* be helpless and in *all* situations. The helplessness model as it stands does not enlighten us at all about this crucial difference between what depressives think and what normal people think.

"In short, Professor Seligman, like the behaviorists he disavows, does not do justice to the way human beings interpret their helplessness and how these interpretations are the key to depression and its treatment. He would do well to acquaint himself with attribution theory," Teasdale concluded.

I was flabbergasted. Teasdale had crystallized, more articulately than I had been able to, my central doubts about my theory.

"Dr. Teasdale is right, I think," I replied. "These objections are substantive and indeed I do not know attribution theory. So I invite Dr. Teasdale to collaborate with me to dispose of the helplessness theory altogether if necessary, or better to refine it so that it might better fit depression."

Teasdale, expecting some clever defense, startled visibly, then said, "I accept." And so John and I began a three-year collaboration.

Chapter Thirteen

Center for
Advanced Study
(1978–1979)

WHEN I RETURNED to Penn from England in January 1976, my research group was swollen with talent, and we were eager to take up John Teasdale's challenge to the helplessness theory of depression. Three remarkable women led my feisty research group: Lyn Yvonne Abramson, in cutoff jeans and outsize tie-dyed blouses, looked like a hippy, which she decidedly was not. Naturally beautiful, she just didn't much care about what she wore. Hailing from rural Minnesota, she mixed some Finnish bloodlines inclined to depression with a dollop of Sioux. She came to Penn as a graduate student by way of a stellar record at the University of Wisconsin. She was deep and scholarly, but completely out of keeping with female graduate students of the era. She was refreshingly assertive, even loud. Her doe-eyed innocence and enthusiasm carried us along. They also marked her as the voice and intellectual leader of the team.

Lyn's closest comrade was Lauren Bersh Alloy. Lauren was the rare Penn undergraduate whose record was so outstanding that she was accepted as a graduate student. Lauren did not take no for an answer. She was a tough Philadelphia kid and had inherited "dauntless" genes: her grandfather's parents were murdered in a Russian pogrom at the

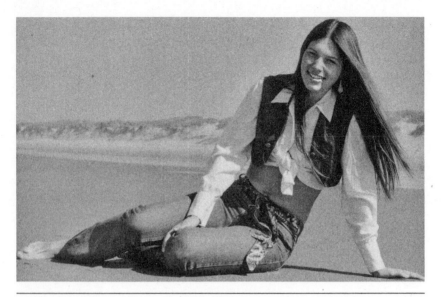

Lyn Y. Abramson was the voice and intellectual leader of my newly formed research group working on the attributional reformulation of the learned helplessness model of depression. Photo courtesy of Lyn Abramson.

turn of the twentieth century, and as a six-year-old, her grandfather had journeyed alone, mostly on foot, to England from Russia. Her father, Phil Bersh, was a well-known, traditionally-minded professor of animal learning at Temple. Unlike the rest of the graduate student body, she actually dressed in fashionable clothes, sported a giant diamond engagement ring, and wore makeup, the very opposite of Lyn. She was actually Dick Solomon's PhD student but was inseparable from Lyn and soon fell into my intellectual penumbra. Together Lauren and Lyn would soon make a discovery that rocked the conventional field of depression.

The third member of the triumvirate (this is the wrong-gender word) was Judy Garber. Judy was fleeing a disastrous graduate student year at Florida State University. She visited Penn and pleaded with me to take her on as an unpaid research assistant for redemption. Our agreement was that if she shined, I would help her restart her career as an academic psychologist. She did shine and soon proved to be invaluable. She carried out the mundane duties, such as feeding the rats their daily chow, but soon became the bookish center of the group.

Lauren Bersh Alloy was Lyn's closet comrade. They went on to win together the Distinguished Scientific Contribution Award of the American Psychological Association, its highest scientific award, for their "sadder but wiser" discoveries. Photo courtesy of Lauren Alloy.

Judy was central because unlike the rest of us she came from a background in social psychology and knew "attribution" theory, which we—clinical and experimental psychologists—did not. She got us to read the literature and then led discussions of attribution theory. I was wowed by her teaching and scholarship, but I was not impressed with attribution theory. "Attribution" is an ambiguous word that here means the causal story that a person tells herself to explain an event, and the theory derives from Julian Rotter's "locus of control" theory.[1] Rotter pointed out that when a bad event occurs, one can attribute its cause either internally to oneself ("I am to blame") or externally, such as to an event, circumstances, or another person ("He was out to get me"). When facing inescapable noise or unsolvable problems, one can see his helplessness as either internal ("I am defective") or external ("This damn problem is unsolvable"). It made sense to us that people who attributed their failure internally would feel unworthy and lose self-esteem, whereas people who attributed the cause of

failure externally would not. So far so good. But attribution of blame was only the jumping-off point of Teasdale's critique.

He further wondered when helplessness would last as opposed to just evaporating and when it would bleed into everything in one's life as opposed to undermining trying ("response initiation") only in the original setting. Judy pointed us in the direction of Bernard Weiner's[2] refinement of attribution theory. Attributions need not be confined to the internal or external. The cause can be thought of as temporary ("I had a hangover") or permanent ("I am stupid"), as specific to the original situation ("I am bad at anagrams") or more global ("I can never solve my problems").

So to respond to John Teasdale, we reformulated the helplessness theory of depression to take into account the way people think about the causes of their helplessness. A person who interprets the cause as internal will feel unworthy and lose self-esteem. A person who interprets the cause as permanent will be helpless long into the future. A person who interprets the cause as global will be helpless in entirely different situations. And crucially, if habitual, this way of thinking is a "depressive attributional style," internal, stable, and global for bad events: "It's me, it's going to last forever, and it's going to undermine everything I do." Nondepressed people who have this unfortunate style, when they encounter setbacks, will become depressed more easily than people without this style. I called the style "pessimism" and hypothesized that it was a risk factor for depression in exactly the same way that smoking was a risk factor for lung cancer and heart disease.

John Teasdale heartily agreed with us, and with him as a coauthor we published the theory.[3] This became a pattern in my own work: when wrong, I tried not to get defensive. I acknowledged my shortcoming in print and, if possible, reformulated or even jettisoned ideas accordingly. I tried to work with my critics, not against them. Unlike a Broadway show in which criticism means a flop, in science it is the key to progress. I have Ludwig Wittgenstein's splendid example here in mind. Wittgenstein's first book—in which, he confided to Bertrand Russell, he had "solved all the problems of philosophy"—was grounded in logical atomism.[4] Midway through his stormy career, he came to

believe that this view of language—that words can correspond to the logical atoms of the world—was wrong. In his last major work published after his death, *Philosophical Investigations*,[5] he recanted and held that the meaning of a word was just its use in the language, not its correspondence to the world. While I suspect that Wittgenstein was a bit of a self-conscious poseur, I believe his openness to changing his mind is the very model of how knowledge progresses.

With the reformulated theory to guide us, we set out to test it on several fronts throughout 1977 and the first half of 1978. The critical member of the research team, Chris Peterson, soon joined us. But before I could really understand just how critical he was, a year of transformation, 1978–1979, awaited me in California.

THE CENTER FOR Advanced Studies in the Behavioral Sciences sits majestically aloof from the world atop a live-oak-dotted hill in Stanford, California. It had been the sought-after destination for young, ambitious scholars going on sabbatical since it was founded twenty-five years before, and I spent my second sabbatical there. Dave Krantz, a distinguished mathematical psychologist, said of it, "It is the first honor I've gotten that wasn't for my *potential.*" There I realized what my Guggenheim Museum dream meant, and there I had my heart broken.

Suzanne Miller and I rented a modern house in pricy Woodside, horse and horsefly country in the wild hills that separated Stanford from the Pacific Ocean. I had left Kerry and my two children the summer before, and Suzanne and I then rented an apartment together in Washington Square in the center of Philadelphia. Ours was a rocky relationship. She left her assistant professorship at the University of Western Ontario to be with me and was scouting for her next job. The way other men looked at her—and, more, the way she looked back—troubled me. I worried that she was still in the romance market and wanted to trade up. Perhaps, I hoped, the slow-paced idyllic atmosphere of the center would settle her down.

More than forty of us were in residence, and the cast of characters included some of the brightest lights of my generation. Jim Heckman, quiet and shy, would go on to win a Nobel Prize in economics. Nan

Keohane would become president of Wellesley and then president of Duke. Marina Whitman, professor of economics, would increase her salary tenfold when she left the center to become financial vice president of General Motors.

Beth Loftus, just beginning her work on defective memory in eyewitness testimony and in alleged sexual abuse, started our year off by sending us each a survey about our opinions on memory. "Do we have all our memories stored up someplace in the brain?"

My reply was typically contentious: "I think we have almost nothing at all stored. I am a bridge player, and I have looked at the queen of spades literally half a million times. I only have the foggiest idea of what she looks like. She is mostly black in color of course, but is she wearing a crown? Carrying a scepter? I don't know. You could put a pearl necklace on her, and I wouldn't notice the difference.

"Outside the first-floor men's room in College Hall at Penn," I continued, "is a large bronze plaque dedicated to the memory of 'Pomp,' Albert Monroe Wilson, a beloved Negro janitor from the nineteenth-century annals. I gave a quiz to the male denizens of College Hall. 'Who is Albert Monroe Wilson?' Despite passing the plaque several times a day, no one could identify Albert Monroe Wilson. Memory is overrated, and computer storage is the wrong model for memory. Unlike any machine, we 'store,' and perhaps only ever know, the *gist* of things."

Days at the center could be contentious, but for the most part the place was paradise—picking fresh figs from the tree outside my carrel for breakfast, writing the morning away, then heading off on an unscheduled adventure at lunch with any of the yeasty people who happened to sit with me: Seymour Kety, Janet Spence, John Whiting, Dick Neustadt, Dave Featherman, Dick Thompson, or Jim Fries. After lunch, the director, Gardner Lindsey, hosted my favorite time of the day, the volleyball game. Gardner had the cushiest of jobs—running the center. He excused himself after one game, saying that he had to go write a letter.

"*D*?" I inquired.

"I actually got a note about you and volleyball," he confided, never short of repartee. "I had mentioned what a powerful spiker you are,

and my correspondent said, 'Of course, but can Seligman set up?'" This stung. I prided myself on setting others up in volleyball and believed I did the same in science with my students and colleagues. But others apparently perceived me as being out only for myself. We were discussing Erik Erikson in a seminar that week, and I wondered now about the end stage of a successful life, the stage of generativity. Was I only a spiker? Would I ever truly reach the stage of setting others up?

I came to the center to write a textbook on abnormal psychology with my friend, Dave Rosenhan. W. W. Norton, the tony New York publisher, guaranteed us each a substantial income, $100,000 spread over five years, as an advance. This was the first real money I'd earned from writing. Dave and I spent hundreds of hours schmoozing about abnormality, and I spent hundreds of hours in my little carrel overlooking Palo Alto, reading and writing. The chapters on depression and anxiety flowed effortlessly, since I'd been thinking about these for a decade. Some of the other chapters were hard slogs. Psychosomatic disorders was one. I read my way through a literature filled with neuromythology and still couldn't put the topic together sensibly. But the chapter on sex came together, and I ventured a new theory on sexual disorders. Any new theory is way out of place in a textbook, but I put it in anyway and refined it in later editions. I proposed that sexual development has five layers, and each can go awry. The deeper the layer, the harder it is to change. Layer 1, the very deepest, is *gender identity*: feeling like a man or a woman. It gets laid down hormonally in the third month of pregnancy, and if the hormonal bath is abnormal, transsexuality—feeling one is a man trapped in a woman's body or vice versa—results. Layer 2 is *object choice*: being attracted to members of the same or the other sex. This too is largely hormonal but gets added a bit later in gestation, with neuroanatomical consequences. Layer 3 is *sexual preference*: the objects (breasts, bottoms) and the fetishes (feet, pain, children) that turn you on. These are acquired in late childhood or early adolescence. Layer 4 is *sex role*: stereotypically masculine or feminine behavior. This is acquired socially through childhood and adult experience. Layer 5 is *sexual performance*: adequacy in intercourse. Disruption here can happen anytime in adulthood. These are layers of *depth*, implying how hard or easy they are

to change, for example in therapy. We have almost no choice about layers 1 and 2. Sexual identity and sexual object choice are difficult if not impossible to change, whereas preferences, roles, and performance are increasingly easier to change. I still believe this theory is largely true, but as far as I know it has never made its way out of our textbook and into sex research or the clinic.[6]

By the middle of 1979, the textbook was drafted. But this turned out not to be the main event of my sabbatical.

I and most of the rest of the cast were "loners" at the center. But one group gathered here to carry out a single purpose, and this group transformed me. These individuals came from, in my view, a low-prestige part of the scientific jungle—applied social science—and I had not, in my narrow world of pure experimental psychology, even heard of any of them.

Their purpose was to found a new field around aging and to make it respectable. "Why," I wondered as I first got to know them, "does the world need a field of aging?"

They launched a volley of answers back at me, answers I found unsettling. First, they said that psychology had so-called developmental psychology, but "development" referred only to infants and toddlers, barely to adolescents, and not at all to the middle-aged or elderly. This narrowness rested on the dubious assumption that not much changed after childhood. Adult development, they contended, was a time of both continuity and more importantly change. My year at the center and my own life demonstrated to me that this was true.

Second, they said that mainstream social science had adopted as self-evident a simplistic and misleading methodology. The routine methods of the mainstream were experimental and cross-sectional, but the laboratory methods suffered from the thorny problems of external validity. They got an A for rigor but a D− for realism. They rarely captured reality and so were rarely taken seriously and applied to issues in the world that mattered.

"Do you really believe, Marty, that the response of giving up when loud noise is inescapable is anything like the response of a mother to the death of her child or the reaction to unemployment or mandatory

retirement?" Even if they were too polite to confront me directly, I had enough imagination to harbor exactly these doubts about my own work.

What they contended was wrong with "cross-sectional" methods was an entirely new challenge for me. All of the experiments I'd done were cross-sectional; we looked at one time slice and assumed continuity into the next time slice of a person's life. But aging was a field that doubted continuity; it suggested that people may change as they age and that what you find early may not hold later.

Cross-sectional studies, my new colleagues contended, are lazy shortcuts that can result in completely wrong conclusions. Let's say you want to know the effect of aging on worrying about money. Further let's say you do a cross-sectional study of three age groups: people born in 1915, 1930, and 1945. The results would be clear-cut, with the oldest group the most worried about money and the youngest group the least worried. You conclude that worrying about money grows with age.

Wrong! The members of the 1915 group were in their formative teenage years when the Great Depression hit, whereas those born in 1930 and 1945 became teenagers at more and even more prosperous times. Financial insecurity is not an age effect but a "cohort" effect, determined not by age per se but by the historical moment when an individual happens to hit adolescence.

An alternate method is much better: a *longitudinal* study that repeatedly tests the very same people as they age. This would reveal no change in financial insecurity as those born in 1915 got older and perhaps even a lessening of their worry about money as they aged. Longitudinal studies are undoubtedly better than cross-sectional studies, but they are hideously expensive and labor intensive. Imagine following several hundred people born in 1915 for fifty years, tracking them down, and trying to convince them to take the same old questionnaires every decade.

My colleagues' third justification for their new field was political: the changing demographics of America. The baby boomers (born between 1946 and 1964) were now the dominant taxpayers and wanted

Congress to fund a science that would tell them how they could age well, with better physical and mental health.

So this aging group gathered at the center with a clear purpose: to establish a respectable scientific field, to seduce the best young scientists into it, and if possible to build support for the fledgling National Institute of Aging (NIA).

This group was indeed trying to seduce me. Flattered, I began to attend their seminars and did the reading, even though a year before I would have labeled them "softheaded." I got to know each of them well. Matilda Riley, a gorgeous silver-haired seventy-year-old and second in command of the NIA, was their official boss, but the power behind the throne was Paul Baltes. Paul grew up in the Rhineland at the end of World War II. His parents had owned a struggling restaurant and put him to work in the kitchen as a kid. When Paul was eight, a drunken, belligerent customer was arguing with his mother at the cash register. Paul came in from the kitchen and talked the customer down. After that, they sent Paul out to deal with difficult customers. Paul grew into a soft-spoken dynamo, the Henry Kissinger of academic psychology, and I was astonished to find myself, surely a difficult customer, listening well to his vehement critique of experimental psychology and even liking him in the process. I started to sip their Kool-Aid.

George Vaillant, a Harvard-bred psychoanalyst and a proper WASP Brahmin, was by his provenance the group member most likely to repel me. He had just published *Adaptation to Life*,[7] the life stories (to date) of the two hundred most "promising" members of the Harvard classes of 1939 through 1944. He was the custodian of the Grant Study, a longitudinal study centered on the outlandish idea of investigating what is right in life as opposed to what cripples life and stultifies growth. It started with the most privileged and talented young people to discover what leads to success and what leads to failure. George's theory of success was "mature defenses." Those Harvard undergraduates who reacted to setbacks with "immature" defenses, such as denial and repression, seemed to fail later in life: broken marriages, alcoholism, and underemployment. Those who reacted "maturely,"

with humor, sublimation, or altruism, went on to lead much more fulfilled and successful lives.

This was all too positive for me. It reminded me of Horatio Alger, Norman Vincent Peale, and the chapel services at the Albany Academy. It felt like the empty "American" propaganda I was wise enough to reject in favor of a career working to undo that which cripples life.

George, however, listened well and was charming, humble, and agreeable, talents that enabled him to interview two hundred Harvard snobs every five years and remain in their good graces. We shared an interest in fine wine and befriended Dick Graff, owner of the renowned boutique vineyard Chalone. George and I were wine groupies, and Dick, for his part, turned out to be a fervent psychology groupie. The three of us became the unofficial sommeliers for the center and gave wine tastings for the class. Dick spent a good deal of time with Suzanne and me. Suzanne flirted openly with him, and Dick confided to me that she was the only female he had ever found attractive. I probably should have taken more notice of her other flirtations, since unbeknownst to me she had already successfully traded up—to Walter Mischel, professor in the Stanford psychology department down the hill. Walter was famous for the ingenious "marshmallow" test.[8] He was a polished, wealthy Viennese émigré and a collector of modern paintings. Within the year, Walter left his wife, Harriet, for Suzanne, and Suzanne left me for Walter.

While I left the center bereft of family and broken of heart, I had nevertheless grown scientifically. I began my year there a snobby dyed-in-the-wool experimental psychologist, convinced that the well-controlled experiment was the royal road to truth. After all, no other method isolated the cause so perfectly. But I had now become convinced that the laboratory experiment came at too great a cost: the variables workable in the laboratory were anemic and too often bore only an unconvincing relationship to the real world. My "aging" friends convinced me that longitudinal methods undertaken outside the laboratory, observing large groups of people across time, had better external validity and that the statistical methods developed for longitudinal studies could also hone in on cause. Study real

people—not just white rats and college sophomores. Study real out-comes—divorce, depression, cancer—not just laboratory analogues. Study how real people actually change over time in their natural habitats.

Study well-being in addition to misery.

These seemed like the "right" questions that the Godhead floating over the Guggenheim Museum wanted me to take on.

Chapter Fourteen

Depression

*B*Y 1980, I was a thirty-eight-year-old bachelor. Having left a wife and two young children and then been jilted by the woman I left them for, I had a major depression. I could do the self-diagnosis. I had a sense of loss, of guilt, and of being a fool. I felt sad much of the time, I lost twenty-five pounds without trying, and I had trouble concentrating on work.

I was not feeling creative, but I was not completely floored. I carried on. I was back at Penn, leading my large research team, and it helped that I had glimpsed a new approach at the center. I was beginning to act on the new vision. I was not helpless, and I was by no means hopeless. After all, I told myself, I became full professor of psychology at the University of Pennsylvania at age thirty-three, likely the youngest in many years. My research was migrating from the dry, clear-headed experimental laboratory to the wet complexity of the longitudinal study of real people as they go through life.

A crucial person was about to bless my life. He appeared because I'd taken a unique route—experimental psychology followed by Mickey Stunkard's and Tim Beck's personally tailored psychiatric residency. With the burgeoning popularity of clinical psychology, my route was becoming known, and others wanted to follow. This was before there were clear paths into the world of clinical psychology, so rigorously trained young academics attracted to the field now wanted to find a way in.

This is how I met Chris Peterson. Chris became my bosom friend and closest colleague until his untimely death at age sixty in 2012. As a second-year assistant professor at Hamilton College, he sent me a handwritten three-page letter:[1] "This is not what I really want to do. I was a math undergraduate and then a social-personality PhD from Illinois. Now I am trapped in a small college in upstate New York teaching eight courses a year. Can I come to Penn and re-tool as a clinical psychologist under your supervision? In exchange I can offer you my body and my offbeat research mind. Pretty please?" I didn't take up the body offer (what he meant by this I would never discover), but his mind was a perfect foil for mine.

Chris was big, six-foot-three and well over 220 pounds. He was shaggy and capacious of mind and of heart. He may not yet have been a clinical psychologist, but he was a personality psychologist and a statistician, and he created questionnaires.

"Chris," I said, "we need a test to measure attributional style. Let's try asking people to rate hypothetical good and bad events along the three dimensions of personal, permanent, and pervasive, and let's try to predict who gets depressed."

"You really don't know test construction, do you, Marty?" Chris said with characteristic patience. "A clever concept is only the very first baby step, Marty. You don't leap from the concept all the way to predicting anything. You first have to create many items and show that the items are 'reliable'—that they correlate with each other. You do this by winnowing out the poor items. That will take a few months and lots of people and lots of money.

"Then you have to retest people and show that the test is 'stable'— that people give roughly the same answers a few months later. That will take another six months. Only then can you test 'validity'—that attributional style correlates with depression. Finally, you can go for the bull's-eye, *predictive validity*—that attributional style actually picks out who, not depressed now, will become depressed later. Bottom line: it is tedious work, and you cannot move at your accustomed near speed of light, Marty."

I groaned and asked Chris if he would lead the project. He, characteristically, said yes.

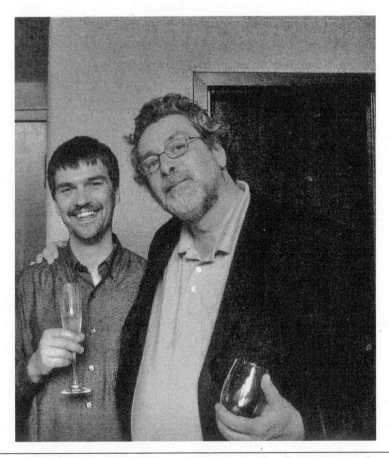

Chris Peterson (1950–2012). Chris, at six-foot-three and well over 220 pounds, was big. He was shaggy, and he was capacious of mind and of heart. He became my closest colleague and my bosom friend. He is pictured here with James Pawelski, director of education at the Positive Psychology Center. Photo courtesy of Mandy Seligman.

After two years of work, we published the Attributional Style Questionnaire (ASQ).[2] It contained twelve well-winnowed questions. Half of them were about bad events: "You can't get all the work done that your boss demands of you." The other half were about good events: "You suddenly become rich." You were to imagine vividly that this happened to you, and then you were to write down what you felt caused it. For example, you wrote down "a bad boss" for the scenario of demanding more work. Then you rated that hypothetical cause on the crucial three dimensions:

EXTERNAL-INTERNAL

Is the cause ("a bad boss") something about you or about other people or circumstances?

Other people or circumstances You

1	2	3	4	5	6	7

You would give "bad boss" a 1. It's not about you at all.

UNSTABLE-STABLE

In the future, when you are working, will this cause again be present?

Never again present Always present

1	2	3	4	5	6	7

You would likely give this a 4, 5, or 6 (unless you were thinking about quitting soon).

SPECIFIC-GLOBAL

Is this cause something that just influences work, or does it also influence other areas of your life?

Just this situation All situations

1	2	3	4	5	6	7

You would likely give this a 1 or 2 unless you brood about it everywhere you go.

As the data on the test were pouring in, Chris posed another question. "Do people *just talking about their lives* make the same kind of attributions that they do when answering a questionnaire that asks about the causes of hypothetical events?"

Oblivious to what this really meant, I dimly recognized this as an "external validity" issue, just like asking if an IQ test actually predicts intelligent decisions in real life. So we asked people who had taken the test to also describe in three hundred words the worst and best events they had recently experienced. One young man might say for example, "My girlfriend, such a moody bitch, dropped me." In three hundred words, it turns out, people typically make three causal statements.

We then gave the statements to raters, who were blind to the person's other statements and blind to the individual's results on the ASQ. The raters would then rate "She is such a moody bitch": The raters gave it 1 for external, 2 for unstable, and 4 for global. Fortunately, the spontaneous attributions people make for real events strongly resemble those they make for hypotheticals on the questionnaire.

Chris wrote a manual for rating spontaneous real attributions,[3] which he called content analysis of verbatim explanations (CAVE), so that other researchers could rate real speech anywhere, anytime. While I did not realize it then, Chris had invented a way to discover the attributional style of people who wouldn't or couldn't take our questionnaires—sports heroes, CEOs, presidents, and the dead.

Using the ASQ, the research team now asked if mildly depressed students had the depressive style we predicted for negative events ("It's me, it's going to last forever, and it's going to undermine everything") and the opposite style for good events ("It's not me, it's going away quickly, and it's only here and now"). The results came in gradually and very strongly confirmed the theory: depressed students had exactly this way of thinking about the causes of good and bad events that befell them.[4]

We developed the parallel test for third- to sixth-grade children, the Children's Attributional Style Questionnaire (CASQ), and found that depressed children had the same pessimistic style as depressed adults.[5]

So far so good, but unbeknownst to me I had now run deeply afoul of the invisible power in the field of depression: organized psychiatry. I first sensed this behind-the-scenes power as an innocent refugee from Cornell, trying to eke out a future as a hanger-on under Mickey Stunkard's benign auspices at Penn. The Department of Psychiatry, I found out, was chronically broke, and without the hard money that the endowed School of Arts and Sciences had, Penn Medicine (and all major schools of medicine) turned to Congress to keep afloat. Without huge research dollars (and with an astonishing 57 percent "overhead" tax tacked on), the faculty of the medical departments would have to give up most of their research to avoid bankruptcy and fall back on the dollars that treating patients brought in. The prestigious

medical faculty was chosen for their research accomplishments and not for their exemplary patient care (just as the prestigious Arts and Sciences faculty was not chosen for its exemplary teaching). The government came to the rescue in 1946 when President Harry Truman signed the National Mental Health Act.

This salvation was christened with a well-intentioned name—the National Institute of Mental Health (NIMH)—that soon became misleading: Despite having "health" in its name and founding charter, NIMH by the late 1970s had become solely about mental illness, and indeed in 2016 it officially defined its mission as the "understanding and treatment of mental illnesses"[6] without mentioning mental *health* at all. You might think this was just innocent semantics, but it was actually a guild-serving sleight of hand, and a book about positive psychology must confront it.

What is mental health? From a traditional medical point of view, mental health is nothing more than the absence of mental illness. So if you are not diagnosed as schizophrenic, depressed, anxious, or suffering from any of the other three-hundred-plus disorders in the American Psychiatric Association's *Diagnostic and Statistical Manual* (*DSM*), you are by default mentally "healthy." This is nonsense of the highest order. From my point of view, mental health is much more than the absence of mental illness; it is the presence of positive emotion, engagement, good relations, meaning, and accomplishment (PERMA). The absence of mental illness does not remotely guarantee mental health of this kind; nor does mental illness wholly preclude mental health. The entire field of positive psychology is about this kind of health and well-being, not about how to avoid illness. I did not know this, of course, during the 1970s, but NIMH's disowning of health had vast scientific and economic consequences.

As I watched *DSM* unfold from a research document into the bible for reimbursement by insurance companies for psychiatric treatment in the late 1970s, I noticed that the words "disorder" and "illness" loomed large. "Major depressive disorder" was now a thing. It was *reified.* I was puzzled, however, since I was working not on disorders but on underlying processes (i.e., helplessness and attributional style)

that might be the basis of a variety of problems in life, including those *DSM* now officially called "disorders."

Not only were the processes no longer funded, but there arose the dogma that mental illnesses were discontinuous from normality. I suspected, however, that depression was on the same spectrum as the normal blues. The more of the twenty-one symptoms (sadness, lack of zest, indecisiveness, weight loss, etc.) in the Beck Depression Inventory and the more intense each one, the more depression. Severe depression, moderate depression, and mild depression differ only quantitatively not qualitatively, just as a midget falls on the short end of the height continuum. Dwarfism, however, in which body parts are out of proportion, is a disorder and not just a case of being very short. The disorder of depression had become, by government fiat, like dwarfism; it was now declared discontinuous from merely having a lot of the symptoms of depression.

With *DSM*, the National Institute of Mental Health was now about disorders and not about the processes that might be the basis of one or more of them. No justification was forthcoming for the assumption that depression had now become a discontinuous disorder, and no public justification was given for the shift of focus from processes to disorders; it just glided through unnoticed. But the real reason was to fund the psychiatry guild that now ran NIMH. The "disorders" became the turf of psychiatry departments, and the funding from NIMH therefore went almost exclusively into their coffers. One did not trespass on their turf with impunity and without obeisance. NIMH brought this to my attention when I applied for a renewal of my large grant that had sailed through for more than a decade.

My renewal was about identifying depressive attributional style, which, I argued, amplified helplessness: if one interprets failure through the lens of personal (it's me), permanent (it's going to last forever), and pervasiveness (it's going to ruin everything), depression results. The NIMH branch chief for depression fired a warning shot across my bow.

"Your proposal is about the symptoms of depression. What does that have to do with depressive *disorder*, Marty?" Bob Hirschfeld, a

future chair of psychiatry in Galveston, Texas, asked me on the telephone. He was trying to help me stave off a rejection. We had been friends for five years and always had been frank with each other, but he was now talking in a code I did not understand. "Why don't you rewrite the proposal to be about the *disorder*, and by the way perhaps you might enlist and pay some collaborators from your psychiatry department."

Housebroken, I complied. My grant was duly funded, and my compliance turned out to be a happy accident. The collaborator we took on from our psychiatry department, someone who did therapy on disorders, was Lester Luborsky. Lester was a psychologist who (unlike me) got stranded in the psychiatry department and therefore was destined to spend his life in a never-ending struggle for funding. Lester investigated the nuts and bolts of psychotherapy sessions. He asked, "What does the therapist say, and how does the patient react?"

"We have invented something for analyzing speech that may help," Chris told Lester and me. Analyzing the verbiage of psychotherapy sessions seemed like a swamp to me, but not to Chris Peterson.

"For our questionnaire project, we validated the test by seeing if people actually spoke in the same way that they filled out the test. So we devised a method for taking every *verbatim* causal statement a person makes and rating how pessimistic it was. So when a person said, 'She left me because I am unlovable,' that cause is personal, permanent, and pervasive; it's very pessimistic. That thought should lead to momentary sadness and maybe, if it's a style, in the long run to depression."

Lester and I got it and did our first case history together.[7] Mr. Q was a twenty-two-year-old with major depressive disorder. He had undergone two hundred sessions of psychoanalytic therapy, and during nine of the sessions, he had a dramatic swing of mood. We extracted sixty-three statements in which Mr. Q. discussed a bad event and gave a cause for it from these nine critical sessions. Four raters, blind to all else, rated each cause for internal, stable, and global on the 1–7 scale. Two therapists rated the tapes of the sessions for the exact moment of the extreme mood shifts.

So, for example, Mr. Q said, "I feel bothered [the bad event] . . . I'm comparing again, and she's stronger than me and brighter than me [the cause]." The four raters agreed: it was internal (Mr. Q was "comparing again"), it was stable ("again" . . . "she's stronger and brighter"), and it was global (it hurt all over). Mr. Q's mood right then dropped precipitously, as the theory predicted.

We contrasted this to Mr. Q saying, "I feel mad at you [bad event] . . . It's your trivial little bit of science fiction, of trying to make reality conform to the jargon you use in your trade [the cause]." The raters here also agreed with each other: it was external (the therapist), it was stable (the way therapy was done), and it was highly specific (just in the therapy session). Mr. Q's mood did not change, as the theory predicted.

So we were complying with NIMH's unwritten rule that we start work on sick people and collaborate with the psychiatry department. We also went into hospitals and tested certifiably depressed patients and nondepressed schizophrenic controls, finding that the depressed patients, but not the schizophrenics, had just the explanatory style we predicted.[8]

These findings were not earthshaking. Perhaps depression caused this pessimistic style, or even more uninterestingly, perhaps the diagnosis of depression partly depended on the presence of this pessimism. In jargon this is "common method variance." If we were getting at the *cause* of depression, and not just boring correlates, this pessimistic style should be present *before* depression strikes, and this style should *predict* who will get depressed once bad events strike. (And even more far-reaching: If we could change this style, would we cure depression?)

Testing causality took us and many other investigators years, but these predictions were largely born out.[9] The basic way to test this was to look at large groups of people across time ("longitudinal" studies). At "time 1" the researcher measured both depression and "explanatory" style (by the 1980s we had jettisoned the nebulous adjective "attributional" and had also begun to call those with the depressive style "pessimists"). Then the researcher merely waited for a few months or years and measured both again. At this later time ("time 2"), the

theory predicted that the pessimists would have become more depressed than those without this pessimistic style, taking the depression at time 1 into account. Dozens of studies tested this and found it to be true. Pessimists were at least twice as at risk for depression as time drifted on.

Another way of testing the theory was to wait for a bad event in reality and see if the pessimists became depressed more easily than nonpessimists given the very same bad event. This technique is called an "experiment of nature." Jerry Metalsky, my "grandson" through Lyn Abramson, who by the early 1980s was a professor at Stony Brook, led a particularly convincing experiment of nature. As the midterm exam for Stony Brook undergraduates taking introductory psychology approached, Metalsky asked them what grade they would be happy or unhappy with. He also measured their explanatory styles and moods before the midterm. Fifty-three of the students then got a disappointingly bad grade. The pessimists among those fifty-three became more depressed than the rest.[10]

"IT'S TOO BAD that we don't have a time machine, so we could go back to before the Great Depression and test these girls for optimism and pessimism," Glen concluded. I was in Heidelberg, meeting with my colleagues from the Social Science Research Council's group on aging. They had successfully seduced me, and I not only drank their Kool-Aid but attended their gatherings. Glen Elder, boyish but silver-haired and still looking the Eagle Scout, was the world's leading sociologist of the family. He gave a paper that afternoon on the longest-running longitudinal study ever done. It had started before the Great Depression, when children from Berkeley were interviewed and tested for their strengths and weaknesses. These children were now about eighty years old and were still cooperating with the researchers. Almost all their families went broke during the Depression. Some families, mostly from the middle class, recovered, but many never did. Glen speculated that it was the pessimistic women who went under and whose health then deteriorated, and it was the optimistic women who bounced back and aged well.

"We do have a time machine, Glen," I shouted as I banged on his bedroom door at five in the morning. The scales had fallen away from my eyes, and I realized for the first time what Chris had invented. Bleary-eyed, Glen opened the door, and I burst in, explaining Chris's new method. "We can go back to the original interviews and CAVE them for pessimism. What did you call the opposite, optimism? I guess we can CAVE for that as well."

This we did, and the time machine worked. We analyzed the dusty, archived Berkeley interviews and found that the lower-class women who aged poorly were pessimists, while middle-class women who aged well had the opposite explanatory style. As a bonus we discovered something about how we get our explanatory styles. In 1970, the women, now grandmothers, were interviewed along with their middle-aged children, and we CAVE'd both sets of interviews. Explanatory style correlated significantly from mother to child but not from father to child. Thus, we discovered, people can acquire their explanatory style by listening to their mothers explain the bad events that befall them and then imitating them.[11]

So my energetic research group, in response to John Teasdale's scathing critique, discovered a risk factor for depression: a pessimistic style of thinking about the causes of setbacks: "It's me, it's going to last, and it's going to undermine everything." This brought us right up to the edge of curing pessimism to see if that might cure depression. But it took us almost another decade before we made this leap.

"MARTY, DEPRESSED PEOPLE are more pessimistic than people who are not depressed, but who is right?" Lauren Alloy asked me. "It's a pretty bad world out there. Maybe depressed people just see the world aright."

Then she said, "Lyn and I are going to test this in the lab." This seemingly innocent idea and their findings ignited a firestorm—still burning—within the field of depression.

You find yourself seated in front of a green light bulb in my lab. There is a button in front of you, and Lauren instructs you to find out how much "control"—from zero to 100 percent—you have over

the green light's going on. You press the button, and the light blinks on. You wait and do nothing, and the light blinks on. You press the button, and nothing happens. You keep this up, and try to figure out how much control you have. The experimenters have programmed the amount of control that is actually possible. When you have 100 percent control, the light blinks on if and only if you press the button. When you have 50 percent control, the light blinks on twice as often if you press the button than if you don't. When you have zero control, the light blinks on at exactly the same rate whether or not you press the button.

To our surprise both depressed and nondepressed people were quite accurate in their assessments when they had some control. The big difference occurred at zero. Depressed people continued to be accurate: "I have zero control," they said. Nondepressed people massively inflated how much control they had when they were actually helpless: "I have 35 percent control" was their average answer when they had no control at all.[12]

In my own depression at that moment, this rang a bell. Tim Beck and all of cognitive therapy told me I was distorting reality, believing things were worse than they really were. But maybe I was accurate about myself and the world: an abysmal failure at love but a promising success at work. Maybe I, too, was sadder but wiser. Years hence I had an opportunity to trade back an ounce of that wisdom for more happiness, and as I write this today, I am glad to have made it.

Master Blaster
(1980–1983)

"*T*HIS PLACE SUCKS," I said to Alan Kors and Dick Solomon at the Chicken Dinner Club. "Penn has all the raw ingredients, but they are not baked into a university. The best conversations of my life were at those dinners at the Wilson Society. They are what a university is."

When Alan arrived as a faculty member in the early 1970s, he and I waxed nostalgic about the life of the mind we led as undergraduates at Princeton. He did history and poetry. I did philosophy and psychology. And we both learned more than a smattering of physics and math and art and politics sitting across the dinner table at the Wilson Society from the faculty and the serious undergraduates in those subjects.

Penn had nothing like this. It had as sparkling a faculty as Princeton, but we never saw each other, except at the occasional faculty senate meeting in which we debated such weighty issues as more parking space. So Alan and I formed the "Chicken Dinner Club," inviting a dozen of the liveliest faculty from across the whole campus to dine on overcooked faculty club chicken once a month. Each of us led one dinner's discussion: Jerre Levy on the split brain, Mark Adams on time travel, Dan Ben Amos on Yiddish humor, Marv Wolfgang on money and happiness, Alan Kors on Delmore Schwartz, Arnold Thackery on Newton, Dick Solomon on addiction.

Having made our little dent into raising Penn faculty morale, we tackled a more entrenched problem: undergraduate philistinism. The whole point, we believed, of a university education was simply to become an intellectual, to become serious about the life of the mind. To our dismay, too many Penn undergraduates, prime candidates once, since they were selected for their academic accomplishments in high school, soon become anti-intellectual party animals. They settled into fraternities, sororities, and dormitories, grouped by age, with no faculty presence outside class. They soon came to think of class, of reading, writing, and learning, as an obligation, but they lived for the real life of Penn—networking and mating—and the two worlds almost never met.

With Dick Solomon for gravitas, we approached Vice Provost Humphrey Tonkin, a scholar with the peculiar specialty of spreading Esperanto across the planet. We pushed for a college house in which faculty lived with the students and created an intellectual and artistic environment therein. Very aware of the undergraduate morass, the administration was eager to experiment. It awarded us a building, a slightly rundown 1950s-era, four-story, ragged-stone affair, which we named Van Pelt College House. Dick had just gone through a messy divorce (his second) and was without a home base, so he became the first master of Van Pelt College. Three years later Alan Kors then paid the price for this bright idea and became the second master of Van·Pelt College. I, now a bachelor with no home, succeeded Alan in September 1980.

I spent the next three years counseling undergraduates about dating, mating, bullying, homosexuality, tolerance, racism, and, once in a while, ideas. I brought distinguished guest speakers to Van Pelt (Norman Mailer found the students "fucking stupid") and hosted seminars (Alan Kors's reading his own poetry was an overflow smash hit). We housed distinguished academics visiting Penn on sabbatical. Two British philosophers, the cigar-smoking Elizabeth Anscombe and Peter ("Logic is the sword of God") Geach, graced us with their presence for a year. They were argumentative, even truculent. This seemed a great opportunity for me to get back in touch with modern philosophy, so puppylike I attended Anscombe's undergraduate lectures.

"The word," she announced, "is merely a printer's artifact." Her theory of language built on this premise. After she spun out her theory, I injected some empirical psychology into the argument.

"If it's an artifact, why then do children first speak in single words?" I queried. Anscombe ignored the question, and Geach looked very annoyed.

At cocktails that evening, Geach stormed up to me. "I don't give a damn what is in your books, Sir." So ended that attempt at reengaging in philosophy. I didn't try again until three decades later, as I tried to move psychology toward a science of the future.

I FOUND THAT I could make deep contact only with the most serious students. Robin Forman was a mathematical whiz and a member of a band that did The Doors almost as well as The Doors themselves. His band played at my "Master Blasters," the master's open house I held periodically with loud music in my attempt to appear less geeky to my students. Robin bore an uncanny resemblance to my college roommate Wilfrid Schmid, Princeton valedictorian of 1964, now gone off to parts unknown.

"Harvard mathematics is my first choice, and I just got accepted, but with $5,000 minus tuition," Robin said, exuding disappointment, when he came to me in April for advice.

"That is an amazing coincidence," I replied. "My roommate, Wilfrid, also first in our class, applied to Harvard almost twenty years ago and was only given $5,000 minus tuition. He asked my advice, and I told him to phone the chairman of math at Harvard and tell him confidently, 'Perhaps, you don't know who I am.' Wilfrid did this and was promptly given a full fellowship at Harvard. Phone the chairman of math at Harvard and tell him, 'Perhaps you don't know who I am,'" I suggested.

"I phoned the chairman of math at Harvard and said exactly those words," Robin reported back to me the next day. "Wilfrid Schmid is the chairman, and he gave me a full fellowship."

BEING A HOUSEMASTER was the hardest job I'd had since selling magazines as a teenager. I rose to the occasion as a salesman, earned a lot (for a teenager), and, most importantly, learned how to sell, a skill

that I used all the time. But I did not rise to the occasion as a house-master. As a lecturer my words were finding a large audience among the students. I was teaching introductory psychology and abnormal psychology to, frankly, rave reviews, and I began to think of myself as a teacher. Three years of daily—and nightly and midnightly—contact with the undergraduates convinced me otherwise. One-on-one, my job—trolling and proselytizing for the life of the mind—did not succeed with the average Penn student. Nor did their issues make contact with me.

I gave popular Master Blasters for the students, and I began to notice that I failed at these conversations more and more, particularly at these parties. I'd never been good at small talk and attributed this to my lack of empathy or slowness of repartee. But another candidate suggested itself.

I volunteered for a "signal detection" experiment in an acoustic chamber. I put on earphones and waited for the "ready" signal. I waited and waited. Finally, the door opened, and the experimenter dismissed me, suggesting that I go to the hospital and have a hearing test. I didn't hear even the loud ready signal. The hearing test confirmed that I was quite deaf. My guess is that my deafness dates back to about age twelve, since I know the lyrics of the rock songs only through 1954 ("Ohhh, yes, I'm the great pretender, laughing and gay like a clown").

So while I had a bit of a physical excuse for my social ineptness at parties, this did not help my lack of rapport with ordinary undergraduates. By the time I stepped down in May 1983, my self-identity had morphed from teacher of young people to teacher of their elders: graduate students, postdocs, and professional psychologists. Moreover, I considered myself a failure as housemaster—the only job I ever had that I completely failed at.

IF SERVING AS housemaster weren't bad enough, Randy Gallistel, the newly elected chairman, asked me to take the most thankless job in the psychology department: director of clinical training. This post had a very troubled history that explains the tightrope I walked for the next fifteen years.

Clinical psychology was the orphan of the great academic departments of psychology. At the decisive 1946 meeting of the Society of Experimental Psychologists, the chairmen of Harvard, Princeton, and Penn declared that they would hire no applied psychologists, and psychology would be a basic science, just like physics. They would bring on no more clinical or industrial psychologists, only psychologists who studied basic, underlying processes. The rest of the prestigious North American departments followed suit. This coincided, however, with massive funding pushing psychology in the opposite direction: the National Institute of Mental Health (NIMH) began to award grants for research on mental illness, and the Veteran's Administration began to hire psychotherapists to treat psychologically wounded soldiers. At the same time as receiving the injection of funds that clinical psychology brought to otherwise strapped psychology departments, the basic academic researchers looked down their noses—with good reason—at these upstarts "pretending" to apply science to troubled people. The good reason was that the therapists were all Freudians—Freud was the only game in therapy-city—and the academics were empirical scientists, the archenemies of the empirically untethered Freudians. This cast a shadow of suspicion over even those people, like Hans Eysenck, Joe Wolpe, Jack Rachman, and Norman R. F. Maier, who did respectable empirical science but applied it. This shadow was (and still is) the basic source of contempt, tension, and misunderstanding between experimental and clinical psychology on the one hand and between psychology and psychiatry departments on the other.

Of all American psychology departments, Penn's was just about the most contemptuous of application when I arrived in 1964, and little changed over the next decade. It included a smattering of clinical graduate students, looked down upon as inferiors by the mathematical psychologists and natural scientists. It was the booming voice of one faculty member, Julie Wishner, the director of clinical training, who I heard opining, "On balance, Seligman should be tenured." Julie had migrated from the frying pan of the psychiatry department, chafing at his second-class citizenship there, only to find himself in the fire of being an applied psychologist in the least applied of psychology

departments. In order to make any headway in this lonely role, he had to out-science the scientists. So he adopted the posture of a psycho-physiologist, who just happened to be interested in schizophrenia, and bad-mouthed the looseness of clinical thinking at every public opportunity. This might have worked before the days of Bob Bush and the very sharp group Bob recruited, but the new guys saw through Julie's act, and the prestige of clinical psychology at Penn sank to a new low.

At the same time as clinical psychology became the sick man of the department, the science behind it (and behind social science generally) was actually getting much, much stronger. When hired in 1972, I had the experimentalists' support (albeit with mixed feelings), because they hoped I was a natural scientist at heart. I had the support of Julie Wishner and the social science wing because the natural scientists ("natural science" being the Penn psychology department's official designation) had certified me kosher but they hoped I was an applied social scientist at heart.

Unlike in the 1960s, when it hired toadies, in the 1970s Penn made junior appointments that greatly raised the scientific profile of my young, applied colleagues. Ruben Gur, an Israeli war hero, along with his MD/PhD wife Raquel, worked at the intersection of neuroscience, anxiety, and schizophrenia. Myrna Schwartz pioneered the new cognitive science to identify the locations of brain damage after a stroke. These individuals did unimpeachable science, but their applied slant tainted them in the eyes of the department.

When Ruben and then Myrna came up for tenure, the natural scientists slaughtered them, even though inferior pure experimental scientists got promoted with relative ease. I worried that we were becoming a department of the retina rather than a department of psychology. Ruben and Myrna got such unfair treatment that I contemplated quitting and interviewed at NIMH for a laboratory chief's job. Their fate was a warning to me as I thought over Randy's offer.

If I became director of clinical training, I could no longer straddle the natural and social sciences or basic and applied science. In the zero-sum game of hiring new professors, I would become, in the eyes of my natural science colleagues, a defector, a relentless and annoying

advocate for applied social and clinical science. I'd watched a decade of this losing battle in department meeting after department meeting. I would have to sacrifice what local prestige I had accumulated and become a whipping boy.

But at bottom, and in this case decisively, I believed that scientific psychology is meaningful only if it applies to human problems. This was the unspoken bone of contention in my last conversation with Bob Bush before his suicide. When Bob said that if I was right, he had "wasted his life," we were arguing about the fundamentals. For Bob mathematics was the king of psychology, and the experimental method was the queen, just as in physics. But for me, psychology first needs to discover sound premises that researchers can only then mathematize and experiment upon. These premises get discovered not from the bottom up but from the top down based on what actually works in the world. Psychology had no convincing application to human problems, so what got considered "basic" was, to put it gently, arbitrary and untethered from reality. Wanking, basically.

My thinking about Pavlovian conditioning and instrumental learning as "basic" processes convinced me of this. What made work on these processes so appealing was the possibility that they might underlie human learning: this was a decent a priori guess, and huge effort (some of it mine) was devoted to understanding both of them. Indeed, these were the premises that Bob Bush had mathematized in his life's work. But such effort was only worthwhile if these processes actually do underlie human learning. If it is not worth doing, it is not worth doing well. To test out that it was worth doing, one needed to reconstruct, to synthesize real learning from these basic "elements." So, for example, take bridge, an instance of actual human cognition. Computer programs that rely only on associations do not get very far playing bridge. Their brute-force approach of merely piling one association on another is too lengthy and too cumbersome. The bridge brain does not work like this. The computer must take radical shortcuts and generate only a few likely hypotheses (e.g., this is either an endplay or a finesse), then test the evidence in order to win at bridge. Brute-force associationism does not work well at chess either. Or in language learning. Or in concept learning. Or in intuition. Or even

in perception. So I was still waiting for any convincing evidence that instrumental learning or Pavlovian conditioning were the building blocks of human learning. Without it, I did not believe that these processes warranted great investment.

Almost all the fiery tussle of department politics was about whether to hire this basic scientist or that applied scientist, and voices for the former consistently won—even when the basic science was untethered from reality. So becoming the advocate of applied psychology may have been a losing battle, but it *was* my battle.

I accepted Randy's offer, and this was the point of no return. Indeed, as I expected, I tried, in one heated faculty meeting after another over the next two decades, to persuade my basic science colleagues to hire talented applied psychologists, and I usually lost the vote. It was a source of 4-a.m. teeth grinding and the gradual erosion of my influence and even some of my friendships. Being born a decade or two after 1942 would have made my job a lot easier, since by about 2010 the corner was turned, and the importance of applied work in psychology dawned (or was forced by undergraduate demand as well as congressional funding) on basic experimental psychologists. The Psychonomic Society, a most intransigent bastion of basic research, came out in favor of "Pasteur's Quadrant," the notion that applicable, but nevertheless very rigorous, research was highly desirable. The British government by the turn of the millennium decided to evaluate and fund its academic departments by impact as well as the traditional, more inbred criteria. (Oh, had I only thought to argue for "impact" rather than "application.") As a result, the great British departments were now snapping up the psychologists they once would have shunned. As I write, a distinguished clinical psychologist occupies the venerable chair of experimental psychology at hoary Oxford.

But "I told you so" is one of the least satisfying phrases in the lexicon.

MY RESEARCH TOOK some very new turns: one was my first venture into the world of business, and the second was predicting sports. My old research team had gone the way of success, with each of the

leaders getting the best academic jobs: Chris Peterson became associate professor at the University of Michigan (and eventually director of clinical training and chaired professor), Lyn Abramson became assistant professor at Stony Brook (and eventually chaired professor at the University of Wisconsin, her alma mater), Lauren Alloy eventually filled her father's shoes as chaired professor at Temple, and Judy Garber went to Minnesota, where she finally got her PhD (eventually becoming a chaired professor at Vanderbilt). My pride in their accomplishments and my expectation that they would carry forward the future of depression research dwarfed my temporary sadness at the loss of their company just down the hall.

A new generation of young scientists who wanted to work with me on the topic of control was forming.

"This is what I want to do with my life," said Peter Schulman. I was teaching abnormal psychology and usually gave an A+ to the best two or three students out of three hundred Penn undergraduates in each class. Along with the A+ I volunteered to help them in their careers. Peter got one of the A+s and came to me to do the volunteering. "I don't want a PhD; I want to help your vision become reality."

Peter became my research coordinator, eventually managing a staff of fifty people and several multi-million-dollar grants. He created structure out of my throw-ten-balls-in-the-air (and-hope-two-will-bounce) approach to science. He was my right arm, the one indispensable person in my scientific life. Without Peter, who is still a crucial part of my life in 2018, I would have retired years ago, since I cannot bring myself to do what he does: negotiate with bureaucrats, broker peace between sparring interests, write progress reports that no one will read, deal with ethics boards, and wade through the swamp of policy in order to help me operate at near light speed.

"Marty," Peter told me just the other day, "what you find soul shriveling and avoid, I find soul enhancing and embrace."

MY FRIENDS IN "AGING" worked by "old-boy" networking, and I found myself a beneficiary. Jack Riley was the husband of Matilda Riley, the second in command at the National Institute of Aging and organizer of the group at the Center for Advanced Study. Jack thought

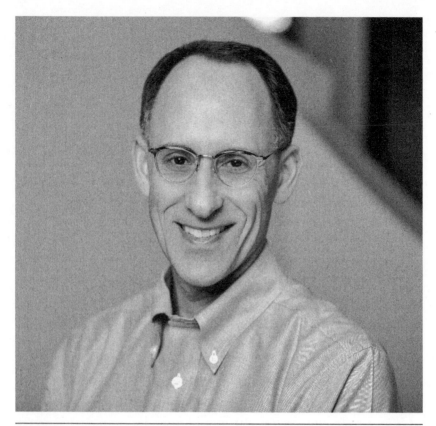

Peter Schulman became my research coordinator, eventually managing a staff of fifty people and several multi-million-dollar grants. He created structure out of my throw-ten-balls-in-the-air (and-hope-two-will-bounce) approach to science. He was my right arm, the one person in my scientific life who was indispensable. Photo courtesy of Peter Schulman.

well of me and, unbeknownst to me, was wealthy and influential. He wanted to make me wealthy, a prospect I had never even entertained.

I received a mysterious invitation to the Rockefeller Estate in Pocantico Hills for the annual meeting of the heads of the big insurance companies. Jack phoned me and told me to accept, which I did. I was impressed by the influence on parade. The CEOs came in limousines, except for the CEO of Prudential, who came by helicopter.

I led a small discussion group, and John Creedon, the CEO of Metropolitan Life, befriended me. John listened well and asked me whether pessimistic people fail more at work. He told me he couldn't

abide the pessimists at Met Life, who got in his way whenever he wanted to do something new. He also mentioned that his salesmen were quitting in droves and that Met Life had a huge retention problem. I had never been this close to a CEO before and was flattered. I was also impressed by John's humility and curiosity.

A few weeks later, I came home from a long day at the office to a ringing telephone. It was a life insurance salesman, and I hung up on him as soon as I figured this out. As I was putting the phone down, it occurred to me what a tough job he had. How did he cope with rejection after rejection? I wrote John and asked him how Met Life inured its salesmen to near-perpetual rejection. He phoned and asked me to come to New York to chat.

"We hire five thousand new salesmen a year, Marty," said John, "and it costs us five thousand dollars to train each one. Half of them quit in the first year, and by the end of three years, eighty percent are gone. Almost no one can take all the rejection."

"So how do you select your salesmen?" I asked.

"We have an IQ of life insurance, called the Career Profile. It asks, 'Do you want to make a lot of money?' 'Do you like to go to parties?' and 'Do you have a lot of relatives?' If you pass, we offer you the job. You mentioned that you have devised a test for pessimism. I wonder if this would help our selection process."

"It does predict who will get depressed in the face of setbacks—the pessimists. So maybe it's the optimists who can brush off rejection best," I ventured.

"Would you try it on some of our sales force? We'll pay you to do it."

Peter Schulman and I went to work. First we found that the top salesmen were much more optimistic on the ASQ than the worst salesmen. Of course their success could be making them more optimistic rather than their optimism making them more successful.

So Met Life underwrote a longitudinal study with three groups, one group very risky indeed. The first group included the five thousand regular salesmen hired after passing the Career Profile. They had also taken the ASQ on being hired, so we could track their sales as a function of optimism as well. Second, Met Life hired a group of about one hundred salesmen who had failed the Career Profile and

done badly on the ASQ, but the managers liked them and thought they had great sales potential. Third, Met Life hired 140 extreme optimists who had failed the Career Profile and did not have the managers' endorsement. They would not have been hired without the study. These were Frankensteinian optimists, since even a "pessimistic" life insurance salesman was way above the national average in optimism. Real pessimists do not apply.

We followed their sales for three years and found that among the regular force, the optimists outsold the pessimists. We also found that the salesmen who only had the managers' endorsement and did badly on the tests failed abysmally. Most importantly, the special force of extreme optimists outsold everyone; at the end of three years, they were still banging away.

So Met Life adopted the ASQ for regular use in hiring its sales force—and paid me royalties.

"I'm rich!" I announced to my mother on the phone.

MY FIRST VENTURE into sports followed from the mechanism of learned helplessness: not trying. A person's belief that nothing he does makes any difference erodes voluntary response initiation. He thinks, "Why bother?" and conserves energy, not attempting difficult voluntary actions. Thus, after defeat, pessimistic individuals will not try as hard and so will do worse than they usually do.

"Whom should we put in the relays?" Nort Thornton and Karen Thornton, the coaches of the US Olympic swimming teams, asked me in 1987. "Bitter experience tells us that the routine move of just putting our fastest swimmers in does not work. The relays follow the individual events, and sometimes if a swimmer—even a great swimmer—flops in the individual events, he [or she] does very badly in the relays. Can you predict who will collapse and who will rise to the occasion after doing badly in the individual events?"

I put this question to Susan Nolen-Hoeksema, newly arrived after finishing at the top of her undergraduate class at Yale. Bob Sternberg, my friend and a professor at Yale, wrote me privately during the admission process and opined that Susan was "headed for greatness." (She eventually became full professor at Stanford and finally at Yale.)

Susan had open-heart surgery as a child, and I sensed a fragility about her, underneath her steely exterior and indefatigable work ethic.

"You used the ASQ to predict life insurance success," Susan said, "so let's use it to predict Olympic swimming. The pessimists might, like rejected salesmen, collapse after defeat, and the optimists might just be energized after defeat."

With Susan, the coaches gave the ASQ to the male and female candidates for the US teams for the 1988 Olympic Games in Seoul, South Korea. The coaches then had swimmers go all out in their best events, then told the swimmers their times were slow by just enough to be undetectable but very disappointing nevertheless. Each swimmer rested up and swam the same event again. As predicted, the pessimists swam the second event about 1 percent slower, and the optimists swam the second event about 1 percent faster.[1] Nort and Karen used this in Seoul, and the United States swept the relays.

Karen Reivich led our next foray into professional sports. Karen was already an undergraduate legend by the time I met her as a student in my huge abnormal psychology course. I knew about her from Penn's director of admissions: in the year she applied, applicants were required to write an essay about the world problem they would solve. Karen wrote her essay about "static cling," an issue trumped up by Madison Avenue to sell laundry detergent. She succeeded Peter Schulman as my A+ student and entered my laboratory after she graduated.

The Olympic swimmers were kind enough to take our questionnaire when asked by their coaches. But most sports heroes, professional basketball players and major league pitchers, would not take questionnaires. So Karen decided to use the CAVE technique on sports page quotes to get their explanatory style. This was immensely tedious, requiring reading the sports pages daily in dozens of national and hometown newspapers for a whole season and extracting and rating every causal statement a player made. Karen was up to the task.

For baseball, Bill James, in his encyclopedic books, had assembled exactly the statistics we needed. We predicted that in tight games, pessimistic pitchers would do worse than they usually did, whereas optimistic pitchers would do better than usual. So Karen formed a

Karen Reivich was already an undergraduate legend by the time I met her as a student in my huge abnormal psychology course: in the year she applied to Penn, applicants were required to write an essay on the world problem that they would solve. Karen wrote her essay about "static cling," an issue churned up by Madison Avenue to sell laundry detergent. Photo courtesy of Karen Reivich.

CAVE profile on major-league pitchers from sports page quotes in the first season and then looked at their earned run average (ERA) during the final three innings of close games in the next season. We found that pessimistic pitchers got worse (their ERAs went up) in the final innings of close games, whereas optimistic pitchers showed the opposite: they got better (their ERAs went down) in the final innings of close games.

We then tried to predict professional basketball: we took two teams from the National Basketball Association (NBA)—the Boston Celtics and our hometown Philadelphia Seventy-Sixers—and we CAVE'd all the sports page quotes from the first season for both teams. The Sixers turned out to be dire pessimists, while the Celtics were sunny optimists. We then looked at the next season and had a tool even better than Bill James's statistics for baseball: handicappers for each NBA game. When one places a bet on a basketball game, one tries to beat the "line," the margin by which the handicappers predict that the team will win or lose. So, for example, the Celtics were basically

better than the New York Knicks, and in a given game between the two, handicappers might predict that the Celtics would win by eight points, the line. If you bet on the Celtics, in order to win you had to bet that they would beat the line (e.g., that they would win by nine or more points).

The line was an exquisite target for us since it took into account all known advantages and disadvantages—for example, the home court advantage or the disadvantage of an injured player. It did not, however, take into account the teams' pessimism or optimism. So we predicted that an optimistic team, in this case the Celtics, after a defeat would rise to the occasion and beat the line, whereas the pessimistic Sixers would collapse after a defeat and lose to the line. This was exactly what happened.

After all the hundreds of hours of reading sports pages, we discovered one more fact. For the Celtics and the Sixers, we need not have worked so hard. Just CAVEing the coaches would have sufficed. The Celtics' coach was an optimist, and the Sixers' coach was a pessimist. So maybe the players got their explanatory style from their coach, and merely knowing about the leader, generally, would predict the performance of followers.

THE OTHER ADVANCE in my research program had to do with cancer and helplessness. Joe Volpicelli and Madelon Visintainer joined my group from the world of medicine. Joe was a Penn MD, a genuine South Philadelphian from a line of proud Italian stonemasons. Madelon was a committed nurse-practitioner from the University of Utah who aimed to make nursing a research-based academic profession. Both believed that helplessness weakened and mastery strengthened the body. I had collected more and more anecdotes in which helpless patients died suddenly and unexpectedly, in contrast to optimistic, masterful patients who beat all the odds and lived despite dire prognoses. But anecdotes are not science: they may be highly exaggerated and, even if truly reported, can involve many other uncontrolled factors. So Madelon and Joe carried out a pioneering rat experiment using the triadic design to test whether helplessness and mastery influenced tumor growth.

Each of three groups of rats got the usual escapable, inescapable, or no shock experience. But before any shock occurred, a malignant tumor with a known "take rate" of 50 percent was implanted on each rat's flank, and thereafter tumor growth was observed. Of the rats that had no shock, 50 percent rejected the tumor, and 50 percent grew the tumor and died. Of the rats that had inescapable shock, only 25 percent rejected the tumor, and 75 percent died. Of the rats that had escapable shock, the results were reversed: 75 percent rejected the tumor, and only 25 percent died.[2]

We published the resultant article in the journal *Science*. It was the only one bearing my name—out of about ten lifetime submissions—that made it into this prestigious venue. Perhaps this was the price of being an adventurous interloper. I have a lifetime batting average (articles accepted by the top journals or grants funded) of about .333. That's a good average for baseball but not for science. In contrast, my colleague Bob Rescorla, a scientists' scientist, has a batting average of 1.000. As far as I know, he has never had either an article or a grant request rejected.

How to explain this vast difference? It is assuredly not because Bob is an optimist—he is not. Rather I think it goes back to Peter Madison's admonishment at Princeton about not being wrong versus not being boring. I've attended faculty meetings with Bob for decades. He has very strong opinions, but he rarely talks, and when he does, everyone listens because he almost never says anything false. He founded the modern field of Pavlovian conditioning and is the best Pavlovian ever, better even than Pavlov. But his field has shriveled and is now dying. Bob retired, resting on his laurels. He did unimpeachable, conclusive science. Few Pavlovians would get into the ring with Bob, and he never tried to reach beyond his grasp. He never tried to extend Pavlovian conditioning beyond its narrow confines. Bob chose not to be wrong. One of his critics said, "Bob is the brightest dull person I ever met." I am forever reaching beyond my grasp. I want to know the furthest boundary of my idea. I often turn out to be wrong, but I am resilient and an optimist about my own work. One of my critics said of me, "Marty is not afraid to be wrong or to sound silly." I chose not to be boring.

The price of being an interloper who tried not to be boring was not just a lot of rejection but also a lot of being ignored. I mentioned before that my learning theory colleagues never thanked me for learned helplessness or for preparedness, and they mostly reacted by ignoring the findings. The tumor-growth article demonstrated conclusively that psychological factors strongly influence malignancy, but the very same thing happened, as impeccable as it was. I thought it was stunningly important, but it was barely followed up (ranking only ninety-fourth in citations of all my three hundred articles), and it forked no lightning.

Part 3

Being

Chapter Sixteen

Mandy (1988–)

MANDY MCCARTHY SELIGMAN is the love of my life. She is the mother of our five children. After thirty years, when I wake up by her side, I am still thrilled to see her. She turned my personal life around and then was the muse who turned me sunward toward positive psychology. And yet I have never written her a love letter.

This is it.

IN MAY 1983 my term as master of Van Pelt College House was up, and I was glad it was over. The lack of privacy and the continual demand at any hour entailed by living with 180 undergraduates—and as many crises—wore me to a frazzle. More than anything, I craved privacy, but I did not crave solitude.

I began to look at houses on the Main Line, the leafy western suburb of Philadelphia. There was a lot of space and privacy there. America's latest oil crisis was in full swing, with cars lined up at gas stations and consumers no longer buying gas-guzzlers. The prices of Main Line houses plummeted, since the prospect of heating a huge home with no insulation made them white elephants.

A real estate agent told me that a "Tudor" built in 1926 by Wallace & Warner, noted local architects of the Roaring Twenties, was coming on the market soon. A more accurate term for its style was "stockbroker bucolic" since this was one of the houses built before the Great Depression to accommodate the large wealthy families from the

Mandy McCarthy Seligman is the love of my life. We married in 1988, and my life turned positive—finally. Photo courtesy of the author.

city on their summer vacations. Woodleigh was a six-bedroom, ten-thousand-square-foot pile with a marble entrance hall and a green marble staircase. The thirty-foot living room, roofed with the darkest of African violet timbers, had perfect acoustics and served as a chamber music setting when Eugene Ormandy, conductor of the Philadelphia Orchestra, occupied the house in the 1940s. It had a winding two-hundred-foot driveway and a row of eight eighty-foot silver beech trees and a hundred-foot oak tree that antedated the house. The smaller trees were entirely overgrown with vines that looked predatory enough to eat human beings.

The owner was Martin Weinberg, the Philadelphia city solicitor and manager of Frank Rizzo's losing campaign to return to his old job as mayor in 1982. Marty was eager to get rid of the huge house. He told me he had never even ventured into the cavernous basement. The house felt like it wanted to be rid of him too so that both it and its present occupant could get on with their lives.

Even with oil-crisis prices, I still couldn't afford it. The down payment was $50,000. I had not even saved $10,000. Irene came up from her small, cheaply furnished condo in Del Ray Beach, Florida, and scrutinized the house. She scratched her fingernail over the checkerboard marble flooring and suggested that it was faux marble (it was not). I was surprised, however, and overwhelmed with gratitude and love when she wrote me a check for $50,000. This must have just about exhausted her life savings. She told me that the best use of money was to give it away exactly when it could make a crucial difference in one's children's lives. I remembered this and followed her example later.

It was wildly impractical, a bachelor's folly, but I bought the house anyway, believing that I would meet a woman who would fill it with kids and with dogs and with love.

The house resisted me. It rained for the first cheerless ten days of my occupancy in May 1983. When the rain finally stopped, I started to rip down the vines on the smaller trees. They did not like this, and I ended up at Lankenau Hospital with poison ivy over 60 percent of my body. I recovered and went off to the Max Planck Institute in Berlin for the summer.

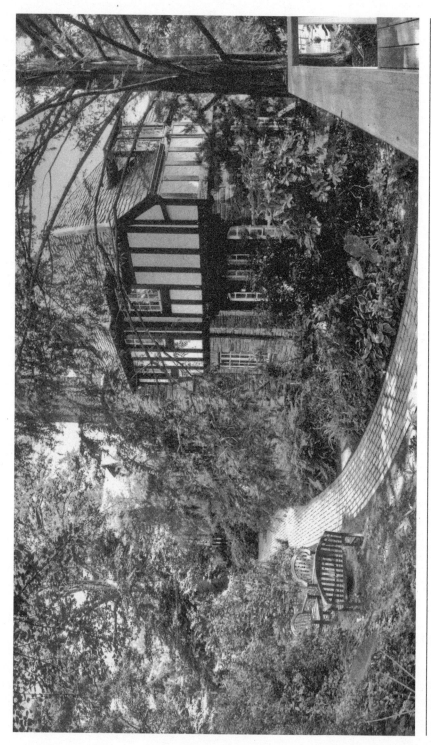

Woodleigh, our house, welcomed Mandy's painting it black and white and trying to convert it into a Cotswold cottage. Photo courtesy of Mandy Seligman.

I returned to discover that the swimming pool leaked perpetually. I could not stop the leak and sued Marty Weinberg for $2,500 for disguising it. He showed up at common pleas court with a retinue of his firm's lawyers. The justice of the peace told him summarily, "Pay the man." This justice of the peace would officiate at my wedding to Mandy five years later. I got the heating bill for February. I called the Philadelphia Electric Company to ask if they had made a decimal point error. They had not.

IN SEPTEMBER 1984 my life turned positive. The new crop of graduate students arrived at Penn. I attended the opening dinner in an off-campus Chinese restaurant and noticed a lovely, petite blonde at the other end of the table, ten seats down. She had almond-shaped blue eyes, a sprinkling of freckles, and a striking resemblance to a slimmer Shirley MacLaine. She did not speak to me then, but she made an appointment to talk about her first-year project.

We sat on a slatted red wood bench outside the laboratory building on a crisp early autumn day to discuss her research. It was our first conversation, and I can even remember the rough-hewn feel of the wooden slats. Her voice enfolded me: she had a British accent, delicate and lilting enough to be soothing, unlike the jangling argumentative tones of the Oxbridge philosophers I knew. She spoke in half sentences and then waited patiently for me to finish them. I eagerly completed her thoughts—with pleasure.

She asked me to be her advisor. I accepted—eagerly.

I snuck a look at her admissions folder. She had an undergraduate degree in social psychology from Kent (Canterbury) and the highest Graduate Record Examination (GRE) scores I'd ever seen. I asked her about her remarkable scores, and she told me she could not remember taking the test, only being in an automobile accident on the way to the test center—she had sleepwalked her way through the GREs with a concussion. She did remark that perhaps getting high scores on multiple-choice exams was genetic. Her father, Dennis McCarthy, had the highest test scores in the United Kingdom when he escaped the Welsh coal valley of his birth by taking the national chartered accountant examinations and so bursting free to London.

She then told me a fragment of her story. (She was reserved, and I am still hearing more fragments almost thirty years later.) At seventeen, sitting in a London café, she "knew" she would come to America. She matriculated at Kent and won the Faculty Prize. She told her advisor that she wanted to go to the United States, and he told her, "People like us don't go to America."

People like us. This was exactly what she wanted to escape: the helplessness and passivity that permeated the United Kingdom following World War II and the yielding up of the empire. She saw it through the eyes of an aspiring student at just the same moment in time that I was seeing it through the eyes of a visiting fellow at the Maudsley Hospital in London. I saw it in the Zen-like forbearance that my British neighbors displayed when the plumber failed to show up or the mail did not arrive. Mandy saw it in the resignation that her friends showed when they went on the dole. She took social psychology at Kent and heard about Martin Seligman and about learned helplessness. Learned helplessness resonated deeply, capturing exactly what she saw all around her, and she knew she was destined to work on it. She heard that one award was available for study in America. "I am not one of those 'people like us,'" Mandy thought when she applied. She got the award. She studied the psychology of language at the University of Indiana with Linda Smith, a Penn PhD, and a former teaching assistant of mine. Linda told her that she should go to graduate school at Penn. She went back to Kent to finish her AB and was admitted to Penn for the PhD.

She sat at the long dinner table ten seats away from me, and another new student pointed me out. Mandy was surprised, since, somehow, she had not known that I was at Penn, but here we both were.

I found myself in a difficult position as her advisor, because I was very attracted to her. This was before the days of rules at Penn forbidding romantic contact between faculty and graduate students, but gossip and shunning accomplished much the same end. Nevertheless, such contact, I felt, would undermine any academic relationship. So I adopted the opposite posture, aloof and severe, more aloof and severe than with my other students.

Aloof and severe did not work. Mandy was my teaching assistant in abnormal psychology. I came into one of her classes unannounced and commented benignly (I thought)—but severely—on some aspect of the latest draft of her article on anorexia. She frowned. I had blundered into criticizing her in front of her students. She out-severe'd and out-aloof'ed me by an order of magnitude. She did not speak to me for a month. Baffled, I woke up each morning feeling that the bottom had dropped out of the universe. It dawned on me that I had a case of something bigger than mere attraction.

An abject apology worked better than severe and aloof.

Mandy studied eating disorders and dieting. She combed through the world literature and found that anorexia and bulimia occur only in cultures, like ours, that have three things: a thin ideal for women, massive dieting among females, and twice as much depression in women as in men. Among cultures that do not have a thin ideal, do not have legions of women dieting (and failing), and have a one-to-one ratio of depression in men and women, there is no anorexia and no bulimia. She theorized that the unrealistic thin ideal for women caused eating disorders: women overdiet to achieve the ideal, and vulnerable females then cascade into bulimia and anorexia. The two-to-one ratio for depression results from females' distress over their body images and failure to achieve the unnaturally thin ideal.[1] This theory was widely cited over the next decade, but Mandy became the only psychologist I know who did not return the *New York Times*'s phone calls.

In May 1987, I gave a talk at Dartmouth on my new theory of dreaming. But I could not concentrate because I had at long last invited Mandy to dinner. I intended to drop the aloof posture and tell her how I felt. I did, and she asked, "Will you be my advisor in the morning?" I said that I would not.

We flew to England. Her father, Dennis, and I went "down the pub," and I asked his permission to marry Mandy. I was seventeen years older than his daughter, he reminded me, and once divorced. Not exactly the ideal groom. He suggested that we wait one year before marrying but consented to my proposing now.

I took Mandy to Le Jardin, a restaurant in Soho with London's most celebrated cellar of very old clarets. I had my mother's diamond engagement ring—the one from Adrian—in my pocket. The evening, however, refused to come off flawlessly.

I looked over Le Jardin's legendary wine list, and the sommelier and I had a long and pretentious discussion. The corks in 1945 had gone bad because of the war, the Pauillacs did not age as well as the St. Estephes, and so on. I could not seem to rein myself in and focus on the main event. I ordered a 1949 Lynch-Bages. It was very expensive and their last bottle. It was brought out with great ceremony and skillfully decanted. I swirled, I swirled again, I inhaled, and I sipped. It was far gone, over the hill. The sommelier, with aplomb, whisked it away. The patrons nearby noticed this and glanced our way surreptitiously. The sommelier handed me the list, and once again we had an overly long discussion of the merits of the 1945s, 1947s, and 1949s. I couldn't shut up. He couldn't shut up. I chose a 1947 Calon-Segur. More ceremony, cork sniffing, and decanting. The other patrons were staring openly. *Oh my God, this one is also bad.* Could I restrain myself and just accept it? Of course not; I enumerated its defects. This time the sommelier tasted it before sending it away. Mandy seemed uncharacteristically impatient. The wine list again. The discussion. "Third bottle," the sommelier said, "you pay half no matter what." I agreed and ordered the 1949 Talbot, not the greatest but the longest-lived of clarets. The ceremony, the decanting, the cork sniffing, and all the nearby patrons now no longer eating and staring.

The Talbot was perfect, heavenly in fact. The sommelier relaxed, Mandy relaxed, and the room broke into polite applause.

I dropped to my knees and took out the ring. Mandy beamed and softly said, "Yes." The room broke into prolonged, booming applause.

ONE YEAR LATER, on September 18, 1988, we were married. The house liked this and permitted us to hold the ceremony within, with Mandy and Dennis walking down her green marble staircase and the vows spoken and clearly heard in her living room. The house tolerated my stuffing insulation into her walls, but she positively adored Mandy's coddling with drapes and cushions and throw pillows. She

especially liked being painted black and white, like the authentic Cotswold Tudor she aspired to be.

We all adjourned to Le Bec Fin for dinner. It was a Sunday, and Georges Perrier had given over his whole establishment to the wedding party. He served us his lighter-than-air mousse of pike in a pale-pink lobster sauce, filet mignon in a marrow-enriched sauce bordelaise, and turbot with white butter. Dick Graff had sent his prized Chalone chardonnay, and we also served the deeply golden "selected late harvest" from Phelps 1976 as well as the Phelps 1979, which was dark brown with over-the-top residual sugar. For the wedding cake, Georges constructed a *croquembouche*, a skyscraper of custard-filled puff pastry balls threaded with caramel, which Mandy and I launched by cracking it open with a bottle of champagne.

The speeches were not perfunctory. Judy Rodin (then dean at Yale and president of Penn six years later), who advised Mandy on her thin-ideal paper, toasted us as "a perfect Penn couple." George Vaillant wished us joy and children and a positive future. With tears in her eyes, Irene silently raised her glass to us all. Dennis spoke about Mandy's courage in leaving England and setting out (just as he had) for a land unknown, knowing not a soul.

WE HONEYMOONED AT an inn down the road in Wayne for one night, and then a few weeks later we rented a house on the fourteenth hole of the Kanapali golf course in Maui for a month. I birdied the hole once and double-bogeyed it about fifty times. We returned to Woodleigh in time for the cold weather and were welcomed by roaring fires in the living room fireplace for the duration of the winter.

"Are you happy?" Mandy asked innocently, as we basked in the glow of the firelight one snowy evening. My irritated peroration took her aback.

"What a stupid question!" I snapped, then, adopting my interrupt-at-your-own-risk professorial mode, continued, "*Happy?* Now there's an empty concept. Ambrose Bierce called it the mythical state attributed by adults to children, by children to adults, and by the living to the dead. 'Happy' is a word used by so many people, so many ideologies, as to be rendered utterly senseless. It's just not a viable notion.

You can't do science on it, and much worse you can't run your life around it. Psychology has been better off since Freud, and Schopenhauer before him told us to forget all about being happy. The best we can ever do in life is to not be miserable, to hold our suffering to as near zero as possible. Now that's a successful life."

Mandy gazed patiently at me. Her serene face showed confidence, and she said just one word: "Wrong."

AS A FORTY-SIX-YEAR-OLD married man, I decided to change my days. Rather than go into the office in the psychology department every day as I'd done for the last fifteen years, I decided to spend more of my time with Mandy. Some of my work required face-to-face contact: teaching students and politicking in the never-ending, disheartening department battle between natural and social science. But much of what I did—writing, reading, directing research projects, conversing with colleagues around the world, and thinking—I could do remotely. I now had a home and wanted to luxuriate therein.

Mandy had asked me if I was happy and I had snapped at her, irritated by the question itself. But I did notice a change: I thought more about positive possibilities in my life now. Until Mandy, I fit the Freud-Schopenhauer ideal perfectly: almost all my emotional thinking was about minimizing my own misery—how to placate an angry colleague, how to galvanize an underproducing student, how to tone my flabby body, or how to be less depressed myself. It occurred to me that the best I could ever do—even if I completely solved all these problems—was arrive at zero. But now I found myself thinking about what might be north of zero in my life: spending more time with Mandy, creating a rose garden in the backyard, listening to the Berlin Philharmonic and Meatloaf more, and playing serious bridge more. I didn't know what, if anything, "happy" meant, but I could distinguish spending my life correcting what was wrong from spending it building what was right. Building a good life as opposed to correcting my shortcomings captured "happier" rather than just "less unhappy."

MANDY FINISHED HER third-year studies and wrote her two "major area" papers. One was the thin-ideal article positing that an unachievable thin ideal for women caused eating disorders. The other

discussed "attachment,"[2] an alien concept for me. "Attachment" came from animal ethology: goslings that "imprint" on their mother (or the first moving goose-like thing they see) "attach." The early ethologists—Konrad Lorenz and Niko Tinbergen—were both behaviorists at heart, and "attachment" was their work-around term for the less scientific, subjective state of "love." "Attachment" then found its way into the psychoanalytic camp to describe the strength of the mother-child bond. The strength of child-mother attachment explains later depression and anxiety and other patterns of neurotic behavior as the child grows up. "Insecurely attached" children, in perpetual fear of abandonment by their unreliable mothers, go on to adult neuroses and become failures in life. They worry that any new love object will abandon them, just as their mother did. "Securely attached" children are confident about their mothers' love—she is reliable and will always love them—and go on to believe in themselves and trust others. This leads to healthy relationships and successful lives.

Mandy took this theory very seriously as a life lesson, and when we had our first child, Lara, Mandy made a crucial decision: she would also stay home, with Lara and with me, rather than do a doctoral dissertation. The *New York Times* phoned and interviewed her. She told the reporter, "I decided not to leave my child to go study attachment."

WE TOOK A second honeymoon, this time to what would become our regular and most cherished vacation spot: Kona Village on the west coast of the Big Island, Hawaii. No television, no radio, just a comfortable *hale* (a South Sea island cottage, pronounced "hahLAY"), Kona coffee, and big families, a few steps from a magnificent coral reef. Lara was just seven months old, and in our *hale* built over a black lava outcropping, she took her first step and said her first word.

I arranged for childcare for Lara so that Mandy and I could have romantic dinners and long walks and cuddly snorkels together—just the two of us. Mandy tearfully declined and paid the babysitter to go away. "I want to be together with you and Lara. I don't want her raised by a stranger," Mandy explained.

Mandy's fireside question, "Are you happy?" and now her decision to restructure our lives around a secure nest both nagged at me. Was she onto a huge missing piece in my work?

This nagging worry had popped up in other, less intimate venues, and I sensed convergence.

MELISSA HUNT, a clinical PhD student of mine, did her first-year research on happiness—not on my students' usual topic of depression. I confessed little enthusiasm for happiness as a research topic, and Melissa asked me why. I reminded her of Phil Brickman's now classic study of twenty-two lottery winners.[3] At first their happiness went up, but after a few months it sank back down to its usual curmudgeonly level.

"Happiness is the just froth on the cappuccino. I want to study the espresso underneath. Depression, anxiety, and anger: that's the espresso," I told Melissa. She was unconvinced.

I HAD BEEN treating patients off and on for more than fifteen years. The unspoken premise was that therapy had succeeded when you helped patients rid themselves of all their sadness, all their anxiety, and all their anger. This followed from Freud's axiom that the best we can ever hope for in life is not to suffer, to confine our misery to as close to zero as possible. While not much of a therapist, I sometimes did good work, and in those cases, my patients' negative emotions were normal by termination. Did I get a happy patient?

No, I got an empty patient.

The convergence was that happiness is more than the absence of unhappiness. There was more to research, more to therapy, and more to theory than just misery and its relief. Most poignantly, there was more to life—my life in particular.

Chapter Seventeen

Learned Optimism
(1989–1993)

I FOUND MYSELF IN Richard Pine's office. Richard was a thirty-year-old Penn graduate and, even at this tender age, a prominent Manhattan literary agent. He was lithe, already balding, and intensely curious about how science can inform the human spirit. He had already sold blockbuster fiction bestsellers and was now looking for science-based nonfiction that might guide readers to fuller lives. Dan Oran, a novelist, my friend, and the manager of our booming Metropolitan Life testing business, had wangled this meeting and told me that people "kill" to get in front of Richard. Richard had read some of my articles, and so we discussed learned helplessness at length. I had never talked with an "agent" before and was surprised by the depth of his knowledge of psychology. He liked the breadth of topics that helplessness bears on—physical health, sports, longevity, business success—but was uneasy about the negative tone underlying all my work: pessimism, depression, helplessness, and anxiety.

"You have a book in you, Marty," Richard said, "a book on optimism."

"But I don't work on optimism," I countered reflexively, as I began my leave-taking. "I work on pessimism." But I couldn't help thinking about the rats, the dogs, and the people who never gave into helplessness. I couldn't help thinking of the rats that had received escapable shock and then fought off tumors even better than rats that had

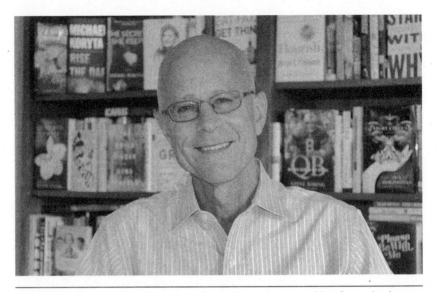

Richard Pine was intensely curious about how science could inform the human spirit. He had already sold blockbuster fiction bestsellers, and he was now looking for science-based nonfiction that might guide readers to fuller lives. He became my advisor and literary agent. Photo courtesy of Richard Pine.

no shock at all. I couldn't help thinking of the swimmers who swam faster after a defeat. I couldn't help thinking of all the people who, after trauma, grew stronger and wiser rather than deteriorating, of all the people who overcame their dismal, impoverished childhoods and rose to success, even to greatness. I couldn't help thinking that my patients needed more skills than just those to fight depression or anxiety. I couldn't help ruing my brusque answer to Mandy's "Are you happy?" and remembering how much comfort I found in Mandy's nest-building.

"People make religions of this stuff. I pray you will write a book on optimism," Richard murmured as I left. On this day I discovered what "agent" meant, and Richard became my agent, trusted advisor, and good friend.

Richard's challenge reawakened the puzzle of why the negative exerts such a hammerlock on the mind. Why did I believe that my work was about pessimism and not optimism, about fear and not courage, about failure and not success, about sadness and not happiness? Of

course the proximate cause was that the agenda of the National Institute of Mental Health was mental illness, and it funded my work. But the power behind the death grip of negativity went much deeper than mere funding.

What is so attractive about original sin—the dogma that deep down we are fallen, that we are rotten to the core? What is so attractive about the theory that people are basically mean and self-seeking? What is so attractive about virtue, sacrifice, and generosity as mere self-serving illusions, frail defenses that compensate for the reality of underlying vice? What is so attractive about Freud's dictum that the best we can ever hope for in life is not to be miserable? Why is journalism governed by "If it bleeds, it leads"? Why are our politics about exposing the ignobility of the candidates and voting for the "least bad" one? Why does victimology almost have a monopoly on government funding with the pursuit of happiness left to the individual?

The literature is unanimous: bad is stronger than good. A severe toothache overrides an enjoyable conversation. A crying baby in the next room preempts lovemaking. The squeaky wheel gets the oil. In the laboratory you solve nine of the ten problems correctly, but you will remember the one you got wrong.

Why?

For one thing, we are bad-weather animals. The most recent geological epoch that shaped human evolution was the Pleistocene, the ice ages: famine, ice, flood, drought, and more ice. What kind of primate survived the ice ages? What happened to the brain that believed "It is a nice day today; I'm sure it will be a nice day tomorrow"? This brain was crushed by tomorrow's ice. The brain that believed "Today may seem like a nice day, but tomorrow comes the trouble" survived and passed its genes down to us. Paranoia—to say nothing of depression, anxiety, and anger—has major survival advantages in a world that is actually full of danger, loss, and injustice.

The human mind is like the human tongue. The tongue's default mode is to swish around the mouth until it finds a cavity and then to worry the defective tooth. The tongue does not look for a perfect tooth and then savor its flawlessness. The tongue is there not to

celebrate what is right but to detect what is wrong and hidden. The default mode of your mind is to swish around your life until it discovers a problem that just might explode into real trouble. It then hones in and plans how to avoid it. The mind did not evolve to celebrate life.

The death grip of the negative exists not just because we are bad-weather animals but also because the negative has an urgency that the positive rarely does. Danger, loss, and trespass tend to arrive suddenly and insist on immediate attention. A stimulating idea, a romantic evening, or a great performance of Mahler's "Resurrection" symphony does not have the shrillness of a fire alarm.

While sadness, fear, and anger surely have evolutionary benefits, they come at a very steep price. If in reality it will be a nice day tomorrow, then the mentality that anxiously broods over the possibility of bad weather cannot bask in the good. If in reality loss is not imminent, then a perpetually gloomy mentality is self-defeating. If in reality other people can be trusted, then the paranoid mentality is self-destructive.

If our world is no longer an ice age, our inherited bad-weather mentality ruins many more lives than it saves.

The upshot is that the pessimistic mind-set needs no advocates and no teaching. People do not need to have the fact that the world is full of loss, danger, and trespass drummed into them. Contrary to cocktail party chatter, there is nothing wise or sophisticated about pessimism. It is the human default—and as we shall see in Chapter 28, it is likely the mammalian default. Pessimism is lazy; it comes easily and naturally. If you actually live in a more benign world than the Pleistocene and want to enjoy your species' hard-earned prosperity, you have to break out of the negative. What needs teaching—what needs nurturance, support, and justification—is an optimistic view of the world. Richard Pine was right: the world needed a book on optimism, and so I began to write one.

Richard sold the book to Sonny Mehta at Alfred A. Knopf, on the basis of little more than an outline and a long writing sample, for what seemed to me a staggering sum. Knopf under Sonny's stewardship was the toniest of publishers, and since I was new to big-league publishing, we hired Tom Congdon (who, Tom told me, ghosted the

bestseller *Jaws*) as my just-in-case ghost. I sent Tom a sample chapter, and he commented extensively. I sent him an even more extensively redone chapter, and he generously told me, "You've got it." So ended the ghosting.

Because I have already told you about the research on optimism and its relation to depression, sports, schoolwork, Met Life, and physical health, there is no need to repeat it here. The book, titled *Learned Optimism*, gave me the freedom to integrate the basic research on learned helplessness and explanatory style with those realms of life. It also contained two other elements: First, I presented the questionnaires we developed for adults and children and encouraged the readers to take the tests, score them, and gain insight into their own levels of pessimism and depression. Second, I presented evidence-based exercises for adults and kids to do that reliably raised optimism and decreased depression.

Disputing pessimistic thoughts is the central skill of learned optimism. A mother finds herself shouting at her children every morning when she sends them off to school. She thinks, "I'm a terrible mother," a permanent, pervasive, and personal explanation that puts her at risk for depression. She learns to dispute this thought realistically. When the kids come home from school, she remembers that she is cheerful, helps them with their homework, and listens patiently to their social problems. She now substitutes "I'm not a morning person" to explain her grouchiness. This explanation, while personal, is temporary and specific, and so it does not produce depression. Essentially learned optimism takes the techniques of cognitive therapy—which are used with very depressed people—and applies them to everyone. The book walked readers step-by-step toward using these skills for themselves and their children.

One major caution ended the book: the need for a sober balance of optimism and pessimism. I did not wish to advocate optimism, recommending its use to counter every trouble. The final chapter discussed "flexible" optimism, a way of thinking that gave pessimism its due. Pessimism has evolution behind it and seems to be the default response to troubles. In a reality full of danger, loss, and trespass, pessimism is a virtue. Having learned the skills of optimism by disputing

catastrophic thoughts, how—in any given situation—do you decide whether to deploy optimism?

Ask yourself, "How dire are the consequences of failure here?" If the consequences are small, use optimism. So, for example, you see an attractive woman at a conference. Should you introduce yourself and try to make friends? Failure here is merely one more rejection in a life full of them. So dispute the thought "Women never like me." When, however, the consequences are major—if your wife finds out, she will divorce you—refrain from learned optimism. We do not want optimistic pilots who might ask, why bother de-icing the plane a second time? The weather is likely going to be fine? The consequence of failure here is catastrophe.

Learned Optimism was duly published in 1990,[1] and I went on my first book tour: *The Today Show*, where Joe Garagiola asked me if the opposite of optimism, helplessness, had ever occurred to me; *Good Morning, Phoenix*, where at 5 a.m. I discovered I was on a spiritualist wake-up show. I called my tough-minded editor, Jon Siegel, who told me that the book was number one in *Newsday* and commented enigmatically, "If you have to have a number, that's a good one." It got a highly positive review in the influential Sunday *New York Times*. The reviewer confessed to being a pessimist and said *Learned Optimism* had "vaulted her out of her funk."[2] This review transformed the book in the eyes of the sales rankers from "nonfiction" to "self-help." For an academic like me, who identifies himself as a scientist, "self-help" was a dreaded category that I would never shake, but it was a boon for bookstores since self-help outsells nonfiction.

I steeled myself as I walked into College Hall a few days after the *Times* review appeared. I was chair of the Arts and Science Personnel Committee. Our job was to review tenure cases, and the committee consisted of crusty traditional academics. I feared the averted eyes and mutterings that awaited me there, but the room broke into applause.

This was a surprise and caused some rethinking. The professors in the humanities led the applause. For them, I discovered, a book, particularly one that emanated from a major New York publisher and then got reviewed in the *Times*, was the acme of success. In the

sciences, a lead article in a specialized journal was the acme of success. My reappraisal was confirmed when no psychologist at Penn said a word to me—not then, not ever—even though the department broke out champagne when my colleague Henry Gleitman published his introductory textbook.

My first impulse was to try to shuck off the label "self-help." Self-improvement, as an explicit genre, began in the nineteenth century and rapidly grew in popularity. In the twentieth century, Dale Carnegie's *How to Win Friends and Influence People* and Norman Vincent Peale's *The Power of Positive Thinking* were huge, long-lived bestsellers. Their popularity with the public was matched only by the scorn they elicited in academia. Like most scornful highbrows, I had never read a "self-help" book, not even Benjamin Franklin's *Autobiography*, but now that I was labeled a self-help writer, I read *How to Win Friends and Influence People*. It was astonishingly good. It really did give the reader ways to make friends, with tips about making other people feel valued (e.g., the most important word in the English language is one's own name). But it was only armchair advice lacking any scientific backing. Popularity and success, not earned the hard way, brought scorn from professors who did careful science but whose words forked no lightning.

But I *was* writing "self-help" and indeed chose my work explicitly to allow people to help themselves. But with one new addition: the tests and exercises came from the very vineyards of science—thousands of subjects, control groups, careful measurement, and peer review. I wrote not *footless* self-help but *evidence-based* self-help, and I believe *Learned Optimism* may have been the first of this genre.

The 1991 Gulf War broke out in Kuwait, and American shopping malls emptied. Even with few shoppers, the book made the lower ranks of the *New York Times* best-seller list for a few weeks, and that was the high-water mark of its popularity. But to my satisfaction it sold steadily and well for the next twenty-five years.

I also wrote *The Optimistic Child* with Karen Reivich, Jane Gillham, and Lisa Jaycox.[3] This book recreated for schoolchildren the tests and exercises we had developed for adults. The four of us completed a major program for teaching optimism in middle school and

found that arming ten- and eleven-year-olds with the skills of optimism markedly lowered their risk for depression and anxiety when they went through puberty. This program became the scientific basis for the field of positive education, which arose fifteen years later and I will discuss in Chapter 23.

The book tour took me to Reverend Pat Robertson's *The 700 Club.* Pat was very hospitable to me, and we appeared together on his call-in show. I was flogging a book about making kids more optimistic, and he had just written a book on the apocalypse—an odd pairing of topics. One caller surprised Pat with her concern: "I need your help, Brother Pat," she said in a deep southern drawl. "I am thinking about getting pregnant, but I understand that nursing mothers don't do very well during an apocalypse."

The grueling book tours notwithstanding, this medium was within my tessitura, and I went to work on my next Knopf book, *What You Can Change and What You Can't.*[4] The idea combined my work on preparedness (some things are learned much more easily than others and some things cannot be learned at all) with all the hard work Dave Rosenhan and I did in writing *Abnormal Psychology.* In the course of our reviewing every psychotherapy and every major drug for every kind of disorder, it dawned on me that some problems are easily treated, and others are untreatable. Yet the public remained in the dark not only about optimal treatments but, worse, about the disorders for which therapy and drugs are a huge waste of time, money, and emotional energy. So I set out to write a sort of *Guide Michelin* to the major disorders and all the major treatments. Given the amount and quality of the evidence, I awarded zero to four stars for each major treatment for each major disorder. So, for example, panic attack, characterized by heart pounding, suffocation, flop sweat, and the feeling that one is about to die, had quite a large number of controlled outcome studies. Untreated it typically was chronic. Antidepressant and antianxiety drugs got three stars for improvement, but the high relapse rate earned them only one and a half stars overall. Cognitive therapy, in contrast, got four stars for both improvement and relapse. For unipolar depression, interpersonal therapy, cognitive therapy, and antidepressant drugs all got three stars on improvement,

and electroconvulsive shock (ECT) got three and a half stars. But they differed on side effects and relapse, with ECT and drugs getting only one and a half stars overall and the psychotherapies earning two and a half stars overall. I have continued to follow the outcome literature in the twenty years since publication, and, dismayingly, there has been almost no progress.

This book did not become a *New York Times* bestseller, but it changed my life more than anything else I ever wrote.

"CONSUMER REPORTS RATES automobiles and dishwashers, as you know, Dr. Seligman, but we now want to wade into murkier waters and rate psychotherapy. Will you help us do it?" The voice on the phone belonged to an editor of this highly credible and commercially disinterested publication. I revered it and turned to it whenever making a big purchase. I was delighted to agree.

The evaluation of psychotherapy was indeed murky. There was almost violent disagreement among outcome researchers and between the warring camps of psychotherapy about how to do it. Early-outcome research looked at patients' satisfaction with therapy. Here the kind of psychotherapy did not seem to matter much, and quite high satisfaction was generally reported. But the numbers were small, and as the importance of insurance and reimbursement grew, there was a call for harder outcomes than mere satisfaction: relief of specific symptoms and cure of the disorder. These harder studies constituted the meat and potatoes of *What You Can Change and What You Can't*, in which specific therapies for specific disorders won. Exposure therapy, for example, relieves obsessive-compulsive disorders well, but nonspecific supportive therapy does not. Behavior therapy does well for curing phobias, but psychoanalysis does not.

Actual clinicians in the field all but ignored these outcome data. Most therapists in the early 1990s were eclectic and psychoanalytically inclined—but not dogmatically so—and dispensed support and acceptance freely. Only a minority used specific techniques for specific problems, such as progressive relaxation for phobias, which my book endorsed. Moreover, many clinicians found *DSM* diagnosis and the very notion of specific disorders alien. A real patient rarely fit into

one diagnostic niche perfectly, and his problems were usually multiple ("comorbid"); for example, anxiety almost always accompanies depression. The goal of many clinicians was not to relieve the symptoms of a specific disorder but to improve the well-being, emotional lives, and functioning of their patients more globally. The field of outcome studies was monopolized by "efficacy" studies, which randomized volunteers into one of two groups: a specific short-term treatment or a plausible but inert control treatment. The big insurance companies ("managed care") followed the efficacy studies for treatment reimbursement and would not pay up if the therapist did not diagnose a specific disorder and then treat it with the specific "efficacious" therapy for the allotted number of sessions. So while efficacy studies fit the needs of short-term reimbursable therapy, the whole notion of the efficacy study was anathema to the long-term therapist whose goal was global mental health.

I cannot overstate the passion that fired this quarrel. Entire livelihoods, as well as the mental health of the nation, depended on this issue, which ripped the 160,000-member American Psychological Association (APA) itself in two. William James's APA had been an organization of paper-reading scientists, but therapists began to join in force after World War II. By the 1970s the therapists had become the majority, and the scientists were in retreat. In the early 1980s the therapists, led by the "dirty dozen," organized a revolt and successfully overthrew the scientists' monopoly on APA governance. Many scientists abruptly quit the association in revulsion and joined the breakaway American Psychological Society. The pivotal issue was now efficacy studies, with most scientists saying yes and most therapists shouting no. Almost every APA president since 1980 had come from the militant therapy side of the aisle.

Consumer Reports (*CR*) wanted to do the largest and most representative study of psychotherapy ever conducted. Its editors had read my book and turned to me because I seemed a disinterested scientific observer. But *CR* did not intend to do an efficacy study. There would be no clinic volunteers, no placebo control group, no random assignment of patients to treatment, no standard diagnostic

workup, and no fixed duration of treatment. Rather *CR* would do an "effectiveness" study, looking at the outcome of therapy as it is done in the real world.

In its annual 1994 survey, *CR* sent out to its 180,000 subscribers around one hundred questions about automobiles and mental illness. The survey asked,

> At any time over the past three years, have you experienced stress or other emotional problems for which you sought help from any of the following: friends, relatives, or a member of the clergy, a mental health professional like a psychologist or a psychiatrist, your family doctor, or a support group?

Of the 18,000 subscribers who responded, 7,000 admitted to such problems; of these, 4,100 had gone to a mental health professional. Led by Mark Kotkin, *CR*'s analysts created a composite outcome measure:

1. Specific improvement ("How much did treatment help with the specific problem that led you to therapy?")
2. Satisfaction ("Overall how satisfied were you with this therapist's treatment of your problems?")
3. Global improvement ("overall emotional state" at the time of the survey compared with the start of treatment: "very poor: I barely managed to deal with things; fairly poor: Life was usually pretty tough for me; so-so: I had my ups and downs; quite good: I had no serious complaints; very good: Life was much the way I liked it to be")

The findings were unexpected, dramatic, and far-reaching, and they catapulted me smack into the middle of the war between therapists and scientists.

The first finding was that treatment by a mental health professional usually worked, and most patients got a lot better. Of the 426 people who were feeling very poor when they began therapy, 87 percent were feeling very good, good, or at least so-so by the time of the

survey. Of the 786 people who were feeling fairly poor at the outset, 92 percent were feeling very good, good, or at least so-so by the time of the survey.

This surprised me: the efficacy studies taken as a whole—many hundreds of them—showed much more modest results. In my best overall estimate, they showed that only about 65 percent of patients got better with either drugs or therapy against an alarming 40 percent placebo rate.

Second, *long-term therapy worked much better than short-term therapy.* This was a big surprise. Long-term therapy was the favorite whipping boy of the science wing of which I was a card-carrying member. Taking years and being very expensive, long-term therapy was thought of as little better than a fraud, a Freudian dinosaur long overdue for extinction. That it should be effective at all, to say nothing of more effective than all the short-term therapies, was a gut shot to efficacy research.

Third, psychologists, psychiatrists, and social workers did equally well, and all did better than marriage counselors; *family doctors did as well as the other professionals in the short run but worse in the long run.* This was another surprise. Therapy of the general supportive and eclectic type dispensed by the average therapist was usually thought of as mere placebo. Academics saw it as another Freudian dinosaur, but the fact that marriage counselors and family doctors did worse suggested that supportive therapy did contain active helpful ingredients.

Fourth, *no specific form of therapy did any better than any other.* This was the biggest surprise. The entire theme of the efficacy studies and of *What You Can Change and What You Can't* was that specific therapies work better on specific disorders: systematic desensitization on phobia, cognitive therapy on depression, exposure on obsessive-compulsive disorder. Was I wrong?

Finally, if *insurance coverage limited the choice of therapist or duration of therapy*, patients did worse. This was cause for upheaval. Managed care had become almost universal in America on the grounds that limiting the duration of therapy and forcing the patient into the right treatment and to the right therapist would save money and

improve Americans' mental health. But these results suggested that it was systematically undermining the mental health of the country.

THE *CONSUMER REPORTS* article unleashed some praise and a torrent of criticism. The praise came from the therapists in the trenches: finally a respected academic had documented and published the fact they were actually doing good work. The torrent of criticism came from my brothers and sisters in the academy, particularly those who devoted their careers to testing the efficacy of specific therapies for specific disorders. Lee Sechrest, one of the most senior advocates of rigorous science about therapy, told an audience that my participation in the *CR* survey was "unforgiveable" and that I was a "traitor." The heart of their criticism was that efficacy studies were the gold standard for verifying what therapy worked and that the *Consumer Reports* survey was trash. Efficacy studies entailed random assignment of patients to therapy or placebo. All were done with a single diagnosis, a manual, and a fixed duration. This meant that they could be replicated in the laboratory. The *CR* survey, on the other hand, being naturalistic, allowed patients to *choose* (heaven forbid) what therapy they got, what therapist they had, and how long they stayed in treatment, and it allowed the therapist to change tack if an approach was not working. Completely uncontrolled trash.

And so, under the gun, I came to grips once again with the problem of external validity: the very issue that had shaken me out of the animal laboratory and into the messier world of real people in their real worlds. This time the issue was not merely academic; the livelihoods of thousands of therapists and, if taken seriously, the very mental health of the nation were at stake.

Even though it looked like good science, the efficacy method—when examined closely—had huge methodological problems that the effectiveness method, used in the *CR* survey, did not. Let's take the problems one at a time.

The point of randomly assigning patients to therapy or a placebo is to spread the unseen and unknown, the confounding characteristics of the sample, evenly across therapy and placebo. So, for example, if

all the patients in the placebo group happened to be introverts or to be very angry or to have rejecting mothers, therapy would do better than placebo, but not because the treatment worked. Random assignment is supposed to even out these confounding characteristics. But a close look shows that it doesn't. Typically in an efficacy study, about twenty patients go into each group. But imagine conservatively that ten personal traits might influence outcomes. If you do the math, random assignment requires hundreds of patients—an unheard-of number—to actually even things out. Random assignment, done with just a few dozen patients, is mere window dressing.

Even worse, an efficacy study forces (randomly "assigns") you into one type of therapy even if you do not want it and do not believe it will work. In the real world you usually choose a therapy and a therapist you believe in. You control what kind of therapy you have. What if success in therapy depends partly on your beliefs and your wholehearted buy-in? Many disorders involve hopelessness, and to the extent that choosing a therapy and a therapist undercuts hopelessness, therapy will work better. So efficacy methods negate the benefits of choice, while effectiveness methods estimate the power of choice accurately.

In real therapy, duration depends on the progress of the patient. In real therapy, the therapist does not follow a manual and can change tack if progress is slow or poor. In real therapy the patient has many problems, not typically a single diagnosable one. And who volunteers for an efficacy study when it is advertised that half of the volunteers will get a placebo? Not your typical patient. So efficacy studies systematically underestimate the usefulness of therapy for real patients in the real world.

I concluded that effectiveness studies, of which the *CR* study was the largest to date, are a decent guide to what works, and efficacy studies are not.[5]

In a stroke I became a pariah to many of my academic colleagues, but I became very popular with therapists.

THE YEAR ENDED tragically for me. Shortly after my election as APA president, I got a call from the sheriff of West Palm Beach, Florida. My mother, he told me, was in the hospital with a broken hip. But

that was not all: she had facial contusions and other bruises. Irene's housekeeper, a middle-aged Romanian immigrant, had been arrested on suspicion of physically abusing her. I flew down to the hospital. When I asked Irene if she'd been beaten, she denied it. I took her back with me to recover in a plush nursing home near our house. Once there Irene confessed the abuse to Mandy and that she had not wanted to tell me lest I worry about her or, even worse, the housekeeper hurt her even more on discovering her tattling.

We celebrated Irene's ninetieth birthday with all her siblings, and she even gave a little speech, saying I had been a "wonderful son." But she went downhill soon thereafter and soon stopped eating altogether.

"Matzo ball soup?" I asked her. She perked up and repeated, "Matzo ball soup!" her first words in days. She smiled and for the next week drank Matzo ball soup through a straw. She died on February 26, 1996. Irene's housekeeper was convicted of abuse, even though a charge of murder or manslaughter might have been warranted, and she received a year's probation with the warning not to apply for work as a caretaker in the future.

In the tumult around Irene's abuse and death, my own emotional life seemed peculiar to me. I could not bring myself to look on her lifeless body, and my aversion had the same defensive quality as when I avoided visiting my paralyzed father in the nursing home forty years before. Nor could I bring myself to pursue charges against her housekeeper, and I declined to appear at her trial. I just wanted to forget. My emotions were blunted, and not until I threw the first earth on Irene's casket as it was lowered did I wrap my cousin, Bobbi, in my arms and finally weep uncontrollably.

Twenty years removed from Irene's death, my memory of her remains distorted. Irene was almost invariably loving and positive. She lived by the doctrine "If you can't say anything nice, don't say anything at all," but in her last years she could be crabby. She once criticized us for wasting money on a bouquet of flowers for her. I find it difficult to conjure up happy, earlier memories of her and treacherously easy to remember the isolated, negative instances from her last, troubled years. I wish I understood this better, since we all want our children to remember us at our best and certainly not at our worst.

Chapter Eighteen

APA (1995–1999)

I HADN'T BEEN PRESIDENT of anything since the ninth grade, and no one had since asked me to run for anything. It was hard not to notice that my friends were assuming high office: Judy Rodin, for example, was elected president of the Eastern Psychological Association. But I had no knowledge about how this was done. Didn't scientific honors and national office just come based on some organic acclamation for work accomplished?

"Sandy," I asked in a moment of naive and abashed candor, "why am I never invited onto prestigious national committees?" My friend, Sandra Scarr, was an all-around professional success, and I envied her. She was chair of the psychology department at the University of Virginia and a prominent researcher on race, poverty, and IQ. She was also politically astute, having evaded the wrath that usually rained down on researchers who found a genetic component to IQ. She was, moreover, the president of the breakaway American Psychological Society.

"These are not knighthoods, Marty. You probably think it is beneath dignity, but scientific honors and national office are not bestowed because you happen to do good science. The dirty little secret is that you have to campaign for them. You have to make allies, and then tell them you want it," Sandy confided. (I am now informed that this is also true of knighthoods.)

So I decided to run for office. I, quietly and blushing all the while, told a few of my friends that I wanted to be president of the Division of Clinical Psychology, Division 12, the largest unit of the American Psychological Association. On my first try, David Barlow, the leading anxiety-therapy researcher, won by a bit, but on my second try in 1993, I was elected easily.

Being president was fun. I liked the people—other clinical researchers for the most part. I liked the venue—three meetings a year in Washington, DC. And I liked the work—moving the agenda, foisted upon me at Penn, of building good clinical science onto the national stage, where the petty politics of departmental infighting was not so personal. My main issue was building support for evidence-based therapy, and with Dave Barlow we oversaw the publication of an influential book on this topic.[1]

Standing up for evidence-based therapy was dandy as far as the academic-based governing board of Division 12 was concerned. But as I began to meet the therapists forced to labor under the insurance companies' reimbursement guidelines derived from efficacy research, I learned that this evidence was not welcome in the trenches. Therapists told me that it provided fodder for the managed care machine that boxed them into overly simple diagnoses, stripped-down brief treatment, lower wages, invasion of patients' privacy, and, worst, termination of therapy too early, without the relief that longer therapy would produce.

These therapists welcomed the *Consumer Reports* study. My newfound popularity with therapists—who formed the largest voting bloc in the American Psychological Association—outweighed my sudden unpopularity with my academic peers.

"I could be elected president of APA," I told Mandy once I saw the *CR* dataset.

"Go for it," she said. "My one condition is that we buy a truck, and everywhere you go as president, you take me and the kids." The family now included Lara, seven, Nikki, almost five, and Darryl, three.

"I AM GOING to run for president of APA, and I need Penn's help," I told Judy Rodin, who was back at the University of Pennsylvania as president of the whole place. After a lightning ascent from department

chair to dean to provost at Yale, she was not chosen as Yale's president, and Penn had the good fortune to steal her back.

"I intend to take it seriously, and I would like you to give me a five-year paid leave from Penn. One year to run, 1996, and if elected, three years to serve, 1997–1999, and one year to recover and retool as a scientist."

"OK," she told me, "I will grant that in exchange for the copyrights on your *Learned Optimism* intellectual property. Penn will license these out to schools and corporations, and that will cover the cost of your leave."

As I left, Judy said, "In the meantime, keep the seat warm for me."

"I AM THINKING about running for president," I told Janet Matthews, a member of the APA board of directors. She kept me abreast of the latest detective page-turners and was well disposed toward me.

"Impossible! The candidates line up years in advance, and the order of succession is already designated. Dick Suinn from Colorado has been chosen for next year."

"Who chose Dick? Isn't this the only office for which all members of APA can vote?" I asked naively.

"The machine chose Dick, and it has run APA ever since taking it over from the scientists fifteen years ago." Janet explained that this machine was a coalition of the leaders of the state associations, the activist practitioners from the council of representatives, and, most importantly, the Council for the Advancement of Private Practice and Sciences (CAPPS). The nominees were handpicked and had served the practice coalition for a long time. This had been true every year for the last fifteen, and so only a tiny fraction of the membership even bothered to vote.

"At any rate," she concluded, "Dick is next, then Stan Moldawsky, the head of CAPPS, then Ron Levant, the next head of CAPPS."

I was appalled. How did sitting on committees in Washington for a decade and networking with the other committees qualify a person to lead all of American psychology? I determined to defy this smug, self-appointed group and win.

I would give myself no excuse for losing. The candidates campaigned, and so did I—not with buttons ("Win with Suinn") or

brochures but with a speech. The main way to meet the therapists was to attend their state conventions, so starting in early 1996, I went to those in New York, California, Florida, Texas, New Jersey, Michigan, and Georgia. I had one edge: what my opposition derided as "name recognition," as if recognition were not earned but somehow a product of Madison Avenue repetition, like "Alka-Seltzer." So, unlike the other hopefuls, I was invited to give a standing-room-only keynote presentation in each of these states. My speech had a theme: that psychotherapy needed better evidence of its effectiveness, evidence of the sort *Consumer Reports* had begun to gather, and that science—as the ally of practice—could provide it. I got standing ovations.

I ventured into the lion's den. In the mid-1970s, a pugnacious no-nonsense psychotherapist named Rogers Wright had led his "dirty dozen," as they proudly called themselves, into a head-on collision with the science wing over who would run APA. The practitioners organized, a tactic that science regarded as undignified and never bothered to do, and Rogers demanded proportional representation in government. Science was blindsided, and by 1980 the practitioners had won and science took a resentful backseat to practice. Rogers was the founding president and chief organizer of what became CAPPS.

Rogers and I met at a deli in rural California and were both surprised and delighted by what we found. Rogers found a scientist sympathetic to practice, and I found a street fighter who wanted to promote independent practice by bolstering it with good science. Rogers felt that his successors had gone too far in reflexively fighting rather than exploiting science, and to my shock he agreed to campaign for me.

As our family drove through Yellowstone Park in late spring of 1996, I went to a pay phone and found out that I had won the election with almost 10,000 votes, three times as many as my nearest opponent. Conceding, Dick Suinn, not ungraciously, labeled me a "force of nature."

Yet, of course, the work was only beginning. A few weeks later I had the lightning bolt conversation with my five-year-old daughter, Nikki, that opens this book, and I made up my mind to use my new post to lead the charge for positive psychology. The opposition was fierce from the start, but like my daughter, I was resolute.

Chapter Nineteen

Inventing Positive Psychology (1998–2001)

"**K**OOL, KOOL, SUPERKOOL, alles SuperKool." The anthem blasted over and over out of the loudspeakers at a German-speaking resort in the Yucatan. It was March 1997, and Mandy had coaxed me into taking a break from my exhausting and sometimes disheartening work as president-elect of the American Psychological Association (APA). I didn't want to get out of bed. Just lying here for the rest of the week seemed like the best way of living through this cut-rate "vacation." Mandy refused to let me just lie there. She knew that getting me moving would produce something better than catatonia.

"Let's drive down the road to Yal Ku, near Akumal," she insisted, pointing to a small blue spot on our tourist map. So the five of us piled into our rental car and motored into the enchanted little village of Akumal. Yal Ku, at its north end, was a "cenote," a lake, mostly underground, formed by the brackish confluence of the sea and the freshwater rivers. It was surrounded by a few very large houses, one owned by the Grateful Dead. Darryl, three, climbed up on my back, and we snorkeled through legions of the fattest, most colorful and playful reef fish I'd ever seen. (It turns out that the fish dine on the excrement that the residents of the big houses flush right into Yal Ku.) We resolved to find an excuse to come someday.

That day was not long in coming.

"I'VE RENTED the Grateful Dead house in the Yucatan, Mike," I told Mihaly Csikszentmihalyi[1] on the phone. "Can you and Isabella cancel your New Year's plans for 1998 and spend the first week with us, inventing positive psychology?"

I had gotten to know Mike well a year before in late January 1997 at the now defunct (eradicated by the tsunami that destroyed Fukushima in 2011) resort of Kona Village, on the Kona-Kailua coast of Hawaii's Big Island. Mike and Isabella happened to be staying there at the same time as the five of us, and Mike and I found ourselves walking and snorkeling together. What I might do as APA president was at the forefront of my mind, and the possibility of a "positive psychology" of the sort foreshadowed by my epiphany with Nikki was now more than just percolating. Mike worked on "flow," that high state of fascination in which time stops for you, you feel completely at home, and you are at one with the music. Flow had to be a centerpiece in any conception of the positive in life. Mike and I talked for hours about what such a "positive psychology" might entail. I asked him to help me create this new field, and he agreed. He was enthusiastic about its prospects.

"I'VE RENTED the Grateful Dead house, Ray," I told Ray and Sandy Fowler on the phone. "Can you spend the first week of the new year with the Csikszentmihalyis and my family inventing positive psychology?"

The nine of us (Mandy and I and our three kids, Mike and Isabella, and Ray and Sandy) awakened in our psychedelically painted bedrooms on January 1, 1998, and the adults spent the week spelling out the elements of a new field and how to found it.

The name. "Positive psychology" won out, not hands down but by default. It sounded too much like the armchair "positive thinking" of Reverend Norman Vincent Peale for a secular, science-based endeavor. "Positive" sounded too *Americanisch* to Mike's coffeehouse European ear. "Psychology" sounded too narrow for a field that might eventually supplement the dismal, remedial concerns of all modern social science. But we couldn't think of a better name.

The substance. We agreed here. The opposite concerns from those of clinical psychology would anchor this new field—achieving the

good life: health and sanity and those things humans choose to pursue when they are not suffering or oppressed.

The people. We were unanimous here as well. Young people were the fulcrum. The old scientists and the old practitioners were sclerotic, overinvested in their way of doing things and making their livings from studying and treating misery. We had to attract the brightest not-yet-tenured scientists to positive psychology, and they needed to have the social skills to become the future leaders of the profession.

The funding. Well, this was uncertain. Psychology relied almost exclusively on the federal government for support. But American politics and federal ideology were steeped in attending to what is wrong—disease—and the good life is not a disease. Hence positive psychology would not be eligible for tax dollars. We would have to work hard here but could explore several avenues. First, I would use my whole APA presidential allotment ($35,000) to hold a gathering of young people on this very spot in January 1999, exactly one year hence. Second, Don Clifton, owner of Gallup, had written to ask if he could back us. Don had written *Soar with Your Strengths*[2] and told me he'd been waiting his whole life for APA to get to work on the positive. I contacted him, and we made concrete plans. Third, the new multi-billion-dollar John Templeton Foundation would soon hold an event in my honor, and I decided to pitch positive psychology to Sir John.

And then I mentioned a bizarre encounter I'd had the previous week with a foundation that would not even tell me its name.

"GO SEE HIM, *definitely*," said Judy Rodin. She was my president now, and I asked her at a cocktail party if she had ever heard of a "PT" who sent mysterious emails. I had gotten one inviting me to come up to Manhattan and chat with him—without explaining why.

So Mari Fitzduff (who was also invited) and I found our way to a grim lower-Manhattan building with no sign on the door. Mari was a Northern Ireland peacemaker and constitution writer who worked with Judy Rodin and me on Judy's commission on civility.

We entered a small, windowless room in which PT and another man sat at a round table, a speaker phone between them. I now

recognized the other person, Joel Fleishman, an amiable law professor from Duke, who worked quietly with us on civility. They introduced themselves but the person at the other end of the speakerphone did not.

"We represent an anonymous foundation," PT began. "We pick winners and you win. We don't micromanage. But you must not reveal our identity" (which they had even not told us anyway).

"Now what would you like to do?" PT continued.

They funded a gathering of fifty scholars of genocide. We convened in Derry, Northern Ireland, because though a genocide had not occurred there, one well might have. Dan Chirot, valedictorian from my Albany Academy days, now a distinguished professor of politics and sociology at the University of Washington, orchestrated the meeting, and we had a terrific week pinning down conditions that prevent genocide.[3]

The story of the anonymous foundation is not over, but before it continues, I must tell you about another foundation that reached out to me.

"CALL THEM UP and tell them you are not for rent," Mandy insisted. I'd received a letter on double-thick stationery from John Templeton Jr., president of the John Templeton Foundation. He proposed that they hold an event in my honor, a Festschrift. I had never heard of this foundation, but Mandy did due diligence. She told me that it was rich—but had a religious agenda.

Following Mandy's instructions to the letter, I told the Templeton executive who answered the phone, "I'm not for rent."

"We do indeed have an agenda," said Arthur Schwartz, as the executive staff appeared in our living room twenty-four hours later. Arthur was their spokesman. "Our agenda is to support research at the border of religion and science."

"But I don't work on religion," I said. "I am a scientist, and I have no axe to grind about theology."

"We understand that, Marty," said Arthur, making a Venn diagram by circling the thumb and forefinger of each hand and overlapping the circles. "You are carving out a positive psychology agenda that

includes good character and positive institutions. Your agenda overlaps with ours in those two spaces. We want to fund you at the overlap, and we will *never* try to co-opt you into our religious agenda."

The John Templeton Foundation has been a major funder of positive psychology for almost two decades, and its representatives have kept their word. I think of them as the Eagle Scouts of philanthropy.

SIR JOHN MARKS TEMPLETON was on his feet. He was in his late eighties, short, balding, and wiry, with an impish smile, and he was leading the applause. It was February 1998, the end of the second day of the Festschrift. It had been an exhilarating event. More than twenty of my colleagues and students delivered speeches: Steve Maier, Chris Peterson, and Barry Schwartz set the tone by tracing my research path from helplessness to hope. Lyn Abramson and Lauren Alloy described how optimism might create invulnerability to depression. Rick Snyder claimed that hope buffered even profound grief over the death of a loved one. Rob DeRubeis reminded us that the negative is integral to the positive. Dave Myers, from the appropriately named Hope College, discussed hope as the cornerstone of happiness, and I concluded with my vision of a new positive psychology.[4]

Sir John took me aside. "I want opinion-makers. Opinion-makers are the key to progress anywhere, and academia is no exception. I value hope, optimism, gratitude, loving-kindness, and forgiveness. My book, *The Worldwide Laws of Life*,[5] is about these universal values. I want science to take these seriously. I want solid empirical science on these topics, and there is no such science now. I want the opinion-makers to create this science. You and I likely differ about religion, but we share these values."

"Science is value-free, Sir John," I cautioned.

"Science will follow the money," Sir John asserted, beaming confidently. "Now send me a proposal so I can help make positive psychology a reality."

"THAT WAS A great meeting you held in Derry, Marty." The voice on the car phone was that of the treasurer of the anonymous foundation. It was a glowing early-autumn afternoon in 1998, and I was

Sir John Marks Templeton told me, "I want opinion-makers. Opinion-makers are the key to progress anywhere, and academia is no exception. I value hope, optimism, gratitude, loving-kindness, and forgiveness. . . . I want science to take these seriously. I want solid empirical science on these topics, and there is no such science now. I want the opinion-makers to create this science. You and I likely differ about religion, but we share these values." He became a river to the new field of positive psychology. Courtesy of the John Templeton Foundation.

driving with Mandy and the kids through Amish country near Lancaster, Pennsylvania. My APA presidential convention the month before had gone swimmingly. I woke up the morning of my speech—it was my fifty-fifth birthday—at the San Francisco convention to the juddering of a small earthquake. In my speech, I announced positive psychology as my central theme and I told the Nikki story. Therapists and researchers alike greeted my presentation warmly. Even the frosty leaders of the Council for the Advancement of Private Practice and Sciences seemed receptive. Jon Kellerman and Dan Goleman gave keynote addresses, and I swelled with gratitude as I gave a presidential

citation to Bob Nozick for a lifetime of philosophical work that might shape the future of psychology. Right after the convention, Mandy, Lara, Nikki, Darryl, and I flew up to Mike Csikszentmihalyi's ranch near the Bitterroot Mountains in Montana for a week of back and forth about the theory of positive psychology. Mike and I dissected the psychology of the present, dividing it into thoughts about the past-present, the present-present, and the future-present. That did not achieve immortality but we did grope our way toward defining the scope of positive psychology as encompassing positive experience, positive character, and positive institutions.

"WHAT DO YOU want to do next?" the voice on my car phone asked. I was taken aback. I had assumed the Derry meeting had ended our work together.

"Next?" I ventured.

"Yes," he replied, "what are you thinking about now?"

I explained a bit about a positive psychology, composed of positive experience, positive character, and positive institutions, but the line broke up repeatedly, and the conversation ended with him saying, "Why don't you come up to Manhattan and tell us about it?"

This time there was a sign on the door: Atlantic Philanthropies. Chuck Feeney, founder of the Duty-Free Shops in every international airport, had given away his entire fortune, some $5 billion, to this foundation to advance opportunity and lasting change for vulnerable people. He had kept only $10 million for himself.

Again, I walked into a room containing PT, Joel Fleishman, and a speaker phone, but the room was now airy, and its huge windows overlooked the East River.

"Now, what is this positive psychology?" Joel asked.

I began my pitch, but after about ten minutes, PT interrupted. "Could you send us two pages about this?" he asked, and as he ushered me out the door, he added, "And don't forget to send a budget."

One month later a check for $1.4 million appeared.

FOR NEW YEAR'S DAY 1999 in Akumal, we rented all the houses around Yal Ku. Mihaly Csikszentmihalyi, Ray Fowler, Don Clifton,

and I hosted six days of conversation among eighteen of the brightest twenty-five to forty-year-olds who worked in or near the field of positive psychology. Here is how it came about.

In January 1998, right after our meeting in the Grateful Dead house, Ray, Mike, and I wrote fifty of the leaders of world social science and asked each for one nominee: "ideal young person: ages 25–40, assistant to young associate professor at a good university, well published and with grant money in a field related to positive psychology; articulate, creative, ambitious, with academic leadership qualities (future department chairs)." We suggested that the single best student they had ever had or their current best young colleague would be perfect.

Forty-five nominations, along with much spontaneous, enthusiastic support for the creation of the field of positive psychology, came from the nominators. We selected, from a truly luminescent group, eighteen people and invited them to attend "a gathering of young, rising academics . . . in Mexico to brainstorm about the major intellectual issues in this field and perhaps to become the nucleus of its future."

All eighteen accepted, and each morning they gave lively presentations in the *palapa*. Each afternoon we walked and snorkeled together. Akumal-1 was an unqualified success. A common evaluation was "the best intellectual experience of my career." All of them said they would return for Akumal-2 in January 2000.

The Akumal eighteen started a listserv, which is still roaring along eighteen years later. They generated an annotated eighty-page bibliography of the field as it stood in 1999 and wrote a long mission statement defining positive psychology as the scientific study of optimal human functioning with the central aim of discovering and promoting the factors that cause individuals and communities to thrive.

"I HAVE A condo on Grand Cayman," Don Clifton told me on the phone. "Please take it for a week and invite the best people in the world to steer positive psychology. Also ask them to plan for an inaugural summit—guest speakers from around the world—in my hometown of Lincoln, Nebraska. This will be the public kickoff for the new field. I'll host it, and Gallup will pay for it."

In the huge hot tub outside Don's condo, the cast of characters soaked.

Don Clifton and I had the least head hair. Unlike Don, I spoke often. Next to Don (I do not have a photo and I am painting this through the fog of memory) was Kathleen Hall Jamieson, founding director of Penn's Annenberg Public Policy Center. Her issue at the moment was increasing civility. The US Congress, in her opinion, was shattering and had lost the capacity to pass constructive legislation; the two sides of the aisle were no longer civil to each other, and downright hate and cycles of revenge were the order of the day. She hoped that positive psychology might come to the rescue.

Dan Robinson sat next to Kathleen. A hybrid philosopher-psychologist from Georgetown, he would not be driven off the bedrock of Aristotle. Anything that positive psychology did that could not be found in Aristotle was suspect.

George Vaillant was on Dan's right. George's view of defenses was changing before our eyes. In his classic work on the Harvard men, he consistently found that those who coped with problems using humor, altruism, anticipation, suppression, and acceptance did best in life. He called these "mature defenses," but as the meeting went on, he began to call them "strengths of character," and these traits lost the tinge of coping against the negative forces of the psyche and transmogrified into good character.

Ed Diener, well over six feet and in fine physical shape, was new to my personal acquaintance. Unlike any of the rest of us, Ed had been working explicitly (and courageously) on happiness. In fifteen years he had moved the empirical study of happiness—he called it "subjective well-being"—from academic laughingstock to respectable psychometric endeavor, and as an emblem of his success, he was now editor in chief of the toughest of all the social journals, *The Journal of Personality and Social Psychology*. He was the methodologist's methodologist. No pushover, he had kept his journal's rejection rate at over 90 percent. He didn't care if Aristotle had said it or not, but it had to be impeccably measured.

Mike Csikszentmihalyi was the same size as Ed, and we could still see evidence of the rock-climbing athlete he had been as a youngster.

The flow that Mike experienced clambering up mountains and ascending sheer cliffs dominated his theorizing, and he insisted that the experience of flow was central to well-being. But was flow, which is characterized by the absence of any thoughts or feelings, part of *subjective* well-being? He told us that when he asked people what they were thinking or feeling in flow, they usually said, "Nothing." Could it be, he mused, that the full attention that flow demands parasitizes all our cognitive and emotional resources and so renders us mindless?

Completing the circle and on my right was my own intellectual hero, Robert Nozick. Bob was now, with his Harvard colleague John Rawls, arguably the leading philosopher in the world. He was fighting off the intestinal cancer that took his life four years later. I worried about inviting him to Cayman for fear that his laser-like style would cut and slash and overwhelm and paralyze our group of slower psychologists. My fear was groundless. Bob was thoroughly constructive—except about Aristotle—and he became the epicenter of the group.

There was only one young person in the hot tub, Derek Isaacowitz, a newly minted PhD of mine, an assistant professor at Brandeis, and our recording secretary. Except for Derek, no one was under fifty, and conscious of this, we all endorsed the young psychologists from Akumal as the heirs to the big tent.

What would positive psychology's subject matter be? We liked the idea of "fulfillment." Surely that would include happiness and its cousins. Ed Diener did not need to convince us of this. Happiness—subjective well-being—is measurable and may even be buildable. But the existence of flow convinced us that positive psychology could not be limited just to the subjective. Flow was a positive fulfillment as well, but we were now using behavioral as well as subjective criteria: "positive" denoted what free people who are not suffering choose. Human beings pursue both the experience of positive emotion and the experience of flow.

So *positive experience* became one "fulfillment" of positive psychology. Was that it? Could we stop with happiness and flow and go home?

"No," Kathleen argued. "Not by a longshot. Sociology is all about the negative institutions, the forces that impede well-being: crime, poverty, racism and the like. How about the positive institutions that allow for well-being? Democracy, free press, strong families, and volunteering, for instance."

We were convinced, and the study of *civic fulfillment* became a pillar of positive psychology.

Bob Nozick now made the case for another pillar, *positive traits*, the individual qualities that enable positive experience.

"Psychiatry," he said, "is the study of insanity, the negative traits that cripple life. Depression, schizophrenia, drug addiction, and the like. What about sanity? What about the traits that are the springboards of positive experience? Creativity, integrity, humor, and courage, for example."

Bob called these traits the *mansions* of life. We spent a long time debating this. How about the state/trait dispute, an ongoing debate in psychology? Are there really enduring personality traits or only temporarily held states of mind? Ed Diener led the way here. He convinced us that there are indeed traits, dispositions to think and behave that transcend time and situation, and that only poor measurement supported "situationism," the argument that all of what drives behavior is in the environment and not in individual character. Integrity, humor, social intelligence, and courage are as real and knowable as schizophrenia, depression, and alcoholism.

What about the arbitrariness of "good" in good character? Surely this changes from culture to culture, epoch to epoch, floating on whatever religion or politics runs the show at the time. We doubted such sweeping relativism and thought the universality of goodness was an empirical issue whose testing we should sponsor.

I took away from Grand Cayman that positive psychology would have three pillars: positive experience, positive traits, and positive institutions. Its task would be to study and to build these pillars.

Our Cayman work was done.

"SHE IS THE *real thing*," whispered Paul Baltes, now director of the Max Planck Institute for Human Development in Berlin. He was

Barbara Fredrickson revealed at the first Gallup summit her "broaden and build" theory: positive emotion broadens the cognitive and behavioral repertoire, and positive emotion builds new strengths. Photo courtesy of the International Positive Psychology Association.

referring to Barbara Fredrickson, who was speaking to about sixty of us at the Gallup Corporation headquarters in Lincoln, Nebraska. It was September 1999, and this was the first international summit of positive psychology, the kickoff Don Clifton had promised. There was an atmosphere of high excitement, as if the audience was glimpsing a new world in every presentation. Barb, a new assistant professor at Michigan, was a statuesque brunette, slow and careful with every word. She was a commanding intellectual presence, and we were on the edge of our seats.

"Evolution has selected negative emotion for fight and flight. Why would evolution have bothered with positive emotion? Why do we have positive feelings?" she mused. She now revealed for the first time her "broaden and build" theory: positive emotion broadens the cognitive and behavioral repertoire and builds new strengths. She had tested the theory and presented evidence for it, such as showing that inducing positive emotion in the laboratory broadened people to holistic, rather than punctate, cognitive processing. Happy people see the wholes more readily than the parts.

"Is she married?" Paul whispered. Margaret, his wife and academic partner of thirty years, had recently died of cancer, and though bereaved, Paul found intellectual power the sexiest of feminine charms.

"She is, unfortunately," I informed Paul as I thought about eros and the hidden, dirty secret of how strongly it powers education, the progress of science, and the life of the mind.

"The force that through the green fuse drives the flower drives my green age," I added, but Paul, who knew Rainer Maria Rilke but not Dylan Thomas, frowned and looked puzzled.

I also met Robert Biswas-Diener. Robert, goateed and handsome, was in his early twenties, the oldest of Ed Diener's five children. Robert would soon become the Indiana Jones of positive psychology. I asked him perfunctorily how he was enjoying the summit, and his answer threw me for a loop.

"I am so proud of my father. I love him so much," He responded. Ed had just given a rousing talk about the measurement of happiness and his uphill struggle over the last two decades to put positive emotion on the academic map. No possible response to his struggle would please Ed more than Robert's, and I have never told Ed what Robert said. I do hope Ed reads this chapter.

SO POSITIVE PSYCHOLOGY was launched by the end of 1999. At a personal level, it began with an epiphany in my garden with Nikki, a vision of what psychology might become. At an institutional level, Ray Fowler, Mike Csikszentmihalyi, and I plotted out a trajectory for the development of the new field, a trajectory that became a reality over the next decade. The Templeton Foundation and Atlantic Philanthropies provided ample, generous funding just at the right time, and most importantly a large group of senior and junior scientists spelled out its mission, and we spread a big tent to welcome scientists and practitioners in.

Chapter Twenty

Good Character
(2000–2004)

VIRTUE WAS A leitmotif of nineteenth-century moral thought, and the psychology of that era cared deeply about virtue. Abraham Lincoln's first inaugural address appealed to the "better angels of our nature" in the vain hope that they would turn Americans away from the looming Civil War. The mental hospitals of the day used "moral therapy" to try to treat the insane. This was not in vain, and cures were indeed reported. But the better-angels morality had a dark side called "vice," and just as it explained good behavior as virtue, it commonly explained bad behavior as vice—bad character. Thinking about virtue and vice was galvanized on May 4, 1886, in Haymarket Square, Chicago.[1] There was a violent confrontation between the laborers of the McCormick factory (mostly immigrants) and the police, seen by labor as the brutal enforcers of management. It turned into a riot, and a bomb exploded, killing seven policemen. The common explanation for the bombing (whose perpetrators were never caught) both in the press and on the tongues of laymen was vice: the immigrants were evil, cruel, brutal, and wanton; they were anarchists. But it did not escape the notice of some of the press and much of the liberal clergy that the conditions of life for these laborers were abysmal: overcrowded, filthy housing, illiteracy, starvation wages, and twelve-hour workdays, six days a week.

Perhaps rather than bad character, the appalling environment that these immigrants suffered had caused their violence. Social science was conceived around this notion: its scientific agenda was to show that perpetrators were not bad people and were not responsible for their apparently "immoral" behavior. Rather the awful conditions they endured drove them to it. So if a toxic environment caused crime and brutality, an enlightened science and politics could eliminate crime merely by improving the environment. If ignorance caused prejudice, universal education would end prejudice. If poverty was not just defined as a lack of money but caused by it, welfare—subsidizing the poor—would end poverty. This was a noble vision indeed, and carrying it out required a change in thinking about human nature. Nurture was doing the dirty work, and we had to dispense altogether with vice and bad character as explanations. The eagerness with which post-Victorians lapped up Karl Marx, Sigmund Freud, and even Charles Darwin stemmed from this vision: Marx blamed labor violence on alienation from work. Freud blamed neurosis on unresolved childhood conflicts. Darwin blamed strife on the primordial struggle to survive. The violent laborers, the unbearable neurotics, the bullies, and a whole host of malefactors were not themselves at fault. Blame lay with how they were nurtured. But along with the bathwater of blaming victims, free will, responsibility, and even virtue also got poured down the drain.

But virtue stayed alive in one corner of social science, psychology—at least until Gordon Allport, from his chair at Harvard, proscribed all reference to character. Virtue—good character—was annoyingly Victorian, distinctly Protestant, and value laden. Psychology, in Allport's view, was a science that described but did not prescribe, and so endorsing a value or a person who displayed good character was not the role of social science. "Personality," a value-free descriptor, replaced "character."[2]

Big mistake. Positive psychology, as I see it, requires character. This field is the study of positive experience, positive institutions, and positive traits. First, why is "trait" indispensable? I am convinced that human beings have dispositions to behave consistently over time and across situations—not 100 percent consistently, of course, but enough

above zero to make calling someone smart or loving or mean or weak sensible—and it is likely a universal across cultures, and all languages likely have words for traits. So traits are undeniable. Second, why "positive"? This word formally means "above indifference" or chosen in preference to nothing, and there are many such preferred traits. Perhaps they vary from culture to culture, but most politics, religions, and cultures that I know of endorse kindness, wisdom, integrity, and courage. Importantly, this does not mean that positive psychology as a science prescribes good character; rather it describes, studies, and asks how to build what is prescribed within the culture. Positive psychology does not do the prescribing; the values of the culture or the individual do that. Positive psychology is an exercise not in changing values but in helping cultures and individuals better achieve what they already value.

Psychiatry-as-usual already had its extensive catalogue of negative traits: the *Diagnostic and Statistical Manual* (*DSM*). The *DSM* catalogued the insanities: schizophrenia, psychopathy, panic disorder, autism, and the like. It listed more than three hundred of them in fact, along with their gender ratios, heritability, course, prognoses, and diagnostic criteria.

"How about a manual of the sanities?" I asked Neal Mayerson. Neal had written to ask if he could fund positive psychology. His parents, Manuel and Rhoda Mayerson, had made their fortune in Cincinnati and turned it to good works under Neal's direction. I was beginning to detect a new pattern of fund-raising after my history of begging the government for research money for disorders for the last forty years. People like Sir John and Dr. Jack Templeton, Chuck Feeney, Don Clifton, and the Mayersons were now giving private, self-made fortunes away to discover and build what is good in life, and the donors were seeking me out, not the other way around. One person, Jim Hovey, even spontaneously wrote me a large check right after a speech I gave at the Union League in Philadelphia. "Do good stuff," Jim said laconically.

Neal asked me for advice about *what* to fund within positive psychology. Whatever we funded must not gather dust in some library, Neal insisted. So he and I convened a two-day meeting of possible

awardees, but none of them hit the bull's-eye for Neal. He wanted a project that would do good but also result in a product that might generate further income for his foundation to then give away. Mindful of the fortune that *DSM* had made for the American Psychiatric Association, a publication that floats much of Big Pharma and a bit of psychotherapy, I suggested a manual of good character—a manual of *sanity.*

"I'll give you a million dollars to produce an un-*DSM* along with a questionnaire to measure character strengths," Neal offered.

"I don't think I can do it, Neal, but I know who can."

IT WAS CHRIS PETERSON's fiftieth birthday, but I was not phoning him ceremonially.

"What are you doing with the rest of your life?" I came right out and asked.

Long silence.

"I'd like you to take a three-year sabbatical from the University of Michigan and come to Penn," I said. Chris was head of Michigan's clinical program, among the top three graduate clinical psychology programs (Yale and UCLA are the other two, with Penn ranking next). He was a legend at Michigan for being enormously generous with his time and knowledge, and everyone loved him. He also had the qualities to make the Mayerson project work: high psychometric expertise, broad scholarship, a deep knowledge of personality and abnormal psychology, stamina, a strong friendship with me, patience, and an overflow of good humor.

"I want you to take charge of writing a *DSM* of good character and virtue, and then I want you to create a questionnaire to measure good character," I said.

Longer silence.

"Yes," said Chris.

CHRIS DROVE HIS aging jalopy from Ann Arbor to Philadelphia (he was afraid of flying) in the fall of 2000 to begin our new collaboration. He listened to talk radio all the way and told me all about Rush Limbaugh. Totaling up the number of hours we spent together and

multiplying by the harmony of each hour, Chris became the longest-running and closest colleague I have ever had.

Our work was pretty one-sided. Chris read and read and thought and thought: early Christian theology, Karl Marx, Buddhist chants, Benjamin Franklin, Islamic virtues. Twice a week over lunch he told me about strengths and virtues across time and space. He told me about the Lakota virtue of generosity. He told me about the Budo virtue, *Rei*, courtesy and etiquette. He told me about Hufflepuff: loyalty and hard work. He told me about the Klingon virtue: to avenge insults against the family for seven generations. We were searching for universals, strengths endorsed by every religion, politics, and culture. It turned out that there was a lot of agreement across history and culture. I listened and reacted, mostly nodding my head approvingly.

We developed the criteria for including a strength in our manual, among them the following:

1. A strength is valued in its own right, not as a means to an end (i.e., intelligence, like perfect pitch, is not a strength valued in its own right; rather it is valued as a means to success).
2. There are paragons and prodigies of the strength and also idiots, people egregiously devoid of the strength.
3. A strength is endorsed universally (or at least ubiquitously).
4. A strength contributes to fulfillment in life.

Chris and I spent hundreds of hours, and I ate hundreds of grilled Reubens, arguing over which candidates fit these criteria. Kindness fit. Wisdom fit. Vitality fit. Social intelligence fit. Tolerance did not, because it was not (universally) valued in Salt Lake City or Mecca. Obedience? The Boy Scouts and Merlin liked it, but the feminist movement did not. Chastity? The Victorians espoused it, but the commune movement rejected it. How about humor? That one was close. Everyone thinks he or she has a sense of humor (universality), and Chris was in fact a remarkable sotto voce stand-up comic. But I was not sure humor was important enough to make the list. Chris wore me down, arguing that humor was a transcendent strength that amplified all the others. We eventually narrowed the list down to

twenty-four strengths and then grouped them, somewhat arbitrarily, under six virtues: wisdom, courage, humanity, justice, temperance, and transcendence.

With the help of more than a dozen experts, one for each strength, we drafted a humungous document (when published[3] it weighed in at about five pounds). After an introduction in which we justified the need for a manual of sanity, we reviewed the history of virtue and the attempts at previous classifications. We then organized the rest of the book around the twenty-four strengths, one chapter for each. Each chapter had a parallel structure, and the chapter on forgiveness and mercy is an example. It opened with a profile of a paragon, Kim Phuc, the naked little girl napalmed by an American plane during the Vietnam War, immortalized in the horrific iconic photograph. She publicly and movingly forgave the pilot when she met him years later. We then defined forgiveness and discussed the philosophical and religious stances on it, as well as contemporary views. We next reviewed the measures of forgiveness (there were two well-honed tests), then the correlates and consequences (e.g., forgiving people have less negative emotion), what was known about how forgiveness develops across the life span (e.g., young children are unforgiving), the factors that inhibit or enable forgiveness (e.g., disagreeable and highly neurotic people are unforgiving), and the gender, national, and cross-cultural factors. Finally we reviewed the interventions that build forgiveness and ended with what was *not* known about forgiveness.

This was merely half of what Chris accomplished in his three-year stint at Penn studying virtue. The other half was empirical. Chris created questionnaires, and he was a statistician. So using these skills he created the Values-in-Action (VIA) Signature Strengths Test.[4] The VIA includes ten items for each of the twenty-four strengths and asks you to rate how closely each item describes you. This results in a rank ordering of your strengths and tells you your five greatest ones. In the fifteen years since Chris created it, more than 3 million people have taken the test in English, and many other people have taken it in German, Chinese, Japanese, and Spanish. In addition to providing individual self-insight, the test is widely used in business, schools, and therapy.

The field of strengths and virtues blossomed empirically. For example, which strengths go along with which careers? Take a look at the figure below, which shows a statistical graph (based on 83,000 people). First, when two strengths are close together, if you have one, you likely have the other. So if you have gratitude, you likely have love and kindness. But if two strengths are far apart, if you have one, you will not likely have the other: kind people are not creative or brave; prudent people have honesty and modesty, but they do not have much zest and hope.

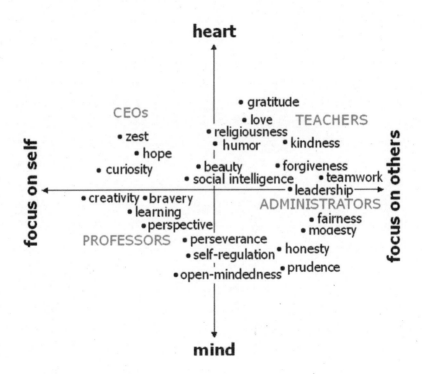

Second, strengths relate to profession. Teachers have kindness, forgiveness, gratitude, and love, but professors lack those strengths. Professors have creativity, bravery, and love of learning, which teachers have in short supply. Administrators are fair, honest, and modest but lack zest, hope, and curiosity. CEOs have these latter strengths but lack fairness, honesty, and modesty. Do not, however, take this figure as career advice. This tells you the strength profile of people

in a profession in general. It does not tell you the strengths of the best practitioners, and the best teachers, for example, have humor and zest, not just love and gratitude.

I cannot give you a citation for this tidbit, however, because Chris told it to me shortly before his sudden death in 2012. With Chris's death, I lost my best and closest colleague, and the field of strength and virtue became bereft.

Flourishing

Chapter Twenty-One

Sixty (2002)

AUGUST 12, 2002.

And so it was my turn to speak at my sixtieth birthday party. Tossing sleepless the night before, I reviewed my life. An anxious child of troubled parents in a world at war. A brainy misfit in a school for rich kids. A foot soldier in the skirmishes with behaviorism. A captain in the battle to steer psychology away from darkness and toward light, drawn into the future rather than driven by the past.

I had built a greenhouse, and we held my sixtieth birthday party in it. The design was imperfect because I forgot a roof opener. So the temperature soared to 140 degrees, and I needed three air-conditioning units in the room to hold the event.

The form of the birthday party was a symposium given by the experts, some of them my friends, on the seventh decade of life. George Vaillant was the master of ceremonies. He was in his third decade of studying success and failure in life among the Harvard men, who themselves were past their sixties. George urged me to marshal my mature defenses, such as I had, to make my way through this tricky decade. Burly Bob Olcott, recently retired from the Albany Academy, reminded us of my (lack of) swimming prowess as displayed at the waterfront of the Stratton Mountain Boy Scout camp, and he seemed to have the benign illusion that I was a decent football lineman. (I was an awful lineman, a physical coward, and I quit as soon as I decently

could.) Ed Diener and Chris Peterson, the youngsters in this crowd, took a comic romp through my curriculum vitae.

Paul Rozin, my brother in arms during thirty years of department battles at Penn, halfway into his own seventh decade, thought of this decade as a sport in the Special Olympics: how much you can still do with what you have left. Lara, twelve, Nikki, ten, and even Darryl, eight, gave short speeches.

"I had thought of my life as an autobiography," I said when my turn came. "An uphill struggle in which I pitted my strengths and skills against a world reluctant to yield up its rewards to me but all too ready to sting and bite.

"What I learned today, from Bob Olcott and Kathleen Hall Jamieson and George Vaillant and Ed Diener and Ray Fowler and Barry Schwartz and Mike Csikszentmihalyi and Lester Luborsky and Chris Peterson—but mostly from Mandy—is that my life is not an autobiography but a biography. The story of how I have been helped through the world by friendship, colleagueship, generosity, and love."

AS THE FIELD of positive psychology burgeoned, I noticed that my life was better—much better. I was happier and getting into better step with the change in psychology itself, and the synchrony between my life and this change is indeed the underlying theme of this book.

But I must untangle why my life was better at age sixty.

The theory of happiness I had at age sixty was simplistic: good externalities plus good internalities equals happiness. I looked at the three great externalities of life: love, work, and play. Each of these was much better now in my own life. Mandy had created a home. The big house was no longer an empty cavern. It was filled with children and Old English sheepdogs (Barney and Rosie). The dogs were unfailingly cheerful, and Mandy was generally a cumulus cloud. We homeschooled our children, not out of ideology but because we were both teachers and our frequent trips did not conform to the school calendar. So we designed our curriculum around our travels and took the kids along. We took them to the Galapagos to learn biology and evolution, but our teaching was imperfect, as we saw when we met Lonesome George, an ancient tortoise who may have been the last of

his species. The conservators explained to us that they were looking desperately for a female for him.

"We're cooking up tortoise Viagra," they told us.

"What's Viagra?" Lara, Nikki, and Darryl asked in unison. Our children had no clue. We had taught them evolution without teaching them about sex. Oops. We took them with us on my many business trips—to Japan, Australia, England, Norway, Germany—and their education emerged not from sitting at a school desk but from reading, from visiting museums, from walking through cities, and from sharing meals with our many fascinating hosts. The kids' prevailing mood, since they were not yet teenagers, was mostly sunny.

The first externality in my life, love, was much better.

My work was much better—mostly because it was no longer *mine*. When Ray Fowler told me that his job as CEO of the American Psychological Association was to bring out the best in his presidents, I realized that my job as president was to bring out the best in my colleagues. This must be Erik Erikson's "generativity" stage, I realized, and I was relieved to have reached it. Stalinism died with Stalin, whereas positive psychology had from the outset many fathers and now many mothers. From the first, we decided to erect a big tent that would comfortably shelter and nurture many agendas: Mike Csikszentmihalyi's on flow, Chris Peterson's and Neal Mayerson's on virtue, Ed Diener's on subjective well-being, George Vaillant's on successful aging, Kathleen Hall Jamieson's on positive civic institutions, and, more recently, Barb Fredrickson's on positive emotion, Jon Haidt's on awe, Sonja Lyubomirsky's on interventions, and Laura King's on meaning. My own prior agenda, prevention of mental illness, was only a wee part, and my main job was to promote everyone else's agendas. I raised money but seemed to be best at asking the right questions at the right time in order to move their agendas forward scientifically. I could listen better, and I could swerve, or even jettison my own interests with advice and criticism.

My critics now called me "nimble," which I took as a compliment. And so the second externality, work, had never been better.

Easily overlooked is the third externality, play. I hosted a poker game once a week and joyfully lost more than $2,000 a year, a fair

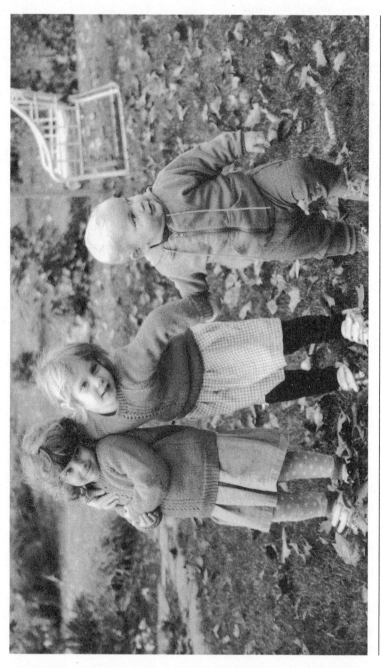

We took Lara, Nikki, and Darryl with us on my many business trips to Japan, Australia, China, England, Norway, Germany, Brazil, and Chile, and their education emerged not from sitting at a school desk but from reading, from visiting museums, from walking through cities, and from sharing meals with our many fascinating hosts. The kids' prevailing mood, since they were not yet teenagers, was mostly sunny. Photo courtesy of Mandy Seligman.

exchange for my only all-male locker-room companionship. But real play for me was bridge, and I had taken up serious tournament bridge again. The game had transformed since my youth. Many of the "bridge bums" who slept in their cars and hoped someone would pay them twenty-five dollars for an afternoon partnership were now multimillionaires. A new profession arose in the 1980s, and bridge genius translated into real money. I would never have guessed the profession: not law, not computer programming, and not poker. It was options trading. Something about the mind of the natural in bridge made him fast and accurate at spotting small discrepancies in stock prices. Bridge players now made up entire flourishing firms, and at least half of the top hundred players in America traded options during the day and competed as major bridge champions at night.

I was not a natural or a bridge genius, but I loved the game, and so to play serious bridge I hired my partners: Paul Soloway, Eric Rodwell, and Mark Lair, three of the all-time greats. They taught me the high-level game, and I was now comfortable sitting down against the best in the world. My Albany Academy class prophecy in 1960 was "Marty Seligman wins a world bridge championship by executing a Vienna Coup." It almost came true: Paul Soloway and I won the world internet championship in 1998 against a team of young, jet-lagged Russians. But there was no Vienna Coup (a rare bridge play comparable almost to a hole-in-one in golf). The next day, however, my son David joined the game, and sure enough, I executed a Vienna Coup.

So my externalities, love, work, and play, were better than they had ever been. In the long history of the words for "happiness" across many languages and cultures, such good externalities should make me a "happy" man, since the words until recently denoted good fortune or luck. But "happiness" in the last two centuries has taken on the internalities of how one feels and how one thinks: subjective well-being. Now you can't be happy unless you also feel good.

My internalities sucked.

They seemed to me about as bad as they had always been from late childhood on. I was still a depressive and a pessimist, the redeeming feature being that such firsthand knowledge helped me greatly in my work. I was not lighthearted and had little in the way of merriment. I

rarely felt joy. I often woke up at four a.m. and brooded. I was a catastrophizer, and when a setback occurred, the worst possible outcome drew my first thought like a magnet. Of course, I knew every trick in the book to counter depression, pessimism, and catastrophizing and to build positive emotion. Indeed, I invented some of them. These worked pretty well for me, but the voices—*You are a loser, you are a failure, you are doomed*—were still there.

So by internalities I was not a happy man.

But there is a redeeming possibility about my gloomy internalities: the interaction of my internals with my externals. My commerce with the world had changed for the better since I got involved in positive psychology. Thanks to Chris, I had now identified my signature strengths—among them creativity and leadership—and I now used them well, albeit far from perfectly, with my fellows. My creativity had two parts: contrarian originality, which had been with me for a long time, and an appreciation of my audience and my collaborators. This appreciation was newer. I knew a lot of psychology now, but more importantly I could connect the dots from one field to the next. I could see what projects might fly and which were quagmires. I could see who the right person for that special place in the jigsaw puzzle was and how to help her arrive there. My leadership style, learned from Ray Fowler, was to bring out the best in others and so to help them achieve their agendas.

Maybe internalities were not all they were cracked up to be. Maybe internalities are almost unchangeable. But by the criterion of good commerce with the world, I was a pretty happy man.

Positivity and
Its Critics (2001–2011)

POSITIVE PSYCHOLOGY EXPLODED in popularity after 2001. I was so accustomed to uphill battles that I was taken aback. Once the field became popular, however, a legion of critics sprang up, some with constructive ideas that advanced it, but more than a few with weak arguments or criticisms that attacked straw men. This chapter tells the story of some of the major advances between 2001 and 2011 and the main criticisms. I first present the progress made and then the criticisms, divided by strong and weak (or even baseless) criticisms, followed by my responses.

Progress

"This positive psychology is becoming quite the thing," said Sam Preston, my dean. Sam was a distinguished demographer and more adventurous than my previous deans. Sam and I were about to embark on an adventure that is still in progress.

"You should have a center, a Positive Psychology Center, Marty. Come see me next week," Sam said over drinks. A "center," in the narrow world of the University of Pennsylvania, sets one free from a "department." A center is interdisciplinary and can have its own grants, missions, and employees, but it cannot make tenure-track professorial

appointments; only departments can do that. Centers historically tend to do the cutting-edge, controversial scientific research, whereas departments tend to be highly conservative, rewarding their faculty for laying one brick safely upon another. Departments usually appoint new faculty who are *nachschleppers* rather than innovators. After years of losing battles over appointing such *nachschleppers*, Sam's get-out-of-jail-free proposal appealed to my entrepreneurial instincts. A center also reports to the dean rather than the department chair, and its "profits" (read "overheads") go to the dean.

"How will we swing it financially?" I asked Sam as we sat down in his spacious, Pennsylvania-memorabilia-lined office.

"I want you to create a new master's degree, Marty, a master of applied positive psychology. You can admit successful adults from the real world as graduate students and then teach them how to apply positive psychology to their lines of work. They can come to Penn in an executive education model: nine long weekends of classes a year, with visiting star professors doing most of the teaching, and a capstone thesis. The students will pay full tuition (around $50,000 in 2018 dollars), and the center will get 30 percent of the surplus, if any, to run itself. 'Surplus' starts at the break-even point of eleven students. And of course you can get your usual grants and contracts."

I ASKED JAMES PAWELSKI to direct the fledgling program. An assistant professor of philosophy and religion at Vanderbilt University, James had been commuting to Penn to audit my courses, and he was incorporating positive psychology into his own undergraduate teaching.

Happily he signed up as director of education, and we began in March 2005 to advertise for students to meet an April 30 deadline, hoping against hope for eleven applicants. We got more than one hundred, and thirty-five of them met Penn's very stiff Ivy League admission requirements. Thirty-four accepted our offer of admission. The Positive Psychology Center and the Master of Applied Positive Psychology[1] (MAPP) program of the University of Pennsylvania were launched.

IN MID-FIFTEENTH CENTURY Florence, Cosimo the Elder was the patron of a new humanism, a flourishing of the arts, learning, and science later known as the Renaissance. In Cosimo Medici's honor, the brand-new Positive Psychology Center held a three-year celebration, Medici 2. In the late spring of each year, the leading senior figures in positive psychology, along with a passel of junior fellows, would live together and meet daily for two months. I chose this season because my roses were blooming, and we would spend many of our hours together enjoying Alchemysts, Climbing Fourth of Julys, Abraham Darbys, and Trojan Victories, all ablaze with the promise of full summer.

Out of Medici 2 emerged some progress.

One big success: Ed Diener led a group working to create "national accounts of well-being." Could we measure how well a nation was doing? Gross domestic product (GDP), the usual contemporary national account, was increasingly out of sync with well-being. GDP measures the total goods and services bought and sold, but GDP fails to distinguish goods and services that promote well-being from those that diminish well-being.

Robert Kennedy in 1968 criticized GDP poignantly and accurately:

> Yet the gross national product does not allow for the health of our children, the quality of their education or the joy of their play. It does not include the beauty of our poetry or the strength of our marriages, the intelligence of our public debate or the integrity of our public officials.
>
> It measures neither our wit nor our courage, neither our wisdom nor our learning, neither our compassion nor our devotion to our country, it measures everything in short, except that which makes life worthwhile.

GDP includes what economists call "regrettables." With every suicide, divorce, or automobile accident, GDP goes up. The funeral expenses, the legal fees, the hospital costs, and the repair bills all add to GDP. The more tobacco sold, the higher the GDP. Moreover, all graphs of national income against life satisfaction yield rapidly

diminishing returns with more income once one is well above the safety net. This is true of national GDP and individual income, with roughly $100,000 per year in the United States being the inflection point at which increasing income brings markedly diminishing increases in happiness.

"It's the economy, stupid," is a stupid account of human flourishing. Ed Diener assumed that we wanted to measure flourishing and that GDP, though a good start historically, was now outmoded. He was after a set of well-being indicators that would complement economic indicators and so assist policymaking for governments and corporations that sought the flourishing of their citizens and employees. I called this goal the "new prosperity."

Ed's visionary initiative resulted first in a landmark paper, "Beyond Money: Toward an Economy of Well-being,"[2] which made this case compellingly. Ed was kind enough to put my name on the paper. Soon thereafter, a gaggle of world-class economists—Richard Layard, Amartya Sen, Ned Phelps, John Helliwell, Jeffrey Sachs, and Joseph Stiglitz—trained their sights on happiness, and once these government-advising economists got into the act, well-being found its way onto the political agenda. Nicolas Sarkozy, the prime minster of France, formed a commission to recommend new measures of national success, and David Cameron, the prime minister of the United Kingdom, announced that he would measure the well-being of UK citizens every three months and hold himself accountable for the success or failure of his policies by changes in well-being. The European Left angrily accused Sarkozy and Cameron of trying to distract people with the sop of "happiness" now that these governments were failing to grow their economies.

In addition to national accounts of well-being, a second bit of progress was the creation of an Authentic Happiness website (www .authentichappiness.org) that contained the major tests of well-being. In the process of creating the website, I broadened my theory of well-being. I had posited three basic elements: positive emotion, engagement, and meaning.[3] An "element" is what free, nonsuffering people choose to pursue for its own sake. But in teaching MAPP and thinking

about what questionnaires to put on the website, I now became convinced that there were five elements of well-being: PERMA.[4]

Positive emotion
Engagement
Relationships
Meaning
Accomplishment

I revised the theory after considering how commonly people pursue achievement doggedly for its own sake: even if it brings no happiness, no flow, no relationships, and no meaning.[5] In 2018 there are now two more claimants as elements: physical health and control. But I am not yet convinced, and five is a more parsimonious number than seven.

The Authentic Happiness website was originally in English, Chinese (both simple and complex characters), and Spanish, and over the years we added German, Japanese, and Korean. The site was widely used in all these languages, but we did not seem to have made it over the Great Internet Wall in China. Although positive psychology became very popular in that country, our website was almost invisible there. We continually added new surveys, refined old ones, and shared our data with researchers around the world. An average of 2,000 new visitors signed up daily, and as of this writing over 4.5 million people have registered from more than two hundred nations. It is a goldmine for researchers, and the findings about signature strengths in the last chapter come from analyzing this website's dataset. We also set up a listserv (friends-of-PP@lists.apa.org), and I invite you to join the still highly active discussions that occur 24/7.

Our new website was marvelous for interventions, both as a way of testing new ones and also as a futuristic way of delivering interventions on a massive scale. As the reader knows from my *Consumer Reports* tale, I spent a lot of effort on what psychotherapies and what drugs worked for what disorders. Testing these was very expensive and very time-consuming. Worse, the results were often inconclusive

THE HOPE CIRCUIT

because live clinical studies can afford only small and unrepresentative volunteer samples. A typical "well-done" efficacy study divides forty clinic volunteers randomly into two groups, with half given an active drug or psychotherapy and half given a plausible placebo. National Institute of Mental Health (NIMH) budgets even for such small studies can run into the low seven figures. Even the *Consumer Reports* survey, with a sample one hundred times this size, cost about this much to run.

The website seemed a much cheaper way of testing new positive interventions with large samples. Can individuals do simple exercises to raise their happiness, and might these exercises also lower depression?

Time magazine did a cover story on positive psychology in January 2005.[6] With Jeff Levy, a Philadelphia MD entrepreneur, we set up another website, Reflective Happiness, for the public to do these exercises. We gave them out free at first and hoped that, if they worked, people would pay a few dollars to subscribe for more exercises.

Reading *Time*, lots of people came and took a free exercise called "Three Blessings": every night for a week, you'd write down three things that went well that day and why they went well. At this point we had lots of evidence from random-assignment placebo-control studies that this exercise reliably lowered depression and raised life satisfaction for as long as six months. I wanted to know if this would work for people who were severely depressed, more depressed than the mildly depressed people who typically came to authentichappiness.org.

The results from the first month were startling. Fifty people fell into the severely depressed range when they registered. Their average depression score was 34, a score bad enough to indicate that these people were in pain: suffering a lot of sadness, crying a lot, very passive, feeling no zest and major loss of pleasure, and usually functioning very poorly, if at all, in work and at home. Thirty-four is close to extreme depression.

These fifty people did the exercise and came back to the website two weeks later to take their second depression test. Their depression scores on average got much better, to 17.2, which is right at the cusp of mild to moderate symptoms. Forty-seven of the fifty people (94

percent) decreased in depression. Their happiness scores, which averaged 53.4 (roughly in the bottom 10 percent) to begin with, zoomed up to 69.8 on average at posttest. This elevated them to the fortieth percentile on happiness, and forty-six of the fifty people (92 percent) increased in happiness.

These results were comparable, perhaps superior, to the effects of medication and psychotherapy in severe depression. My colleague, Robert DeRubeis, a leading outcome researcher in depression, shared some of his typical findings with me for rough-and-ready comparison: over four weeks, combined cognitive therapy and medication decreased depressive symptoms from 34.1 to 19.6 (n = 134) versus a placebo, which went from 34.8 to 24.4 (n = 49).

I was cautious about these dramatic results. I did not run out and shout that web exercises could cure severe depression, since our method had plenty of flaws: no random assignment, no placebo control, no diagnosis of major depression, and no long follow-up. And of course, unlike the usual severely depressed person arriving at therapy, these people came with high *Time*-induced hopes.

Even with such promising initial findings, use of the website dropped, and not enough paying subscriptions came in to keep the business afloat for more than one year. We failed to raise additional funding. Reflective Happiness flopped as a business, and I never published these results, but I left this arena impressed by the potential of web therapy for depression. Two of my graduate students, Acacia Parks and Stephen Schueller, took up the cause, but its long-term future was hard to predict. There are not enough face-to-face therapists to cope with the sheer amount of depression in our society, so it should be viable. It was dirt cheap and could be mass-distributed, and in my heart of hearts I believed it was almost as effective as psychotherapy and medication. So why would web therapy not prevail?

The competition was stiff, and the playing field was not level. Psychiatrists, clinical psychologists, social workers, and marriage and family counselors formed often self-protective guilds. The pharmaceutical companies raked in huge profits for their antidepressant drugs and did not welcome being undercut. But another, almost

entirely unnoticed factor was even more important than this competition: a discrepancy between patent law and copyright law in the United States that has stifled—perhaps killed—the development of psychotherapy. If you discover a drug that works at all in depression, you can patent it, corner the market, and make out like a bandit. If you discover a psychotherapy or an exercise that works just as well or even much better, you cannot make serious money. You can only copyright the words. "Fair use" law means that if a competitor merely changes a few words, calling the exercise "What Went Well" rather than "Three Blessings," and makes a few other cosmetic refinements, that competitor is in business. Big Pharma's patent monopoly endows it with a massive war chest to trumpet its drugs, even if they are only marginally effective. Our initial results from the web exercise were at least as good as those for any antidepressant drug, but we could not raise enough money to keep the website going, and the public was deprived of a likely effective antidepressant treatment. The reason: Who would invest in a product that, if effective, could be so easily and legally ripped off? So there was minimal financial incentive to develop and promote effective psychotherapy and verbal exercises for mental illness. Once you do all the work and pour your money into promulgating them, any wealthy company could come along, change a few words, out-advertise you, create a jazzier website, and run you out of business.

I COUNTED THE website a success, even if the business failed, for it led to positive psychotherapy.

Tayyab Rashid and his new wife, Afroze, came from Pakistan to take their PhDs at Fairleigh Dickinson University, and then Tayyab charmed his way into becoming my postdoctoral fellow at the Positive Psychology Center. He did not want to make a lot of money; he wanted to do a lot of good. Pakistan, it seemed to me, needed a megadose of positive psychology, and when the time was ripe, Afroze and Tayyab were my candidates to lead it.

"Let's bundle all these web exercises together into the hands of skilled therapists and test them in face-to-face therapy with severe depressives," Tayyab suggested. It was the next step, but I expressed

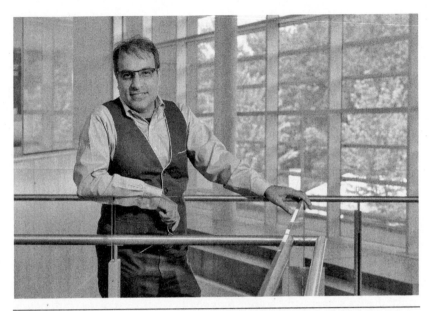

Tayyab Rashid tested a fourteen-session ensemble of positive psychotherapy against antidepressant medications and against cognitive therapy with diagnosed major depression. It was superior to both. Photo courtesy of Tayyab Rashid.

doubt that it would work. Undeterred, Tayyab boldly tested positive psychotherapy against antidepressant medications and cognitive therapy over fourteen sessions with patients diagnosed with major depression.

"Well, it worked, Marty," Tayyab told me as he spread the data sheets all over my work table. "Look at this." He had carried out a full-blown pilot study with severe depressives: eleven clients in individual positive psychotherapy, nine in treatment-as-usual, and twelve in treatment-as-usual plus antidepressant drugs. The results were startling: positive psychotherapy worked markedly better on all measures than the usual treatment and better than the usual treatment plus drugs.[7]

Given these very encouraging data, we applied for a grant from NIMH. It was turned down administratively without even the bother of any reviews. Annoyed, I saw NIMH more and more in the service only of neuroscience and Big Pharma. It had by now given up on psychotherapy. Discouraged, Tayyab decamped for Toronto, Canada,

where he carried out study after study, each showing good effects of positive psychotherapy. We reviewed fifteen randomized trials in *Positive Psychotherapy: A Manual*.[8] But in the absence of the expensive, definitive, larger-scale, random-assignment outcome studies, which only NIMH could afford to fund, I remained an optimist about positive psychotherapy but skeptical that it would become as widespread as it deserves to be in my lifetime.

Critics and Criticisms

Unlike in theater, where harsh criticism will shut down a Broadway show, criticism in science is a main driver of progress. Knowing this, I have always welcomed critics and shunned ass-kissers. That said, I have never met anyone with "thick skin," and in truth criticism almost always smarts and sometimes really wounds. For me it depends on the kind of criticism. Oddly, the weaker the criticism, the more it bothers me. The strongest criticisms—such as Dick Herrnstein's "Animals only learn responses—they don't learn *that* anything" in references to learned helplessness theory—sting, but they invigorate me. They are testable and will eventually prove right or wrong. For strong criticisms, truth will out. The weaker criticisms—such as "Positive psychology is individualistic and selfish, ignoring as it does other people"—wake me up at 4 a.m. grinding my teeth. The really weak ones, the attacks on straw men, such as "Positive psychology is oblivious to misery," drive me up the wall. And the ad hominem attacks that cast me as the Darth Vader of psychology make me wish I had stuck to playing bridge.

I categorize the criticisms as "strong" or "weak." I also touch on some of the "really nasty" stuff from the trolls who roam the internet.

Strong Criticisms

Positive psychology tells us nothing that my grandmother, St. Augustine, and my Sunday school teacher did not already know.

I heard this criticism often when positive psychology was young, so I made a list of things I did not know before it came along. Here is part of the list of surprises I made ten years ago in a reply to John

Lanchester's "Well, duh" criticism of the obviousness of positive psychology published in the *New Yorker* (February 27, 2006):

- Optimistic people are much less likely to die of heart attacks than pessimists, controlling for all known physical risk factors.[9]
- Women who display genuine (Duchenne) smiles to the class photographer at age eighteen go on to have fewer divorces and more marital satisfaction than those who display fake smiles.[10]
- Externalities (e.g., weather, money, health, marriage, religion), totaled together, account for no more than 15 percent of the variance in life satisfaction.[11]
- Specific exercises increase happiness and decrease depression six months later, while other plausible exercises are mere placebos.[12]
- The pursuit of meaning and engagement is much more predictive of life satisfaction than the pursuit of pleasure.[13]
- Self-discipline is twice as good a predictor of high school grades as IQ.[14]
- Happy teenagers go on to earn very substantially more income fifteen years later than less happy teenagers, equating for income, grades, and other obvious factors.[15]
- People experience more "flow" at work than at home.[16]

And here are a few more "I'll be darned" items I've discovered since then:

- People who prefer meaning (*eudamonia*) to pleasure (*hedonia*) have a distinguishable genetic profile.[17]
- The belief that income inequality is fair goes a long way to canceling the negative effect of income inequality on life satisfaction.[18]
- Conservatives report themselves happier than liberals do.[19]
- Mindfulness training makes you more resilient.[20]

POSITIVE PSYCHOLOGY IS just old wine in new bottles. Abraham Maslow and the humanistic psychology movement said it all forty years ago.

Indeed the humanistic psychologists were furious with me and the positive psychology movement. They felt slighted and not properly acknowledged. They laid into me mercilessly.

Their anger was more than partly justified. Abraham Maslow first used the term "positive psychology," and his thinking was iconoclastic and antedated some of our main ideas. In our inaugural article on positive psychology,[21] Mike Csikszentmihalyi and I foolishly lumped humanistic psychology together with crystal healing and aromatherapy, and for my part I apologize for this unwarranted slight.

On the other hand, Abraham Maslow came too early. Scientific psychology did not take him seriously. Maslow himself recognized that he wanted scientific respect above all, and his research assistant, Bob Gable, in a revealing personal letter in 2001, wrote me, "Abe would have been happier with something that never happened—a return phone call from Fred Skinner." Rather than carry out mainstream science on his ideas, his followers, calling themselves humanistic psychologists, developed their own qualitative and nonexperimental methods. Humanistic psychology's then radical ideas about happiness, combined with its less-than-rigorous methods, made it doubly difficult for science to digest—hence its present status as a scientific backwater separate from positive psychology.[22] Positive psychology keeps some of the radical ideas but uses conventional, rigorous methods.

In point of fact, spotty scholar that I am, I had not read much Maslow, and so his writings played little role in my own thinking. Had I invoked Maslow, however appropriately, it would have been window dressing. Positive psychology arose directly from my take on the shortcomings of mainstream clinical and experimental science.

POSITIVE PSYCHOLOGY IS unnecessary. Psychology-as-usual aims to get rid of what is bad. Human well-being follows automatically when all that is bad is fixed.

Is the good simply the absence of the bad?

There are three kinds of opposites:
The first is when both extremes lie on the *same continuum*. Temperature is like this. Hot and cold are opposites, but they only

differ as a matter, literally, of degree. Hot is just less cold, and cold is just less hot.

The second kind of opposite is when *one side is well understood* but the other side is nothing more than the absence of the first side. "Colored" and "colorless" are like this: "colorless" has no meaning except the absence of color.

The third is when each side *forms its own distinct world* with properties not deducible from the absence of the properties of the other world. Civility is an example. The presence of civility leads to cooperation, friendship, and loyalty. Civility is a positive-sum game. Incivility leads to revenge, hate, and divorce. Incivility is a negative-sum game. Civility and incivility are different in kind, not just in degree. The benefits of civility are more than just the absence of revenge, hate, and divorce, and the costs of incivility are more than just the absence of cooperation, friendship, and loyalty.

Good and bad, positive and negative are this third kind of opposite. The good and the bad each form their own unique worlds. e e cummings said it best in his 1935 poem "love is a place":

> *yes is a world*
> *& in this world of*
> *yes live*
> *(skillfully curled)*
> *all worlds*

"The basic mission of journalism is to uncover what is hidden," declared Bill Moyers to the audience. What Bill Moyers thought about journalism was holy writ among American journalists, and he was the speaker at the Annenberg Public Policy Center at Penn. Kathleen Hall Jamieson, the director, chose me to be a discussant.

"Imagine, Mr. Moyers, that journalism was wholly successful, and it uncovered everything that was hidden. Even further, imagine that journalism uncovered everything that was wrong and hidden and further that journalism corrected everything that was wrong," I said. "Where would you have gotten to?

"You would have gotten all the way up to . . . *zero*," I paused for effect. "Not getting it wrong does not equal getting it right. Has journalism no positive values? What is journalism's positive vision? What is praiseworthy? Heroic? Virtuous? Is there not a world above zero, a world that journalism should envision, praise, nurture, and help to birth?"

Bill Moyers took this seriously, and we then spent an entire dinner wondering how positive journalism could ever take off. We were joined by David Eisenhower, a faculty member at Penn and the grandson of President Dwight Eisenhower, and most importantly by his wife, Julie Nixon Eisenhower. She opined that her father, Richard Nixon, was brought down by unremittingly negative journalism and remarked on the almost complete absence of any counterbalancing journalism about his virtues and strengths. History has been kinder to him in this regard, but the ceaseless drumbeat of negativity and scandal overwhelmed him.

There is, of course, a long tradition of "positive" journalism, but it is derided as fluff. Many journalists, in addition to digging up dirt, write positive stories. These show up in the food section, in local columns, in "feel-good" stories, and in what used to be called the "women's pages." In its strongest and most widely read form, positive journalism inhabits the sports pages. It is often said that writing about heroism and virtue and skill cannot be as commercially successful as uncovering scandal, but the popularity of the sports pages should tell us that "If it bleeds, it leads" is not necessary for commercial success.

Positive psychology stood all the usual questions on their heads for me, and my mantra was now "Not getting it wrong does not equal getting it right." The tradition I cut my teeth on, learning-theory-as-usual, made this mistake big time. From E. L. Thorndike's cats in the puzzle box through B. F. Skinner's pigeons pecking lighted keys, learning was said to be "trial and error." The animal only gradually eliminated all that was wrong (the error trials) and eventually whittled its "response" down to the right one. (The emblematic story tells of Skinner lecturing to Harvard undergraduates, who conspired to perk up and look interested only when Skinner moved toward the left corner of the stage. Skinner, so the legend goes, eventually wound up frozen in that

corner.) The gradualness of the "learning curve" in animals seemed to support this. But the apparently gradual curve is often just an artifact of averaging a lot of sudden step functions of different animals. So if ten rats are learning to press a bar for food, and each rat suddenly "gets" it by "insight," but each on a different trial, suddenly—not gradually—learning what's right, the averaged curve will look gradual even if composed only of insight functions (e.g., rat 1 gets it on trial 2, rat 2 gets it on trial 5, rat 3 gets it on trial 12, etc.). In a classic experiment,[23] the experimenter nodded his head with approval whenever subjects said words that ended in *s*. Averaged learning to say *s* appeared gradual, but when results were broken down subject by subject, no learning occurred at all until the subject could verbalize the insight that words ending in *s*, or plural words, got head nodding. Then the subject jumped to 100 percent right. Nature just cannot work by the enormously inefficient way of gradually eliminating all possible errors. The poor animal would be long dead before getting it right. Evolution will favor cognitive mechanisms that help us to leap to the right answer, and animals (and people) surely have evolved to get there more directly than by first eliminating all the wrong pathways.

In its modern cognitive incarnation, the elimination-of-errors school, led perhaps unwittingly by Danny Kahneman,[24] made much out of ridding ourselves of cognitive errors. The "recency" error, for example, makes us over-remember the most recent event at the expense of failing to take into account the average over the longer past, and the "availability" error has us overweighting what is most attention grabbing. By eliminating these errors, so Kahneman alleged, we will become more accurate. Eliminating errors is surely a big help to accuracy, but it misses the boat about insight. Coming up with the right answer usually involves much more than just eliminating all these errors. We often just *see* what is right long before all errors are eliminated, and this insightful leap is at the heart of nothing less than creativity itself.

That the positive adds properties over and above the absence of the negative is very important for psychotherapy. When I first became a therapist, I was taught, following the dogma of Freud and Schopenhauer, that the best we can do is not suffer, so I aimed to help patients

get rid of all of their negatives: anger, sadness, and anxiety. That done, therapy ended. Once in a while, we did very good work, and these dysphorias cleared up completely. Did I get happiness? No, I got an empty patient, because the skills for cultivating positive emotion, engagement, meaning, and good relationships differ entirely from those used to fight anger, anxiety, and depression.

So getting what is good in life entails a lot more than just eliminating what is bad.

POSITIVE PSYCHOLOGY UNDERRATES the importance of the external world. To build more well-being, just allocate more money to making the world a better place, and please don't mess with people's psyches.

Using money, usually tax money, to make a better external world has been the rallying cry of social scientists and liberal politicians since the Haymarket Square Riot of 1884. Since poverty is at the root of unhappiness, throw money at it, and unhappiness will disappear. Since ignorance is at the root of prejudice, spend more on education, and prejudice will disappear. Since deprivation is at the root of crime, undo deprivation, and crime will disappear.

Who would dare speak against this?

This objection has some strong and some weak points. More money sometimes works. Crime goes down during boom times and up when times are hard. Prejudice seems to be on the decline, but it is not at all clear that prosperity rather than the rule of law and simple goodness has played much of a role. Happiness, however, does not seem to change much with income, once people are above the safety net. So, for those below the safety net, more money will produce more well-being. For those above the safety net, more money sometimes might build more well-being, particularly if explicitly spent on producing more well-being rather than less ill-being.

Over the last 130 years, almost all the financial subsidies have been poured into alleviating ill-being: defense, hospitals, and welfare are examples. These have worked but have not produced more well-being, only less ill-being. A world that takes well-being seriously and uses money to promote positive institutions—strong families, beautiful surroundings, democracy, uplifting entertainment, deep, lifelong

education, women's reproductive rights, and engrossing, active sports, for example—will increase well-being directly.

The strongest version of the importance of the external world is the "objective list" theory of happiness,[25] which lodges happiness outside psychology and onto a list of "truly valuable" things in the real world. Happiness in a human life consists of achieving worthwhile pursuits: career accomplishment, friendship, freedom from disease and pain, material comfort, civic spirit, beauty, education, love, knowledge, and good conscience. Consider the thousands of abandoned children living on the streets of Luanda. As the *New York Times* tells us, "Dressed in rags, they spend nights in the sandy strip along the bay, and their days foraging for food through mounds of garbage." Their lives, consumed with meeting momentary needs, adventurous roving in gangs, and casual sex, with little thought for tomorrow, might actually be subjectively "happy" and have high "life satisfaction." Very few people would classify such an existence as "happy," however, since these children are deprived of most things that would go on anybody's list of what is worthwhile in life. So there is much truth in the view that making the external world better increases happiness, and I for one take the quality of the external world as seriously as the quality of the internal world as a cause of happiness.

Weak Criticisms

Positive psychology is WEIRD: it is based on Western, educated, industrial, rich, and democratic societies.[26] Positive psychology needs to be cross-cultural.

These critics have not done enough homework. Positive psychology, in fact, involves research on well-being in more than two hundred nations and from every major culture. A subfield and book series, *Cross-cultural Advancements in Positive Psychology*,[27] seek a deep understanding of the way culture influences differences in well-being.

MAKING MORE MONEY is the solution to achieving more well-being. Above the safety net, more income does not really have diminishing returns on life satisfaction. If you replot the y-axis to log income (a transformation that acknowledges that a raise of $10,000

for someone who earns only $10,000 has more impact than a $10,000 raise for someone who makes $100,000), you get a straight line heading continually upward, with more income always producing more life satisfaction. So an individual or a nation wanting more happiness just needs to make more money.[28]

It is not the economy, stupid, and this is a statistical trick. A replotted straight line does indeed yield no satiation of well-being by more income. So what? This does not remotely mean that you should always try to earn more and more money if you want more and more happiness. Spending that time with your friends or family or in leisure will likely produce more happiness, once you are well above the safety net, than will spending that same amount of time making more money. So if you earn $100,000 a year now and could boost it to $120,000 by working for six more weekends next year, forget it. Your life satisfaction will increase more if you spend those six weekends with friends and family or on your hobby.

WE NEED NOT more optimism but more realism. Optimism created our last major recession, and we need to counter it with a big dose of realistic pessimism.[29]

Barbara Ehrenreich has been an unrelenting critic of mine, beginning with her article "I Hate Hope."[30] She places the blame for the economic downturn in 2007 on positive thinking. Motivational gurus, like Oprah, Joel Osteen, and Tony Robbins, she tells us, revved the consumers up into buying more than they could afford to repay. Academics—she likens me to the Wizard of Oz—provided the scientific props for these hucksters. What we need, Ehrenreich tells us, is realism, not optimism. Indeed, cultivating realism, rather than positivity, is her theme song.

The view that optimism caused the economic meltdown of 2007 is pure twaddle. Rather, optimism causes the stock market to go up, and pessimism causes it to go down. I am not an economist, but I think stocks (and derivatives and goods generally) go up in price when people are optimistic about their future worth and go down when people are pessimistic about their future worth.

Ehrenreich is confused about reality itself. There are two kinds of reality. One kind is not reflexive; it is not influenced by what human

beings think, desire, expect, or wish for. What time the sun rises tomorrow, whether there is adequate laboratory space for your research, and whether there will be a terrorist attack in Mumbai are all *nonreflexive realities*. In none of these do your thoughts and wishes influence what happens. These are Ehrenreich realities.

The other kind of reality, *reflexive reality*, is influenced and sometimes even determined by people's expectations and perceptions. How bright the teacher thinks a student is influences how she does in class. How much our mates think we love them influences how well we get along with them. Perception and expectation strongly influence market price, an eminently reflexive reality: how much you are willing to pay reflects more than a judgment of the real value of stock; you are also judging the market's perception of the future value of the stock. When investors are optimistic about the market's perception of the stock's future value, its price goes up. When investors are very pessimistic about the market's perception of the future value of a stock, its price melts down.

So, a footless optimism among buyers who believed the real estate market would go up forever surely contributed to the meltdown. In general, however, optimism causes stocks to rise; pessimism causes them to fall. A viral pessimism, just as unrealistic as the footless optimism it displaced, then contributed massively to the economic meltdown. So I believe that both the viral pessimism and the underlying nonreflexive reality of financially unsound subprime mortgage loans contributed to the meltdown. To attribute the meltdown to optimism is pure Ehrenreich fantasy.

Something more insidious than economics really lies behind Ehrenreich's exhortation for more reality. Ehrenreich wants a world with no psychological influences, in which human well-being follows only from class, war, and money, not from beliefs and expectations. By definition, then, she needs to ignore the enormous number of reflexive realities in which a person's thoughts and feelings influence the future. My life's work is entirely about such reflexive realities, and so Ehrenreich has found in me the right bête noire.

POSITIVE PSYCHOLOGY IS Pollyannaism rewarmed. It ignores suffering and misery and all the bad stuff in the world.

This is a straw man, lobbed by writers who have not read beyond the name "positive psychology" and have certainly not read the 1913 bestseller *Pollyanna*. I and many of the practitioners and scientists in positive psychology came right out of work on misery and suffering. I devoted thirty-five years of my life to undoing depression and helplessness. I found that merely getting rid of the bad stuff was not enough, and so I advocated working on what makes life worth living as well. Positive psychology complements, but does not displace, working to rid the world of what cripples life.

I CANNOT BRING myself to list all the accusations that the trolls of the internet have clubbed me with. Here's one sample, to give you a flavor of what gets my teeth grinding: one person after numerous nasty blog posts about me and positive psychology, sent me an email with the subject line "An Olive Branch." His olive branch: "I will refrain from accusing you of plagiarism if you will help me get elected president of the APA Division of Humanistic Psychology."

IT IS MUCH better to be criticized than to be ignored, and the fact that critics are legion tells me that positive psychology is genuinely popular. A search for "positive psychology" brings up more than 1 million results on Google. My free Authentic Happiness site (www.authentichappiness.org) has registered almost 5 million people. Many hundreds of college courses teach positive psychology (including the once most popular course at Harvard). Almost every major newspaper and magazine in English has featured positive psychology. Thousands of researchers and practitioners call themselves "positive psychologists." There are thousands of refereed journal articles on positive psychology and more than two hundred books, several of them bestsellers, translated into many languages. My books alone have been translated into almost fifty. The topic has garnered at least $200 million in grants and contracts. There are more than twenty national and regional positive psychology organizations[31] and a several-thousand-member International Positive Psychology Association.

I unblushingly identify myself as a positive psychologist.

Why is positive psychology popular? Why now? One explanation is that the world is better, much better, than it used to be. The world

is much wealthier than fifty years ago. Even the poor nations have seen more than 1 billion people lifted out of poverty. Prosperity, of course, moves us to aim for more than just alleviating misery—we aim toward what is good in life. Public health, modern medicine, and the green revolution surely mean there is per capita less physical suffering today than ever before on this planet. In fact, you have to be blinded by ideology not to see that almost everything we care about (except mental health) is better now: less pollution, more democracy, more human rights, less violence,[32] longer life expectancy, lower child mortality, more music, more education, tastier food, healthier bodies, and more poetry.

We may already be in the epoch of positive-sum-games that Robert Wright envisions in *Nonzero*.[33] Human progress, while undeniable—unless you happen to be a professor of cultural anthropology or literature at a major American, British, or French university—is nevertheless fragile. There are forces that, if they prevail, would undo progress and unleash apocalypse on the human race. Or worldwide depression might occur. Or nuclear catastrophe. Or unknown unknowns. But if the trend ongoing since World War II continues, we need a psychology that is conscious of, measures, and builds wellbeing. A psychology of misery no longer suffices for the human future.

A final reason for the popularity of positive psychology is gender. Psychology, when I first encountered it more than fifty years ago, was male. Only 20 percent of graduate students then were women. The hot topics, not surprisingly after two world wars and a great depression, were typically masculine: conflict, dominance, competition, stress, authoritarianism, and the like. The popularity of agency and control, of learned helplessness itself, had a male feel to it. It did not occur to the stress theorists of the time that the reaction to bad events might be not only fight or flight but also, as Shelley Taylor "discovered," tend and befriend.[34] The gender percentages are now flip-flopped, and almost 80 percent of graduate students are female. The subject matter is also feminized: cooperation, positive emotion, engagement, trust, relationships, and love. Positive psychology is likely a major beneficiary of the gender revolution in psychology.

Chapter Twenty-Three

Positive Education
(1990–)

"*I*N TWO WORDS or fewer, what do you most want for your children?" Anthony Seldon asked the assembled gathering at the Lawrenceville School in New Jersey.

"Happiness, meaning, contentment, fulfillment, joy, health, enthusiasm, courage, stick-to-it-iveness," we called out, the words cascading over each other. The occasion was a June 2007 meeting of teachers from around the world, and our theme was how to build "nonintellectual" strengths—meaning, engagement, optimism, positive emotion—into schools. Anthony was headmaster at the prestigious Wellington School in the United Kingdom, a biographer of John Major and Tony Blair, and a historian of the Tory Party. He had launched a well-publicized program in his school, one that heavily featured meditation, and he was a spell-binding orator.

"Now in two words or fewer, what do schools teach?" he asked us.

"Discipline, numeracy, hard work, science, literacy, conformity." The words seeped out with embarrassed hesitation.

"Notice," he said, "there is no overlap between the two lists. Now imagine that well-being, joy, meaning, fulfillment, engagement . . . the whole first list could be taught without compromising the traditional goals of school, the achievement list."

Anthony had defined a new kind of education, and I thought its name must be "positive education."

This is its history.

In the 1990s, Susan Nolen-Hoeksema, Joan Girgus, and I tested whether pessimism predisposed young schoolchildren to depression, just as it predisposed adults. It sure did.[1] The belief that personal, permanent, and pervasive factors caused bad events robustly predicted depression and poor school achievement over the following year among eight- to eleven-year-olds. Pessimism is a risk factor for depression in schoolchildren in exactly the same sense that smoking is a risk factor for lung cancer, and, actually, pessimism is considerably bigger as a risk factor.

We thought prevention, not therapy, was a better strategy to deal with depression. Parking an ambulance at the bottom of a cliff to help those who fall off is a much worse strategy than preventing the fall in the first place. Could we teach children at risk for depression to argue against unrealistic pessimistic thoughts, just as cognitive therapy teaches adults already in therapy to become more optimistic? Would this prevent depression? This question led us to develop the first Penn Prevention Program for children, and this was the moment, in the winter of 1990, when positive education began.

Jane Gillham, having completed her postdoc at the Yale Child Study Center after a PhD with me, Lisa Jaycox, just finishing her PhD with me, and Karen Reivich devised a twelve-week, two-hour-per-week prevention program for middle school students. They wrote a minute-by-minute manual, and we screened two hundred fifth and sixth graders to find the seventy kids most at risk for depression.[2]

We then followed the kids for two years into puberty—when the epidemic of depression first takes hold. Before the program started, 25 percent of the kids in both the prevention group and the untreated control group had moderate to severe depressive symptoms. By the end of the program, twelve weeks later, the prevention group had dropped to 13 percent, but the control group stayed at 23 percent. Two years later only 22 percent of the prevention group had moderate to severe symptoms, but a whopping 44 percent of the control group did. This was a 100 percent effect. The principal cause was a change

from pessimism to optimism in the prevention group, and this was exactly what we taught the kids.

The key to learning optimism is learning how to recognize and then dispute unrealistic catastrophic thoughts. In *Learned Optimism* I described how we taught adults to do this. With children we used the same principles but with cartoons and comedy and snacks. Here the child takes a dire permanent explanation ("They are always picking on me"), which leads to lasting sadness, and he improvises a contrasting explanation ("They are in a mean mood because they just lost their baseball game"), which leads to only transient sadness. We also taught social skills, such as negotiation, and how to take another kid's perspective.

My graduate students and staff were great teachers of how to teach optimism to children, but there were not enough of us to go around, so we began to train schoolteachers and measured how well they did at preventing depression. Based on the amount of depression prevented and the amount of optimism learned by their students, teachers did as well as we did. By 2016, twenty years down the road, the Penn Prevention Program had been replicated many times across the globe, with rich kids, poor kids, white kids, black kids, and Asian kids in English, German, Dutch, and Chinese. The prevention of depression, as well as anxiety, was reliable but "small" to "moderate" in size; in one meta-analysis, no significant findings appeared.[3]

The Penn Prevention Program taught resilience and was the forerunner of positive education, but it predated positive psychology, whose tools were not available until after 2002. Disputing catastrophic thoughts is a major tool of psychotherapy-as-usual—getting rid of negatives to good effect. But it is not directly about building positive emotion or engagement or good relationships or meaning or achievement. Positive education—it was not yet named—would aim to build these directly.

OUR EXPLORATION OF noncognitive factors in school received a giant boost with the arrival of Angela Duckworth. Angela joined as a first-year Penn graduate student in September 2002. She had been an urban schoolteacher, McKinsey consultant, NGO head, and

Marshall Fellow at Oxford. She had an unfashionable take on why some talented kids do badly in school, and others, less talented, shine: character.

Conventional wisdom and political correctness had for almost a century blamed the teachers, the schools, the classroom size, the textbooks, the funding, the politicians, and the parents for students' failure—faulting anything or anyone but the students themselves. What? Blame the victim. Blame the character of the students?

Angela bit into this as soon as she entered Penn. The element of character that fascinated her was self-discipline. Her subjects were the students of Masterman High School, the magnet school in downtown Philadelphia. Masterman accepted promising students beginning in the fifth grade, but many of them washed out, and the real competition began in the ninth grade. Angela wanted to find out how self-discipline compared with IQ in predicting who would make it. She created a new composite measure of self-discipline, gave it to all kids, and found that self-disciplined eighth graders went on to earn higher grades, score higher on achievement tests, spend more time on their homework, start it earlier, and watch less television. Self-discipline out-predicted IQ by about a factor of two.[4]

This attracted the notice of two prominent American headmasters from schools at opposite ends of the economic spectrum. One was David Levin, head of the Knowledge Is Power Program, the KIPP schools, a charter organization with more than 180 schools. These college preparatory schools, made up of poor black and Hispanic kids, had an impressive record of success: 8,000 college alumni. Their motto was "Work hard, be nice." David's partner was Dominic Randolph, the British-educated headmaster of the elite Riverdale School in northern Manhattan. Together they wanted to bring positive psychology into their schools and specifically programs of character education. They visited us at Penn, and we began a fruitful collaboration. We focused on creating the "right-hand side" of the report card, measuring the character strengths of zest, self-control, optimism, gratitude, and social intelligence.

Angela caught fire and was launched on a glittering career measuring self-discipline and its extreme cousin, grit: never giving up.

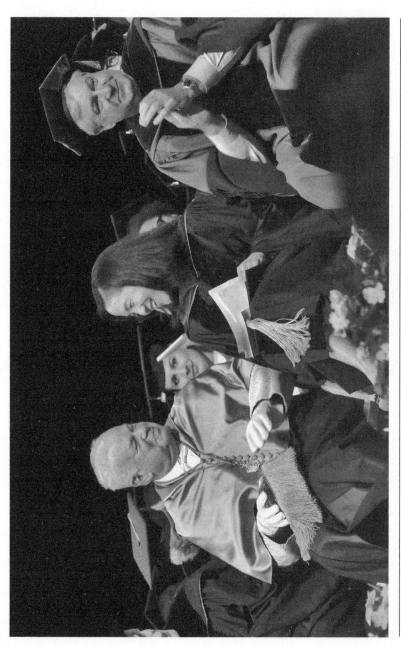

Angela Lee Duckworth joined as a first-year Penn graduate student in September 2002. She had been an urban schoolteacher, McKinsey consultant, NGO head, and Marshall Fellow at Oxford. She had an unfashionable take on why some talented kids do badly in school, and others, less talented, shine: character. Photo courtesy of the University of Pennsylvania College of Liberal and Professional Studies.

As I write, Angela's first book, *Grit: The Power of Passion and Perseverance*, is in its twenty-fifth week on the *New York Times* best-seller list, and she is now a major player in positive education and beyond.

MANDY AND I helicoptered from a tiny float in the middle of the Yarra River in Melbourne to the front lawn of Trent Barry's sprawling house. Trent was an advisor to the Geelong Grammar School (GGS), one of the two leading private schools in Australia. Trent phoned me during my Australian speaking tour in February 2006 and asked if I might detour to GGS. The school was at the climax of a $16 million campaign to build a well-being center, and a few remarks by me to the donors, Trent thought, would raise the last $2 million.

Not shy these Aussies, I thought.

"Imagine positive education," I intoned, thinking of Anthony Seldon, as I concluded my speech to the donors. There—I had finally given voice to my vision of schoolchildren who experience pleasure, engagement, good relationships, and meaning and are also high achievers—and I had named the movement.

The $2 million was raised that very day, and the principal donor, Helen Hanbury (Rupert Murdoch's big sister), told GGS, "Not another gym. I want *well-being* for the children!"

A few months later, in response to Mrs. Hanbury's death-bed request, GGS sent a delegation to the Penn Positive Psychology Center and asked Karen Reivich and me how, if we had carte blanche, Penn would create positive education at GGS. We also were not shy and told them we would

- train all the two hundred teachers and the staff in positive psychology, strengths, and resilience;
- arrange visiting lectures from the major figures in world positive psychology;
- appoint a full-time director of positive education;
- have a curriculum designer lead the faculty in creating a K–12 syllabus in positive psychology.

They agreed on the spot to all of these.

"And by the way," I added, "Mandy and I and my kids will come and live at GGS."

So on a baking summer day in January 2007, Mandy, the kids—with Carly and Jenny, we now had five—and I arrived at GGS (where air conditioning was a rarity). Darryl, in tenth grade, and Nikki, in eleventh grade, boarded at the school. Karen Reivich and fifteen of my applied positive psychology master's students arrived the same day to begin a two-week positive education training of the faculty and staff, more than one hundred of whom had, without pay, given up two weeks of their precious summer vacation to attend.

The first day began inauspiciously. The new headmaster, Stephen Meek, was the very model of a British headmaster: chilly, stiff as a broom, skeptical, and barely welcoming. I couldn't blame him: the previous headmaster, Nicholas Sampson, now off to head Marlborough in the United Kingdom, had imposed positive education on his successor. Stephen inherited this burden and its serious expense. The rest of the ten days went swimmingly, however: the teachers learned about resilience, then about strengths, and finally about social skills. First they learned to use these skills in their own lives, and then we covered how to teach them to kids. The big effect was the rejuvenation of the teachers, and I saw it in Stephen Meek. By the end of the workshop, he was glowing, all smiles, hugging people, and effusively asking them about their signature strengths. Years later, his wife, Christine, confided to me that I had changed Stephen's life.

The Seligmans had a smashing sabbatical. We lived in the chaplain's house in the middle of campus, and because Nikki and Darryl were boarders, we had a constant stream of student visitors sampling better food, air conditioning, and family life. Darryl became a rugger, and we motored with his team all over the state of Victoria. Nikki broke the strict GGS rules the very first weekend but was forgiven. Ray Fowler, Barb Fredrickson, Roy Baumeister, Diane Tice, Kathleen Vohs, Kate Hays, Stephen Post, and a stream of distinguished positive psychologists paid long visits. The faculty, under the supervision of Randy Ernst, a Golden Apple high school teacher from Kansas City, devised the first K–12 positive education curriculum. When we finally departed in June 2007, Geelong Grammar School had become

the foremost bastion of positive education in the world.[5] Since then, its faculty, under a full-time director of positive education, has taught positive psychology to teachers from all over Australia, and the University of Melbourne now gives a master's degree in positive education.

IN THE MEDIEVAL monastery, the abbot bridged the sacred and the secular, sorting out the monks as well as dealing with the crass interests of the state. Sir Richard Layard, a modern abbot, was a world-class economist, professor at the London School of Economics, major theorist of happiness, and Labour Party leader; he and his wife, Mollie, were one of only two couples who by dint of merit were in the House of Lords. For the last two decades, Richard had made it his job to take promising ideas from psychology and persuade the British body politic to act on them. With David Clark, professor at Oxford, he coaxed Parliament to allocate more than £1 billion to train thousands of new cognitive therapists to treat depression.[6]

"I am going to take the Penn Prevention Program to the schools of the UK," Richard declared as we walked the back streets of Glasgow on a break from a meeting in which we shared the podium.

"That would be great, Richard. I think we may have enough data to try a small pilot replication in Liverpool."

"You don't get it, do you, Marty," said Richard in his affable way. "Like most academics you believe that government adopts policy when the scientific data mount and mount to an irresistible point. In all my years in politics, I have never seen such a case. Government acts when the data are sufficient and the political will is there. Your data are sufficient, and the political will is here, and I am going to take your prevention program to the schools of the UK."

He began to raise funding for training programs for UK teachers, and these were launched in twenty schools in South Tyneside and Manchester in 2007. By this writing thousands of British teachers have been trained and have gone on to teach resilience to tens of thousands of kids.

One most heartening development in positive education came from India. Steve Leventhal had made the mission of his foundation,

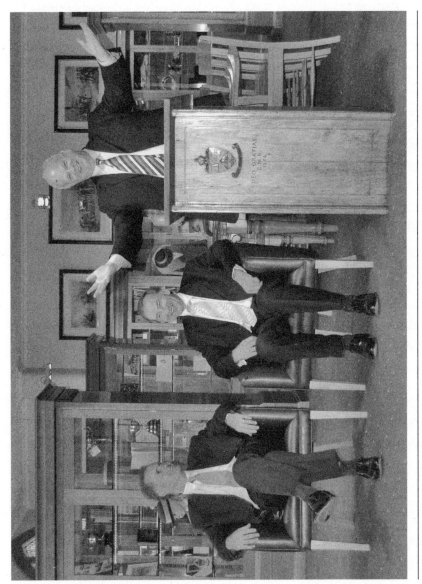

The Seligmans had a smashing sabbatical. We lived in the chaplain's house in the middle of campus, and because Nikki and Darryl were boarders, we had a constant stream of student visitors sampling better food, air conditioning, and family life. Photo courtesy of Geelong Grammar School.

CorStone, the teaching of the very poorest of girls from the slums of India. His group taught positive psychology to 30,000 "untouchable" girls in the state of Bihar and found improved emotional resilience, health knowledge, attitudes toward gender equality, and use of clean water.[7]

Hector Escamilla, president of Tecmilenio University in Monterrey, Mexico, decided to embrace positive education for the entire university. He founded a well-being institute and a well-being ecosystem, and all of the more than 53,000 students on thirty campuses throughout Mexico took courses in positive psychology. And Sir Anthony Seldon, now the vice chancellor of the University of Buckingham, declared it the first happiness university in Britain.

THE PREMIER OF South Australia appoints the thinker in residence of Adelaide. The program was designed to bring innovation to the state and, in the case of my appointment, to raise the well-being of all South Australians. Their well-being was already pretty high, and Adelaide was perennially ranked as one of the most livable cities in the world.

"Nothing really bad has ever happened to Adelaide," the lord mayor told me, "no typhoon, no terrorism, no serial killer, no drought, no bankruptcy, and no epidemic. We are the only large city in the world so blessed. We have the usual urban problems, of course, some poverty, some crime, some racial tension, some unemployment, but except for the really hot summer, Adelaide is a Garden of Eden."

We were given a house at the very center of the Garden, the former headmaster's quarters at Saint Peter's College,[8] where we lived among 1,200 boys. Our two youngest daughters, Carly (seven) and Jenny (four), were the only young females on campus, and they knew it. The house, surrounded by a greensward of cricket pitches, was adjacent to a huge botanical garden. We were at home here for the three Februaries between 2012 and 2014.

Saint's was the other top private school in Australia. Between them, GGS and Saint's had graduated many of Australia's prime ministers and Nobel laureates. Simon Murray, the energetic headmaster, and Mathew White, the director of well-being and positive education,

had brought me there to help reinvent an already great school around positive education. They recruited Karen Reivich and the Penn team to teach the teachers, sponsored a star-studded lecture series still ongoing six years later, infused a language of strengths rather than pathology among the students and teachers, and introduced David Cooperrider's Appreciative Inquiry[9] as a vehicle of school-wide communication. Simon Murray founded Positive Education Schools of Australia (PESA), an association now comprising more than two hundred schools.[10] Simon was committed to spreading positive education to the state schools, and teachers and principals from throughout South Australia were trained at Saint's.

The premier, Jay Weatherill, decided to measure well-being regularly throughout the entire state, and his administration introduced positive psychology interventions into the mental health services and the hospitals.[11]

"ALL OF THEM, Alejandro, every last one?" I asked Alejandro Braun Adler, my most promising senior undergraduate. For his honors thesis, he worked on the psychological well-being of Asian refugees in South Philadelphia. He was from Mexico City, and his future would be international. He wanted to steer the world toward greater well-being and was a born diplomat. So for his PhD he applied to doctoral programs in political science—and only political science. Despite a sterling record, including the award for the best senior thesis in psychology at Penn, every program rejected him. Interlopers from psychology unwelcome, I assumed; too much overspecialization, not like the 1960s when Penn Psychology eagerly accepted me straight from receiving a philosophy undergraduate degree. The interlopers do the creative work, and as an inveterate—usually unwelcome—interloper, I was on Alejandro's side.

"You're a born psychologist, Alejandro." Too laissez-faire, as usual, I regretted not pushing him harder to apply for a psychology doctorate. "Would you consider applying late for a PhD in psychology here?"

He was desperate and gratefully agreed. I phoned our director of graduate studies, who reminded me that the deadline had passed, and the entering class for 2011 was set. I had only asked the powers that be

Alejandro Braun Adler. To round out the most massive dissertation I have ever super-
vised, Alejandro found in Bhutan, Mexico, and Peru that his well-being curriculum
increased both well-being and academic performance as measured fifteen months
later. Photo courtesy of Alejandro Adler.

to consider a candidate belatedly once before, and that was for Angela
Duckworth, a decade earlier. Angela worked out splendidly and was
now a chaired professor in our department, the first directly inbred
one since I was hired forty years before—and I'd had to absent my-
self at Cornell and in Penn Psychiatry before Penn Psychology would
consider me. After a tussle over tuition dollars (the director insisted
that I put skin in the game and have my grants pay his tuition), Ale-
jandro got in.

"I want to expand positive education internationally," I told Ale-
jandro after giving him the good news. "This may fit your ambitions."

Alejandro went off to Bhutan in 2011, beginning a graduate ca-
reer in which he spent almost as much time on airplanes as at Penn.
Bhutan, a small Himalayan country, was especially well suited to our
first nationwide positive education program. The fourth king, Jigme

Singye Wangchuck, had declared in 1972, "Gross national happiness is more important than gross national product." This idea drives public policy, and the Bhutanese Ministry of Education defines its mission as educating for gross national happiness (GNH). The ministry invited us to codevelop a GNH curriculum, and Alejandro led the project. The curriculum for grades seven through twelve was fifteen months in duration and targeted ten life skills:

1. Mindfulness: having calm awareness of thoughts, emotions, and surroundings
2. Empathy: identifying what others are feeling and thinking
3. Self-awareness: understanding one's own strengths, talents, limitations, and goals
4. Coping with emotions: identifying, understanding, and managing emotions
5. Communication: being active and constructive with others
6. Interpersonal relationships: interacting healthily and lovingly with friends and family
7. Creative thinking: developing novel and useful ideas
8. Critical thinking: analyzing, applying, synthesizing, and evaluating information as a guide to beliefs and actions
9. Decision making: choosing the best beliefs or action plans from available options
10. Problem solving: learning shortcuts to solve theoretical and practical problems

OUR STUDY INVOLVED eighteen entire schools. Eleven schools (5,347 students) were treatment schools, and seven schools (3,138 students) were the controls. We told the principals and teachers in both groups of schools that we were training them to teach the GNH curriculum. The students in both groups of schools received the same number of classroom hours during the real and placebo fifteen-month life-skills course: two hours per week. All principals and teachers in the eleven treatment schools received training during a ten-day GNH curriculum retreat. The trainers were psychologists from my center plus nine staff members from Bhutan's Ministry of

Education; a training manual (*Educating for GNH*) was used. The trainers taught the principals and teachers how to practice the skills in their own lives and how to teach the ten life skills to their students. Teachers learned to infuse their academic subjects (e.g., math, science, and reading) with the ten life skills. Literature instruction, for instance, employed a "GNH lens" to identify strengths and virtues in characters from novels, which students were then encouraged to use in their daily lives. The principals and teachers from the schools in the control group received training during a four-day placebo GNH curriculum retreat during which they learned about how to teach nutrition, psychology, and human anatomy.

We measured students' well-being and national standardized exam scores at the end of the fifteen-month course and then twelve months later. Well-being rose and was significantly higher in the treated schools than in the placebo schools. Most importantly, academic achievement—as measured by the national exams—rose and remained much higher in the treated schools. We also found that student engagement and perseverance accounted for most of the superiority of the treatment.[12]

Bhutan adopted this curriculum for all the schools in the nation.

ALEJANDRO'S NEXT TARGET was his home country of Mexico. The governor of the state of Jalisco initiated a constellation of programs to build well-being, and the Ministry of Education partnered with us to conduct a random-assignment, placebo-controlled study of positive education. We had seventy schools with a total of 68,762 students. Alejandro and the ministry modified the Bhutan curriculum for Mexico. It comprised the parallel ten elements from Bhutan.

Our staff, using an extensive training manual, taught thirty-five Mexican trainers, each with a background in psychology and education, how to teach teachers these life skills and how to infuse them into their academic courses. These thirty-five trainers went on to teach the principals and teachers of thirty-five schools, chosen at random. The same trainers taught the principals and teachers about nutrition, psychology, and human anatomy in thirty-five control schools.

Fifteen months later the children from the well-being schools had higher well-being and significantly higher standardized test scores than those in the placebo schools. Again, greater engagement and perseverance seemed to have caused the improved grades. The academic effect was somewhat smaller than in Bhutan, likely because there was now an additional layer of training between our experienced trainers and the actual teachers.[13]

To round out the most massive dissertation I have ever supervised, Alejandro, in partnership with the World Bank, then did Peru—this time with 694 schools and 694,153 students. The design mirrored that in Mexico and Bhutan, and the curriculum paralleled Mexico's. There was, however, one more layer to dilute the training. Our Penn trainers taught 28 Peruvian trainers, who then taught 590 local trainers, who in turn trained the principals and teachers from the 694 schools.

The curriculum increased both well-being and academic performance, as measured fifteen months later. Engagement and perseverance of the students once again mediated, and with yet another layer of dilution, the effect on academic performance, while highly significant, was smaller.[14]

CHANGING THE EDUCATIONAL system of the world is daunting. Teachers and principals are heavily invested in what they already teach, and unions entrench policies that make transformation nearly impossible. The main objection that Alejandro and I heard time and again was that schools were about creating paths to college and the workplace. Any program that taught well-being to schoolchildren had to replace some useful program already in place. The school day had only so many hours, and money was insufficient to support what already existed. Making kids happier might therefore subtract from traditional academic success. Alejandro's data showed convincingly that young people with higher well-being actually did better in their academic courses. They became more engaged in school and grittier in their schoolwork. I believe the students did so because teaching positive psychology rejuvenated the teachers themselves and made them easier for the students to engage.

From my point of view, improvement in grades is a welcome by-product of positive education. But regardless of its influence on success, more well-being is every young person's birthright, and we now know that it can and should be taught. I believe that much of the future of positive psychology will rest on the fulcrum of positive education.

Chapter Twenty-Four

CIA (2002)

The Navy formed a high-powered medical team.
In particular, it invited Professor Seligman to
Guantánamo. This practitioner is a celebrity, re-
nowned for his works on depression. His books on
optimism and confidence are international best-
sellers. It was he who oversaw the experiments on
human guinea pigs. . . . U.S. torturers, under Pro-
fessor Seligman's supervision, experimented and
perfected every single coercive technique.

THIERRY MEYSSAN, "THE SECRET BEHIND
GUANTÁNAMO," VOLTAIRENET.ORG, 2010.

"*H*OW DOES IT feel to be the spiritual father of American tor-
ture?" the anonymous email read. It was a crisp late-summer day in
2015, and I was with Mandy and the kids at the Philadelphia Art Mu-
seum. How did it feel? It felt like I had been punched in the gut, and I
crumpled onto a bench.

Unlike the wildly false quote that begins this chapter, this email
hurt. I would never aid or abet torture. I believe my very purpose in
being alive is to increase the amount of well-being in the world, and
I have worked my whole life to decrease helplessness in the world. So
as I got up from the bench, clutching my gut, I decided that I would
devote a chapter of this book to narrating what actually happened.

I had made it a practice to try never to get defensive when my science was criticized, since science advances by criticism. But this criticism was not about my science; it was personal and moral, as well as untrue, and so this will be the only chapter that will feel defensive to my readers.

Here in a nutshell is what happened: in the spring of 2002, James Mitchell, Bruce Jessen, and Kirk Hubbard of the CIA asked me how the research on learned helplessness could help captured Americans resist and evade torture and interrogation. They never asked about how to use learned helplessness with detainees and never mentioned the interrogation of detainees. Mitchell and Jessen later created an enhanced interrogation program, and it was falsely reported that they based some of its brutal techniques on the theory of learned helplessness. I played no role at all in these developments, and I am grieved and horrified that brutal interrogations might employ scientific research conducted to relieve helplessness and depression.

NOW THE DETAILED history.

My reaction to 9/11 was typical of most Americans'. It was the first frontal attack on American soil since Pearl Harbor, and I worried that it was the opening shot of full-scale war. What could I do to help my country? I had no high government or military contacts; nor did I know much about Islam or terrorism. I did, however, have good convening power among academics. I called my friend and donor Jim Hovey and asked if he would underwrite my convening a group of academics to make recommendations to the White House about how to counter Islamic extremism. Jim agreed readily.

So a group of twelve professors met at my house on December 15 and 16, 2001. Four people from the American intelligence community also showed up. I did not invite them, and I do not know who did. We wanted to send the White House unsolicited recommendations to help the nation in a time of great need. Our topic was how to win a lasting victory against global terrorism. I made no recommendations myself: I served as secretary and compiled the recommendations of the other invitees. We probably sent them to the White House, but I

never received any response from the government about this meeting or the report.

The four intelligence people introduced themselves (Steven Band and Steven Etter from the FBI and Kirk Hubbard and James Mitchell from the CIA), but they were totally silent throughout. I did not have a conversation that I can recall with any of them—except during one break James Mitchell told me, quite gushingly, in a thirty-second conversation how much he admired my work. He did not elaborate. His remark was striking, and I proudly told Mandy about it that night.

There was not a single mention of interrogation, torture, or detainees during the meeting.

The most unrelenting of my critics call this meeting the "misty origin" of the torture program and my complicity in it.[1] But there is no basis for this other than my being in the same room with James Mitchell and Kirk Hubbard for two days.

In 2008 Jane Mayer, a *New Yorker* writer, made the first allegations that I had aided torture.

> Professor Seligman's disavowal actually adds a rather interesting new fact to the story of how the psychology profession played a role in the CIA's "special" interrogation program. In "The Dark Side," I established by interviewing him, that he had personally spoken for three hours at the Navy's SERE School in San Diego, in April of 2002, at a somewhat mysterious confab organized in part by the head of Behavioral Science at the CIA.
>
> . . . Seligman, it seems, agreed to participate in what he says was an unexplained private high-level CIA meeting, held on the campus of the part of the Navy that runs a secret program emulating torture. . . .
>
> Professor Seligman says he has no idea why he was called in from his academic position in Pennsylvania, to suddenly appear at this CIA event. He just showed up and talked for three hours about how dogs, when exposed to horrible treatment, give up all hope, and become compliant. Why the CIA wanted

to know about this at this point, he says he never asked. But somehow—and this is what is news as far as I know . . . Professor Seligman does know that in his audience were the two psychologists who soon after became the key advisers to the CIA's "enhanced" interrogation program: James Mitchell and Bruce Jessen. So, Professor Seligman, must have had some contact with them, since he knew they were in his audience. Did he speak with them? What did they talk about?

. . . So did Seligman assist the U.S. Torture program? I am careful not to say so in "The Dark Side,"—I just recount the facts of his odd visit to the SERE school.[2]

As far as I am concerned, Mayer does not "recount the facts" and her claim of an "interview" with me is a half-truth. We had an email exchange in December 2007, a few months before publication of her book *The Dark Side*.[3] I emailed her several paragraphs on December 21, 2007, and also said, "I can try to answer your email queries."

She emailed back, "I'll send a few questions your way shortly. I have a lunch appointment in a moment, but when I get back I'll send off an email. Again, thank you for any help on this."

She never wrote me again, and so we never had a substantial interview. I have a complete record of our correspondence (I have been careful to do all my interviews about these matters in writing so there would be a public record if needed). Her statement "Professor Seligman says he has no idea why he was called in from his academic position in Pennsylvania, to suddenly appear at this CIA event" is absolutely not supported by the facts.

Here are the facts of my dealings with the CIA in 2002 and thereafter.

In mid-February 2002, Bruce Jessen, on behalf of the Joint Personnel Recovery Agency (JPRA), invited me to give a talk at the annual conference of the Survival, Evasion, Resistance and Escape (SERE) community. He sent along a collection of papers on how our troops were trained to resist interrogation and survive captivity. He asked to meet with me in April to discuss the contents of the talk and signed the letter as "Senior DoD SERE Psychologist."

Two meetings then took place at my house. I have a clear memory of the first but no memory of the second. Kirk Hubbard and a female lawyer (whose name I do not remember) came to my house, and we had a roughly two-hour conversation. They asked me at length about learned helplessness (procedures, generalization, time course, immunization, biology, and therapy). I went through all this material in detail with them. They told me that they were interested in how what was known about helplessness might help Americans when captured to resist and evade torture and interrogation. They suggested that I make this the topic of my speech to JPRA at the San Diego Naval Base in mid-May.

The next meeting likely occurred later in April 2002. I have had to turn to others to document that it actually happened. The meeting was at my house with Kirk Hubbard, James Mitchell, and Bruce Jessen. I have wracked my brain for almost a decade trying to conjure up any memory at all of this meeting, but with no success. Nor do I have any record of it in my date books. Of all the events I report in this chapter, this is the only one that I do not remember. So for its existence and the account of what happened at the meeting, I have to rely on external sources.

Greg Bloche, a professor of law at Georgetown, interviewed a CIA source who confirmed the existence of such a meeting "sometime in the spring of 2002," and the source said that I had a "classic approach-avoidance conflict regarding helping [them]."[4] I think the source was Kirk Hubbard, since he also affirmed the existence of this meeting to David Hoffman for the Hoffman Report to the American Psychological Association (APA).[5] The APA Board of Directors commissioned the Hoffman Report in 2015 as an "independent investigation" into APA's role in the enhanced interrogation program.

David Hoffman asked me by email in 2015 about the existence of such a meeting in preparing his report. Here is what I emailed him:

> I continued to be puzzled about the visit with Hubbard, Mitchell and Jessen in April 2002, since I have no memory of it. So I wrote Kirk Hubbard and sent him all my recent correspondence with you, asking him to comment on its accuracy

in toto. Here's his response: "I reviewed your responses to David Hoffman. And I am pleased that I am not the only person whose memory isn't as clear as I would wish! I believe all of your responses are accurate except for a couple of things. There was a second meeting at your home on April 3, 2002 with Mitchell, Jessen and myself attending. The purpose was to ask you to discuss Positive Psychology at an upcoming JPRA conference in May 2002, to which you agreed. As you note <u>there has never been any discussion with you regarding any aspect of interrogation that I am aware of</u>. [Underlining is mine] And I verified that with Jim Mitchell. Second, I did give you a glass vase on April 3, 2002. It was probably worth under $50.00 and, since I paid for it, it was a personal gift from me not the CIA."

So I surmise from this that there must have been such a meeting and such a gift, since I cannot think of any reason why Hubbard would make this up. Most important to me, Hubbard (and through him, Mitchell) both confirmed that "there has never been any discussion with you regarding any aspect of interrogation."

Despite my having no memory of the meeting, I believe it occurred because (1) Bruce Jessen asked me to meet with him on that date; (2) Hubbard and Mitchell told Hoffman that there was such a meeting and I can't think of any reason they would lie; and (3) I can remember meeting Mitchell only twice and Jessen only twice: Mitchell at my house in December 2001 and also presumably in April 2002, and Jessen at the JPRA meeting on May 17, 2002, and also presumably at my house in April 2002. (Neither Mitchell nor Jessen was present at the first meeting at my home in early 2002, and I do not think Mitchell was at the JPRA meeting.)

Jeffrey Kaye, a psychologist and anti-torture activist, sees my failure to remember this meeting as evidence of a cover-up.[6] It would be exculpating and convenient for me to remember this meeting and its contents, but the simple truth is that I do not.

So what was said at this meeting?

I assume, but I cannot be certain, that I went through exactly the same material about the research literature on learned helplessness as I did with Kirk Hubbard and the lawyer and as I also did subsequently at the JPRA meeting in May. On those other occasions I outlined the procedures for inducing helplessness in the laboratory, the generalization to other laboratory settings, when it is temporary and when it is permanent, how to immunize against it, its neurobiology, and how to do therapy to cure it.

I am certain that they did not mention detainees, interrogation of detainees, or using learned helplessness on our prisoners. Had they mentioned any of these at any time, alarm bells would have sounded, I would surely have remembered it, and the meeting would have stood out in my memory. Hubbard and Mitchell testified to Hoffman, "There has never been any discussion with you regarding any aspect of interrogation." My conversations with Hubbard and the lawyer in April and at the JPRA meeting were entirely about how the knowledge of learned helplessness could help captured American personnel and not about using learned helplessness on detainees. My motivation was entirely to help captive Americans.

Here is what the Hoffman Report concluded about my role:

> Combining the statements made to us by Seligman, Hubbard, and Mitchell, it appears that Hubbard met with Seligman at his house on two occasions—once along with Mitchell and Jessen, and once along with two other CIA psychologists or attorneys. At these meetings, learned helplessness was discussed (in substantial detail during at least one of the meetings), and Seligman was invited to speak to a SERE conference in San Diego about learned helplessness. Our evidence shows that Mitchell was very interested in the application of the learned helplessness theory to interrogations of uncooperative detainees. Hubbard and Mitchell say that they never discussed interrogations with Seligman and did not provide him information about the interrogation program. Seligman agrees and says he thought their interest in learned

helplessness related to its insights for captured US personnel who are trained through the SERE program to resist providing information in interrogations.[7]

On May 17, 2002, I gave the promised three-hour lecture at the San Diego Naval Base to an audience of about one hundred people, presumably from the Department of Defense (DoD). I spoke in detail about the scientific literature on learned helplessness and how captured American troops and American personnel might use what was known to resist torture and evade interrogation by their captors. I was surprised to learn that I was barred from all sessions except mine, since I had no security clearance.

My speech in San Diego was pro bono, but JPRA reimbursed me for my airfare and hotel. Kirk Hubbard was in the audience, as, I believe, was Bruce Jessen. I do not remember seeing James Mitchell there. Hubbard and I and the same lawyer who visited my house had an outdoor lunch at the Hotel Coronado before my speech. Our conversation concerned what learned helplessness tells us about how captured American personnel could resist and evade torture and interrogation. There was no mention of detainees.

IN 2016 TAMSIN SHAW wrote a hostile article about me in the *New York Review of Books*. She said, "The extent of Seligman's further involvement has not been established, but in an e-mail sent by Hubbard in 2004, he expressed gratitude for Seligman's help 'over the past four years.'"[8]

Was I involved with the CIA after my speech on May 17, 2002?

This question first arose when James Risen, a well-known *New York Times* reporter, was writing *Pay Any Price*,[9] the book that gave rise to APA's commissioning the Hoffman Report. Risen asked me about the gratitude to me expressed by Kirk Hubbard in an email to Scott Gerwehr. Here is my email exchange with Risen from December 12, 2012:

Hi, Mr. Seligman. I am finally finishing up my book that I contacted you about last year. I am doing a chapter about

interrogation policy and the mental health professions, and as part of that I've looked into the life of a Rand researcher named Scott Gerwehr who I think you may have known. He died in 2008, and I have obtained many of the emails that he wrote or received while he worked on deception detection research, often on contracts for the CIA and other government agencies. The emails are mostly of interest to me not because of anything Gerwehr did, but because they seem to provide a glimpse into a network of behavioral science professionals who were in and out of the intelligence community during the Bush years. Some of the emails relate to you, and one in particular, caught my eye. It was an email Kirk Hubbard of the CIA wrote to Gerwehr and other people in March, 2004. In it, he wrote that "My office director would not even reimburse me for circa $100 bucks for CIA logo t-shirts and ball caps for Marty Seligman's five kids! He's helped out a lot over the past four years so I thought that was the least I could do. But no, has to come out of my own pocket! And people wonder why I am so cynical!" This is a fairly pedestrian email, but I would like to ask you about Hubbard's suggestion that you had been helping the CIA for the previous few years. I was particularly struck by this since you had previously told me that you had nothing to do with the CIA's interrogation program. So I was wondering if you were working with the agency on other matters.

I emailed Risen the same day. Here's the text:

I do not have any memory of Mr. Gerwehr. I got no hat or T-shirts for my kids, nor any other token of gratitude from the CIA. The only thing Kirk Hubbard might be referring to was my lecture in May 2002 in San Diego (which was sponsored by SERE, not as far as I know by the CIA). I had lunch with Hubbard, at the Coronado I think. It was friendly and I told him at length about my work on learned helplessness, in the

context of our soldiers and diplomats resisting captivity. Or perhaps he is referring to the meeting at my house in December 2001 (which had nothing to do with interrogation—but with how our global policies could counter Islamic Jihad). He was there as well. All of our conversation was friendly. You might ask Hubbard what he was referring to. I did no work for the CIA during the Bush era, not on interrogations, not on anything else. Maybe this is naive, but can't you just ask the CIA to verify this?

I emailed Kirk Hubbard the next day and asked him to verify for Risen what is above. Hubbard emailed me back on December 14, 2012. Here's the text:

Yes, the below does conform with my memory. I did not purchase any hats or t-shirts for your children because I was disgusted that the office director would not reimburse me and I was, sadly, too cheap to pay for them myself. The SERE conference in San Diego was not sponsored in any way by the CIA. And I can verify that you were never on contract to do work for the CIA.

So the reason that, as Shaw comments, "the extent of Seligman's further involvement has not been established" is that there wasn't any. I had no other substantive interactions with Hubbard, Mitchell, Jessen, the female lawyer, the CIA, or any related agency after the May 17, 2002, JPRA meeting in San Diego.

IT WAS SAID that Mitchell and Jessen based their "enhanced interrogation" program on learned helplessness. Mitchell denied this, and in a December 9, 2016, email to me, referring to his book *Enhanced Interrogation*,[10] he said, "For the first time the CIA is allowing me to say that I did not base my approach on learned helplessness." In my view learned helplessness is not relevant to what the program did. As described in the press,[11] enhanced interrogation involved beatings, sleep deprivation, waterboarding, and a host of cruel techniques.

This is old-fashioned brutality, and its effects are not the same thing as learned helplessness. Learned helplessness is about bad (or good) events that continue regardless of what you do; its defining feature is that nothing you do matters. The bad events continue regardless of your actions. In contrast, the implicit bargain in such interrogation is that if the prisoners tell the truth, the brutality will stop, and this is exactly the bargain that Mitchell described in his book.

Further—and I qualify what follows by saying that I have never seen an interrogation; nor do I know the literature on interrogation—I think that the goal of interrogation is to get at the truth. The interrogator and the subject have a bargain: if the subject tells the truth, he will get better treatment (or a reduced sentence or better food or more sleep). Learned helplessness rests on the belief that nothing the subject does matters at all—it does not matter if he tells the truth, or lies, or is silent, or says what the interrogator wants to hear. So using enhanced interrogation to produce learned helplessness would make no sense. That outcome would totally undermine the bargain by making the prisoner believe that it did not matter whether he told the truth. It would make the prisoner more passive and depressed, but it would not lead to disclosure.

The irrelevance of learned helplessness aside, Tamsin Shaw suggested that I should have foreseen that the CIA would use my information about learned helplessness for ill purposes.

> Martin Seligman has repeatedly insisted that he is an opponent of torture. He tells us in his letter that he "strongly disapproves" of it. If he found himself at the very center of the terrible episode in our recent history in which the United States inflicted brutal torture on detainees in the Abu Ghraib prison, the Guantánamo Bay detention camp, and at CIA black sites, this was, he maintains, entirely unwittingly. And yet, since he was at the center of this episode, being in direct contact with the architects of the CIA's torture program at the moment of its devising, there are some clear questions that a declared opponent of torture might have asked in his position.[12]

That I was "at the very center of this terrible episode" is pure Shaw fantasy. As far as I can see, I was not even marginally involved. But what of the "clear questions" that I, as an opponent of torture, should have asked Mitchell or Jessen?

JPRA and the CIA approached me in early 2002 to ask what I knew about learned helplessness in order to help train our soldiers and diplomats to resist torture and interrogation when captured. The entire discussion was about helping Americans. Detainees were never mentioned. Interrogating—to say nothing of torturing—detainees was never mentioned. Needless to say, I wish no wars ever had to be fought and that the brutal business of war and the horrible torture that sometimes accompanies it never happened. But since the world is still a dangerous place, we have to deal with the awful reality that our soldiers might be tortured. That does *not* mean that I believe we should torture our enemies. I most emphatically don't—for reasons both moral and practical. I am, however, a patriotic American, eager to help my country in a time of great need, and I took the questions Mitchell or Jessen asked at face value.

Why should I not have? Shaw wants me to have foreseen that these people might use my information to brutally interrogate and torture detainees. I am not particularly naive, but this did not occur to me. Nor, do I think, would it have occurred to anyone without 20/20 hindsight coupled with a conspiracy theory about the Department of Defense.

Shaw sees my failure to confront the CIA and refuse them help in early 2002 as a moral failure. She believes that psychologists should better foresee how what they say and what they write might be misused.

The irony of her accusation leads to my concluding remarks.

I have been puzzled about the unrelenting attack on my actions and my character that these events unleashed. Despite repeated investigations and a mass of evidence that I was not complicit, the theory that I helped to design and carry out a program of torture continues. Nothing found counts as disconfirmation in the eyes of the attackers.

Here's why I surmise that the attacks continue nevertheless.

I was asked right after 9/11 to help captured American soldiers evade and resist torture—which I gladly did, foreseeing that the likely consequence would be less suffering by our soldiers. But an organized cadre of antiwar activists did not want to look properly at the facts or my motives. In the hands of Tamsin Shaw, Jeffrey Kaye, Roy Eidelson, Bryant Welch, Steven Soldz, Steven Reisner, Jean Maria Arrigo, and their Coalition for an Ethical Psychology, this presented a capital opportunity to accuse a prominent scientist (and former APA president) of aiding and abetting the torture of detainees. A smear campaign, guilt by association, and quarter-truths notwithstanding, I speculate that they hoped to exploit my case to forward their agenda: undermining psychologists' willingness to help the US military. While I did not foresee the possibility that some might use my knowledge in truly awful ways, I believe that these antiwar activists foresaw one very likely consequence of their maligning my actions. In the future, when asked by legitimate government officials to serve the United States of America, young psychologists will be more likely to refuse lest they be similarly defamed should their knowledge be misused.

This same group of antiwar psychologists succeeded on a larger scale in 2015. They staged a coup d'état in an attempt to take over the American Psychological Association.

For the last fifty years, APA has had three overlapping constituencies. The original and most venerable comprised the scientists. In the 1970s, the independent therapists overtook the scientists in numbers, and governance fell to them in the coup d'état staged by the self-named "dirty dozen." My presidency in 1998 marked a brief respite and some sharing of power between the practitioners and the scientists.

But there has always been a third, less conspicuous constituency: the social activists. Indeed, many of the therapists and scientists share their ideals. I do as well, particularly on race and gender issues. The agenda of the social activists, broadly speaking, is "human rights." Psychologists are left of center politically, and explaining this would itself require a whole chapter. Suffice it to say that one major factor is the psychologists' laudable task of helping people in trouble, the

downtrodden, people who need advocates and defenders. So it is no surprise that APA has been conspicuous in advocacy for, and devoted major resources to, affirmative action, women's issues, and gay rights. But the social activists, particularly the far-left, antiwar wing, have always taken a backseat to the therapists and the scientists and even to the moderate social activists.

All this changed in 2015. James Risen's *Pay Any Price* accused APA of complicity in the George W. Bush administration's enhanced interrogation program. The allegation made the front page of the *New York Times*. The *New York Times* attacking organized psychology—*mon dieu*! This was the moment, and attacking APA as a puppet of the Bush administration became the moral high ground that the antiwar activists used to orchestrate regime change. They declared an emergency and demanded an investigation of APA's "collusion" with the Bush administration. The board of directors, under President Nadine Kaslow and President-elect Susan McDaniel, acceded. At the cost of $4.5 million, they hired David Hoffman, a Democratic prosecutor from Chicago, to carry out an independent investigation. Hoffman regularly consulted the antiwar activists, but not the accused, and gave them premature access to the report. In July 2015, "unknown" parties prematurely leaked the Hoffman Report to the *New York Times* before those "named" could defend themselves. Those "named" (I was not one of them) never received their promised right of response and correction. The Hoffman Report was interpreted as concluding that APA officials "colluded" with the Department of Defense to sanction torture and that APA's "currying favor" was motivated by the desire for DoD contracts and grants. The governance of APA, along with several past presidents, was condemned. (To my relief, the testimony of Hubbard and Mitchell, it seemed, had exculpated me.) Within days, the high administration of APA either resigned or was fired, and Nadine Kaslow, as president, endorsed the report and issued an apology to the nation.

The actions, policies and the lack of independence from government influence described in the Hoffman report

represented a failure to live up to our core values. We profoundly regret, and apologize for, the behavior and the consequences that ensued. Our members, our profession and our organization expected, and deserved, better.[13]

APA promised to clean up its act and take human rights more seriously. Psychologists were forever banned from participating in DoD interrogations, regardless of how legitimate the request or how desperate the national need.

I have not been in the APA loop since 2000, so I have no firsthand knowledge of what actually happened in Washington, DC. But as a reader of the report and the firestorm of pros and cons that ensued,[14] the takeaway—that APA "colluded" with DoD to sanction torture, motivated by dollars—looks flimsy to me. Not flimsy is the fact that APA governance moved toward the antimilitary left. It is no coincidence that the very same people who falsely accused me of aiding and abetting torture and, as we shall see in the next chapter, opposed resilience training for American soldiers were at the center of the Hoffman episode. As I write, those "named" have sued APA and Hoffman for malicious libel.[15] The plaintiffs allege that Hoffman, Kaslow, and McDaniel actively colluded with Stephen Soldz, Steven Reisner, and the antiwar APA Left and engaged in a malicious and knowingly false smear campaign. That Hoffman took his lead from the antiwar Left is entirely plausible given his questions of me—for example, "Describe all other items of value you received from the government between September 11, 2001 and December 2008. Please include all gifts received from Kirk Hubbard and/or Jim Mitchell, including any vases and CIA-labeled paraphernalia." The outcome of the coup, the lawsuit, and who will control APA's $100 million budget and lead its 100,000 members is very much in doubt.

One thing is not in doubt. The antiwar activists have scared the pants off many APA members. Psychologists—scientists, practitioners, and centrist social activists—have learned that cooperating with the government, particularly with the Department of Defense, is dangerous to one's career. Such cooperation invites a smear

campaign from the antiwar activists. Undermining psychologists' willingness to help the government is, I believe, the basic intention of this group.

We cannot know what the future holds, but, unfashionable as it is, I strongly believe that when in doubt, we should err on the side of helping our nation.

Chapter Twenty-Five

Army (2008–2017)

AT EITHER END of the long table sat a brigadier general. Both were women. In the middle of the table sat a constellation of two- and three-star generals. They were all men. The four-star chief of staff of the US Army walked in. Everyone jumped to attention, and I, the only civilian, stumbled to my feet. General George Casey took the chair in the middle, across from me. It was December 2008, and the war was raging in Iraq. President George W. Bush had, with fulsome praise, kicked General Casey upstairs from the battlefield to the Pentagon, to be replaced in the field by General David Petraeus. Petraeus's surge seemed to be taking hold, but mental illness plagued the army itself—hence my invitation to the Pentagon.

"Suicide, drug abuse, posttraumatic stress disorder, panic, depression, divorce," began General Casey, speaking deliberately but with an undertone of skepticism. "What does positive psychology say about all that, Dr. Seligman?"

"The human reaction to awful events like combat, Sir, is bell-shaped," I began, reflexively using the honorific that I learned in the battalion at the Albany Academy for Boys. "You have just described the left-hand side of the bell, the different names for the ways in which people's lives are ruined. But most people are *resilient*, which means they go through a tough time in combat and then a few months later, by all our physical and psychological measures, they are back where they were before combat.

"More important and much less publicized," I continued while focusing my eyes on a major general without a left leg, "is *posttraumatic growth*, the right-hand side of the bell curve. These are the soldiers who go through a terrible time in combat but one year later are stronger—by our physical and psychological measures—than they were to begin with. The army is not a hospital, and of course you should continue to spend the billions of dollars it takes to help those who have their lives ruined, but my advice, Sir, is to move the whole curve rightward, toward posttraumatic growth."

"The general staff has done its homework, Dr. Seligman," General Casey replied. I could see from the books they were carrying, including my latest, that they were well prepped. "I intend to create an army that is just as psychologically fit as physically fit. We have read your work on positive education. We know that you teach teachers the skills of resilience and positive psychology and that you have found that young people who learn your material from their teachers have less depression and more well-being. That's the army way. We have 40,000 teachers in the army."

"You do, Sir?"

"The drill sergeants," he said with finality, and then, unlike you and me, who, when we have a good idea, try to convince our colleagues, General Casey now commanded, "I want the drill sergeants taught the skills of resilience and positive psychology, and the drill sergeants will then teach the 1.3 million soldiers. From this day forward, resilience and positive psychology will be taught and measured throughout the entire United States Army. I intend to create an army that is just as psychologically fit as physically fit.

"To do this I want you to work with one of the brigadier generals, Dr. Seligman."

I glanced at Brigadier General Loree Sutton, the army's chief psychiatrist, at the left end of the table. I had heard a bit about her; it was said she was staging Greek tragedies with traumatized soldiers as her actors, getting them to open up and pour out their hidden emotions. This was not my kind of intervention. But General Casey, to my relief, pointed to the right end of the table.

"Dr. Seligman, meet Rhonda Cornum. Rhonda is the chief urologist of the army, and I want you to work with her to create 'Comprehensive Soldier Fitness.' Report back to me in sixty days."

"I will be delighted to work with a star neurologist, Sir," I answered.

"*Urologist*," Rhonda corrected, and on this off-note began one of the farthest-reaching collaborations of my life.

TWO DAYS LATER Rhonda drove her RV up from the Pentagon to my office at Penn's Positive Psychology Center to plan. At five-foot-two and one hundred pounds, she was pert, with short-brown hair, and dressed in unflattering army camouflage.

She was laconic and used humor to drive home her points. "Better is the enemy of the good," she told me when I suggested too many experts. "He needs some adult supervision," she said when I recommended a captain. She was also a war hero, the only female general to hold the Purple Heart, having been wounded in combat.

During Operation Desert Storm she went on a rescue mission. Her helicopter was shot down, and all the men jumped on her to protect the physician with their bodies. Unfortunately, the bullets were coming up from below, and all but Rhonda and one other soldier died. She suffered two broken arms, a broken finger, a gunshot wound, and other injuries. She was taken prisoner and sexually molested. Saddam Hussein and President George H. W. Bush negotiated her release.

"It's too bad you're a woman, Major," the welcoming colonel told her when she arrived back in Saudi Arabia from prison, "otherwise you could be a general." A general she became and—as I discovered somewhat later, seeing how at Fort Leavenworth 1,200 majors and colonels had risen to their feet applauding her—not just any general but the poster child general.

Creating a psychologically fit army required two things. First we needed a measure of psychological fitness, not just the usual measures of unfitness: mental illness, indiscipline, substance abuse, felonies, dishonorable discharges. We needed good measures of a soldier's well-being, resilience, character strengths, social support,

sense of purpose, growth, and positive emotion—the positive sides of a soldier's life, since Comprehensive Soldier Fitness (CSF) aimed explicitly to increase the well-being of all soldiers not just to reduce negatives. Second, we needed a plan for building well-being and resilience, a plan to move the entire army toward the right-hand side of the bell curve—toward posttraumatic growth.

For the first, we convened a meeting of measurers the very next week, right before Christmas 2008, in my office. I came down with the flu, and they excused me after my opening remarks. Chris Peterson chaired the meeting along with Colonel Carl Castro. Nansook Park, Chris Peterson's right hand, was the workhorse. Taking the best items from a variety of personality inventories, they constructed a 120-item Global Assessment Tool (GAT) and started the pilot work right away.

"REPORT," GENERAL CASEY instructed. Same lunch table, same generals—it was mid-February 2009, and I was jet-lagged, just back from teaching positive psychology to Geelong Grammar School teachers in Australia.

"We developed a questionnaire to assess soldiers' well-being, resilience, and character strengths, as well as the usual deficits and problems," Rhonda said, "and we piloted it with ten thousand soldiers, Sir." She actually called 10,000 subjects *pilot* work.

"Good work, General Cornum. What are you and Marty [I blushed when General Casey used my first name] going to do by way of building resilience and positive psychology in the army?"

"We'd like to run a pilot study with one hundred drill sergeants and five thousand soldiers," Rhonda said. She and I had discussed this at length and decided to go slowly and carefully. "Each sergeant will teach fifty soldiers resilience skills and then for the next year we will gather data—"

"We are at war, General Cornum," interrupted General Casey. "I don't want a pilot study. I want you to teach and measure resilience and positive psychology in the whole army now."

"Move out, Soldier!" he said and left the table. We snapped to our feet.

So Rhonda and I had three huge tasks. The first, creating a viable test of resilience and well-being for more than 1 million soldiers, was well underway. The second was to craft an intervention that had a shot, in the absence of serious pilot work, at building resilience in soldiers. The third was to measure—in the midst of war—if soldiers were actually learning more resilience.

Karen Reivich now enlisted to build the intervention. Karen had been teaching resilience and positive psychology to hundreds of schoolteachers, most recently at the Geelong Grammar School. The drill sergeants were indeed teachers, but of a very different stripe. How could we modify the extensive manuals we used to teach teachers in peacetime to teach drill sergeants in the middle of a hot war?

We needed to combine what we'd learned teaching civilian teachers with the issues that overwhelmed soldiers in Iraq and Afghanistan. So Karen mixed two teams together: the first comprised our five best teachers of ordinary schoolteachers, and the second consisted of soldiers, from colonels to corporals, all of whom had served on the front lines. We had already created massive minute-by-minute manuals for teaching schoolteachers and modified them to teach drill sergeants. In an eight-day program for schoolteachers we started first by teaching the teachers to use the skills of resilience and positive psychology in their own lives and only then taught them how to teach the skills to schoolchildren. So we planned to first teach the sergeants to use the skills on themselves and then develop the techniques for teaching the soldiers.

We were surprised by the similarity in the issues faced by both soldiers and civilians. Before meeting the soldier team to redo the manuals, we assumed new material would deal primarily with firefights, roadside bombings, and dealing with hostile as well as innocent civilians. How can you remain resilient when your best buddy has just been decapitated?

We were soon disabused of this CNN-stereotyped warfare in Iraq.

"This is the first war in which soldiers have cellphones," a major reminded us. "Before a battle a worried private will call his girlfriend in Saint Louis, and they will have a huge fight. When we see suicide

attempts or posttraumatic stress, troubles back at home loom as large as firefights in Iraq."

So as we wrote the new manuals for the drill sergeants, we coupled examples from army life and ordinary home life. Take for example an exercise to correct *catastrophization* (the worst possible interpretation applied to an ambiguous situation) by transforming it into a more realistic interpretation. The exercise, called "Put It in Perspective," aimed to lower the panic and anxiety set off by the worst interpretation of a bad event.

Army life:

> You and your squad are out on a land navigation course. It is twenty minutes past the midnight deadline, and one of your soldiers has not shown up.
>
> Step one is to list the worst possibilities:
> * He's got heat stroke.
> * He's probably dead.
> * It's my fault, and I will rot in jail the rest of my life.
>
> Step two is to list the best possibilities:
> * He's taking a nap.
> * He's 100 meters away and will be here in a few minutes.
>
> Step three is to list the most likely possibilities:
> * He got lost.
> * He's hitchhiking back.
> * I will have to report him, and the captain will bawl me out.
>
> Now develop a plan for dealing with the most likely outcomes.
> * Find out who saw him last.
> * Send out a couple of guys with a vehicle to look for him.

Home life:

> You phone you girlfriend late at night in the United States, and she does not answer.
>
> Worst outcome?
> - She's out on a date with another man.
> - She's having an affair.
> - It's all over.
>
> Best outcome?
> - She's asleep and does not hear the phone.
> - She's staying overnight at her mother's house.
>
> Most likely outcome?
> - She's gone out drinking with her girlfriends.
> - She's tempted by other guys.
>
> Now formulate a plan for dealing with the most likely outcomes.
> - Outline an understanding script about how lonely you both are.
> - Rehearse it with your best buddy.

THE MANUAL STARTED with a panoply of such resilience, or "mental toughness," exercises. This took up the first two or three days of the program. In the next two days, the sergeants (20 percent of whom were female) learned to identify their signature strengths, as well as the strengths of the soldiers in their platoons, and how to deploy the range of strengths to carry out actual missions. Finally, we taught "building strong relationships," a scientifically informed version of inculcating leadership skills. So, for example, we taught how to impart effective praise. When you recognized someone and offered praise, we suggested naming the specific strength, strategy, effort, or skill that had led to the good outcome. It just takes another sentence. Naming the strength does three things:

- Demonstrates you were really watching
- Demonstrates authenticity
- Enables winning streaks

We piloted the program successfully with several hundred drill sergeants, and after months of negotiations, the army and Penn entered into a $30 million contract to train thousands of drill sergeants and other noncommissioned officers over the next three years. My work was entirely pro bono.

Accordingly, once a month about 180 drill sergeants showed up at the Penn Sheraton Hotel for a nine-day course. As of this writing, we have trained more than 40,000 trainers. They were not shy and were more candid critics than our polite, housebroken schoolteachers. The sergeants were typically black or Hispanic soldiers originally from tough urban neighborhoods and had done three often heroic tours of duty in Iraq or Afghanistan. They had seen it all and were forthright about their opinions.

I should say that after going to faculty meetings for fifty years, I have yet to meet a faculty member I would trust my life to. In the course of this work, I have now met dozens of sergeants that I would trust my life to.

I will present some numbers about the effectiveness of this training below, but the sergeants' reactions were dramatic and more to the point. At the outset of the first hour, they were leaning away from us with facial expressions that ranged from stolid indifference to sucking on a lemon. They were thinking something like, "What is this emasculating psychobabble that we have been ordered up to Philadelphia to listen to?" By the end of the first hour, they were leaning forward, intrigued. By the end of the last day, three-quarters of them had volunteered to become trainers of trainers, the next level of teaching. Their average rating of the entire program was about 4.9 out of 5.0, and the modal and emblematic comment was "This is the single best course I have had in twenty years in the army."

The drill sergeants told us many times that these skills were "life-saving," but my guess is that the real effect was on the home front.

One morning I came in very early to the Sheraton and sat down to breakfast. A master sergeant whom I had met the day before, when we taught active constructive responding to good events, joined me.

"I couldn't wait to tell you that something really cool happened last night after class, Sir," he said, barely restraining himself. "I called home, and my son answered. He was so excited. He hit a home run in Little League and won the game. We chatted for about five minutes, and then he said, 'Dad, is this really you?'"

These skills are useful on the battlefield, but they are at least as useful at home with the people you love. One sergeant told me that taking this course when he was younger would have saved his marriage.

We planned carefully to get good data on whether the program actually worked, using untreated control groups and random assignment of sergeants to training or no training. We originally designed the rollout of the training so that 10,000 soldiers would have resilience training and 10,000 controls would not, a nice clean experiment. But the reality of war thwarted us. The sergeants' reception to this course was so overwhelmingly positive that the generals sped up the rollout, wiping out our neat control group. So our well-designed experiment went up in smoke. In the meantime, the army decided to create a giant electronic database housed in Monterrey, California, and for the very first time at least thirty siloes of data—formerly separated and unanalyzable—millions of soldiers were merged into the Person-Event Data Environment. This became a national treasure for civilian and military medical research, and you will hear more about its power for scientific discovery in the next chapter. In the absence of a controlled experiment, Major Paul Lester and his team of statisticians in Monterrey did their very best to get before- and after-deployment data to see if resilience-trained soldiers actually fared better.

Looking at soldiers' psychological status before and after deployment to Iraq or Afghanistan, they found that the soldiers (n = 6,739) who had resilience training improved in emotional fitness, active coping, and optimism and catastrophized less in contrast to the soldiers

(n = 3,218) who had no resilience training and actually dropped in these measures by the end of their deployments.[1]

Since these were self-reported data, the army under Major Lester went on to look at the diagnosis of mental illness. Significantly fewer soldiers who had resilience training were diagnosed with posttraumatic stress disorder, anxiety, and depression, and the rate of substance abuse was halved.[2] Based on these findings the Department of the Army declared the program "effective" and institutionalized it throughout the service.[3] The program is now available to the families of soldiers as well as to the soldiers themselves.

At the outset I told the generals that I wanted to migrate the program to the army and not have the army dependent on me and the University of Pennsylvania. So each month we picked out the most skilled sergeants to become trainers of trainers. They then delivered the resilience training to other sergeants on army bases throughout the world. By now we have at least five hundred skilled trainers of trainers, most of whom were sergeants.

Given these successes, I was surprised by the harshness of the criticism the program unleashed. But I was not surprised by who the critics were. They were the very same people who accused me of designing the enhanced interrogation program for the CIA. Here are their criticisms and my responses.

IT SHOULD NOT have been undertaken, or if undertaken, it should have been done much more slowly. According to R. Eidelson, M. Pilisuk, and S. Soldz,

> It is highly unusual for the effectiveness of such a huge and consequential intervention program not to be convincingly demonstrated first in carefully conducted, randomized, controlled trials—before being rolled out under less controlled conditions. Such preliminary studies are far from a mere formality.[4]

General Cornum and I proposed to first do a big pilot study on 5,000 soldiers, but the chief of staff overruled us. In his view, a pilot

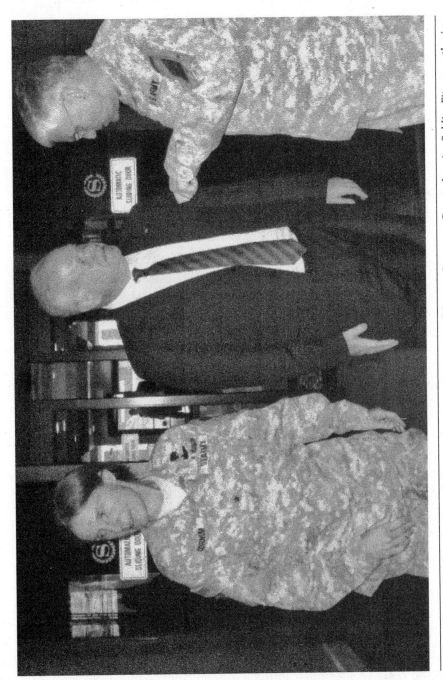

Brigadier General Rhonda Cornum, the author, and Army Chief of Staff George Casey at a Comprehensive Soldier Fitness gathering. Photo courtesy of Rhonda Cornum.

study would take years, and the results would come in too late to help our soldiers in Iraq and Afghanistan. There were, however, twenty-one replications of the procedures on middle and high school students.[5] In the absence of any resilience program that met Eidelson, Pilisuk, and Soldz's requirements, General Casey, we believe, made the wise choice: a program reasonably likely to work rather than no program at all or one that came too late.

IT DID NOT work, and it was a waste of money. The Institute of Medicine report *Preventing Psychological Disorders in Service Members and Their Families*[6] said,

> More recently, in another internal non-peer-reviewed report, The Comprehensive Soldier and Family Fitness Program Evaluation Report #4: Evaluation of Resilience Training and Mental and Behavioral Health Outcomes, Harms et al. (2013) examined psychological health diagnosis outcomes for 7,230 soldiers who received the GAT before Master Resiliency Training was initiated (October 2010) and again approximately 6 months later (about April 2011). . . . Findings revealed . . . no difference in diagnosis among those receiving the intervention.

This is an egregious error. Here is what Report Number 4 showed for the diagnosis of mental disorders in these 7,230 soldiers:

1. In the Master Resilience Training (MRT) condition, the diagnosis of substance abuse occurred in 1.16 percent of soldiers, whereas in the nontraining condition, the diagnosis of substance abuse occurred in 2.85 percent of soldiers. MRT more than halved substance abuse.

Projected across 1 million soldiers (there were 1.1 million soldiers in the army at the time), this would equate to 11,600 as opposed to 28,500 cases of substance abuse, a difference of 16,900. If each case cost the army $20,000 (I am making this number up, but it is likely a

substantial underestimate), MRT would save the army $340 million—to say nothing of massively reducing suffering.

2. In the MRT condition 4.44 percent of soldiers were diagnosed with posttraumatic stress disorder, panic, or depression. In the nontraining condition 5.07 percent were so diagnosed. Projected across 1 million soldiers, 44,400 cases would have occurred with MRT and 50,700 with no MRT, a difference of 6,300 cases. If each case costs the army $20,000 (again my made-up number but conservative), MRT would save the army $125 million—to say nothing of reducing suffering.

COMPREHENSIVE SOLDIER FITNESS is unethical. R. Eidelson, M. Pilisuk, and S. Soldz wrote,

> No evidence was provided indicating that CSF received preliminary review by an independent ethics review board. This is particularly disturbing since the program includes components that are mandatory for all U.S. soldiers. The discarding of informed consent protections is a serious violation of the Nuremberg Code established after World War II in response to the actions of Nazi doctors.[7]

Here is how the army responded to congressional staffers about this:

> According to Army Regulation 70-25 (Use of Volunteers as Subjects of Research, 1990, p. 17), research is defined as: "A systematic investigation that is designed to develop or contribute to generalized knowledge. *The term does not include individual or group training of military personnel such as combat readiness, effectiveness, proficiency, or fitness exercises.*" As CSF is a training program that supports and impacts all Soldiers and there is no expressed intent to create generalized knowledge, the program does not fit the definition of research. [Italics mine]

CSF has the same status as training programs that require all soldiers to do morning physical training, and to attend classes about how to recognize signs of suicide and sexual harassment, how to resist when captured, or why to wear safety belts when driving. These programs do not require informed consent.

CSF HARMS SOLDIERS. According to Eidelson, Pilisuk, and Soldz,

> There are, however, other ethically fraught possibilities . . . "moral injury" . . . the challenges and consequences soldiers face in response to "perpetrating, failing to prevent, bearing witness to, or learning about acts that transgress deeply held moral beliefs and expectations." Resilience training could, for example, harm our soldiers by making them more likely to engage in combat actions that adversely affect their psychological health. Missing from CSF is a component devoted to helping soldiers grapple with the profound ethical dilemmas involved in their duties, including killing in furtherance of state policy.[8]

Similarly, Bruce Levine, a blogger, ranked CSF number six on his list of the ten worst abuses of psychiatry and psychology.[9] Why? Because it subverted "U.S. Soldiers' resistance to the military-industrial complex." As the only evidence that this might be so, he wrote, "In one role-play used in this program, a sergeant is asked to take his exhausted men on one more difficult mission, and the sergeant is initially angry and complains that 'it's not fair'; but in the role play, his 'rehabilitation' involves reinterpreting the order as a compliment."

Here is what the Office of Comprehensive Soldier Fitness stated in response to congressional inquiry about these allegations:

> The authors of the article expressed concern that CSF training might actually cause harm. Current data analyses show that there is no evidence that CSF causes harm (Office of Comprehensive Soldier Fitness, 2011). These critics wanted a program that would lead soldiers to oppose American foreign

policy, to defy orders, and to avoid combat. CSF does not bear on any of these—one way or another. Rather the results showed that soldiers who participated in CSF training

1. Had greater emotional fitness
2. Were more adaptable
3. Thought in less catastrophic terms when faced with adversity
4. Employed their core character strengths more often
5. Had better coping skills
6. Were more optimistic
7. Perceived the Army as being more supportive of their family's needs.

CSF WAS A reward for my assisting the CIA torture program. Daniel Tencer wrote,

> A psychologist whose research was used in constructing the US's program to torture terrorism suspects has been granted a $31-million no-bid Army contract to provide "resilience training" to US soldiers.
>
> Mark Benjamin at Salon.com reports that University of Pennsylvania psychologist Martin Seligman's research "formed the psychological underpinnings of the Bush administration's torture program."
>
> The Army awarded the "sole source" contract in February to the University of Pennsylvania for resilience training, or teaching soldiers to better cope with the psychological strain of multiple combat tours. The university's Positive Psychology Center, directed by famed psychologist Martin Seligman, is conducting the resilience training.[10]

The clear implication is that Comprehensive Soldier Fitness was some kind of nefarious reward for my allegedly helping construct the enhanced interrogation program. But I did not assist or abet the interrogation program, so there could have been no such "reward." Nor

was my work on learned helplessness the basis of the enhanced in-terrogation program.[11] Since helping the US Army make our soldiers more resilient has been one of the personal and professional high points of my life, I find this accusation unjust and insulting.

Here are the facts. The University of Pennsylvania received a sole-source, no-bid $31-million contract to train US Army personnel in resilience and positive psychology. This was sole-source, no-bid be-cause there existed no other known entities besides Penn to compete for this contract. The chief of staff of the army, George Casey, viewed this as very urgent. He was in a rush to get such a program started to help our troops as soon as possible. I believe the army decided to sole-source the contract for the following reasons:

- Penn was the only known entity that had done extensive train-ing and published extensive peer-reviewed research on resil-ience training.
- Penn was the only known entity that had extensive experience in the training of trainers in resilience.
- The army could identify no other competing entity.
- General Casey wanted the program expedited.

Army procurement and Penn negotiated for many months, and there was never any mention of past work that I might have done with DoD or Intelligence (I had not done any such work).

The only contract I ever held with the CIA or any other relevant group was in the early 1980s analyzing the speeches of world leaders for optimism and pessimism. Other than this, I have never before or since had a contract with any intelligence agency or any other relevant public or private agency. I have never held any security clearance.

ALMOST ALL THE criticisms came from people who opposed Amer-ican foreign policy and our military interventions in the Middle East. So I must say two things in closing this chapter.

First, it is malice to invoke the Nuremberg Code, the Nazi doctors, and ethical violation in the criticism of CSF. Such allegations, how-ever baseless, have a chilling effect on those many psychologists who

want to help our soldiers and the government in these trying times. Some will wonder, *Might I get accused of ethical violations?* and so be deterred from service. I want to encourage scientists and mental health practitioners to come to the aid of our government, and I urge them not to let this tactic deter them.

Second, these critics accuse me of "blind patriotism." My patriotism is not at all blind: I view the United States as the country that gave my relatives, persecuted unto death in Europe, a sanctuary where their children and grandchildren would flourish. I view the US Army as the force that stood between me and the Nazi gas chambers, and thus I count my days with the sergeants and the generals as the most fulfilling of my life.

Physical Health
(2007–2017)

MY SEARCH FOR protective factors against physical illness began in 2007 when Paul Tarini visited me. Paul ran the Pioneer Portfolio of the Robert Wood Johnson Foundation, the leading private funder of American medical research.

"The foundation likes what you've done with mental health, Dr. Seligman. You argued—with lots of data—that mental health is more than just the absence of mental illness; it is the presence of positive emotion, meaning and engagement. What is physical health?" Paul asked me rhetorically. "Is it just the absence of physical illness, or is it the presence of some real thing? We would like you to create a field of positive health, a field that will explore protective factors."

I welcomed this job and needed at least two shining lights to attempt it. I knew one already: Chris Peterson. I snagged him into re-analyzing existing studies, probing for protective factors—over and above risk factors. For the other person, I wanted the world's leading cardiovascular epidemiologist, since heart disease seemed a prime area to look for protective psychological factors.

"Who is the world's leading cardiovascular epidemiologist?" I asked Jim Marks, the executive vice president of the Robert Wood Johnson Foundation.

"That would be Darwin Labarthe," he said without hesitation.

Darwin Labarthe! I had lost track of Darwin, the founder of Wilson Lodge and hero of my Princeton days. I had never met him then, just worshipped from afar. Darwin's life's work, it turned out, had been the eradication of heart disease, and he believed that prevention—the earlier the better—was the way to do it. Cardiovascular medicine had reduced death risk from heart attack and stroke in America by almost half in my lifetime, and Darwin's mission was to reduce it to zero. He believed in "primordial prevention," positive health from gestation on. I asked Darwin to join positive health, and he consented eagerly, quite appreciative of my praise for what he did at Princeton fifty years before. A circle was completed in my life.

We laid out our mission statement:

> Positive Health empirically identifies health assets by deter-mining factors that predict health and illness over and above conventional risk factors. *Biological health assets* might in-clude, for example, high heart rate variability, high levels of HDL, and cardiorespiratory fitness.
>
> *Subjective health assets* might include positive emotions, life satisfaction, hope, optimism, and a sense of meaning and purpose.
>
> *Functional health assets* might include close friends and family members; a stable marriage; meaningful work; partic-ipation in a social community; and the ability to carry out work, family, and social roles.
>
> Health assets are desirable in their own right, but research has clearly demonstrated the relevance of biological assets and suggested the importance of functional health assets to overall health. Still to be determined is whether and how sub-jective health assets contribute to health-related outcomes, including:
>
> - Longevity
> - Morbidity
> - Quality-adjusted life years
> - Prognosis when illness strikes
> - Health care utilization and cost[1]

Chris, along with Laura Kubzansky, a young professor of public health at Harvard, Eric Kim, and Julie Boehm, led the analysis for subjective health assets. There existed many well-executed long-term studies of heart disease, but they were heavily biased toward the negative, measuring—almost exclusively—risk factors: depression, divorce, unemployment, anxiety, hostility, and the like. They failed to measure the good things in life. But here and there snippets yielded clues to positive protection.

Six studies fit our criteria of good science with some minimal measures of positive factors, and we analyzed these closely. Our reanalyses found that all of these revealed heretofore hidden protective factors.

The Whitehall II Cohort found[2] that optimism and emotional vitality were both associated with a modest but consistently reduced risk of incident coronary heart disease (CHD). It also found that protection was evident for satisfaction in job, family, sex life, and self, but not for love, leisure, or standard of living.

We reanalyzed the Normative Aging Study and found that high self-regulation reduced the risk of nonfatal myocardial infarction and CHD death compared to lower levels.

We reanalyzed the Health and Retirement Study and found that higher optimism predicted a 10 percent lower incidence of stroke in a two-year follow-up of 6,044 adults. Optimism stayed significant even after fully adjusting for demographic, behavioral, biological, and psychological stroke risk factors.

We reanalyzed other variables from the Health and Retirement Study and found that purpose in life predicted 21 percent lower risk of subsequent heart attack among 1,546 participants with cardiovascular disease two years later, controlling for psychological and biological risk factors.

This was the beginning. Optimism emerged so frequently as a protective factor for CHD in the reanalyses that Laura Kubzansky and Julie Boehm went on to review all the major studies of optimism and heart disease and published a landmark *Psychological Bulletin* paper.[3] The twenty or so such studies painted a consistent and compelling picture of pessimism as a huge risk factor for, and optimism as a huge protective factor against, cardiovascular disease.

Here is just one representative and well-done study: the Women's Health Initiative. It followed 97,000 women, healthy at the outset, for eight years. As usual in careful epidemiological studies, it measured age, race, education, religious attendance, health, body mass, alcohol consumption, smoking, blood pressure, and cholesterol at the start. Optimism was measured by the well-validated Life Orientation Test,[4] which asked ten straightforward questions, such as "In unclear times, I usually expect the best," and "If something can go wrong for me, it will." Importantly, depressive symptoms were also held constant, since pessimism might stem from depression. The most optimistic quarter had 30 percent fewer coronary deaths than the bottom quarter. The trend of fewer deaths, both cardiac and all-cause deaths, held across the entire continuum of optimism, indicating that optimism protects and pessimism hurts. This was true holding all the other risk factors—including depressive symptoms—constant.[5]

We knew that optimists smoked less, had less depression, and were happier than pessimists, but these studies showed that optimism mattered over and above all of these factors in preventing heart disease. By what mind-body mechanism did optimism matter so much for heart disease and not so much—if at all—for cancer or even infectious illness? Here's my best guess.

In the next chapter, I introduce the idea of prospection, the ubiquitous mental activity of envisioning future scenarios about our lives. You are likely doing just this right now, taking this very sentence and projecting its possible use into your marriage, your teaching, or your health, since prospecting is an ineluctable hallmark of human thinking. Optimism, unlike the momentary high spirits of hedonic happiness, is a trait, a mental disposition to prospect positive scenarios about the future, and pessimism is a disposition to prospect negative futures. These scenarios occupy us many hours every day. Just as strong external events are accompanied by cardiovascular consequences, so likely are prospections. Anxiety-inducing real events and anger-inducing real events and sadness-inducing real events all result in pronounced sympathetic activity and difficulty relaxing, states that injure the heart in the long run. Pleasant, relaxing, victorious real events result in parasympathetic activity and good vagal tone, states

that are good for the heart. The same holds for vividly imagined future events: the pessimist, just sitting at her desk, is roiling in anger, anxiety, and sadness-inducing prospection and suffering its injurious cardiac effects, while the optimist is basking in positive futures and their healthy cardiac effects. Done every day for a whole lifetime, this adds up.

If this is how optimism helps and pessimism hurts the heart, a very cost-effective intervention follows. Just change pessimism into optimism in cardiovascular patients, as the Penn Resiliency Program did with soldiers and kids and as Tayyab Rashid did in positive psychotherapy. Indeed, one recent Iranian study did this.[6] Reza Nikrahan and his bold colleagues gave sixty-nine coronary patients six weeks of positive psychology interventions and followed them for fifteen weeks, looking at coronary biomarkers: they found better cortisol response, a sign of heart health, than in the controls. No one has ever done this with the prevention of death as the outcome.

Given the size of optimism's protective effects (they are rather larger than those of not smoking), their consistency (every single study shows that optimism protects), and how readily pessimism can be turned toward optimism, I've been advocating a major study of training optimism to prevent cardiovascular disease and death. I still have not gotten past first base, and positive health's inability to penetrate conventional medical thinking and its journals is the single most frustrating obstacle in my scientific career.

Our journal rejection rate from the Robert Wood Johnson Foundation project at the prestigious medical outlets has been close to 80 percent, and I see a double standard in action. Studies that show positive psychological protective factors get rejected out of hand, but those that deny positive protection get accepted and publicized. Here's a recent example from the *Lancet*, a highly prestigious journal that has rejected every one of our submissions outright.

A very substantial literature makes a compelling case that happy people live longer[7] and that happiness influences longevity. Literally scores of meticulous studies in psychology journals document this, and there are almost no exceptions. In 2016 the *Lancet* trumpeted its article "Happiness and Unhappiness Have No Direct Effect on

Mortality."[8] The investigators reported that among 719,671 British women, of whom 31,531 died over a ten-year follow-up, self-reported unhappiness failed to predict who would die—once self-reported poor health was removed statistically. Self-reported poor health predicts death, the article concluded; unhappiness does not.

Oh, my God, I thought when reporters called me for comment. Could all the previous scores of studies have been wrong?

No. The *Lancet* study, for all its "1 million women," was very poorly done, and looking at it as disinterestedly as I can, I am sure no rigorous psychology journal would have accepted it. The authors asked only one unhappiness question in a 316-item survey. It was the 306th item, following hundreds of questions about medications, diet, and ill health (400,000 women quit before reaching this item). The women were fifty-nine years old on average when they answered the unhappiness question and the current poor health questions. There is excellent reason to believe that unhappiness would influence the reporting of poor health at age fifty-nine and that a lifetime of unhappiness, by the well-documented mechanisms of unhappiness producing worse sleep, less exercise, more smoking, and fewer friends, in the first fifty-nine years of life would strongly cause self-reported and actual poor health at age fifty-nine. A trio of distinguished psychologists published a damning critique, which concluded, "We believe what the authors of the *Lancet* study found was not whether happiness is related to longevity but this: Whether a one-item happiness question will predict a shortened life in healthy middle-aged women, if you delete how happiness has affected their health for their first six decades and if you erase the influence of key pathways to health such as social support, smoking and body mass index."[9]

So I here want to complain publicly about the leading medical journals.

Psychologists are unwelcome interlopers in the world of medical science. Medicine is dominated by the belief that psychological factors do not cause medical outcomes or only do so by way of biological processes—even if the psychological factors are known and measured and the biological factors are completely unknown. This creates an extraordinary double standard. Studies showing that unhappiness and pessimism cause death—and even more, studies showing that

happiness and optimism prevent death—in our experience face almost insuperable obstacles to publication in the best medical journals. Sloppier studies that deny psychological causation are readily published.

Someday we will discover the unknown biological correlates of happiness, optimism, and vitality and how they impinge on the body. In the next chapter I put a promising candidate forward. For now, however, we presently know how to measure—and most importantly, how to change—these causal psychological states for the better. There should be widespread programs to raise the optimism, happiness, and vitality of medical patients—right now.

The double standard in the medical literature, I believe, squelches this, at a cost of millions of lives a year.

AS OF 2011 we had been extracting and reanalyzing the few positive, protective items from the existing literature on risk factors. We correlated them to cardiovascular disease, and the protective factors were surprisingly predictive. But now a new question emerged: Wouldn't it be much better if there existed a longitudinal study of hundreds of thousands of healthy people that measured health and illness as well as the panoply of protective factors?

Out of the blue, the US Army decided to create just this. It consolidated its personnel and medical records into one huge system, the Person-Event Data Environment (PDE). This was a big step forward for the Department of Defense (DoD) since there had existed at least thirty separate siloes of data, almost inaccessible to one another. The different siloes included all the medical records, promotions, suicides, crimes, medal awards, wounds, annual evaluations, commendations, instances of family violence, and much more, but they did not talk to one another. The Global Assessment Tool (GAT) that Chris Peterson and Carl Castro developed in 2009 was in one of the siloes and contained data on psychological protective factors, such as strengths and well-being, as well as psychological risk factors, such as catastrophization, for more than 1 million soldiers. If we could access the PDE, we would no longer need to scavenge through old studies to find out, for example, if soldiers with a strong sense of meaning recovered from surgery faster, controlling for the severity of the injury. Or if soldiers who catastrophized tended to get posttraumatic stress disorder,

controlling for depression and intensity of combat.[10] We could define the "optimally healthy soldier" by asking how optimal health comes about and how to maintain it. This—and so much more—lay in the PDE, waiting for scientists to analyze.

We seized the moment. The army, Penn, and the Robert Wood Johnson Foundation all saw the PDE as a national treasure, an unparalleled resource for answering medical and scientific questions never answerable before. The foundation called a meeting at its Princeton headquarters and the surgeon general of the army helicoptered in. Rhonda Cornum, Darwin Labarthe, and I drove. So the Positive Psychology Center, the US Army, and the Robert Wood Johnson Foundation launched a new project to harvest the low-hanging fruit in the PDE and then to create an infrastructure so that civilian and military scientists could ask the great questions of the PDE.

This launch gave us a lot to celebrate and much to discuss, and so we scheduled a steering committee meeting for October 9–10, 2012. Soon after we got our big news, tragedy struck. On October 9th, Chris Peterson died suddenly, likely of a heart attack, while sitting on his balcony having a last cigarette before leaving for the meeting.

LINDA NEWSTED, my secretary, rushed into my office. She was weeping. "They just found Chris on his balcony. He's dddd . . . he's not alive."

I had just lost my dear friend and my closest colleague. He knew me very well, perhaps better than anyone, except Mandy. But strangely, I never knew him. I never knew his sexuality or even that he smoked. I was without words for the next few weeks. I lapsed into stunned silence during my eulogy at the positive psychology summit three weeks later, and my students had to cover for me. In the obit that Nansook and I jointly wrote, we said,

> "Other people matter. Period," said Chris Peterson when asked for a concise definition of "Positive Psychology," the field he helped to found and then helped to guide through the first decade of the 21st Century. He researched, taught, and lived positive psychology. . . .

Within hours of his death a cascade of hundreds of re-
membrances filled the ether and their main theme was how
and why Chris was so loved. He left giant footprints not only
in positive psychology, but also in the lives of so many people
that he touched through his life. . . .

He loved people. He walked the positive psychology walk.
He was genuinely interested in getting to know others. He
made everyone around him feel comfortable and respected.
He was an understated, humble, and generous person. It was
no accident that his Michigan nickname was "Mother The-
resa." He always found joy in letting other people shine and
sharing the credit with others. He had a gift for seeing the
best in each person. He also had a strong sense of fairness
and duty without being rigid. He did not allow his personal
feelings to obscure his judgment. He always had fun what-
ever he did, and also brought fun for others. Although his
scholarly contributions are significant, his lasting legacy will
be what he shared with other people. So many of us are in-
debted to him for being better researchers, better teachers
and better people. Other people mattered to Chris, and he
to others.[11]

Now five years after Chris's death, the words of G. H. Hardy[12] ring
true for me:

I still say to myself when I am depressed, and find myself
forced to listen to pompous and tiresome people, "Well, I
have done one thing you could never have done, and that is to
have collaborated with both Littlewood and Ramanujan on
something like equal terms."

Indeed the best days of my life were spent collaborating with Chris-
topher Peterson on something like equal terms.

POSITIVE PSYCHOLOGY SUFFERED a second crushing blow in
December 2012. Ray Fowler, my friend and my only mentor in my

adulthood, had stepped down as CEO of the American Psychology Association (APA) after fifteen years. He had turned APA around, and its finances and membership had never been in better shape. It was a 160,000-member body with a surplus of $100 million. He now turned his energy to positive health and had a special mission. In my opinion, positive psychology is the invention of pointy-headed, unathletic, middle-aged men, and it is almost entirely neck-up. But so much of what makes life worth living is neck-down:

> It is a freezing December night in Washington, and I have just attended a very long and tedious board of directors meeting. I am invited by the younger set to watch amateur tango dancing in an unheated barn. The dancers are amazing, and I am transfixed by their beauty and grace. Hours pass. At two in the morning, a gorgeous female who moves like a panther asks me to dance.
>
> "I only do words," I say declining.

Ray decided to make neck-down positive psychology his cause. He added exercise to psychological protective factors and changed my life with an hour-long speech at Geelong Grammar School in 2008. He lectured on the evidence for 10,000 steps per day creating cardiovascular fitness. The lecture itself was a bit tedious, what with all that data, but the next day many of us went into town and bought pedometers. I have walked 10,000 steps per day almost every day since then. (Oops, only 7,124 so far today.) Having been through the APA wars, Ray became our senior political advisor when we founded the International Positive Psychology Association, and he was on the steering committee of my Robert Wood Johnson Foundation positive health grants. His project was to add positive psychology and positive health to the medical school curriculum, and he created a new curriculum for physicians.

More than anything Ray was determined to make it to one hundred. He made us all read *Blue Zones*,[13] Dan Buettner's intriguing study of places where lots of people live to be centenarians. He was in great physical shape, the perennial winner of the over-sixty APA marathon. He modestly said he won because the competition thinned

out every year. At Akumal, besides walking and running us off our feet, he was always the first one into the ocean for a very long swim and snorkel. We tagged along like goslings.

Mandy and I were about to fly to San Diego for Ray's eighty-second birthday in 2012, when his wife Sandy told us that he had suffered a massive stroke. Partly paralyzed like my father, Ray never really spoke again. I tried to talk with him on the phone, but to no avail, and as with my father, I was too phobic to visit him. Ray died in 2015, nursed faithfully by Sandy and surrounded by his large, loving family until the very end.

Here is what I wrote to the listserv Friends of Positive Psychology:

> Ray Fowler's death is a grievous loss to Psychology, to Positive Psychology, and to me personally. Ray was the long-serving CEO of the American Psychological Association, recruited when he was President, in a successful attempt to rescue APA from desperate financial and political troubles. He said his greatest virtue was that he suffered fools gladly (I know I was one of them). After he retired as CEO, then in his seventies, he found a new career in Positive Psychology. His main interest was the psychological benefits of exercise. He pedometerized all of his friends and walked and ran us off our feet until we flourished or dropped. He encouraged me to run for APA president. He exhorted me to become a transformational rather than a transactional leader, and he held my hand in the creation of Positive Psychology as a discipline. He was a cherished mentor and he was my good friend.

Chris and Ray, both personality theorists, would have loved what happened next in positive health, and I mourn not being able to tell them about it.

Positive Psychology Marries Big Data

Google Zeitgeist 2010, a meeting of the top Google people and their richest clients—Motorola, Time-Warner, Zappos—was held in an upscale adobe hotel in Paradise Valley, Arizona. There was a lot of

margarita drinking and loud music, and the people were astonishingly young. An elder, I was out of my element, but I was a keynote speaker. My address followed that of an unremittingly pessimistic economist who predicted worldwide economic collapse and a dire future. In contrast I decried self-fulfilling pessimism and predicted continuing, if balky, human progress.

But I was really there because I had a big idea, and I wanted to road-test it with Google Earth. I hoped to measure the well-being of the world cheaply and in real time.

I have used questionnaires all my life, but warily. Questionnaires suck when it comes to getting at what I really want to know. I want to know, for example, how much meaning you have in your life. But the only tool I've had until recently is to ask straight out, on a scale of one to ten, "How much meaning do you have in life?" with one being "none" and ten being "full of meaning." I can ask the same question in different ways (e.g., "How much purpose do you have in life?") to bolster "reliability," but the problem of validity—is what you say true?—remains. Here are just a few of the problems of questionnaires:

- You might lie.
- You might detect what hypothesis I am pushing (e.g., depressed people have little meaning, particularly if the meaning question follows a depression inventory), and you might then go out of your way to confirm or disconfirm it.
- You might "reputation manage."
- You might just not answer and leave. This happens all too often.
- You might not understand what "having meaning in life" means.
- The questionnaire puts its words into your mouth as opposed to using the words you spontaneously use.

All this is even worse if I want to know your "personality." Are you an extrovert? So I ask, "Do you like to go to parties?" and "Do you start conversations with strangers?" These questions are subject to all the problems above, yet are alleged to be the "ground truth" of personality.

The jargon for these problems is that questionnaires are "reactive" and "intrusive" as opposed to spontaneous and unobtrusive. There is a better way to get closer to ground truth: what is actually going through your head, the words and phrases you say to yourself all day long. The new social media throw open a picture window on those words and phrases—at last a better way in.

"How happy are people in the Bay Area? Are people in San Francisco happier than people in Berkeley?" I asked one of the head programmers for Google Earth over a Dr. Pepper.

"I haven't the slightest idea," he said.

"Let's find out," I said, whipping out a list of about twenty happiness words that I got from my thesaurus: happy, joy, cheerful, content, smile, glad, sunny, and so on. "Could you use the Google search engine and pinpoint the frequency of the happy words by location?"

"I was up half the night," he told me the next morning as he handed me a colored-in map of the Bay Area, "and here are the data. The red areas use the most 'happy' words and the blue areas the fewest."

We showed Larry Page, Google's laconic CEO, these results, and he blessed the endeavor. My collaboration with Google was short-lived, however, because the company insisted on using its search engine rather than extracting words from Gmail. When people use a search engine to look up "happy" or "love," however, unlike when they search for "cough" or "flu," it is usually because they don't have happiness or love, not because they do.

I then went full blast after Big Data as a better way of measuring psychological states and traits. First I brought Lyle Ungar on board. Lyle was a professor of computer science and math prodigy, and unlike many of his colleagues, he also understood and even liked psychology—especially positivity, which he exuded. He viewed the "meaning" of a word not by obsolete necessary and sufficient conditions (a bachelor is defined as an unmarried man). Rather he asked how a word was actually used in the social media. He combed through millions of tweets and looked for the words that actually co-occur with "bachelor," up to five words on either side. To my mind, Lyle had brilliantly quantified Ludwig Wittgenstein's revolutionary insight that

the meaning of a word is its use in the language.[14] Lyle was eager to collaborate and brimming over with insights about how to mine Big Data to measure well-being and personality.

We recruited Andrew Schwartz, a dyed-in-the-wool computational linguist, as a postdoc to manage the project, and we landed Johannes Eichstaedt. Johannes was a phenomenon, a young polymath. When not climbing the Himalayas or meditating, he did physics, math, linguistics, neuroscience, and psychology. He took his master's in applied positive psychology with me in 2011, finishing at the top of the class, and was admitted as a PhD student to the Penn psychology department.

Led by Andy Schwartz, the team applied to the Templeton Religion Trust for a grant to map the well-being of the world and in 2014 received $3.8 million to do this. The data poured in, and they convinced me that we had opened a new world of psychological measurement, one that would complement and possibly replace questionnaires. Take a look.

The figure just below shows a word cloud derived from the Facebook statuses of 40,000 women. The larger the word, the more it distinguished women from men.

The next figure shows the word cloud for 40,000 men.

Yes, my dear, this is what he was actually thinking.

Merely looking blindly at Facebook or Twitter, we were right about the gender of the author 92 percent of the time. When I first saw the gender word clouds, I staggered and had to sit down. I felt like I was peering right into the frontal lobes of men and women. No personality test ever gave me this kind of illumination. Where does this leave personality itself? Personality after all gives us a shorthand for predicting what a person will think or do.

The next two figures show the expurgated word clouds for "neurotic" and "nonneurotic" people:

high neuroticism

The nonneurotic word cloud is a portrait of high emotional stability—psychological health and well-being—unlike any I have seen before. What is ground truth here anyway? Is it the result of a personality test that comes up "neurotic," or is it the top word cloud in the figure?

The next figure shows the word clouds for middle-aged people organized by topic—there are easily computed statistics for discovering the topics that people talk about.

Johannes, in his first year as a graduate student, made a major discovery about cardiovascular death.[15] He used the US county-by-county cardiovascular death rate from the Centers for Disease Control and Prevention for 2010 and localized 82 million tweets by county of origin. He then asked if he could predict death rate in a county just from Twitter language and compared this to predictions of death rate using the usual risk factors.

Twitter alone out-predicted the ten leading risk factors combined (income, education, smoking, diabetes, hypertension, obesity, etc.) for cardiovascular death. The content of young people's tweets predicted cardiovascular death of the older people at an astonishingly high level of .67.

The next figure shows the word cloud for counties at high risk.

And the last figure shows the word cloud for counties protected from cardiovascular death.

These were merely correlations, but could the word clouds be causal? Do the words that run through your head activate the cardio-vascular system malignantly or benignly—all day long? If yes, then changing what you think and what you say and what you write might be a royal road to physical health.

Our search for positive health uncovered protective factors that tell us that health actually is not just the absence of illness but the presence of something. By serendipity the search for these protective factors opened a new window on the mind, and just perhaps the very words and phrases that you say to yourself day and night determine your physical health.

Part 5

Looking into
the Future

Homo Prospectus
(2008–2016)

"*H*OLINESS, CAN I say what bothers me about Buddhism?" I asked the Dalai Lama. He was unflappably positive, and my question did not ruffle him a bit. We were on stage at a meeting titled "Mind and Its Potential" in Sydney, Australia, on a scorching summer day in December 2009. His Holiness was rarely challenged, and I tried to perk up an overly reverential and sleepy discussion with a deep issue that was on my mind much of the time.

"Buddhism urges us to live in the present and to be mindful of the present," I continued. "I don't agree. We are not beings who dwell in the present. Our minds brim with futures. This is not to be fought. The future is our nature. We are creatures who are drawn into the future."

WHERE WAS THIS outlandish idea coming from?

Traditional psychology's emphasis on the present and the past had been bothering me since the founding of positive psychology. At first just the glaring omission of the positive bothered me. Traditional psychology tried to undo what was wrong, or tried to derive what was right from what was not wrong, or neglected what was right altogether. Positive psychology corrected this imbalance. But I suspected an even more fundamental shortcoming: the future. Traditional

psychology tells us that we are creatures of the past and the present, which in turn give rise to the future. Psychology-as-usual studies memory, a person's past, as well as motivation and perception, the present. Predicting a person's future actions will directly fall out from knowing his past and his present—somehow.

This picture does violence to my own mental life. I don't think much about the past, and I certainly don't bask in the present. The present is too brief to dwell in. Rather I spend an enormous amount of my time imagining futures, daydreaming what-ifs, turning possible scenarios over and over, upside down, and backward, and the older I get the more time I spend in the future.

The name of our species bothers me as well. *Homo sapiens* means "wise man" or "knowing man," but in contrast to *Homo habilis*, "handy man," and *Homo erectus*, "upright man," this name is not a description but an aspiration. And not one that we live up to. What do we actually do well that every other species does poorly? Language, toolmaking, killing, rationality, tasting bad to predators, cooperation—are all candidates. But when we look closely at other mammals, birds, and even social insects, our uniqueness fades. So with Dan Gilbert, professor of social psychology at Harvard,[1] I believe that the unrivaled human ability of imagining futures—"prospection"—uniquely describes our species.

We prospect the future uniquely well, and this ability might ultimately make the aspiration of wisdom a reality. Hence, we are better named *Homo prospectus*.[2]

This promotes prospection to the front and center of psychological science. In the traditional view, if you want to know what I will do in the future, you need know, in principle, four things:

My history
My genetic makeup
The present stimuli
My present drives and motives

Psychoanalysis, behaviorism, and most of cognitive psychology accept this. But I do not. I have been working on *agency*, one way or

another, from learned helplessness on, all my life, and in thinking about prospection, agency comes into focus most clearly. Here is the great blind spot of the traditional framework that has gnawed at me for fifty years: it leaves out human agency and its very fulcrum, a mind that *metabolizes* the past and present to create the future and then chooses among possible futures.

There cannot be a positive psychology without prospection.

I first broached this idea with Roy Baumeister in 2008. We were working together on mental energy—another sorely neglected topic in psychology, orphaned by the field's abandonment of Freud's hydraulic theory of emotional life. The baby of energy got thrown out with the bathwater of Freud's concept of repression. Roy had resuscitated energy to explain his memorable chocolate-chip cookie finding. His subjects sat in front of a freshly baked plate of them but were told that they were in the "radish group," which meant they could eat as many radishes as they wanted but must not eat any cookies. Following this excruciating resisting of temptation, Roy's subjects did worse at puzzles that required trying and persistence.[3] They were depleted of mental energy. Roy and I tossed around the idea that consciousness uses energy and we should try to measure how much.

Roy suggested that consciousness is for imagining possible futures (like eating a chocolate-chip cookie and then feeling guilty). I fell in love with this idea, and a couple of drafts about consciousness as simulating futures changed hands. In the meantime, Roy published a learned *Psychological Review* article in which this slant on consciousness appeared briefly but was swamped almost to invisibility by other bowings and scrapings to the reviewers.[4]

In October 2010, Chris Peterson and Nansook Park used their campus clout to organize well-being as the University of Michigan's theme for the year. There were happiness banners everywhere, and I was invited to deliver the Tanner Lecture in philosophy about positive psychology. Over lunch, I met Chandra Sripada, an assistant professor of both philosophy and psychiatry. Chandra, meticulous of dress and speech, turned out to be a working neuroscientist in addition. He mapped out network architecture by the connectivity from one area to another. I had never before met anyone who combined philosophy,

psychiatry, neuroscience, and psychology, and as I would discover over the next six years, Chandra was a polymath—one of only a half dozen I have ever met.

He was shocked that I had never heard of the *default network* and opened my eyes to the wondrous discovery of a reliable brain circuit that could well be how the brain does its simulations of possible futures.

"There must be at least one thousand studies of the brain on a particular external task like mental arithmetic or anagrams," Chandra began over our cafeteria lo mein. "But you always have to run a 'rest' period for contrast. During 'rest' you tell the subject just to lie there and not do anything."

I nodded my head.

"The circuits that light up for mental arithmetic are pretty noisy, not quite a dead end, but a messy signal-to-noise search. But what lights up at so-called rest is uniform and reliable, so it is called the 'default' circuit, what the brain defaults to at rest.

"Now here is the shocker. This is not some sort of empty rest. This is the same circuit that lights up when you ask the person to imagine a personal future."[5]

My epiphany light bulb went on. This must be the circuit that does the simulations that Roy and I thought consciousness was all about.

That evening the Michigan professors of philosophy and psychology dined together over many bottles of an indifferent red wine. I was seated next to Peter Railton, a well-known moral philosopher. Peter told me that he worked on desire. Desire, Peter said, is about forming a positive image of a possible future. Desire exemplifies being drawn into the future rather than being pushed by the past. At this point, I was called on to say a few words, and I recalled Morton White's[6] unfilled promise that philosophy should someday rejoin its orphaned child, psychology.

"We all pay lip service to interdisciplinary work," I said. "Let's go around the room and say as a result of this day what we will now do differently? Peter Railton and I will start. We're going to write an article together on being drawn into the future rather than driven by the past."

This was the very first that Railton had heard of our project. Nevertheless, it actually began a few days later. Railton and Sripada sent me several articles to read, and within two weeks, I sent them the very first of what would become twenty drafts, which culminated in our article[7] and ultimately our book *Homo Prospectus*.[8] In this first pass, I confessed my doubts about traditional psychology and how a framework that put prospection front and center would lead to better psychology.

I suggested where a new psychology should start. The hard determinism of traditional psychology is a will-of-the-wisp because all science is at best statistical. No science can ever be billiard-ball deterministic, and even the "simple" problem of where three balls colliding will end up is only approximated statistically. Knowing the genes, the past history, and the present stimuli—even to a statistical asymptote (imagine it achieves the never-achieved 0.99 accuracy)—will not come close to deducing what the person will go on to do in any real-time sequence, because .99 × .99 × .99 × .99 all too rapidly approaches zero prediction. Therefore, discovering what the person expects, intends, and desires in the future is usually a better starting-off point than asking about past behavior. If you want to know what I will do next Saturday night, the best place to start is by asking what I intend to do next Saturday night, not what I did last Saturday night and the Saturday night before.

I gave "what consciousness is" my first try. Human consciousness is the seat of agency. Agency consists in running simulations of possible futures and deciding among them. Agency is prospecting the future, and expectation, choice, decision, preference, desire, and free will are all processes of prospection. Maybe all this happens in the default network.

My bottom line was that human action is drawn by the future and influenced, but not driven, by the past. All of this seemed pretty naive to Railton, the meticulous philosopher, and it seemed out of touch to Sripada, the working neuroscientist, and they began to rework these ideas into a more scholarly and sophisticated form.

Enter the Eagle Scouts of philanthropy: the John Templeton Foundation. The foundation regularly asked me to spot initiatives that were

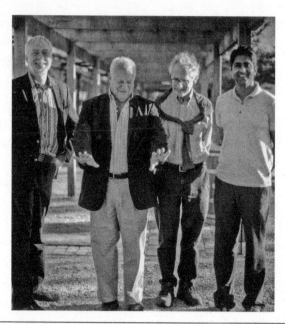

Spending weeks at a time with Roy Baumeister, Peter Railton, and Chandra Sripada was like going to graduate school all over again, but in a brand-new discipline: prospective psychology. Photo courtesy of Mandy Seligman.

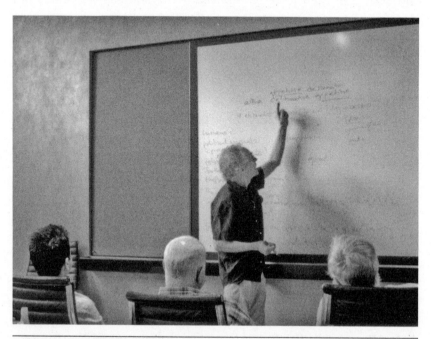

Peter Railton teaching us (Chandra Sripada, the author, and Roy Baumeister) about moral realism.

adventurous, good science, unlikely to be funded by disease agencies like the National Institute of Mental Health, and compatible with Sir John Templeton's vision of a science of human flourishing.

Barnaby Marsh and Chris Stawski (both then advisors to Jack Templeton, Sir John's neurosurgeon son, who succeeded to the presidency after Sir John's death) took me to lunch, and I explained the idea of prospection at length.

"This is just the kind of science that Sir John loved," was their first reaction. "Sir John thought that imagination—future-mindedness—was the key to success." In due course, the Templeton Foundation funded the four of us to write *Homo Prospectus* and to do laboratory psychology and neuroscience on prospection. They actually doubled down and created a $3-million research competition for the measurement, mechanisms, applications, and improvement of prospection.

We went to work and wrote draft after draft of our first paper. Peter and I struggled over almost every line. He wanted every sentence to be true on its own, but I wanted them to be readable. Peter added qualifiers to achieve reviewer-friendly prose. I cut out half his qualifiers to get reader-friendly prose. He stuffed them back in. We ultimately sent it in to the leading theoretical journal in psychology, the *Psychological Review.* The editor told me it was "the most interesting paper he had read since becoming editor," but it was not theoretical enough. We then sent it to the *Psychological Bulletin.* The editor said that it was one of the most interesting papers he had read since becoming editor, but it did not review the literature exhaustively enough. We then sent it to *Perspectives on Psychological Science,* also a leading journal. The editor, Bobbie Spellman, said she could publish anything she wanted if it was really good, and this paper was really good. She published it.

Spending weeks at a time with Roy, Chandra, and Peter was like going to graduate school all over again—but in a brand-new discipline. The rest of this chapter shares some of what I learned and what made me wish I was twenty-one again.

WHAT IF PERCEPTION *is not the registration of what is present but a useful hallucination of what to expect?* The modern understanding

of vision differs vastly from what I was taught. The visual system of the brain is a column, where the bottom of the column gets almost point for point what the retina registers. The next layer then gets a more abstract version, and abstraction deepens on up to the top layer. The top layer is extremely abstract, housing schemas for detecting such entities as a table or even a basketball, for example. Strangely, however, there are ten times as many connections going down from the top as there are up from the bottom.

Why?

Our eyes jerk three times every second, but the world stays stable. Top-down instructions to the lower layers explain this stability. You watch a film of people passing a basketball around and are instructed to count the number of passes. A gorilla walks across the court. Half the observers do not see the gorilla. The top layer tells the layers below that this is basketball: amplify the basketball-relevant elements and inhibit gorilla elements. What we see is not reality printing itself on our eyes but a hallucination of what we expect to see next, a projection into the future.[9]

WHAT IF MEMORY is not a file drawer of films and photographs but a changing collection of possibilities most relevant to the future? In writing this book, I have been astonished by how flawed my memory is. I decided to write first and fact-check later. I had already written so much about the topics that if I read what I originally wrote, my rendering would be boring for me and not nearly fresh enough for you. So when I finally went about fact-checking—by looking at datebooks, articles, books, and emails and asking living witnesses—I found disturbingly many errors. Bob Kaiser, for example, insists that it was a purple 1947 Chevrolet, not a green 1948 Ford, that we raced around our drag track. And that it cost thirty-five dollars, not fifty. But I can still see the grill of our green Ford so clearly.

This isn't Alzheimer's creeping up on me. It is a brute fact about memory, and Ulric Neisser pinned this down with his study of the *Challenger* disaster. Twenty-four hours after it happened, the students in his introductory psychology class wrote down where they were, what they were doing, and how they felt when they heard the tragic

news. Two and a half years later, they answered the same questions and also said how confident they were about their responses. There were gaping discrepancies, and only a quarter of the students even remembered filling out the first questionnaire. Despite the memory lapses, many students were completely confident about their completely false recollections.[10]

Perhaps the fallibility of memory is not a bug but an essential feature. Errors of memory, shifting and shuffling bits of our old memories, might enable us to draw different lessons from the past, lessons that are necessary for a better future.

WHAT IF FREE will is not about willing? The key to prospection is that we are constantly imagining possible futures and that each scenario comes with a valence—how much we like or dislike it. Here's what Chandra utterly persuaded me of:

> I believe the proper form of a philosophical theory of free will is a "distinctive mark" theory. Consider the question of what makes a Ferrari fast. It is unhelpful to cite the pressing of the accelerator as what accounts for the Ferrari's fastness. While it is true that accelerator pressing is necessary for the Ferrari to cruise down the road at 100 miles an hour, citing this factor misses the point of the question. Accelerators must be pressed in Ferraris and non-Ferraris alike. The question of what makes a Ferrari fast is rather a request for information about what is special or distinctive that makes a Ferrari speedier than other cars. A proper answer must say something, not about the pressing of the accelerator, or the tightness of lug nuts, or the lack of corrosion on the spark plugs, or all the things that are necessary for a Ferrari to go fast, but rather must say something about the distinguishing basis for the Ferrari's speediness. That is, it should say something about the Ferrari's engine, and in particular its size or power or its unique engineering. The philosophical question of free will is similar. Of all the attributes and qualities of an agent that are necessary for freedom, what is the distinctive mark

that makes certain creatures—presumably humans, but per-
haps other creatures as well—free?

That mark is the latitude of the scenarios we imagine. Humans,
unlike any other species, imagine futures that stretch and stretch.
They stretch over time—even whole lifetimes. They stretch over com-
plex sequences—linear and branching. They stretch to hypotheticals
and counterfactuals—What if life does not depend on carbon? What
if the Vikings had had gunpowder?

The scope of our freedom, then, is exactly the latitude of our
imaginings.

Willing now shrinks almost to invisibility. We simply enact the
scenario with the highest valence. How we calculate valence remains
unknown but is a proper subject for the future study of free will.

WHY DO WE *feel anything at all?* This is called the "hard" problem of
consciousness[11] because it is . . . well, so damn hard. Machines don't
need to feel anything to do their business perfectly. The mechanical
tortoise is programmed to register when it runs low on electricity
and to return to its nest and plug in. It doesn't need to experience
anything at all—not weariness, not homesickness. What does our
subjective world of experience—which is so close to being our very
identity—add?

Here are the competing scenarios that crossed my mind in a matter
of seconds recently:

1. I could go on the internet and play bridge. Who might be avail-
 able? Mark Lair, but he's usually at lunch. Peter Friedland, he's in
 Taiwan, probably going to sleep, but there are a few lesser lights
 likely to be available. They make errors. Anyway, I've wasted a
 lot of time playing bridge lately.
2. I might help Mandy teach Carly and Jenny about the Silk Road.
 I don't know much about Asia. But the kids would love it, and
 I haven't spent any time with them today. Mandy might find it
 intrusive, having prepared the lesson. But she thinks I have not
 done my share of teaching lately.

3. I might make myself some lunch. There's some Moroccan chicken left over in the fridge. It's pretty high calorie though. And I'm meeting Phil Voss for dinner at Le Bec Fin in only five hours. But I could order only their three-course meal. Maybe Mandy was saving the chicken for the kids' dinner.

4. I could keep working on this damn paper. But I'm having trouble thinking through examples of compelling counterfactual mental simulations. Maybe a bridge break will help. But this is a pretty good example, maybe I should keep plugging. Why bother? I don't have a deadline, since this paper is for my own amusement. Peter Railton will be disappointed if I don't follow up soon.

5. All those tulip bulbs need planting. I could use the exercise, particularly with Le Bec Fin coming up. The temperature is good, but the ground is soggy. Tulips can be planted even if it gets really cold, no rush. They might rot. I did lift weights for twenty minutes already today. But I could use some fresh air. It would calm me down. I need it particularly after my argument with the dean.

Notice how multidimensional these simulations are and also how incommensurable they seem. By what measure does the pleasure of playing bridge with Mark Lair stack up against the annoyance of letting tulip bulbs rot or the satisfaction of seeing bright tulips in six months or the anticipation of Moroccan chicken or guilt about not working out? Subjective feeling is the brain's common currency for value, and it lets us compare possible futures. A capacity for vivid conscious simulation could feed into a final common path for comparisons. There is also the genuine constraint that we must often make decisions very quickly, and we may use acting in response to subjective feeling as the streamlined readout to compare futures.

We also need to compare the present, which is cloaked in feeling, to possible futures. You walk into the tavern, paycheck in hand, and must compare the pleasure of drinking now to the ensuing fight with your wife and the pain of sleeping on the couch all weekend. That these prospections are also cloaked with feeling allows us to compare

directly the present to the future as well as to compare one possible future to another.

THE FINAL THING I learned from working with Roy, Peter, and Chandra had to do with creativity itself and how it fares with aging, a topic of obvious concern to me.

Can creativity increase with age?[12] Creativity employs an exquisite kind of prospection: imagining something original and surprising and useful that is not present to the senses. The research literature strongly suggests that creativity wanes as we get old.

I am in mind of that day in Oxford in 1975 when John Teasdale and I began our reformulation of learned helplessness together. Our public agreement to do this did not end the day. Another encounter right afterward echoed many years beyond the collaboration that John and I had just undertaken. As I am seventy-five, this encounter is particularly resonant right now.

I was invited to dinner at Donald Broadbent's chicly modern house in an Oxford suburb. Jerry Bruner was the other guest. Not one for social chitchat and mindful of the uniqueness of this opportunity, I raised a topic that I was very curious about. At age thirty-two, I worried that I had peaked, and much research suggests that the mid-thirties are the high-water mark of scientific creativity. I knew the careers of the two luminaries I was dining with. Donald was about fifty and did his great work on dichotic listening at about my age. Jerry was almost sixty and had done his great work on thought going beyond the data given twenty-five years before, in his early thirties as well. Truth to tell, I was less impressed by what they had done since.

"It's an honor to be with the two of you this evening," I said. "I am a fan of both of your careers, and I know your work pretty well and *when* you did it. Now tell me honestly, when were you at your most creative?"

"*Right now!*" they roared in unison.

Even more strikingly, when I recently asked Aaron Beck, in his mid-nineties, the same question, he responded with exactly those words. And when I ask myself the very same question, I answer, "Right now." I wonder if we were all harboring a benign, defensive illusion.

That creativity might increase well into later life flies in the face of the data. Much research shows that creativity peaks within a couple of decades of the start of a career, earlier with mathematics and poetry, later in science, history, and philosophy.[13]

Here's the damage that aging does,[14] and I can testify to each of these personally:

- We're slower. Neural conduction speed decreases markedly.
- We're forgetful. Memory is much worse.
- We're tired. Stamina decreases.
- We're rigid. Hardening of the categories increases.
- We're banal. Originality decreases.[15]

Wait, originality—divergent thinking—decreases? Doesn't that end the discussion? Creativity requires originality, which in turn requires prospection, which in turn requires imagination. Paving my driveway with salami is an original idea, but it is useless. Creativity demands more than originality; also requires usefulness and a good sense of who will make use of the idea, the audience. "Audience" can refer to a literal audience in the arts but often alludes to the gatekeeping members of the discipline in academia.

What gets better with age that might outweigh all these losses?

First, knowledge itself increases. Even though I have forgotten a huge amount, I know more in total now. I know, for example, almost automatically about how to use Big Data to get around the artifacts of questionnaires and why the default network might be the imagination network.

I not only know more facts from my own discipline, but I know more generally. I recently took Jenny and Carly to the architecturally magnificent Native American Museum in Washington, DC. On hearing that European diseases carried by Christopher Columbus's sailors had decimated the native Carib population, Jenny, then seven, asked, "Why weren't the European sailors killed off by Carib diseases?" The answer is crossroads. Europe of the fifteenth century had stood at the crossroads of many civilizations for 2,000 years. With the diversity of people who traipsed through Europe as traders, soldiers, and slaves

came the diversity of their diseases. This host of plagues honed the immune systems of Europeans; those who survived had the ability to fight off a great variety of diseases and passed on their disease-fighting genes. The Carib "Indians," highly interbred, did not have the dubious benefit of encountering one different plague after another in their immunological history, and so they were devastated.

It is not just the immune system that thrives with diversity; ideas do too. Crossroads thinking is general knowledge and underpins creativity. Jared Diamond points out that Tasmanian Aborigines were at a cognitive disadvantage compared with Australian Aborigines. Tasmania is cut off by the almost impassable Tasman Strait, whereas geography does not block trade across Australia. The sophistication of Australian tools increased across 2,000 years, whereas that of Tasmanian tools deteriorated.[16] Creativity sharpens tools and also brings different ways of thinking to make connections among seemingly unrelated concepts.

Crossroads thinking implies diversity. If experience consists only of repeated examples of the same thing, it adds little. I was at a faculty meeting about forty years ago, and Frank Irwin, then the grand old man of our department, said, "I've had twenty years of experience with this" (what "this" was, I forget). Assistant professor Frank Norman, then a young Turk, said, "There's twenty years of experience, Dr. Irwin, and there's one year of experience twenty times."

BESIDES MORE SPECIFIC and general knowledge, a second benefit of age for creativity is that shortcuts and guidelines get better.

The story about Isaac Newton and the apple is apparently true, but not the apple-falling-off-the-tree version that we learned at school. One evening when Newton was at his family's farm during the plague years, he was at his desk. An apple sat on the surface and the moon rose behind it, occupying the same visual space. Aha! Newton wondered if same force that holds the moon in orbit could draw the apple to the ground.[17] Newton was a "natural." Really wondrous here is the scaffolding that permitted him to perceive the apple and the moon in just that perfect way to point toward gravity and the inverse-square law.

Newton had this scaffolding in place in his early twenties. How could so much scaffolding have been erected so early? It is commonly said that Newton was a genius, and with that statement the mystery is thrown back on another mystery: the brain, a gift, God, birth from Zeus's brow, or "talent." Angela Duckworth has demystified talent at least a bit.[18] Talent is the rate at which a skill is acquired. Newton was fast and could soak up information more quickly than the rest of us. He had knowledge-based shortcuts that allowed him to see to the bottom faster and with less input.

I think an alternate explanation of Newton calls not on a gift from the gods but on experience: shortcuts. My guess is that Newton's being a "natural" came from continual reverie about physics and mathematics, and this huge amount of "time on task" created the shortcuts that permitted him to see that the apple plus the moon equals gravity.

While I am certainly no Newton, I have been through so much in my continual daily reverie about psychological issues that I have an immense latticework of shortcuts that allow me to leap from one building to the next with ease. Newton had it at twenty-two, but it took me decades to build.

For example, I used to read every word of a journal article laboriously. Now I just scan because I can infer huge swaths of what the whole article contains. I know that if Bob Rescorla wrote it, I don't have to worry about the adequacy of the control groups. These kinds of shortcuts save me a lot of time that I can put to better use elsewhere.

BESIDES SHORTCUTS THAT save time, guidelines more formally called "heuristics" likely get better with age. Many guidelines are about what not to do—negative heuristics that tell you how to avoid errors. "Recency," for example, is one: if a long friendship has just ended on a bitter note, you will underestimate how worthwhile the friendship was, relative to a lower-quality friendship that just petered out. I use some negative heuristics specific to doing psychology:

- If the theory contains "self-[esteem, efficacy, worth, compassion]," hold on to your wallet.
- If you need fancy statistics to see a result, think twice.

- If an article ends with "more research is needed," be skeptical.
- If "qualitative study" or "focus group" appears, stop reading.

I use negative heuristics in daily life: don't promise more than you can deliver; never be sarcastic; check your work repeatedly; don't be late; when in doubt stand on principle. These are some of the "thou shalt nots" by which I have learned to live.

But I repeat a major caveat in the context of the heuristics that may improve with age: not getting it wrong does not equal getting it right. There are positive heuristics that are more important than negative heuristics, and these likely get better with age.

Imagine making a speech with no grammatical errors. Or writing a memoir in which you say nothing untrue. Or serving a meal in which nothing tastes bad. Or proving a theorem in which every statement is true. Or playing a Beethoven piano sonata with no mistakes. Or chairing a meeting in which no one is discourteous. None of these guarantees a good speech, a good book, a good meal, a good proof, a good performance, or a good meeting.

Guidelines of the form "thou shalt" create goodness, right, beauty, and truth over and above the mere absence of badness, wrong, ugliness, or falsehood. Discovering positive heuristics is a much harder task than discovering shortcuts to avoid errors, and unlike negative heuristics, positive heuristics are at the heart of creativity.

Enumerating them is well beyond me, but here are a few I have learned to use in psychology:

- A good theory makes surprising counterintuitive predictions (e.g., treating depression as prospection gone awry will work better than correcting false beliefs about the past and the present).
- Begin with an anecdote that distills the idea (e.g., "Sauce béarnaise used to be my favorite sauce") and only then challenge the reader with the details of experiments and theory.
- Drill down to the most basic assumption and ask, if it were false, what would follow (e.g., What if early-childhood trauma has only minor effects on adult personality? Then adolescence might be the crucial time that wreaks the tectonic changes in

who we will become, and intervening then will do more good than early-childhood interventions).

- A good piece of science tells the reader that something she thought was false is true, or something she thought was true is false. You will read about a whopper that stands learned helplessness on its head in the next chapter.

Beyond allowing one to glean more knowledge and better shortcuts and guidelines, aging helps counterbalance the losses with a keener sense of audience. Creativity requires the accurate evaluation that the original and surprising idea will be useful, beneficial, and desired by the relevant audience.[19] "Audience" is both literal, as in the arts and commerce, and figurative, in the case of academic disciplines. Here "audience" refers to the gatekeepers—the individuals who have the power to decide which contributions are creative. Isaac Newton at age twenty-three had an exquisite sense of audience. Returning from two plague years at home, he had written three papers: one on optics, one on calculus, and one on gravitation. His audience was his mentor, Sir Isaac Barrow, who responded by resigning his Lucasian professorship in 1669 in favor of Newton. (Oh, to have such a student! Oh, to have such objectivity!)

Writing about creativity offers an example of the importance of audience. Creativity is an overworked topic, and almost everything has been said about it. For an article about creativity to see the light of day, it is a good idea to first send a draft to Dean Simonton, Mihaly Csikszentmihalyi, Teresa Amabile, and Howard Gardner and patiently wait for their comments. Their work needs to be cited (favorably if possible) and their papers read carefully. I blush to say that I have failed to do this all too often in my eagerness to get on to my next work. Dick Solomon had a much better grasp of this principle than I. He always sent his drafts out to the gatekeepers first, and blessed with Harold Schlosberg on one shoulder and Walter Hunter on the other, commenting on each sentence, Dick had a great sense of audience.

Ideas that are a half step ahead of the audience are good "normal" science, and the journals are filled with these. While usually boring

to read, they provide the cumulative bricks. Papers that are two steps ahead of the gatekeepers are rejected as outlandish. If you wish to succeed in normal science, stay just one step ahead, but do venture an occasional one-and-one-half-step paper to keep your sense of self-respect.

I ASKED THE Dalai Lama what follows if we are not of the present but are drawn into the future. He was sympathetic and encouraged me to pursue it. With Peter, Chandra, and Roy, over the next five years, we put prospection front and center, and this illuminated several huge issues in psychology and neuroscience that were completely opaque in the framework in which the past and the present determine the future. Consciousness became the process by which humans envision the future. The default network became the imagination network. Subjectivity became the common currency we use to compare future scenarios. Freedom of the will became the latitude of the scenarios we envisage. Creativity became the combination of original and surprising prospections coupled with a keen sense of audience, meaning that creativity can increase with age and might be teachable at any age.

Even though it may be a myth, I end this chapter with this story.

On Nov. 18, 1995, Itzhak Perlman, the violinist, came on stage to give a concert at Avery Fisher Hall at Lincoln Center in New York City. If you have ever been to a Perlman concert, you know that getting on stage is no small achievement for him. He was stricken with polio as a child, and so he has braces on both legs and walks with the aid of two crutches.

To see him walk across the stage one step at a time, painfully and slowly, is an unforgettable sight. He walks painfully, yet majestically, until he reaches his chair. Then he sits down, slowly, puts his crutches on the floor, undoes the clasps on his legs, tucks one foot back and extends the other foot forward. Then he bends down and picks up the violin, puts it under his chin, nods to the conductor and proceeds to play. . . .

But this time, something went wrong. Just as he finished the first few bars, one of the strings on his violin broke. You could hear it snap—it went off like gunfire across the room. There was no mistaking what that sound meant. . . .

He waited a moment, closed his eyes then signaled the conductor to begin again. The orchestra began, and he played from where he had left off. He played with overwhelming passion and power and purity.

Of course, anyone knows that it is impossible to play a symphonic work with just three strings. I know that, and you know that, but that night Itzhak Perlman refused to know that. You could see him modulating, changing, re-composing the piece in his head. At one point, it sounded like he was detuning the strings to get new sounds from them that they had never made before.

When he finished, there was an awesome silence in the room. And then people rose and cheered. There was an extraordinary outburst of applause from every corner of the auditorium. We were all on our feet, screaming and cheering, doing everything we could to show how much we appreciated what he had done.

He smiled, wiped the sweat from this brow, raised his bow to quiet us, and then he said, not boastfully, but in a quiet, pensive, reverent tone, "You know, sometimes it is the artist's task to find out how much music you can still make with what you have left."[20]

Chapter Twenty-Eight

The Hope Circuit (2016)

AFTER FINISHING OUR PhDs at Penn in the late 1960s, Steve Maier and I went in opposite directions. I spun outward from learned helplessness, applying it to larger and larger targets: human depression, physical illness, psychotherapy, schools, businesses, the army, and, as you will soon read, even a flourishing human future. Steve went inward. He essentially switched fields and retrained as a serious neuroscientist studying how the brain circuits in rats influence behavior. He did not return to helplessness until the 1990s. When he did, he changed everything.

Steve took an assistant professorship in the University of Illinois's psychology department in 1968. He had a weird teaching style, but it won the undergraduate teaching award. He did not lecture; he only answered questions. I met Greg Kimble, a venerable learning theorist, and he told me about a new department he was forming at the University of Colorado in Boulder. He asked me if I was interested. I had just been tenured at Penn and was not moving again. Steve, I recalled, loved the outdoors, so I told Greg, "Try Steve Maier." Greg did, and Steve left the plains of Illinois for the mountains of Colorado, where he stayed for the rest of his career—hiking and bicycling through these mountains on weekends. He molted, no longer a flabby city kid, and even in his mid-seventies, he is, annoyingly, a model of trim, muscular fitness.

Steve went on to make the most important discovery in our field, and his discoveries turned learned helplessness on its head. He showed that the arrow of causality that we had postulated was wrong and that it was not helplessness but control and mastery that were learned. He discovered the brain circuits that produce and prevent helplessness, and their functions are wildly different from what we had expected all those years ago. How Steve discovered this is a mite technical but the prettiest example of neuroscience that I know, so I urge the reader to bear with the telling. This chapter recounts his story; I play the role of admirer. The years I'd spent working on positive psychology gave me a special appreciation for just how profound his findings were.

I first need to remind you what our theory said originally and what we discovered fifty years ago. Our theory essentially claimed that animals learned that nothing they did mattered, and so they expected that nothing they did in the future would matter. This expectation of helplessness undermined trying to escape bad events in the future. Our evidence came from the triadic design: in the first phase, one group (ESC) of animals got escapable shock, a second group got exactly the same pattern of shock but the shock continued regardless of what they did (INESC), and a third group got no shock (Zero). In the second phase all the animals went to a shuttle box, usually twenty-four hours after the first phase. Most of the animals in the INESC group then failed to escape in the shuttle box; they just lay there passively. Almost all the animals in the ESC and Zero groups learned to escape shock well in the shuttle box.

Steve, of course, was eager to know what the brain of the rat was doing, but good tools for looking closely at brain circuitry only got developed in the 1990s. Steve wondered where to start and reasoned backward from the passive behavior and heightened anxiety in the INESC group. Helpless rats showed aborted fight and flight and increased anxiety (panic), and the brain structures for these were known by the 1990s: the dorsal periaqueductal gray controls fight or flight and the amygdala controls panic. It looked as if INESC rats had inhibited dorsal periaqueductal gray function and exaggerated amygdala function.

And there is a structure—the dorsal raphe nucleus (DRN)—that projects to both, inhibiting one and potentiating the other. It does this by releasing serotonin, 5-HT, which in turn leads to the release of 5-HT in the amygdala and dorsal periaqueductal gray down the line. This produces passivity and panic.

To my non-neuroscience reader: I am going to simplify and keep to the bare bones of what you need to know about the brain to appreciate how Steve did it. The dorsal raphe nucleus is one structure you will need to remember and the transmitter, 5-HT (serotonin), is another, because activating the DRN directly and getting its release of 5-HT produces just the same deficits—panic and inhibited fight-or-flight response—as inescapable shock does.

So Steve reasoned that if inescapable shock produces a powerful activation of the DRN 5-HT neurons leading to the release of 5-HT in the amygdala and dorsal periaqueductal gray, then the DRN might be the crucial node in INESC producing learned helplessness. But it would also have to be true that escapable shock does not activate the DRN.

Got it so far? If not, stop scanning, slow down, and reread the previous paragraph.

Steve's group then demonstrated exactly this: inescapable shock activates the neurons in the DRN that contain 5-HT, and exactly equal escapable shock does not.[1]

Yet, to withstand scientific scrutiny, these findings alone were not enough. The fact that INESC shock activated DRN 5-HT neurons did not mean that this process is either necessary or sufficient to produce helplessness. So next Steve showed that DRN activation was necessary for helplessness to occur and that it was sufficient. In other words, DRN activation always produced helplessness, and nothing else did. He determined necessity by blocking the DRN activation produced by inescapable shock with lesions or injection of drugs to the DRN.[2] These prevented inescapable shock from producing its usual poor escape and panic: rats that got INESC but had the DRN blocked were not helpless.

He determined sufficiency simply by injecting drugs that activate 5-HT neurons into the DRN, producing the same passivity and panic

as does INESC shock. Rats that got no shock at all but had an excited DRN were helpless.

So the activation of the DRN is necessary and sufficient to produce passivity and panic.

(Pause. If your hold on this material is shaky, go back and read the last page again.)

To this point, Steve's experiments had shown only the brain chemistry behind the behaviors we'd witnessed decades before. But now a new question arose, one that we couldn't have considered in 1964 because neuroscience hadn't come far enough: Why does the DRN respond only if the shock is inescapable? The obvious option is that the DRN detects that shock is inescapable. However, the DRN is a tiny brainstem structure (perhaps 20,000 to 30,000 neurons in the rat, 150,000 cells in the human), and so it is unlikely to have the processing power to detect no control. The next possibility is that the DRN receives greater excitatory input during inescapable than during escapable shock, thereby leading to more activation with inescapable shock. But this turned out not to be so.

If the rats were not learning helplessness, only one obvious possibility remained: that being helpless was a natural, unlearned, default response to prolonged shock. This, in turn, meant that the presence of control must somehow be learned high up in the cortex, and this learning must turn off the DRN and so abort helplessness. In other words, helplessness wasn't learned; control was. Steve tested this theory and confirmed it was true. Through further experiments he located the actual pathway—within the medial prefrontal cortex (MPFC)—that was the agent of the change we'd seen all those years before. The MPFC-DRN pathway was the key, and it didn't teach those rats helplessness; it taught them control.

Steve showed that turning this pathway on or off chemically overrode the external contingencies. He first taught rats to escape by turning a wheel. They did this perfectly well, even when the MPFC-DRN pathway was turned off chemically. But crucially they were later helpless in the shuttle box. Completing the tour de force, he first made the rats passive and helpless, because their wheel turning did

not matter. But he turned this pathway on chemically during the helplessness. Crucially these rats were not helpless later in the shuttle box.[3]

The development of a new circuit that sent the information about control to turn off the DRN required the production of new proteins, and Steve's group showed that blocking new protein synthesis in the MPFC after escapable shock allowed helplessness to later occur.[4] That is, even though the subjects exerted control and the MPFC was activated, the rats were helpless later unless new proteins could be formed. These particular proteins, called plasticity proteins, were indeed induced in the MPFC by escapable shock.[5] So Steve concluded that the MPFC-DRN pathway was modified in the several hours after the experience of escapable shock, and this altered pathway was crucial to the expectation that shock would be controllable in the future.

Keep this newly formed MPFC-DRN pathway in mind. What in the world is it?

Steve's findings turned learned helplessness on its head. Helplessness wasn't learned; only control was. Did this mean our first great finding was a mistake? What did the original learned helplessness theory get right, and what did it get wrong?

As the original theory claimed, organisms do indeed learn about the dimension of control, and this dimension is critical. However, the dimension detected and learned about was the presence, not the absence, of control. This did not mean that animals were born helpless, but it did mean that they became helpless when faced with sustained negative experiences. The passivity and panic that followed INESC for several days was an unlearned reaction to prolonged aversive stimulation. This meant that helplessness is not learned; it is some kind of mammalian default response to bad things. Steve had showed that learning about control aborted this default process. He'd discovered a pathway for defeating helplessness.

Clearly, this was a substantial revision to the theory we developed fifty years ago. When we found that dogs given inescapable shock later failed to learn to escape in a shuttle box, but that dogs given escapable shock later escaped normally, the ideas we developed were

our guess about what is most adaptive for dogs, rats, and people. We reasoned that active coping was best because this would minimize bad events, and so we assumed that organisms would initially expect control to be possible and try to escape. If the stressor proved to be uncontrollable, organisms would then learn this and expect it to be true in the future, with this expectation of uncontrollability undermining trying. However, the neural data do not support this. Instead, the presence of control is the active ingredient, leading to the inhibition of default DRN giving up.

Perhaps this counterintuitive arrangement makes more sense if we consider evolution. For our ancient ancestors, threats engaged defensive reflexes, and these reflexes cost energy. If the reflexes were unsuccessful, it would be adaptive to shut them down and conserve energy for adjustments that promote survival, such as altering the immune system to better fight any infection or wound that might occur. Primitive organisms, such as reptiles, do not have the sensory apparatus to detect threats at a great distance; nor do they have complex responding to deploy for control. Bad events for primitive organisms are generally uncontrollable by any available voluntary behavior, and so primitive organisms do not need mechanisms to detect controllability. Thus, the success of defensive reflexes is likely related to how long the existing threat lasts—if it is prolonged, then passivity and conservation would be adaptive, with energy being shifted to physiological adjustments to threat. It is important that 5-HT is phylogenetically ancient and has, from the beginning, been involved in shifting the balance of the flow of energy.

As organisms became more complex in evolution, they began to detect and identify threats at a distance. And so they developed rich behavioral and cognitive skills to control threats. Control became available even against prolonged threats. So passivity and other energy adjustments set in motion by the continuation of threat should shut down when control works.

Thus, when high mammals encounter a threat, here is what happens. First, defensive reflexes occur, activating the DRN. 5-HT builds if the threat continues long enough, and if 5-HT reaches some threshold, voluntary trying is shut down, and energy flow is shifted.

However, detection of control shuts down the DRN so that trying will continue. Further, when control exists, plasticity occurs in the MPFC-DRN circuit so that the system now learns, reacting to bad events as if they are escapable, thereby prolonging trying. This is why expert athletes, soldiers, and pilots are calm under pressure. Their brains detect and expect control when others panic and freeze.

In short, control is a relatively recent adaptation in evolutionary history. Our experiments showed just how powerful it can be, and Steve's showed exactly where in the brain it lodged.

THERE ARE TWO main takeaways. The first is that our default response to prolonged bad events is helplessness and heightened anxiety. The second is that our higher cortical processes inhibit this default helplessness. These higher cortical processes buffer against, but do not annihilate, the default passivity of the DRN.

This paints an up-from-helplessness neural picture that fits human development well. As a species we are born helpless, and as infants and toddlers we stay immature for a very long time. Indeed, this slow maturation may be crucial to our success as a species. Perhaps during this time we are gradually learning more and more control. Importantly rats that learn mastery early in life resist helplessness when exposed to inescapable shock later in life, and it is exactly the MPFC-DRN pathway that prevents this later helplessness.[6] Early experience with control immunizes us against the ravages of uncontrollability later in life, perhaps through this pathway. But I still wondered exactly what psychological process this all-important circuit was.

All this has major implications for therapy. Therapy that tries to undo trauma is not likely to work. Trauma is here to stay. Treatment that dwells on past trauma and present misery without emphasizing planning for a better future may be for naught. Consider the classes of therapy in which the patient reviews a past trauma in order to gain insight into its causes or to have catharsis about it. The circuitry suggests that merely confronting, understanding and reliving the trauma cannot achieve much. Confronting the past is not the province only of psychodynamic therapy; it is also common in popular cognitive-behavioral therapies: discussion of rumination, discussion of memory

biases like selective filtering (where the patient only attended to a neg-ative part of something that happened and ignored the positive parts), behavior-chain analysis (where the patient looks at all the steps that led up to an eating or drinking binge and considers how those steps set him up to "fail"), and catastrophizing about the present are all modern techniques that work on the present without necessarily ad-dressing the future. A skilled and experienced therapist can lead a pa-tient through these exercises about the past and the present with the added, explicit purpose of changing future behavior, such as better recognizing triggers for past maladaptive responses in order to avoid those triggers in the future or gaining insight into catastrophizing in order to learn how to be more optimistic. So therapy that explicitly creates end runs around trauma, buffers against it, and uses the past and the present as vehicles for planning a better future is more likely to work.

This circuit also implies something that—skeptical about the overselling of neuroscience—I have never countenanced before: that there may come a day when we can treat depression by turning on the MPFC-DRN pathway directly or by turning off the DRN directly. Steve's discoveries were about rats, of course. But human beings have quite similar structures. Right now we do not have anything like the tools to identify these circuits in human beings. Nor do we have the tools to turn on or turn off these structures by drugs or transmagnetic stimulation or optogenetics (the use of light to stimulate neurons). But that day will soon come, and depression and panic in humans—I say this for the very first time—might become curable.

It is gratifying to have lived long enough and to be in a vibrant enough science to find out you were wrong. Helplessness is not learned as we first thought; it is the default reaction of mammals to prolonged bad events. What is vouchsafed to humans, however, is a magnificent cortex, a top-down structure that learns mastery over bad events. We can learn—and teach—that future bad events will be controllable, and this will buffer us against helplessness and anxiety.

THIS DISCOVERY WAS profound. But I still didn't fully grasp what this circuit really was until the middle of a long, strange night.

I had been mulling over Steve's data for more than a year. We were writing a *Psychological Review* article together,[7] but I was still bewildered. I felt the MPFC-DRN circuit was tremendously important, that it made evolutionary sense, and that it was more important even than Steve thought, but I couldn't put my finger on why.

My friend and patron Jack Templeton died of brain cancer on May 22, 2015. Jack and I still had so much unfinished business to do together: to increase the creativity of the next generation, to raise positive psychology to the next level, and to understand the biology of hope and how it relates to spiritual flourishing. He had been a rock of support for all of these.

His memorial service was scheduled for June 11, 2015, at 10:30 a.m. at an evangelical Presbyterian church in nearby Bryn Mawr. A thousand people from all over the world would come—representatives of all the good works that Jack supported—and I planned to be there as well.

But on June 10, Mandy took me to hospital. There was a cyst on my spine, and I was having trouble walking. I'd had a similar episode a year before, and surgery to remove the cyst had kept me in bed for almost a month. I recovered completely, and the cyst was benign. The surgeons now operated while visualizing my spinal cord in real time—an amazing new technique—and the new cyst was aspirated. I came out of general anesthesia after midnight. All was well—the cyst was benign again—but I was advised to stay in bed for the next few days. Mandy put me to bed at 1 a.m.

Three hours later I awoke suddenly from a deep sleep, completely alert. My very first thought was that I knew what the MPFC-DRN circuit was. I just knew it. It was the hope circuit. All this fell suddenly into place. I didn't know the details yet, but I knew I was right and rushed downstairs to write an email to Steve. I started the email at 5:35 a.m. and finished at 5:57 a.m. At the moment I put my finger on the send button, all the electricity in Lower Merion Township died.

A scene from the movie *Field of Dreams* crossed my mind. The protagonist, Ray, tells his wife Annie, "When primal forces of nature tell you to do something, the prudent thing is not to quibble over details."

I want to tell Jack Templeton about a discovery he would have loved. Jack and I talked often about a science of hope and its relation to faith. Jack wanted there to be a "hope circuit" in the brain, and I can tell him now that there is. Photo courtesy of the John Templeton Foundation.

The power came back on at 6:20 a.m., and I hit send. The email was delivered to Steve.

I next opened my snail mail and read a note of thanks from Mathew White, sent with a copy of his new book on positive education at Saint Peter's College in Adelaide.[8] I glanced at the chapter on positive Christianity and read, "Religion and science are opposed but only in the same sense in which my thumb and forefinger are opposed—and between the two, one can grasp everything." This was the focal issue for Jack and his father, Sir John Templeton. I burst into tears and had a command hallucination to put on a suit and go to the memorial service. Which I did.

I arrived at the church shortly before the service began and saw Jack's widow, Pina. I told her about my midnight epiphany. She told me that I should testify. There were two eulogies for Jack scheduled, and I should give a third. So after Stephen Post's eulogy, I was announced.

"I want to tell Jack what happened to me this morning and to tell Jack about a discovery he would have loved. Jack and I talked often about a science of hope and its relation to faith."

I narrated the surgery, the sudden awakening, the MPFC-DRN mystery, and the blackout. Finally I added, "Between science and religion one can grasp everything."

"Jack wanted there to be a 'hope circuit' in the brain, and I can tell him now that there is," I concluded.

There was a stunned silence. I left the church and went home to bed. I stayed there for days.

Chapter Twenty-Nine

Turning the World

*F*IRST, DURING MY LIFETIME psychology abandoned behaviorism and took cognition seriously. Second, during my lifetime psychology turned its attention from misery toward happiness. Third, during my lifetime psychology finally took evolution and the brain seriously. And fourth, during my lifetime psychology moved from its obsession with the past to researching how the brain thinks about the future.

But how much does cognitive psychology matter? How much does evolutionary psychology matter? How much does positive psychology matter? How much does a psychology of prospection matter? How much does a hope circuit matter?

And how much did my role in these transformations matter?

These are questions a memoirist cannot evade. On most days, my answer is "not much." Each of them was likely a mere baby step in scientific and cultural progress, either to be soon forgotten, or overtaken by the next fad, or in the best case assimilated, with the proper footnote, into the next step in scientific progress. Each of them likely would have occurred without me, only a bit later. Any realistic person likely believes something like this about his or her own work, and it would not be worth writing a chapter to echo such a commonplace sentiment.

And yet . . .

On a really good day, I think these ideas do matter for the long future and that my role was crucial. This chapter talks about what I

believe on a really good day—first what I believe about my role and how I personally changed over my life, then what I believe about how important these changes in psychology are for the long human future.

My Role

At my fiftieth college reunion in May 2014, I sat on a panel of well-known Princeton alumni. "Career trajectory" was the topic.

"I wrote about cooking, and it really felt good, so I wrote more funny stories about food," a *New York Times* columnist said.

"I picked up the banjo, and the audience loved it, so I devoted myself to playing blues," a popular musician said.

Their prevailing narrative was "I tried this . . . it felt good, so I did it more" or "I tried that . . . people didn't like it, so I stopped," and so, blown hither and thither by their proclivities, by prevailing winds, and internal and external rewards and punishments, they arrived at their professions.

"Not me," I said. "I was called."

THE BELIEF THAT one is called by the future is a common human experience. Moses's Burning Bush is the paradigm. But many of the rest of us have such experiences. When Gallup asked Americans if they'd had a "profound religious experience or awakening that changed the direction" of their lives, 41 percent agreed that the statement "*completely* applie[d] to them," and 30 to 40 percent felt they had a calling.[1] I number myself among them. I was around thirty, newly tenured at the University of Pennsylvania, an animal experimental psychologist, and a dyed-in-the-wool learning theorist. My teacher, Aaron Beck, warned me that if I continued on this path, I would "waste my life," and a numinous dream then rattled me enough to change my trajectory.

I have paid attention to dreams and epiphanies for my entire scientific career. When I first saw a helpless dog in the fall of 1964, I "saw" almost to the end the implications of this discovery and its future

directions, although it took fifty years and a new neuroscience to pin them down.

Positive psychology as well. On a late winter day in 2002, I was walking near the Lincoln Memorial in a cold and hard rain with David Larson. We were huddling together under an umbrella after a meeting in Washington. David would die about two weeks later, suddenly, at the age of fifty-four. Having never met him before, I told him that I admired the bold steps he'd taken as an executive at the National Institute of Mental Health. David founded a branch to investigate the relationship of health to spirituality, a topic quite out of keeping with the institute's usual priorities. After an uphill battle, David won, and while not a lot of money got channeled into this, it was a breakthrough in the otherwise remedial, pedestrian projects funded by the government.

"How did you think the idea up?" I asked.

"I didn't, Marty," he replied. "I was told to do it. How about you and positive psychology?"

"I was told to do it."

WHY ME? WHY NOT Al Bandura, Richard Lazarus, Julian Rotter, Mike Csikszentmihalyi, or Ed Diener? All of these scientists were farther along, fruitfully investigating the positive side of life. Any of them might have invited other scientists and practitioners of the positive into the big tent and so ignited the movement. That I was president of the American Psychological Association (APA), a very bully pulpit, and in need of a transformational theme mattered. That I emerged from working on the really bad stuff—helplessness, depression, panic—mattered. I could see and name the missing piece—the positive—because of this stark contrast with the demoralizing awfulness I usually worked on. That I had serious doubts about what was "basic" mattered, and so I was less purely academic than my peers, having struggled uphill for twenty years in advocating the application of psychology to the real world.

Positive psychology had only a mere outline, not a master plan. Deciding to run for president of APA was not the culmination of long

deliberation. A recurring joyful image of a fetus floating above the Earth from the movie *2001* somehow propelled it. With Mike Csikszentmihalyi and Ray Fowler in early January of 1998, we sketched out what the new field would need to thrive: funding, just the right leaders, and the young people. These all fell into place without our doggedly pursuing them: Atlantic Philanthropies, Templeton, Jim Hovey, Gallup, and Neal Mayerson all came to me, not vice versa. Bob Nozick, Chris Peterson, Ed Diener, Kathleen Hall Jamieson, and George Vaillant hopped on board without much urging. Barb Fredrickson, Jon Haidt, Laura King, Sonja Lyubomirsky, James Pawelski, and a dozen other talented young scientists answered the call and stayed the course.

Prospection also had the same feel: Roy Baumeister's idea that consciousness is for imagining futures, Chandra Sripada's unveiling of the default network, my impulse to announce without even asking him that Peter Railton and I would write an article about being drawn into the future, and the Templeton Foundation's jumping in with $8 million to support an idea not even half baked.

Finally, the hope circuit. I could not fit the jigsaw puzzle together, but it emerged out of general anesthesia, a blackout, and an evangelical memorial service. This was even weirder than the rest.

The history of positive psychology is better described as the alignment of the planets than as the execution of a plan. I made the right speeches at the right times, but odd as it sounds, I consistently and completely underprepared. For the first Nikki speech and my APA presidential address, and on many other occasions, I waited for the words to come, and the words came.

So what was my role? "Vehicle," "catalyst," and "attractor" all come to mind. But on my good days, I like to think I was a "natural." In bridge, as I mentioned, among the high experts a few are naturals; the cards just fly off their hands, and they cannot always explain what they did. But their plays are consistently right. Peter Madison early spotted this in me, and I recognized it—in this case being a natural was about having good ideas in psychology. From my APA presidency on, I became a natural inspirer, and I acquired charisma.

In bridge the cards fly off the hands of naturals. The great plays express the shortcuts the player has built over long experience plus more than adequate talent, and nothing more. No higher power is at work in bridge. And I do not intend to invoke a higher power in my life course. But I do not intend to deny it. The words, nevertheless, were put into my mouth.

THE THEME OF this book will not have escaped you: the trajectory of my own life and the trajectory of psychology itself are parallel and they influenced each other. Psychology as I first found it in 1964 had, by 2018, rejected the premises that were blinding it. Psychology is no longer just about misery. It is about happiness as well. Psychology no longer disregards natural selection. Psychology no longer uncritically accepts determinism, that we are frog-marched into the future by our past, especially by childhood. It is also about how healthy and free people hope for, plan, and choose among possible futures. Psychology no longer believes that consciousness is mere froth. It accepts that conscious thoughts can drive sadness, fear, and anger, as well as joy and hope. In short, psychology no longer misses everything that makes life worth living. Psychology, finally, gets it.

As do I. How have I changed from the time of my first academic post in 1967 until now, and how do these changes parallel the changes in psychology?

I am still an old-fashioned intellectual, and my loyalty lies with the big questions. But the questions I venture into are bigger and harder now, with those about creativity and imagination, well-being and the future of the planet, destiny, time travel, and God coming only at the end.[2]

I am a no longer a dedicated skeptic. While still loyal to the side that needs defenders, I think skepticism is overrated. Science has its verificationists, the people who work on confirming or disconfirming others' ideas, but science also needs its question posers, those who can ask the right question at the right time and then point in the general direction of a fruitful answer. These people are perhaps naturals. The sense in which I am still a skeptic is now about science

itself. The human mental apparatus has evolved to solve survival and reproduction problems. It has not evolved to know the truth or to perceive ultimate reality. Human beings can know about only the tiniest edge of what is true.

I am still in a bit of a hurry. I want to finish things, and I still take shortcuts. I am still wrapped up in my own thoughts, and I still do psychology almost every waking moment. But I do not know what—if anything—comes next for me, and so I am more content to polish and rewrite.

I am no longer ambitious. I am more conscious of the awards and honors that I have not gotten than of those I have. But this is a 4 a.m. annoyance, not a vexation or plague. My big ambition as an undergraduate was to be like Ludwig Wittgenstein, surrounded by devoted students and followers. This actually came to pass and has very much taken the edge off any hunger for prizes. It is a gratifying state of affairs in the abstract, but it is primarily of practical importance, because it makes it more likely that my work will be carried into the next generation.

I have acquired some charisma. My public lectures sometimes are received—to my surprise—with standing ovations and even sometimes with tears of joy. I had a bit of this as a young psychologist, but it was just my own enthusiasm that was contagious. Now the ideas themselves are inspiring. But at seventy-five I have begun to worry about creeping dementia. I now average thirty minutes a week trying to find where I parked my car. Dick Solomon swore me to a secret pact when I was in my thirties and he was in his sixties.

"Marty," he said over scotch at the faculty club, "I am worried that I am starting to talk rot and that my lectures are not cutting-edge. The saddest thing about dementia is that the judgment of capacity deteriorates in lockstep with the deterioration of that capacity. So as my student and now close colleague I want you to promise me that if this starts to happen to me, you will tell me, and then I will shut up and retire."

As it happened, Dick died at age seventy-seven in 1995, before I detected any waning of his powers. But had I, I would have carried

out my promise, and I now need to find a young colleague to take the pledge for me.

I am a leader. Now less centered on my own agenda, I attend well to the agendas of others. When I was younger, my advocacy was rightly seen as self-promoting. Now it is rightly seen as generative. I see the strengths of the colleagues and students around me and so better guide them toward achieving their own goals. I can point the way toward new, promising scientific futures, and I can recruit and mobilize those who will achieve them.

I am no longer negative. I am actually quite positive. I now ask questions about what is best in life: positive emotion, meaning, human progress, virtue, and the long future of flourishing. My critical antennae are still up, but I pay much less attention to their tantrums. I never squash others. I do not get spontaneously depressed or anxious often—except when a specific bad event looms. I now have more than my fair share of contentment. I rate my PERMA very high: on a one-to-ten scale, I rate my positive emotion a six, my engagement a ten, my relationships a six, my sense of meaning a ten, and my accomplishment a ten. In 1967, had I conceived of PERMA, all of my scores would have been much lower. I am optimistic and usually filled with hope about the future.

My personal life is much better. Mandy brings me joy and inspires my academic life. I work at home and so am with Mandy and my children almost all day every day, and they are sunshine. Jenny, the youngest, brightens every single day for me. About eight years ago, Matthieu Ricard, my friend and a renowned Buddhist monk, decided to teach loving-kindness mediation to Tim Beck and to me. We sat with Matthieu in my poker room, and he told us to imagine someone we loved and then to expand the feeling outward. Jenny, then age five, happened to walk into the room, and this made the meditation simple for me. So I found that loving-kindness meditation worked. Tim thought it was hogwash.

THE CHANGE IN my own life and the change in psychology are intertwined. Both grew from despair to hope, from darkness, through

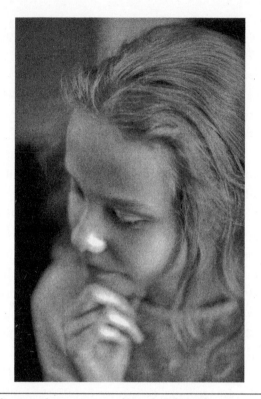

Jenny Emma Seligman. Photo courtesy of Mandy Seligman.

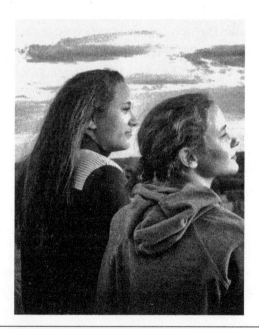

Carly and Jenny Seligman. Photo courtesy of Mandy Seligman.

shadow, toward light. This is the theme, the very sense, of this book. But a third thing also happened.

The world got better.

The Tiger

The setting is no less than the Canterbury Cathedral. I convened a prospection meeting in October 2014 to consider "being called." There were about a dozen participants. All of us recognized how common is the feeling of "calling," but we differed about what it means. For the secular among us—Amy Wresniewski, Bob Wright, David Yaden, George Vaillant—the feeling is a mere efflorescence of natural selection. It is adaptive for the species to undertake vision-ary missions and partake of a marching in step that tunes the group. Human beings have been selected for such spirituality—to think our-selves part of something larger and more important that we are. This kind of calling, adaptive as it is, however, is for the secular just a ben-eficial illusion. For the divines among us—Hugh Kempster, founder of Mystics Anonymous; Jonathan Sacks, chief rabbi of England; Kevin Rudd, prime minister of Australia; Thérèse Rein, former first lady of Australia and a positive psychologist; and Theo McCall, exponent of positive Anglicanism—being called is no illusion. Some people are actually called into the future, by the future itself or by God. Dreams and visions are mediums of the call.

On the third day, the divines asked, "Why are the pews empty?" In my view the Christianity of the crucifix, of sin and repentance, is hugely consoling but thrives best in a world of misery. In a world with less and less suffering, the crucifix loses much of its appeal. But there is a new, competing Christianity—a Christianity without the crucifix, a Christianity of love and gratitude and kindness. The schism in An-glicanism (and in Catholicism) between South America and Africa, on the one hand, and Europe and North America, on the other, is exactly about this. As medical, agricultural, and social progress and a tolerant diversity continue to relieve misery in the world, a positive Christianity and a positive Judaism and a positive Islam, I venture, will thrive.

This impulse to build what is positive in life, to raise temples yet undone, is by no means confined to religion. Our world is becoming more and more secular, but secular morality and surely our politics leave a moral vacuum. Toward what does the moral compass point? In the absence of divine reward or divine instruction, upon what rock can we justify morality? What principle is grand enough and believable enough to live one's life around?

I believe that the moral compass points to well-being, in the sense of PERMA, and that this aspiration is sufficiently grand and believable.[3] What does every culture, every religion, every politics agree upon? What does every parent want for his or her children? What can almost everyone say yes to? We can all say yes to more positive emotion. We can all say yes to being more engaged at work, with those we love, and in leisure. We can all say yes to better relationships with our fellow human beings, our fellow animals, and our planet. We can all say yes to more meaning in life. And we can all say yes to more noble accomplishment.

Human history has, until recently, been a tale of woe: warfare, plague, famine, injustice, poverty, ignorance, and violent death. The last half century has witnessed, if not the eradication, a great reduction of these ills. When the world is a vale of tears, it is natural that politics, religion, science, medicine, and the arts should concern themselves with defense and damage. But what happens when the world is no longer a vale of tears?

Florence of the fifteenth century is our beacon: no plague, no famine, civil harmony, peace, and extraordinary wealth. The city prospers under the genius of Medici leadership. Cosimo the Elder asks the city to debate what it should do with its financial surplus, how it should best use its great good fortune. Florence decides to invest in beauty and science, creating what two hundred years later we called the Renaissance. Our world, emerging at last from its vale of tears, now stands on the brink of a Florentine moment. Until now our institutions—political, religious, artistic, medical, and scientific—have seen their mission as reducing misery. They have succeeded in this laudable mission,[4] imperfectly perhaps, but well enough that we must now ask, "What next?" It is perilously easy to forget these huge advances

and to slip into our glib and quotidian catastrophizing about what "terrible times" we live in now. I exhort us to be more fully conscious of these positives, for in their belief that less suffering was the best we could aspire to, Freud and Schopenhauer led us into personal, scientific, moral, and political dead ends. We have much more to aspire to than less suffering. We can also aspire to more PERMA, more well-being, and more happiness. It is vouchsafed to us not only to witness the turning of the world but to actually turn the world toward well-being. We can remake politics, religion, the arts, medicine, and science into the engines of well-being.

"I AM an administrator," said Serene Jones, president of the Union Theological Seminary, on the final day of our meeting in the Canterbury Cathedral, "so I have administrative dreams.

"My academic field," Serene continued, "is the Reformation of the sixteenth century and the subsequent Thirty Years' War. Once every five hundred years, an idea arises so powerful that it sweeps away everything. It uproots and then replaces all the old, entrenched political and religious structures. That the building of well-being might become the moral touchstone of the way forward is, I believe, a once-in-five-hundred-years idea."

She continued, now narrating her dream.

> I get a call from the New York City Police. A tiger, they tell me, has escaped from the Central Park Zoo. So as an administrator, I make sure the gates of the seminary are closed, the students are up in their dorm, and the security people are out front. I then get another call from the police, and they tell me that I will be relieved to hear that the tiger has been captured.
>
> I look up from my desk, and I see out the window a humongous tiger coming down the hill. It is so gigantic that it is going to crush the seminary, flat. I feel expectation and joy and hope.

We will go out into the world and plant gardens and orchards to the horizons, we will build roads through the mountains and across the deserts, and terrace the mountains and irrigate the deserts until there will be garden everywhere, and plenty for all, and there will be no more empires or kingdoms, no more caliphs, sultans, emirs, khans, or zamindars, no more kings or queens or princes, no more quadis or mullahs or ulema, no more slavery and no more usury, no more property and no more taxes, no more rich and no more poor, no killing or maiming or torture or execution, no more jailers and no more prisoners, no more generals, soldiers, armies or navies, no more patriarchy, no more caste, no more hunger, no more suffering than what life brings us for being born and having to die, and then we will see for the first time what kind of creatures we really are.

—KIM STANLEY ROBINSON,
THE YEARS OF RICE AND SALT

Photo courtesy of Mandy Seligman.

ACKNOWLEDGMENTS

This is the easiest acknowledgments section I have ever written, since the book is peopled by those I want to thank. In addition, and with respect to writing the book itself, there are several people I want to single out: Richard Pine, who read a draft biographical chapter and told me that only I could write deeply on the subject of me. Sam Hughes, who wrote that original biographical chapter that got me to write it myself. Sam read and commented helpfully on several early drafts and urged me to continue on my own. My sister, Beth Brezner, read several drafts, as did my brother-in-law, Jerry. Beth said he laughed out loud occasionally, and she corrected numerous errors and reminded me of incidents now included. Dan Chirot, Bob Kaiser, Doug North, Paul Monaco, Ken Kudon, Alan Klein, and Jonathon Gordon all sent me corrections and memories of our schooldays. My oldest child, Amanda Irene Seligman, a skilled editor in her professional capacity as a historian, read two entire drafts and commented encouragingly and extensively. Her blue ink far outweighed her red ink—the best of editorial virtues. George Vaillant read early parts and applauded loudly, adding energy that kept me going in some rough spots, as did Senia Maymin, Scott Kaufman, Betty Sue Flowers, Serene Jones, and Martha Stout (who advised me not to change a single word). Jeanette Elstein and Peter Schulman helped a great deal in the gathering and editing of the photos. Ben Adams, my editor, came on board, and I wrestled him to the ground, whereupon he stood up

and was enormously constructive. Jen Kelland, my copy editor, told me that reading this book reminded her why she loved her job, and this one comment made light work of proofing four hundred pages. The love of my life, Mandy, read every word several times, provided photos, and supported me all the day long.

NOTES

NOTES TO CHAPTER 2
1. E. Abbott, *Flatland* (London: Seeley, 1884).
2. S. Freud, *New Introductory Lectures on Psychoanalysis*, trans. James Strachey (Oxford, UK: W. W. Norton, 1965), 202.

NOTES TO CHAPTER 3
1. M. Seligman, D. Chirot, and J. Albert, "Graduation," *Fish and Pumpkin* 22 (1960): 5. My only published poem.

NOTES TO CHAPTER 4
1. A. Whitehead and B. Russell, *Principia mathematica* (Cambridge: Cambridge University Press, 1910).
2. L. Wittgenstein, *Tractatus logico-philosophicus* (London: Kegan Paul, 1922).
3. D. Edmonds and J. Eidinow, *Wittgenstein's Poker: The Story of a Ten-Minute Argument Between Two Great Philosophers* (New York: Perennial, 2002).
4. M. E. P. Seligman and B. A. Campbell, "Effect of Intensity and Duration of Punishment on Extinction of an Avoidance Response," *Journal of Comparative and Physiological Psychology* 59 (1965): 295–297.
5. Alessandra Stanley, "Poet Told All; Therapist Provides the Record," *New York Times*, July 15, 1991, http://www.nytimes.com/1991/07/15/books/poet-told-all-therapist-provides-the-record.html.
Sexton's moving poem opens:

> *You, Doctor Martin, walk*
> *from breakfast to madness. Late August,*
> *I speed through the antiseptic tunnel*

> *where the moving dead still talk*
> *of pushing their bones against the thrust*
> *of cure.*

6. Peter told me in the 1980s that he burned it, along with all the other life stories he spent so much effort compiling. His concern was our privacy, but like Anne Sexton, I wish he had preserved mine.

NOTES TO CHAPTER 5

1. W. James, "Does Consciousness Exist?," *Journal of Philosophy, Psychology, and Scientific Methods* 1 (1904): 477–491.

2. Pavlov called it the *"conditional* reflex," marking the fact that the mechanism was future oriented, but the American W. Horsley Gantt egregiously mistranslated this as the *"conditioned* reflex," crucially omitting its forward-looking orientation. I. P. Pavlov, *Lectures on Conditioned Reflexes: Twenty-Five Years of Objective Study of the Higher Nervous Activity*, trans. W. Horsley Gantt with G. Volbroth (New York: International Publishers, 1928).

3. D. Coon, "Eponymy, Obscurity, Twitmyer, and Pavlov," *Journal of the History of the Behavioral Sciences* 18 (1982): 255–262.

4. J. B. Watson, "Psychology as the Behaviorist Views It," *Psychological Review* 20 (1913): 158–177.

5. E. L. Thorndike, "Some Experiments on Animal Intelligence," *Science* 7 (1898), 813–818.

NOTES TO CHAPTER 6

1. J. B. Overmier and R. C. Leaf, "Effects of Discriminative Pavlovian Fear Conditioning upon Previously or Subsequently Acquired Avoidance Responding," *Journal of Comparative and Physiological Psychology* 60 (1965): 213–217.

2. N. Chomsky, "A Review of B. F. Skinner's Verbal Behavior," *Language* 35 (1959): 26–54.

3. B. F. Skinner, *Verbal Behavior* (Boston, MA: Copley, 1957).

4. U. Neisser, *Cognitive Psychology* (Appleton, WI: Appleton-Century-Crofts, 1966).

5. M. Seligman and S. Maier, "Failure to Escape Traumatic Shock," *Journal of Experimental Psychology* 74 (1967): 1–9.

6. Seligman and Maier, "Failure to Escape Traumatic Shock."

7. S. Maier, M. Seligman, and R. Solomon, "Pavlovian Fear Conditioning and Learned Helplessness," in *Punishment*, ed. B. A. Campbell and R. M. Church. New York: Appleton-Century-Crofts, 1969 (299–343).

8. M. E. P. Seligman, S. F. Maier, and J. Geer, "The Alleviation of Learned Helplessness in Dogs," *Journal of Abnormal Psychology* 73 (1968): 256–262.

9. P. Singer, *The Expanding Circle: Ethics and Sociobiology* (New York: Farrar, Straus and Giroux, 1981).

10. M. A. Visintainer, J. R. Volpicelli, and M. E. P. Seligman, "Tumor Rejection in Rats After Inescapable or Escapable Shock," *Science* 216 (1982): 437–439.

NOTES TO CHAPTER 7

1. For a history, see M. Seligman, E. Walker, and D. Rosenhan, *Abnormal Psychology*, 4th ed. (New York: Norton, 2001).

2. S. Freud, "Analysis of a Phobia of a Five-Year-Old Boy," in *Case Histories 1*, Pelican Freud Library vol. 8, (Harmondsworth, UK: Pelican, 1977; orig. 1909), 169–306.

3. J. Wolpe, Psychotherapy by Reciprocal Inhibition (Stanford, CA: Stanford University Press, 1958).

4. S. Maier, "Failure to Escape Traumatic Electric Shock: Incompatible Skeletal-Motor Responses or Learned Helplessness?," *Learning and Motivation* 1 (1970): 157–169.

NOTES TO CHAPTER 8

1. I. Pavlov, *Conditioned Reflexes and Psychiatry* (New York: International Publishers, 1941).

2. N. R. F. Maier, *Frustration* (Ann Arbor: University of Michigan Press, 1949).

3. J. Garcia and R. Koelling, "Relation of Cue to Consequence in Avoidance Learning," *Psychonomic Science* 4 (1966): 123–124.

4. J. Watson, *Behaviorism*, rev. ed. (Chicago: University of Chicago Press, 1930).

5. The dialogues with my students and with others in this book are only my reconstructions of conversations and events. They are not verbatim and may be inaccurate in the detail of time and place. They are meant to capture the gist of the events and the personae of the speakers as closely as possible.

6. M. Seligman and J. Hager, *The Biological Boundaries of Learning* (Appleton, WI: Appleton-Century-Crofts, 1972). M. Seligman, "On the Generality of the Laws of Learning," *Psychological Review* 77 (1970): 406–417.

7. T. Sowell, *Inside American Education* (New York: Free Press, 1993).

8. T. Kuhn, *The Structure of Scientific Revolutions* (Chicago: University of Chicago Press, 1962).

9. Sagan, *Contact* (New York: Simon and Schuster, 1985).

10. M. E. P. Seligman and D. Groves, "Non-transient Learned Helplessness," *Psychonomic Science* 19 (1970): 191–192.

11. A. Jensen, "How Much Can We Boost IQ and Achievement," *Harvard Educational Review* 39 (1969): 1–123.

NOTES TO CHAPTER 9

1. A. T. Beck, *Depression* (New York: Hoeber, 1967).

2. A. T. Beck et al., *Cognitive Therapy of Depression* (New York: Guilford, 1979).

3. M. E. P. Seligman, "Depression and Learned Helplessness," in *The Psychology of Depression: Contemporary Theory and Research*, ed. R. J. Friedman and M. M. Katz (New York: Winston-Wiley, 1974).

4. M. E. P. Seligman, "On the Generality of the Laws of Learning," *Psychological Review* 77 (1970): 406–418.

5. Ultimately gathered together in R. Rescorla, "Pavlovian Conditioning: It's Not What You Think It Is," *American Psychologist* 43 (1988): 151–160.

6. M. E. P. Seligman, "Phobias and Preparedness," Behavior Therapy 2 (1971): 307–320.

NOTES TO CHAPTER 10

1. J. Weiss, "Effects of Coping Responses on Stress," *Journal of Comparative and Physiological Psychology* 65 (1968): 251–260.

2. J. V. Brady, "Ulcers in Executive Monkeys," *Scientific American* 199 (1958): 95–100.

3. J. L. Kavanau, "Behavior of Captive White-Footed Mice," *Science* 155 (1967): 1623–1639.

4. E. Langer and J. Rodin, "The Effects of Choice and Personal Responsibility for the Aged: A Field Experiment in an Institutional Setting," *Journal of Personality and Social Psychology* 34 (1976): 191–198.

5. R. White, "Motivation Reconsidered: The Concept of Competence," *Psychological Review* 66 (1959): 297–333.

6. J. Rotter, "Generalized Expectancies for Internal Versus External Control of Reinforcement," *Psychological Monographs* 80 (1966): 1–28.

7. A. Bandura, "Self-Efficacy: Toward a Unifying Theory of Behavioral Change," *Psychological Review* 84 (1977): 191–215.

8. R. Lazarus, J. Averill, and E. Opton, "The Psychology of Coping: Issues of Research and Assessment," in *Coping and Adaptation*, ed. G. V. Coehlo, D. Hamburg, and J. Adams (New York: Basic Books, 1974), 249–315.

9. S. Maier and M. Seligman, "Learned Helplessness: Theory and Evidence," *Journal of Experimental Psychology*: General 105 (1976): 3–46.

10. Maier and Seligman, "Learned Helplessness." But keep in mind, when you read chapter 28 and find out that our dogs and rats did not learn helplessness under trauma, that animals and people certainly can, under more benign circumstances, learn that they have no control as demonstrated by the nontraumatic experiments.

11. D. Hiroto and M. Seligman, "Generality of Learned Helplessness in Man," *Journal of Personality and Social Psychology* 31 (1975): 311–327.

NOTES TO CHAPTER 11

1. Joan Oliver Goldsmith's marvelous little book *How Do We Keep from Singing: Music and the Passionate Life* (2002) contains a chapter titled "Tessitura," which is my inspiration on this topic.

2. R. Solomon and L. Turner, "Discriminative Classical Conditioning in Dogs Paralyzed by Curare Can Later Control Discriminative Avoidance Responses in the Normal State," *Psychological Review* 69 (1962): 202–219. Do note the length of the title itself.

3. F. Irwin and W. Smith, "Value, Cost, and Information as Determiners of Decision," *Journal of Experimental Psychology* 54 (1957): 229–232.

4. *American Psychological Association Publication Manual* (Washington, DC: American Psychological Association Press, 2010). This publication, perennially on the best-seller list, provided serious income to the APA.

5. R. Rescorla and R. Solomon, "Two-Process Learning Theory: Relationships Between Pavlovian Conditioning and Instrumental Learning," *Psychological Review* 74 (1967): 151–187.

6. M. Seligman and J. Johnston, "A Cognitive Theory of Avoidance Learning," in *Contemporary Approaches to Conditioning and Learning*, ed. F. J. McGuigan and D. B. Lumsden (Washington, DC: Winston and Sons, 1973), 69–110.

7. R. Solomon, L. Kamin, and L. Wynne, "Traumatic Avoidance Learning: The Outcomes of Several Extinction Procedures with Dogs," *Journal of Abnormal and Social Psychology* 48 (1953): 291–302.

8. R. Rescorla, "Pavlovian Conditioning: It's Not What You Think It Is," *American Psychologist* 43 (1988): 151–160.

NOTES TO CHAPTER 12

1. H. Eysenck, obituary of Michel Gauquelin, *Independent*, June 20, 1991.

2. I. Marks, *Fears and Phobias* (New York: Academic Press, 1969).

3. A. Ohman et al., "The Premise of Equipotentiality in Human Classical Conditioning: Conditioned Electrodermal Responses to Potentially Phobic Stimuli," *Journal of Experimental Psychology: General* 105 (1976): 313–337.

4. S. Rachman and M. Seligman, "Unprepared Phobias: Be Prepared," *Behaviour Research and Therapy* 14 (1976): 333–338.

5. J. Durac, *A Matter of Taste* (London: Deutsch & Co, 1975).

6. S. J. Rachman, "*A Matter of Taste*: J. Durac," *Behaviour Research and Therapy* 14 (1975): 94.

7. M. Seligman, *Helplessness: On Depression, Development, and Death* (San Francisco: W. H. Freeman, 1975).

NOTES TO CHAPTER 13

1. J. Rotter, "Generalized Expectancies for Internal Versus External Control of Reinforcement," *Psychological Monographs* 80 (1966): 1–28.

2. B. Weiner, "'Spontaneous' Causal Thinking," *Psychological Bulletin* 97 (1985): 74–84.

3. L. Abramson, M. Seligman, and J. Teasdale, "Learned Helplessness in Humans: Critique and Reformulation," *Journal of Abnormal Psychology* 87 (1978): 49–74.

4. L. Wittgenstein, *Tractatus Logico-Philosophicus* (New York: Harcourt Brace, 1922).

5. L. Wittgenstein, *Philosophical Investigations* (Lanham, MD: Rowman & Littlefield, 1953).

6. For the most complete statement, see Chapter 13 in M. Seligman, E. Walker, and D. Rosenhan, *Abnormal Psychology*, 4th ed. (New York: Norton, 2001).

7. G. Vaillant Adaptation to Life (Boston: Little, Brown, 1977).

8. W. Mischel, E. Ebbesen, and A. R. Zeiss, "Cognitive and Attentional Mechanisms in Delay of Gratification," *Journal of Personality and Social Psychology* 21 (1972): 204–218.

NOTES TO CHAPTER 14

1. I am reconstructing the gist of the letter from memory, since the original disappeared long ago.

2. C. Peterson et al., "The Attributional Style Questionnaire," *Cognitive Therapy and Research* 6 (1982): 287–300. The references for much of the work on the ASQ can be found in C. Peterson and M. Seligman, "Causal Explanations as a Risk Factor for Depression: Theory and Evidence," *Psychological Review* 91 (1984): 347–374.

3. C. Peterson and M. Seligman, "Content Analysis of Verbatim Explanations: The CAVE Technique for Assessing Explanatory Style" (unpublished paper, 1984).

4. M. Seligman et al., "Depressive Attributional Style," *Journal of Abnormal Psychology* 88 (1979): 242–247.

5. M. Seligman et al., "Attributional Style and Depressive Symptoms Among Children," *Journal of Abnormal Psychology* 93 (1984): 235–238.

6. "Mission," National Institute of Mental Health, accessed September 4, 2017, http://www.nih.gov/about-nih/what-we-do/nih-almanac /national-institute-mental-health-nimh.

7. C. Peterson, L. Luborsky, and M. Seligman, "Attributions and Depressive Mood Shifts: A Case Study Using the Symptom-Context Method," *Journal of Abnormal Psychology* 92 (1983): 96–103.

8. C. Raps et al., "Attributional Style Among Depressed Patients," *Journal of Abnormal Psychology* 91 (1982): 102–103.

9. C. Peterson and M. Seligman, "Content Analysis of Verbatim Explanations."

10. G. Metalsky et al., "Attributional Styles and Life Events in the Classroom: Vulnerability and Invulnerability to Depressive Mood Reactions," *Journal of Personality and Social Psychology* 43 (1982): 612–617.

11. M. E. P. Seligman and G. Elder, "Learned Helplessness and Life-Span Development," in *Human Development and the Life Course: Multidisciplinary Perspectives*, ed. A. Sorenson, F. Weinert, L. Sherrod (Hillsdale, NJ: Erlbaum, 1985), 377–427.

12. L. Alloy and L. Abramson, "Judgment of Contingency in Depressed and Nondepressed Students: Sadder but Wiser?," *Journal of Experimental Psychology*: General 108 (1979): 441–485.

NOTES TO CHAPTER 15

1. M. E. P. Seligman et al., "Explanatory Style as a Mechanism of Disappointing Athletic Performance," *Psychological Science* 1 (1990): 143–146.

2. M. Visintainer, J. Volpicelli, and M. Seligman, "Tumor Rejection in Rats After Inescapable or Escapable Shock," *Science* 216 (1982): 437–439.

NOTES TO CHAPTER 16

1. M. McCarthy, "The Thin Ideal, Depression and Eating Disorders in Women," *Behaviour Research and Therapy* 28 (1990): 205–215.

2. For a useful review of the origins and growth of attachment theory from Konrad Lorenz to John Bowlby to Mary Ainsworth, see

I. Bretherton, "The Origins of Attachment Theory: John Bowlby and Mary Ainsworth," *Developmental Psychology* 28 (1992): 759–775.

3. P. Brickman, D. Coates, and R. Janoff-Bulman, "Lottery Winners and Accident Victims: Is Happiness Relative?," *Journal of Personality and Social Psychology* 36 (1978): 917–927.

NOTES TO CHAPTER 17

1. M. Seligman, *Learned Optimism* (New York: Knopf, 1990).

2. M. Sandmaier, "Don't Worry, Be Happy," *New York Times Book Review*, January 20, 1991.

3. M. Seligman et al., *The Optimistic Child* (Boston: Houghton Mifflin, 1996).

4. M. Seligman, *What You Can Change and What You Can't* (New York: Knopf, 1994).

5. M. Seligman, "The Effectiveness of Psychotherapy: The Consumer Reports Study," *American Psychologist* 50 (1995): 965–974. M. Seligman, "Science as an Ally of Practice," *American Psychologist* 51 (1996): 1072–1079.

NOTES TO CHAPTER 18

1. P. Nathan and J. Gorman, eds., *A Guide to Treatments That Work* (New York: Oxford University Press, 1998).

NOTES TO CHAPTER 19

1. An etymological digression: Mike is a lineal descendant of Genghis Khan, and the surname derives from his family's town of origin in Hungary: St. Michael of Csiks. It is pronounced "cheeks sent me high."

2. D. Clifton and P. Nelson, *Soar with Your Strengths* (New York: Dell, 1992).

3. D. Chirot and M. Seligman, eds., *Ethnopolitical Warfare: Causes, Consequences, and Possible Solutions* (Washington, DC: APA Books, 2001).

4. J. Gillham, *The Science of Optimism and Hope: Research Essays in Honor of Martin E. P. Seligman* (Philadelphia: Templeton Press, 2000).

5. J. Templeton, *Worldwide Laws of Life* (Philadelphia: Templeton Press, 1997).

NOTES TO CHAPTER 20

1. See B. Kuklick, *Churchmen and Philosophers* (New Haven, CT: Yale University Press, 1985), especially Chapter 15, for the narration and implications of the Haymarket Square Riot for the founding of social science.

2. G. Allport, "Personality and Character," *Psychological Bulletin* 18 (1921): 441–455.

3. C. Peterson and M. Seligman, *Character Strengths and Virtues* (Washington, DC: APA Press and New York: Oxford University Press, 2004).

4. You can take it for free at authentichappiness.org

NOTES TO CHAPTER 22

1. "Master of Applied Positive Psychology," University of Pennsylvania, accessed September 4, 2017, http://www.sas.upenn.edu/lps/graduate /mapp. If you are so called, please do apply. It is the single best learning experience in positive psychology.

2. E. Diener and M. E. P. Seligman, "Beyond Money: Toward an Economy of Well-being," *Psychological Science in the Public Interest* 5 (2004): 1–31.

3. M. Seligman, *Authentic Happiness* (New York: Free Press, 2002).

4. I thank a valuable member of the friends-of-PP list-serve, Judy Krings, for thinking up the catchy acronym "PERMA" and generously allowing me to use it.

5. M. Seligman, *Flourish* (New York: Free Press, 2011).

6. C. Wallis, "The New Science of Happiness," *Time*, January 9, 2005.

7. M. Seligman, A. Parks, and T. Rashid, "Positive Psychotherapy," *American Psychologist* 61 (2006): 774–788.

8. For a meta-analysis of thirty-nine studies of positive interventions, see L. Boller et al., "Positive Psychology Interventions: A Meta-analysis of Randomized Controlled Studies," *BMC Public Health* 13 (2013): 119. For the latest, see also C. Chaves et al., "A Comparative Study on the Efficacy of a Positive Psychology Intervention and a Cognitive Behavioral Therapy for Clinical Depression," *Cognitive Therapy and Research* 41 (2016): 1–17.

9. J. Boehm and L. Kubzansky, "The Heart's Content: The Association Between Positive Psychological Well-being and Cardiovascular Health," *Psychological Bulletin* 138 (2012): 655–691.

10. L. Harker and D. Keltner, "Expressions of Positive Emotion in Women's College Yearbook Pictures and Their Relationship to Personality and Life Outcomes Across Adulthood," *Journal of Personality and Social Psychology* 80 (2001): 112–124.

11. D. Schkade and D. Kahneman, "Does Living in California Make People Happy?," *Psychological Science* 9 (1998): 340–346.

12. M. E. P. Seligman et al., "Positive Psychology Progress: Empirical Validation of Interventions," *American Psychologist* 60 (2005): 410–421.

13. V. Huta and R. Ryan, "Pursuing Pleasure or Virtue: The Differential and Overlapping Well-being Benefits of Hedonic and Eudaimonic Motives," *Happiness Studies* 11 (2010): 735–762.

14. A. L. Duckworth and M. E. P. Seligman, "Self-discipline Outdoes IQ in Predicting Academic Performance of Adolescents," *Psychological Science* 16 (2006): 939–944.

15. E. Diener and M. E. P. Seligman, "Very Happy People," *Psychological Science* 13 (2002): 81–84.

16. M. Csikszentmihalyi, *Finding Flow* (New York: Basic Books, 1997).

17. B. Fredrickson et al., "A Functional Genomic Perspective on Human Well-being," *PNAS* 110 (2013): 13684–13689.

18. S. Oishi, S. Kesebir, and E. Diener, "Income Inequality and Happiness," *Psychological Science* 22 (2011): 1095–1100.

19. P. Taylor, C. Funk, and P. Craighill, "Are We Happy Yet?," Pew Research Center, February 13, 2006.

20. R. Davidson, *The Emotional Life of Your Brain* (New York: Penguin, 2012).

21. M. Seligman and M. Csikszentmihalyi, "Positive Psychology: An Introduction," *American Psychologist* 35 (2000): 5–14.

22. A. Waterman, "The Humanistic Psychology–Positive Psychology Divide: Contrasts in Philosophical Foundations," *American Psychologist* 68 (2013): 124–133.

23. C. Spielberger and L. DeNike, "Awareness in Verbal Conditioning," *Journal of Personality* 30 (Supplement 3) (1962): 73–101.

24. D. Kahneman, *Thinking, Fast and Slow* (New York: Farrar, Straus, and Giroux, 2011).

25. M. Nussbaum, "Human Functioning and Social Justice: In Defense of Aristotelian Essentialism," *Political Theory* 20 (1992): 202–246. A. Sen, *Commodities and Capabilities* (Amsterdam: North-Holland, 1985).

26. J. Henrich, S. J. Heine, and A. Norenzayan, "The Weirdest People in the World?," *Behavioral and Brain Sciences* 33 (2010): 61–135.

27. A. Delle Fave, Cross-cultural Advancements in Positive Psychology (New York: Springer, 2010). See also T. Lomas, "Positive Cross-cultural Psychology: Exploring Similarity and Difference in Constructions and Experiences of Wellbeing," *International Journal of Wellbeing* 5, no. 4 (2015): 60–77. P. Wong, "Cross-cultural Positive Psychology," *Encyclopedia of Cross-cultural Psychology*, ed. K. Keith (Oxford, UK: Wiley Blackwell Publishers, 2013).

28. B. Stevenson and J. Wolfers, "Economic Growth and Subjective Well-being: Reassessing the Easterlin Paradox," *Brookings Papers on Economic Activity* 39 (2008): 1–102.

29. B. Ehrenreich, *Bright-Sided: How the Relentless Promotion of Positive Thinking Has Undermined America* (New York: Holt, 2009).

30. B. Ehrenreich, "Pathologies of Hope," *Harper's Magazine*, February 1, 2007.

31. "Positive Psychology Associations," IPPA, accessed September 4, 2017, http://www.ippanetwork.org/associations.

32. I recommend Stephen Pinker's *The Better Angels of Our Nature* (New York: Penguin, 2012) for those who doubt that there is less, much less, violence now than in the past, and I particularly recommend Johan Norberg's *Progress* (London: One World, 2016) for a discussion of all the realms of life in which progress has been substantial in the last two hundred years. Pinker's newest book, *Enlightenment Now*, will come out in February 2018. It is *Better Angels* on vitamin pills.

33. R. Wright, *Nonzero: The Logic of Human Destiny* (New York: Pantheon, 2000).

34. S. Taylor et al., "Biobehavioral Responses to Stress in Females: Tend-and-Befriend, not Fight-or-Flight," *Psychological Review* 107 (2000): 411–429.

NOTES TO CHAPTER 23

1. S. Nolen-Hoeksema, J. Girgus, and M. Seligman, "Predictors and Consequences of Childhood Depressive Symptoms," *Journal of Abnormal Psychology* 101 (1992): 405–422.

2. M. Seligman et al., *The Optimistic Child* (Boston: Houghton-Mifflin, 1995).

3. J. Horowitz and J. Garber, "The Prevention of Depressive Symptoms in Children and Adolescents: A Meta-analytic Review," *Journal of Consulting and Clinical Psychology* 74 (2006): 401–415. S. Brunwasser, J. Gillham, and E. Kim, "A Meta-analytic Review of the Penn Resiliency Program's Effect on Depressive Symptoms," *Journal of Consulting and Clinical Psychology* 77 (2009): 1042–1054. But for the nonsignificant results, see A. Bastounis et al., "The Effectiveness of the Penn Resiliency Programme (PRP) and Its Adapted Versions in Reducing Depression and Anxiety and Improving Explanatory Style: A Systematic Review and Meta-analysis," *Journal of Adolescence* 52 (2016): 37–48.

4. A. L. Duckworth and M. E. P. Seligman, "Self-discipline Outdoes IQ in Predicting Academic Performance of Adolescents," *Psychological Science* 16 (2005): 939–944.

5. M. Norrish, *Positive Education: The Geelong Grammar School Journey* (Oxford: Oxford University Press, 2015).

6. R. Layard and D. Clark, *Thrive* (London: Penguin, 2014).

7. "Girls First | Bihar, India," CorStone, accessed September 4, 2017, http://corstone.org/girls-first-bihar-india.

8. M. White and S. Murray, *Evidence-Based Approaches to Positive Education* (New York: Springer, 2016).

9. D. Cooperrider and D. Whitney, *Appreciative Inquiry* (San Francisco: Berrett-Koehler, 2005).

10. "PESA: Updates from Positive Education Schools Association," IPEN, May 29, 2015, http://www.ipositive-education.net/pesa-updates-from-positive-education-schools-association. Based on the PESA model, the International Positive Education Network (IPEN) held its first "festival" in Dallas, from July 17 to 20, 2016. More than eight hundred people from thirty nations attended. Sir Anthony Seldon was the president, and Lord James O'Shaugnessy was the chair. The festival was sponsored by *Success Magazine* and *Live Happy Magazine*. The second festival will be held in Dallas in June 2018.

11. M. Seligman, *Building a State of Well-Being* (Adelaide: Department of Premier and Cabinet, 2013).

12. A. Adler, "Teaching Life Skills Increases Well-being and Academic Performance: Evidence from Bhutan, Mexico, and Peru" (PhD diss., University of Pennsylvania, 2016).

13. Adler, "Teaching Life Skills."

14. Adler, "Teaching Life Skills."

NOTES TO CHAPTER 24

1. J. Kaye, "NYT Misses Full Story on Mitchell-Jessen," *Firedoglake*, August 13, 2009.

2. J. Mayer, "Mayer on Seligman," *Atlantic*, July 17, 2008.

3. See J. Mayer, *The Dark Side* (New York: Doubleday, 2008). See also J. Mayer, "The Experiment," *New Yorker*, July 11, 2005.

4. G. Bloche, *The Hippocratic Myth: Why Doctors Are Under Pressure to Ration Care* (New York: St. Martin's Press, 2011).

5. D. Hoffman et al., "Report to the Special Committee of the Board of Directors of the American Psychological Association: Independent Review Relating to APA Ethics Guidelines, National Security Interrogations, and Torture," APA, 2015, http://www.apa.org/independent-review/APA-FINAL-Report-7.2.15.pdf.

6. J. Kaye, "Top US Psychologist Allegedly Met with James Mitchell in Days Before Zubaydah Torture," *Firedoglake*, December 8, 2013.

7. Hoffman "Report to the American Psychological Association," 48–49.

8. T. Shaw, "Learned Helplessness and Torture: An Exchange," *New York Review of Books*, April 7, 2016.

9. J. Risen, *Pay Any Price: Greed, Power and Endless War* (Boston: Houghton Mifflin Harcourt, 2014).

10. J. Mitchell, *Enhanced Interrogation* (New York: Penguin, 2016). For those interested in the details of this program, I highly recommend this book.

11. For a detailed example, see M. Apuzzo, S. Fink, and J. Risen, "How U.S. Torture Left Legacy of Damaged Minds," *New York Times*, October 9, 2016.

12. Shaw, "Learned Helplessness."

13. "Press Release and Recommended Actions: Independent Review Cites Collusion Among APA Individuals and Defense Department Officials in Policy on Interrogation Techniques," APA, July 10, 2015, http://www.apa.org/news/press/releases/2015/07/independent-review-release.aspx.

14. "Information and Resources Regarding the 'Hoffman Report' Independent Review," Division 19, accessed September 4, 2017, http://www.division19students.org/hoffman-report.html.

15. Electronically filed, Court of Common Pleas, February 16, 2017, 12:31:28 p.m., Case Number: 2017 CV 00839 Docket ID: 30555815, Gregory A. Brush, Clerk of Courts, Montgomery County, Ohio.

NOTES TO CHAPTER 25

1. P. Lester et al., "The Comprehensive Soldier Fitness Program Evaluation: Report Number 3: Longitudinal Analysis of the Impact of Master Resilience Training on Self-reported Resilience and Physical Health," University of Nebraska, Lincoln, 2011, http://digitalcommons.unl.edu/cgi/viewcontent.cgi?article=1009&context=pdharms.

2. P. Harms et al., "The Comprehensive Soldier and Family Fitness Evaluation: Report Number 4. Evaluation of Resilience Training and Mental and Behavioral Health Outcomes," University of Nebraska, Lincoln, 2013, http://digitalcommons.unl.edu/pdharms/10.

3. D. Vergun, "Study Concludes Master Resilience Training Effective," Army.mil, January 24, 2012.

4. R. Eidelson, M. Pilisuk, and S. Soldz, "The Dark Side of Comprehensive Soldier Fitness," *The Psysr Blog*, April 5, 2011, http://www.psysr.org/blog/2011/04/05/the-dark-side-of-comprehensive-soldier-fitness.

5. S. M. Brunwasser, J. E. Gillham, and E. S. Kim, "A Meta-analytic Review of the Penn Resiliency Program's Effect on Depressive Symptoms," *Journal of Consulting and Clinical Psychology* 77 (2009): 1042–1054.

6. L. Denning, M. Meisnere, and K. Warner, *Preventing Psychological Disorders in Service Members and Their Families: An Assessment of Programs* (Washington, DC: Institute of Medicine, National Academies Press, 2014).

7. Eidelson, Pilisuk, and Soldz, "The Dark Side of Comprehensive Soldier Fitness."

8. Eidelson, Pilisuk, and Soldz, "The Dark Side of Comprehensive Soldier Fitness."

9. B. Levine, "10 of the Worst Abuses of the Psychiatric and Psychological Professions in American History," *Alternet*, September 24, 2015, https://www.alternet.org/news-amp-politics/10-worst-abuses-psychiatric-and-psychological-professions-american-history.

10. D. Tencer, Global Research, October 14, 2010.

11. See note 8, chapter 24.

NOTES TO CHAPTER 26

1. M. Seligman et al., "Positive Health and Health Assets: Re-analysis of Longitudinal Datasets," Positive Health, 2012, http://positivehealthresearch.org/sites/positivehealthresearch.org/files/PH_Whitepaper_Layout_Web.pdf.

2. J. Boehm et al., "A Prospective Study of Positive Psychological Well-Being and Coronary Heart Disease," *Health Psychology* 30 (2011): 259–267.

3. J. Boehm and L. Kubzansky, "The Heart's Content: The Association Between Positive Psychological Well-being and Cardiovascular Health," *Psychological Bulletin* 138 (2012): 655–691.

4. C. S. Carver, M. F. Scheier, and S. C. Segerstrom, "Optimism," *Clinical Psychology Review* 30 (2010): 879–889.

5. H. Tindle et al., "Optimism, Cynical Hostility, and Incident Coronary Heart Disease and Mortality in the Women's Health Initiative," *Circulation* 118 (2009): 1145–1146. I reviewed all these studies in M. Seligman, *Flourish* (New York: Free Press, 2011).

6. G. Nikrahan et al., "Effects of Positive Psychology Interventions on Risk Biomarkers in Coronary Patients: A Randomized, Wait-List Controlled Pilot Trial," *Psychosomatics* 57 (2016): 359–368.

7. E. Diener and M. Chan, "Happy People Live Longer: Subjective Well-being Contributes to Health and Longevity," *Applied Psychology: Health and Well-Being* 3 (2011): 1–43.

8. B. Liu et al., "Does Happiness Itself Directly Effect Mortality? The Prospective UK Million Women Study," *The Lancet* 387 (2015): 874–881.

9. E. Diener, S. Pressman, and S. Lyubomirsky, "Can 1 Million Women Be Wrong About Happiness and Health?" *Los Angeles Times*, December 17, 2015.

10. And so it does, big time. M. Seligman et al., "Catastrophic Thinking Predicts PTSD: From a New Authoritative Army Database," submitted

2018. Soldiers who were strong catastrophizers and faced intense combat were over 300 percent more likely to come down later with PTSD. Since catastrophization can be mitigated by our resilience program and can be identified in advance, this could lead to a major reduction in PTSD.

11. N. Park and M. E. Seligman, "Christopher M. Peterson (1950–2012)," *American Psychologist* 68, no. 5 (2013): 403.

12. G. H. Hardy, *A Mathematician's Apology* (Cambridge: Cambridge University Press, 1967).

13. D. Buettner, *Blue Zones* (New York: National Geographic, 2008).

14. L. Wittgenstein, *Philosophical Investigations* (Oxford: Blackwell, 1953), 43.

15. J. C. Eichstaedt et al., "Psychological Language on Twitter Predicts County-Level Heart Disease Mortality," *Psychological Science* 26 (2014): 159–169.

NOTES TO CHAPTER 27

1. D. Gilbert, *Stumbling on Happiness* (New York: Knopf, 2008).

2. I am informed that the more correct Latin is *Homo prospiciens*. But it is too late now to change the book's title to the grammatically correct one.

3. R. Baumeister et al., "Ego Depletion: Is the Active Self a Limited Resource?," *Journal of Personality and Social Psychology* 74 (1998): 1252–1265.

4. R. Baumeister and E. Masicampo, "Conscious Thought Is for Facilitating Social and Cultural Interactions: How Mental Simulations Serve the Animal-Cultural Interface," *Psychological Review* 117 (2010): 945–971. Roy held the world's record for the number of publications in the nit-picky *Journal of Personality and Social Psychology* and so probably became a master of bowing and scraping. Strangely enough, however, his is one of the most original minds I know.

5. M. E. Raichle et al., "A Default Mode of Brain Function," *Proceedings of the National Academy of Sciences* 98 (2001): 676–682. R. L. Buckner, J. R. Andrews-Hanna, and D. L. Schacter, "The Brain's Default Network: Anatomy, Function, and Relevance to Disease," *Annals of the New York Academy of Sciences* 1124 (2008): 1–38. R. Buckner and D. Carroll, "Self-projection and the Brain," *Trends in Cognitive Science* 11 (2007): 49–57.

6. M. White, *Toward Reunion in Philosophy* (Cambridge, MA: Harvard University Press, 1956).

7. M. Seligman et al., "Navigating into the Future or Driven by the Past," *Perspectives on Psychological Science* 8 (2013): 119–141.

8. M. Seligman et al., *Homo Prospectus* (New York: Oxford, 2016).

9. J. Hawkins and S. Blakeslee, *On Intelligence* (New York: Times Books, 2004).

10. U. Neisser and N. Harsch, "Phantom Flashbulbs: False Recognitions of Hearing the News about *Challenger*," in *Affect and Accuracy in Recall: Studies of "Flashbulb" Memories*, ed. E. Winograd and U. Neisser (New York: Cambridge University Press, 1992), 9–31.

11. D. Chalmers, "Facing Up to the Problem of Consciousness," *Journal of Consciousness Studies* 2 (1995): 200–219.

12. See the "Creativity" chapter by M. Seligman, with M. Forgeard and S. Kaufman, in *Homo Prospectus* (New York: Oxford, 2016).

13. H. Zuckerman, *Scientific Elite: Nobel Laureates in the U.S.* (New York: Free Press, 1977).

14. T. Salthouse, *A Theory of Cognitive Aging* (New York: Elsevier, 1985).

15. R. R. McCrae, D. Arenberg, and P. T. Costa, "Declines in Divergent Thinking with Age: Cross-sectional, Longitudinal, and Cross-sequential Analyses," *Psychology and Aging* 2 (1987): 130–137.

16. J. Diamond, *Guns, Germs, and Steel: The Fate of Human Societies* (New York: W. W. Norton, 1997).

17. J. Gleick, *Isaac Newton* (New York: Vintage, 2004).

18. A. Duckworth, J. Eichstaedt, and L. Ungar, "The Mechanics of Human Achievement," *Social and Personality Psychology Compass* 9 (2015): 353–369.

19. M. Csikszentmihalyi, *Creativity: Flow and the Psychology of Discovery and Invention* (New York: HarperCollins, 1996).

20. J. Riemer, "Perlman Makes His Music the Hard Way," *Houston Chronicle*, February 10, 2001.

NOTES TO CHAPTER 28

1. R. Grahn et al., "Blockade of Alpha1 Adrenoreceptors in the Dorsal Raphe Nucleus Prevents Enhanced Conditioned Fear and Impaired Escape Performance Following Uncontrollable Stressor Exposure in Rats," *Behavioural Brain Research* 134 (2002): 387–392.

2. For the details of these techniques and others that follow, see S. Maier and M. Seligman, "Learned Helplessness Revisited Fifty Years Later: Insights from Neuroscience," *Psychological Review* 123 (2016): 349–367.

3. M. Baratta et al., "Selective Activation of Dorsal Raphe Nucleus-Projecting Neurons in the Ventral Medial Prefrontal Cortex by Controllable Stress," *European Journal of Neuroscience* 30 (2009): 1111–1116.

4. J. Amat et al., "Prior Experience with Behavioral Control over Stress Blocks the Behavioral Effects of Later Uncontrollable Stress: Role of the

Ventral Medial Prefrontal Cortex," *Journal of Neuroscience* 26 (2006): 13264–13272.

5. J. Christianson et al., "Learned Stressor Resistance Requires Extracellular Signal-Regulated Kinase in the Prefrontal Cortex," *Frontiers in Behavioral Neuroscience* 8 (2014): 348.

6. Amat et al., "Prior Experience with Behavioral Control over Stress."

7. Maier and Seligman, "Learned Helplessness Revisited Fifty Years Later."

8. M. White and A. Murray, eds., *Evidence-Based Approaches in Positive Education: Implementing a Strategic Framework for Well-being in Schools* (New York: Springer, 2015).

NOTES TO CHAPTER 29

1. "Religious Awakenings Bolster Americans' Faith," Gallup, January 14, 2003, http://www.gallup.com/poll/7582/religious-awakenings-bolster -americans-faith.aspx. R. Duffy and W. Sedlacek, "What Is Most Important to Student's Long-Term Career Choices: Analyzing 10-Year Trends and Group Differences," *Journal of Career Development* 34 (2007): 149–163. A. Wrzesniewski et al., "Jobs, Careers, and Callings: People's Relation to Their Work," *Journal of Research in Personality* 31 (1997): 21–33.

2. M. E. P. Seligman, "Introduction: How Are We Called into The Future?," in *Being Called: Scientific, Secular, and Sacred Perspectives*, ed. D. B. Yaden et al. (Santa Barbara, CA: Praeger, 2015) xvii–xxvi. M. Seligman, "God Comes at the End," *Spirituality in Clinical Practice* 1 (2014): 67–70. See chapter 10 of M. E. P. Seligman et al., *Homo Prospectus* (New York: Oxford University Press, 2016).

3. R. Layard, "Promoting Secular Ethics," in *World Happiness Report Update 2016*, ed. J. F. Helliwell, R. Layard, and J. Sachs (New York: UN Sustainable Development Solutions Network, 2016), http://worldhappiness .report/ed/2016. I am in almost total agreement with this essay, with one exception: Layard argues that happiness, subjective well-being, is the unitary measure of the aim of secular ethics. I believe it is but that PERMA, which is broader and combines objective measures with subjective measures, is the path to happiness.

4. I must again recommend Johan Norberg's *Progress* (London: OneWorld, 2016) to the doubters.

INDEX

Credit: Mandy Seligman

Martin E. P. Seligman, PhD, is the Zellerbach Family Professor of Psychology at the University of Pennsylvania, director of the Positive Psychology Center, and former president of the American Psychological Association. Among his thirty books are *Learned Optimism* and *Flourish*.

PublicAffairs is a publishing house founded in 1997. It is a tribute to the standards, values, and flair of three persons who have served as mentors to countless reporters, writers, editors, and book people of all kinds, including me.

I. F. STONE, proprietor of *I. F. Stone's Weekly*, combined a commitment to the First Amendment with entrepreneurial zeal and reporting skill and became one of the great independent journalists in American history. At the age of eighty, Izzy published *The Trial of Socrates*, which was a national bestseller. He wrote the book after he taught himself ancient Greek.

BENJAMIN C. BRADLEE was for nearly thirty years the charismatic editorial leader of *The Washington Post*. It was Ben who gave the *Post* the range and courage to pursue such historic issues as Watergate. He supported his reporters with a tenacity that made them fearless and it is no accident that so many became authors of influential, best-selling books.

ROBERT L. BERNSTEIN, the chief executive of Random House for more than a quarter century, guided one of the nation's premier publishing houses. Bob was personally responsible for many books of political dissent and argument that challenged tyranny around the globe. He is also the founder and longtime chair of Human Rights Watch, one of the most respected human rights organizations in the world.

· · ·

For fifty years, the banner of Public Affairs Press was carried by its owner Morris B. Schnapper, who published Gandhi, Nasser, Toynbee, Truman, and about 1,500 other authors. In 1983, Schnapper was described by *The Washington Post* as "a redoubtable gadfly." His legacy will endure in the books to come.

Peter Osnos, *Founder*